Avant-Garde Performance and the Limits of Criticism

THEATER: THEORY/TEXT/PERFORMANCE
Enoch Brater, Series Editor

Recent Titles:

AVANT-GARDE PERFORMANCE & THE LIMITS OF CRITICISM

Approaching the Living Theatre,
Happenings/Fluxus, and
the Black Arts Movement

Mike Sell

The University of Michigan Press
Ann Arbor

Copyright © by the University of Michigan 2005
All rights reserved
Published in the United States of America by
The University of Michigan Press
Manufactured in the United States of America
⊛ Printed on acid-free paper

2008   2007   2006   2005   4   3   2   1

A CIP catalog record for this book is available from the British Library.

Library of Congress Cataloging-in-Publication Data

Sell, Mike, 1967–
    Avant-garde performance and the limits of criticism : approaching
the Living Theatre, happenings/Fluxus, and the Black Arts movement /
Mike Sell.
        p.   cm. — (Theater—theory/text/performance)
    Originated in the author's dissertation.
    Includes bibliographical references and index.
    ISBN-13: 978-0-472-11495-5 (cloth : alk. paper)
    ISBN-10: 0-472-11495-6 (cloth : alk. paper)
      1. Living Theatre (New York, N.Y.)   2. Fluxus (Group of artists)
3. Black Arts movement.   4. Avant-garde (Aesthetics)—United States—
History—20th century.   I. Title.   II. Series.
PN2297.L5S45   2005
792'.09747'1—dc22   2005016628

Acknowledgments

Because this project began as a dissertation, there are a great many people and institutions to thank. First, the English departments at the University of Michigan, Millikin University, and Indiana University of Pennsylvania. The librarians at Michigan's Labadie Collection, Nina Myatt and Scott Sanders of Antioch's Antiochiana Collection, and the Interlibrary Loan department at IUP helped track down books, articles, and documents. The Rackham Graduate School afforded me three semesters away from teaching at a crucial moment in the project's development, and the College of Humanities and Social Sciences of IUP afforded assistance with conference travel. The Graduate Employees Organization at the University of Michigan played a significant role, too, particularly regarding my understanding of the significance of organizational theory in the avant-garde moments I explore.

The opportunity to present sections of the book was given by the American Society for Theater Research, the Association for Theatre in Higher Education, the Modern Language Association, the Midwestern Modern Language Association, the Performance Studies Conference, and the organizers of the 2000 Notre Dame conference "Rethinking the Avant-Garde." My special thanks to seminar participants who read and discussed my work at ASTR in 1999, 2000, and 2003. Early versions of material appearing herein were first published in *African American Performance and Theatre History: A Critical Reader,* ed. Harry Elam, Jr., and David Krasner (New York: Oxford University Press, 2001); *Contours of the Theatrical Avant-Garde: Performance and Textuality,* ed. James Harding (Ann Arbor: University of Michigan Press, 2000); *On-Stage Studies; Rethinking Marxism;* and *Theatre Journal.* My thanks to the editors and reviewers for their insightful critiques.

Carl Cox, Juan Atkins, Richie Hawtin, and Derrick May helped me better understand the relationship between innovative art and cultural formation after the 1960s. Laurie Cannady assisted with the index, and Kevin Sanders chased down plays and contact information for the chapter on the Black Arts Movement. Portions of this book were read and critiqued by

David Downing, Harry Elam, Jr., Maurice Kilwein-Guevara, Ian Leong, Baubie Paschal, Sally Robinson, P. A. Skantze, Kelly Thomas, and Leigh Woods. Ed Bullins, Askia Touré, and Kalamu Ya Salaam all gave generously of their time and energy, as did undergraduate and graduate students at IUP in the three courses on the black arts movement I taught in the spring of 2003. Rosaly Roffman underlined for me the importance of the issues explored herein, particularly from the perspective of those who have long lived in the margins. David Krasner and James Smethurst were invaluable resources and critical voices as I wrote and revised the case study of the Black Arts Movement.

I've benefited from time spent with committed, caring mentors. Enoch Brater, director of the dissertation, helped me find an effective balance between theoretical rigor and theatrical concreteness. His skeptical encouragement and insistence on clarity of expression are touchstones. LeAnn Fields, my editor at the University of Michigan, helped me shape an ungainly manuscript into a book and, not coincidentally, helped me shape my sense of my own role in the field of dramatic, theatrical, and performance studies. I am not the first to have had such help from her. Lastly, my gratitude goes to James Harding, whose presence is palpable throughout these case studies. He is a friend, colleague, and mentor.

Roy and Carol Trifilio, my parents-in-law, have generously given me time and space to write this book at their beautiful home on Lake Michigan. My love to them. My own parents, Thomas and Sandra Sell, taught me to be curious and helped me understand the responsibilities of teaching.

Lastly, Kate Trifilio, who worked hard to support the writing of this book, caring for a home, and raising our boys River, Brando, and Dylan. She is my constant inspiration.

Contents

Introduction
The Revolution Will Not Be Theorized

In other words, it is impossible to address this reading without first of all addressing the cultural code which refuses it, without first of all acknowledging that we are nothing but the products of this code, and that, in the course of our reading . . . , whether we like it or not, we are actually complicit, even in our desire to understand, with the various types of censure we might have set ourselves against to begin with.

—Marcelin Pleynet, "The Readability of Sade" (1968)

I think we can regard the past eighty or so years in the arts . . . not as a series of islands with names ending in *ism*, but as forming a still little-explored continent whose jagged coastline we have begun to leave astern without knowing whether the land is habitable.

—Roger Shattuck, introduction to Maurice Nadeau's
The History of Surrealism (1965 ed.)

The Birth of the Avant-Garde (Again . . .)

We live in an era of unprecedented avant-garde activity and equally unprecedented tactics for monitoring and policing it—and there's nothing especially new about that situation. The minuet of cultural innovation and improved security strategies has been a constant among artists, activists, bureaucrats, and moral pundits for almost two centuries. In academic studies of the avant-garde, the minuet of vanguard and cop has twirled to a very specific tune: the sad, often nostalgic strains of the eulogy. There is probably no other field of study that must contend so often with declarations that its object is defunct. To study the avant-garde, it seems, one must study the death of the avant-garde. Yet, with the kind of brutal irony that would have struck French symbolist and German Dadaist alike (not to mention Mark Twain), the death of the avant-garde has proven, once again, to have been declared prematurely.

The September 11, 2001, attacks on the World Trade Center and the Pentagon office building were engineered by men described by their leader,

Osama bin Laden, as an "Islamic vanguard," and bin Laden himself has been profoundly influenced by a theorist of Islamic vanguardism little known to, and often misunderstood by, non-Muslims, Sayyid Qutb. Qutb's work fuses the Leninist model of party organization with indigenous Islamic models based on the Prophet's secret early work with the small community later to be known as Muhammad's Companions.[1] In November 2001, the work of another vanguard came to international attention (though, like bin Laden's crew, it had been working quietly for years behind the scenes): the "special forces" of the U.S. military, a strategic model directly descended from Napoleon's elite military engineering cadres, but with an understanding of the role of cultural factors (tribal loyalties, ethnic affiliations, etc.), of the dynamic of local tactics and global strategy, and of command-control-communication strategies that would have thrilled the Frenchman's generals.

As the news broke on the eleventh, I was preparing a lesson plan on Rachilde's *The Crystal Spider* (1892), an intensely violent symbolist play that deploys rapidly shifting verbal imagery and a horrific theatrical stunt (an anorectic young man crashes into a mirror, ripping open his throat) to undermine cherished institutions of the fin de siècle French bourgeoisie: masculinity, love, the family, money. At the same time Rachilde was writing her play, bombs were being dropped in urban centers across Europe by the intransigent wing of the international anarchist movement. The connection between avant-garde theater, drama, and performance and the bombing of banks and government buildings is no coincidence. Rachilde's salon was fluent in the language of cultural radicalism, a language that circulated freely among radicals of all ideological stripes. This sharing went beyond concepts and vocabulary. Much like the droppers of bombs, one of Rachilde's favored arenas for action was the spectacle of daily life, where she enjoyed a scandalous reputation as a transvestite, sexual experimenter, and free thinker. She shared the streets of Paris with more utilitarian compeers who effectively disrupted the superficial tranquility of urban life with nitrogen-compound bombs. Not surprisingly, when the crackdown on the terrorists began, Rachilde and her literary compeers, whether bomb throwers or not, sympathizers or not, experienced profound levels of harassment and oppression.

Reading Rachilde, bin Laden, and the highly trained young men of the U.S. Navy, Army, and Marines together, it becomes clear that the stage of the avant-garde has never been abandoned; rather, the spotlight has shifted. One of the aims of this book is to describe exactly how complicated the cultural terrain of the avant-garde was, is, and will be given the greater and greater intertwining of technology, subjectivity, and cultural production, an intertwining enabled in part by the institutions of higher education and scholarship. Likewise, I hope to show, through careful examination of three avant-garde moments that demonstrate varied responses to the technical, cultural, and informational shifts catalyzed by the U.S./Soviet Cold War (1945–90), how the complexity of avant-garde activism, which experienced a profound intensification during the 1950s and 1960s, represents real limits to scholarly efforts to historicize and critique it. To invoke Donna Haraway, avant-garde activism, especially when it utilizes performance modes such as spoken word, theater, or dance, resists translation into a "common language in which all resistance to instrumental control disappears and heterogeneity can be submitted to disassembly, reassembly, investment, and exchange."[2]

In the 1960s, radical cultural production in regions around the globe took on forms that systematically and intentionally challenged the institutional and ideological foundations of liberal and authoritarian political regimes alike. However, unlike previous manifestations of the avant-garde imperative, these enjoyed the benefit of historical and institutional self-consciousness—in other words, an intimate knowledge of exactly how good academic criticism, scholarship, and pedagogy were at making sense of the challenge of the avant-garde, and exactly how good academic research was at devising techniques to battle existing avant-gardes (e.g., the development of surveillance technologies at the University of Wisconsin–Madison used to track down Che Guevara during his last guerrilla campaign in Bolivia). The birth of the field of avant-garde studies roughly coincided with the first two decades of the Cold War and was signaled by a rash of exhibitions, catalogs, retrospectives, changes in the curricula in art history and in literary studies, and the publication of three groundbreaking texts on the subject: Hans Magnus Enzensberger's "The Aporias of the Avant-Garde" (1962), the English translation of Renato Poggioli's *Teoria dell'arte d'avanguardia* (1968), and Donald Drew Egbert's *Social Radicalism and the Arts: Western Europe* (1970). The consequence of this abrupt spike in knowledge of the avant-garde was not a domestication of the avant-garde, but rather a translation into terms that made sense within institutional contexts that were witnessing increasing demand (and funding) for academic programs that could effectively integrate cultural production and technical innovation.

The nature of that translation can't be understood without attending to larger social, political, and cultural contexts. The politicization and commodification of daily life, the rise of a mass-mediated leisure society, the advent of social movements based in newly formulated or formerly denigrated social identities, the rapid rate of scientific discovery, and the development of new communications technologies implied to many that the idea of an artist or an artistic community taking a stand against oppression and reflecting that stand in an aesthetic creation was, though not defunct, at least in need of extensive renovation. For critics and scholars who wished to keep the heritage of the avant-garde alive—who wished to vitalize the tradition of revolt, refusal, and subversion developed by naturalists, symbolists, Dadas, vorticists, lettristes, Blue Blousers, proletcult agitators, Communist poets and musicians, and others—but who didn't want to simply repeat the past, the need to invent new approaches, whether aesthetic or critical-scholarly, was imperative. One of the key practical and theoretical innovations of the period concerned the critical and scholarly communities themselves. The innovative period in avant-garde history we know now as "The 60s" was characterized by both the cultivation and the systematic sundering of communication lines between artists and the academic community of scholars, critics, and teachers.

By examining the efforts of cultural radicals during the sixties to open up or tear down oppressive symbolic, discursive, and institutional systems during a period of remarkable innovation and creation of symbolic, discursive, and institutional systems, we can learn much about the possibilities and limitations of similar efforts in our own times. That this period saw such rich and troubled relations between avant-gardes and academia makes it all the more relevant. Examining avant-garde performance and the limits of criticism in the 1960s, we can learn much about the role of teachers, scholars, and critics in the conservation, translation, and policing of avant-gardes. In a note attached to his essay "Cecil Taylor *Floating Garden*," Fred Moten notes that critical method can easily devastate the progressive interrogation, destruction, and revision of a culture's symbol systems. Easily, but not necessarily. "The question remains whether and how to mark (visually, spatially, in the absence of sound, the sound in my head) digression, citation, extension, improvisation in the kind of writing that has no name other than 'literary criticism.'" The avant-gardes of the 1960s, in sum, took the foundational innovations of the historical avant-gardes (Dada and surrealism, in particular) to a new level—and did so with the assistance, both benign and malevolent, of academics. If, as Peter Bürger has demonstrated, the historical avant-gardes were the first to recognize and thematize the institutional conditions of art, the avant-gardes of the 1960s thematized institutions that Bürger himself fails to recognize: his own institutions, the institutions of criticism, scholarship, and pedagogy.

One of the assumptions of this book is that the avant-garde did not die during the 1960s, nor did it simply repeat the achievements and failures of the past in some kind of conceptually empty "neo" gesture, as Bürger and a great many others contend. Quite the contrary, the avant-garde is still alive today and equipped with a self-consciousness informed by the kinds of penetrating critiques mounted against the avant-garde since the mid-1950s. Recent theoretical developments in the fields of literary studies, performance theory, theater history, and visual culture studies, along with social developments in conjunction with new musical forms (e.g., techno and hip-hop) and the increasing strength of global trade structures and actions against it confirm the vitality—if not the necessity—of radical cultural actions conceived within the historical and conceptual fields of the avant-garde. Such actions possess both the material and symbolic force to generate popular unrest, to change the terms of the social conversation, and to afford a conceptual and linguistic matrix conducive to affiliation, for both the Right and the Left. However, even today, after yet another round of police actions against youth in the name of parental authority and drug interdiction, after the symbolic actions at World Trade Organization meetings in Seattle and Genoa, after the collapse of the World Trade Center, and after the stunning successes of fundamentalist movements around the globe, the majority opinion of scholars and historians still weighs in on the side of the eulogists.[3]

Thus, many of the readers of this book will probably disagree with its basic assumption. There's good reason for this view. The past four decades of art, literary, and performance criticism have demonstrated at length that discussion of the avant-garde must inevitably confront disturbing subplots in its story: the implicit militarism of the term; its long acquaintance with misogyny, colonialist primitivism, and cultural imperialism; its inflated claims to originality; its promiscuity with Stalinism, fascism, radical-chic capitalism; its romance with the vanguard party model; and, finally, terrorism. Such criticism can't be dismissed, certainly, but if we admit the profound flaws inherent to the avant-garde model, what's the use of holding onto it? To answer this question, it's germane to examine a crucial period in the development of today's military-economic-cultural-technical situation. During the middle years of the Cold War, avant-garde individuals, groups, and movements consciously and systematically positioned both their work and the conditions in which that work was encountered by audiences in conscious relationship to art, literary, and performance critics and scholars and the institutions in which they worked. As part of this positioning, these new avant-gardes also considered the historical reception of their forebears.

The case studies that constitute this book will identify and examine the limits of criticism when faced with movements cognizant of the institutions of criticism. The subjects of these case studies are not meant to be viewed as typical; quite the contrary. They can be viewed, however, as emblematic for the ways they effectively situate, thematize, and engage with the discourses and institutions of criticism, scholarship, and pedagogy. Critics, scholars, and teachers of the avant-garde during the Cold War—and in our own times—generally fail to recognize how lines of communication between the avant-garde and academic critics and scholars became the subject of critique, innovation, and subversion. There is an oddly disembodied quality to much commentary on the avant-garde, a refusal to consider the institutionality of that commentary even when dealing with avant-garde movements that made institutionality a central concern of their work. There are notable exceptions to this rule, which I'll discuss soon.

If Cold War avant-gardes purposefully complicated the methods and models of their critics and scholars, they also complicated understandings of the "political" during their times. The conjunction of institutional self-consciousness and rethinking of the political is not coincidental and not wholly a matter of choice. Cold War avant-gardes had to maneuver through a shifting landscape of social, economic, cultural, and technical reformation, a landscape that was shifting as the consequence of a purposeful, systematic attack by the government on older left-wing coalitions and organizations. Cultural radicals maneuvered across a rapidly growing art market bolstered by an academic system of critics, scholars, and teachers who were both knowledgeable of and sympathetic with the pre-World-War-II avant-gardes—and equally cognizant of developments within contemporary art (such as abstract expressionism).

Very few critics and scholars have taken seriously this complex interaction among the avant-garde tradition, the unique ideological and material conditions of the Cold War, the rise of the counterculture, the institutional impact of the counterculture, and the development of new critical and scholarly methods and disciplines. Only two critics contemporary with such developments did so and with a persistent focus on their own institutional positions: Marcelin Pleynet and Roger Shattuck, selections of whose work start off this introduction. Shattuck is correctly regarded as a foundational scholar of the avant-garde. *The Banquet Years* (1968) is a book whose critical methods are no longer in vogue, but whose blend of richly textured, urbane anecdote and sophisticated formalist analysis, organized around four key figures in the Parisian fin de siècle, is still required reading. Pleynet, on the other hand, was part of a key group in vanguard intellectual history whose methods are in many ways fundamental to contemporary critical theory. The *Tel Quel* group systematically shifted the way theoretical inquiry works in the field of cultural criticism and literary study. The critique mounted by

Kristeva, Derrida, Foucault, Barthes, and others in the journal's pages both presaged and salvaged the revolutionary moment of 1968, preserving in textual, theoretical form the situated struggle of vanguard communities.

Notably, both critics explicitly reject the methodological approaches of the eulogists; Shattuck by delving into anecdote, Pleynet into poststructuralist *écriture*. To the latter first. Well aware of the new avant-gardes outside his Paris office in 1968 and the new generation of critics and scholars traipsing through his office, Pleynet writes in the journal *Tel Quel* that any act of reading subversive or revolutionary art, literature, and theory will necessarily entangle itself in "multiplicitous articulations of textual contradictions" that must, inevitably, lead to the democratization of the reading process itself.[4] Bad news for the professional critic, for sure; after all, the democratization of reading tends to undermine the professional critic's authority, as Roland Barthes makes clear in his essay "The Death of the Author," published that same year.[5]

Pleynet revels in the revolutionary excess of the moment. Shattuck, on the other hand, plays ironically the role of disappointed colonialist in his introduction to the 1965 reissue of Maurice Nadeau's *History of Surrealism* (first ed., 1944). He portrays himself and his fellow historians of the avant-garde in an almost melancholy fashion, as if taking a glance back at a shadowy continent, ruing their failure to ascertain "the topography and resources"[6] of radical cultural movements that slowly, inevitably recede beyond the horizon. Unlike Pleynet, Shattuck is ultimately disappointed by his inability to map the radical cultural movements of the past, an inability he views as harming the progressive development of democratic society. The arguments, methods, and metaphors of these two are worth exploring at length, particularly given their commitment to irony. They allow us to see how critics in the sixties were limited by the conceptual, methodological, and institutional structures of their historical moment and geopolitical situation as well as how they were constrained by transhistorical, structural conditions that impact avant-garde scholarship and criticism at all times.

Pleynet and Shattuck help us understand that there are real stakes in the theorization of the relationships among the avant-garde tradition, the critic-scholar and her discourses, and the historical moment. This is why they both refuse to cross certain conceptual and representational boundaries in their essays. They help us to better understand that our critical and scholarly efforts, even at their most rigorous and rigorously self-conscious, can't see beyond certain horizons. Such limits are foundational to criticism and scholarship, and they can be easily exploited by those who oppose the individual critic-scholar or the institutions in which she works. When faced with events, artworks, and situations that challenge the basic assumptions, methods, and institutional bases of criticism and scholarship, why would we expect to be able to overcome a degree of blindness or the necessity of using metaphors?

What are the specific limits of criticism identified, transgressed, or respected by Pleynet and Shattuck? In response to dominant methods and models used by his contemporaries to study the works of the marquis de Sade, Pleynet argues that anyone "reading the radical" inevitably finds herself in play with three demands, demands that transform even the most sensitive, sympathetic, and critical reading into an elaborate apology for conservatism. This conservatism isn't something one can simply avoid, Pleynet cautions—one can't simply decide not to be conservative in this respect. The very decision to play the game of criticism and scholarship means that we're willing to play by a certain set of institutionalized rules, some of which are explicit, some tacit. Pleynet addresses three of these limits: (1) the necessity of resolving contradiction, (2) the necessity of objective analysis, and (3) (a corollary of 2) the necessity of avoiding nonacademic entanglements with the subject. Given these limits, he asks, how can we ever read Sade? In fact, Sade can never be read in a noncontradictory, objective, impersonal way, Pleynet claims, since his writings purposefully and systematically hamper such an effort. As a consequence, Pleynet argues, Sade has never been released from the chains and towers of the Bastille, only now the prison has been replaced by a literary criticism that doesn't adequately account for the social, cultural, and economic implications of its own game rules. For Pleynet, a truly radical literary historian must read differently, must read not only the literature but the literary critic, too, especially if the critic wishes to support (as Pleynet does) on the level of academic discourse the street-level actions of the students who shut down France in 1968, the year his essay appeared in print. For those interested in being more than a belletristic capo, Pleynet concludes, there is a possibility of reading the radical, of releasing Sade from his chains. This way of reading would intensify the contradictions of the literature and ultimately democratize the conditions for critical reading, leaving the professional critic in the dust.

From the Bastille to the colony. Shattuck's essay gets us thinking in other directions; specifically, about other kinds of structural and institutional limits relating to the critic's emotional engagement with the topic and the institutions in which he works. Shattuck is no less aware than Pleynet of the challenge of radical art; however, he is more concerned with the question of memory and the nostalgic adoration that bourgeois culture feels for what it destroys. For him, surrealism is little more than a "promontory" that extends from a kind of vast, unknown continent of subversive culture, a heart of darkness whose obscurity is defined as much by forgetting as by misunderstanding. Surrealism, he asserts, is threatened, first and foremost, by the forgetting of the conflicts, contradictions, and critical methods of the movement. This theoretical vacuum he hopes will be partly described by the book for which he's writing the introduction: Maurice Nadeau's *History of Surrealism,* the first on the movement, and the first to take seriously surrealism's rigorous reappraisal of art, theory, politics, and everyday life. If Pleynet criticizes the politically, methodologically, and unconsciously conservative critical establishment, Shattuck criticizes an emotionally conservative, overrational society bolstered by the objectivist methodologies of higher education. For him, surrealism's greatest accomplishments are to be found in very different territories, in humor, love, and other intense emotional experiences easily forgotten by the critic, scholar, and teacher.

Pleynet and Shattuck hint at a way of thinking about the avant-garde that differs significantly from those who argue that the avant-garde is dead or who carry on with its translation with no regard to institutional dimensions. Unwilling to consign the avant-garde tradition to the grave—and equally unwilling to consign the avant-garde to a radicalism limited to an internal debate about art and its institutions[7]—they hint at possibilities that have been largely ignored by avant-garde scholars and critics since their time. Shattuck notes that the idea that the avant-garde was "benign" and "reabsorbed" was a "common assumption" by 1964 (11). The irony is that this opinion was strengthened, not weakened, by the increasingly widespread presence of surrealism in American culture; for example, in galleries, art history courses, and advertising. He writes that "a new round of histories, studies, editions, and exhibits" of avant-garde works "makes it not easier but harder than ever to get a straight answer" about whether the avant-garde was still a viable concern. As a consequence, the heritage of surrealism as both a theoretical movement and a revolutionary expansion of humor and love was threatened, left behind in mystery. Shattuck warns us about the consequences of such a forgetting: "I happen to believe that real importance attaches to the estimate we now make of Surrealism. Like progressive education and pacifism, it lies close to the center of our immediate heritage; we ignore those matters at our own peril" (11).

Both Pleynet and Shattuck assume that historicizing the avant-garde raises questions about how critics, scholars, and the institutions in which they work relate to radical cultural movements in their own times. Again, we should note that this is a rare moment of self-reflexivity among the scholars and critics of the avant-garde; in my research, I've found only a few critics who've demonstrated a similar self-consciousness, notably Renato Poggioli in *Theory of the Avant-Garde,* Paul Mann in *The Theory Death of the Avant-Garde,* and Kristine Stiles in her series of essays on destruction in art.[8] Most critics and scholars of the avant-garde seem to assume that they are neutral, disembodied observers of the event. Corollary to this assumption is another: that the avant-garde event is a discrete, bounded moment in the past. One reason for such assumptions is surely the close relationship of academics and the avant-garde, a relationship no more strong than in the 1940s and 1950s. The close relationship of artists and critics in the Cold War era helped to promote a sense of common esprit de corps. As a consequence, Gregory Battcock argues, the dominant art trends of the 1940s and 1950s were "a critic's art rather than an art of rebellion."[9] Battcock implies that critics aren't interested in rebellion; however, critics of the avant-garde, if not always interested in rebellion, have consistently focused on the question of politics, especially such crucial concerns as freedom of expression, thought, and action.

Nevertheless, the way such critical collaborations occurred was inevitably determined by the unique conditions of the Cold War. Robert Motherwell, who was not only an abstract expressionist painter but also a critic and historian of the avant-garde, pondered in 1944 the loss of certain social and political connections that had formerly sustained the avant-garde: "The artist's problem is *with what to identify himself.* The middle class is decaying, and, as a conscious entity, the working class does not exist. Hence the tendency of modern painters to paint for each other."[10] The critic and scholar are no less vulnerable to the problems of identification.

In distinct ways, Pleynet and Shattuck refuse to consign the avant-garde to the past and do so by engaging precisely with such questions of identification. Both insist that the radical past is also the radical present and a set of possibilities for the future. Both attempt to describe a way of thinking about the avant-garde that refuses to sew up all the loose ends. They maintain a certain openness and critical irony in their thinking about the avant-garde, an openness to the possibilities and limits produced by the breakdown of older identities anchored in preexisting affiliations among critics, artists, and social groups. How do they work within these possibilities and limitations? For both, the horizons of the avant-garde are best characterized as open, as open to *contradiction;* in other words, the avant-garde's revolt against the mainstream is multiplicitous, ambivalent, ironic, and excessive, never able to be fully captured by critique and scholarship. Unlike the artists described by Motherwell, there is a purposeful, positive-minded refusal of identification in these two essays. The reticence and caution of these texts provide a liberating sense of failure, the kind of liberation that comes when we finally understand the limits of our tools.

How can contradiction be both a method and a limit? Pleynet affords one possibility, arguing (in line with Barthes, Kristeva, Derrida, and others who theorized the exemptions and excesses of *jouissance* and *l'écriture*) that texts by writers like Sade purposefully play on the border between the universalizing gestures of modernism and the singularity of fetishism and subversive "perversion," generating difficult questions about their and our societies, and sparking the search for utopia. While conservative critics consigned Sade's work to the limbo of history (e.g., he wrote in such-and-such a time and is relevant as an example of such-and-such a trend of that time) and individual style (the mark of his rugged singularity), Pleynet prefers to view Sade's work as a "series of questions which will not reduce its transgressive violence" (111). As a radical critic searching for new concepts and methods of critique, Pleynet argues that Sade's work is best understood as a representational strategy that is both modernist and countermodernist; best understood, in short, as embodied activity, as writerly performance. He quotes Sade: "The simplest movements of our bodies are enigmas as difficult to decipher as thoughts, for whoever thinks upon them" (115).

Coming from a very different political, institutional, and theoretical vantage point, Shattuck is less concerned with the contradictions of political action than he is with the unstable, fluid *emotional* charge of radical cultural activity, a charge that fits uneasily with traditional academic language and critical standards. He writes, "The two domains, then, to which Surrealism made a lasting contribution are love and laughter. Other activities of the group look less important now" (26). Though we might disagree with the latter part of that judgment, his focus on affective charge fulfills, no doubt, a necessity that he himself feels lacking in the intellectual environment of his times.

Quite explicitly, Shattuck writes his introduction in response to the success enjoyed by existentialist philosophy, its artistic offshoots in American higher education after World War II, and its role as a catalyst for "cool." Existentialism, Shattuck argues, has, due to its "imposing terminology and a certain high seriousness . . . already been coupled to the other coaches of intellectual history" (23). Neither academic circles nor the students who pass through them can give any space for "the disequilibrium and latent pressure" of surrealism's revolutionary love and laughter (23). Unlike Jean-Paul Sartre's insistent focus on intellectual synthesis, categorical clarity, and totalizing views of human life, surrealism refuses to synthesize ("not to obliterate or climb higher than the big contradictions, but to stand firmly upon them as the surest ground" [22–23]) and refuses to leave behind the problems of emotional life, especially desire.[11] "Little wonder," Shattuck concludes, looking ahead to a discussion of love and laughter, "that [surrealism] has become one of the hardest lessons to present in the institutionalized arena of higher education in the United States" (23).

Both Pleynet and Shattuck assert that contradiction isn't something to be avoided; rather, it is a symptom of vitality, the mark of a latent radicalism that can put to question all aspects of life, including the life of the critic and scholar. They focus on contradiction in order to open space for a reconsideration of the avant-garde that can at once renovate the modes and methods of scholarship and criticism while at the same time keeping open the possibility of avant-gardism as a critical method even after scholarship and criticism has had their say. Pleynet paraphrases the Comte de Lautréamont's oft-quoted call for poetry to be made by all, but swings it in the direction of literary criticism: "To say of Sade that he is readable is to say that he is *still* to be read, and by all" (119). And that is the end of the essay—as if this kind of radically democratic reading can't be captured by an essay, not even in allegorical terms, only introduced, then left to continue on its own. Shattuck, we recall, considers surrealism to be as weighty an issue for his generation as progressive education and pacifism. However, surrealism, and by extension every avant-garde movement, recedes from the view of the critical and scholarly just as surely as love and laughter.

In both essays, we find an interest in playing around certain limits to the critical and scholarly methods and categories of their day, and a wise recognition that those limits can't be crossed, at least for the time being. The kind of playful reticence that we find in their work marks the virtuous failure of their projects, a virtuous failure to claim a way to represent in academic language the specific form that Sade and surrealism might take at the present time. The issue here isn't just ethical or methodological—both critics are aware of what's happening outside their windows. Unlike those who declared the avant-garde dead, Pleynet and Shattuck recognize something distinctly unprecedented happening around them, something that forces them toward an unprecedented level of critical self-reflexivity as they contemplate their subject matter. This self-reflexivity is due in part to the recognition that something is happening "out there," something more than a little aware of these dutiful, remarkable scholars.

The Conceptual Crisis of the Counterculture

In virtually all writings on the avant-garde during the first two decades of the Cold War, we discover an occasionally explicit but mostly tacit acknowledgment of a crisis: a social crisis, a crisis of progressive artistic activity, a crisis of critical standards, a crisis of the critic's authority. To apply Shattuck's metaphor to the works of what must be considered a school unto itself, the Eulogist School of Avant-Garde Studies, we can detect an unmapped continent looming in the haze of discourse: the counterculture. What do I mean by "counterculture"? The answer is not easy, particularly since I want to keep in play the ways that Pleynet and Shattuck deal with the avant-garde (as contradiction, as emotionally charged subject matter). In other words, we need to be as conscious of the limits of concepts and categories as we are of the necessity for clarity of concepts and categories. However, before moving into that kind of self-conscious play, we can establish some common terms and concerns.

The writer who first coined the term *counterculture,* Theodore Roszak, explicitly viewed it as a categorical crisis for academic critics and scholars. This was why he was coining the term—it enabled him to write about something that didn't fit into the language of sociology. This crisis was due to the counterculture's unprecedented social, cultural, and historical being. Unlike previous radical communities and social trends, Roszak argues, the counterculture "arose not out of misery but out of plenty; its role was to explore a new range of issues raised by an unprecedented increase in the standard of living."[12] Not only were the conditions of revolt unprecedented (though "plenty" wasn't as widespread as Roszak would have us believe), but "the very weakness of conventional ideological politics in the United States led the counter culture to its unique insight" (xiii). According to Roszak, one of the most profound challenges posed by the counterculture was its systematic criticism of dominant theories of leadership and leadership training, a criticism that resulted in new organizational structures, some based on participatory democracy and decentered decision making. Demographic changes also produced new kinds of political identities and affiliations that put older analytical methods to the stake. For example, the increasingly right-wing tendencies of working-class organizations such as the AFL-CIO helped promote the development of political groups that focused on the specific needs of youth, students, minorities, and other communities excluded from the Cold War economic boom.

But the social and historical dimensions of countercultural exceptionalism, an exceptionalism not all historians are willing to accept, are not the most significant. As Shattuck implies, emotional experience and emotional intelligence played a significant role in the self-definition of countercultural communities. A perfect example of this kind of emotional, experiential self-definition would be the Student Non-Violent Coordinating Committee

(SNCC), an initially integrated organization that played a significant supporting role for Martin Luther King Jr's efforts in the southern United States during the early 1960s, a role played effectively and enthusiastically until 1965, when, outraged by the assassination of Malcolm X and under intense pressure from radical organizations such as the Revolutionary Action Movement (RAM), it split from the left-liberal King's organization and embraced a culturally radical Black Nationalism. Though the organization's move to nationalism was catalyzed by X's death and the pressure of RAM agent Askia Touré, the move had been prepared by the frustrating pace of nonviolent activism and party politics.[13]

It was also spurred by changes in the way members of the organization began to conceive identity, experience, and culture, issues that were not considered by the Congress of Racial Equality (CORE) as a significant strategic or tactical concern. In an effort to devise a more effective organizational structure and an equally effective recruitment strategy, many of SNCC's members began to focus on the assumptions implicit in SNCC's organizational structure and how those assumptions ran against the culturally specific ways of thinking about self, community, and progressive transformation that were gaining strength among the group's African American members. The conclusion was reached that the shape of the organization contradicted the experience of the majority of its members and of most of the people the organization served. As a consequence, in 1965, all non–African Americans were expelled from the group.

The expulsion was justified by the leaders of SNCC in terms germane to a discussion of the limits of criticism. In the corporately written "SNCC Speaks for Itself" (1965–66), we read: "The myth that the Negro is somehow incapable of liberating himself, is lazy, etc., came out of the American experience. . . . Any white person who comes into the movement has these concepts in his mind about black people, if only subconsciously. He cannot escape them because the whole society has geared his subconscious in that direction."[14] Fortunately, the writers expand their analysis beyond this fairly muddy notion of "subconsciousness." The impact of whites on the movement, they argue, is a complex one related to questions of "identification." The presence of whites, they write, impacts expression, hampers the development of leadership skills among African Americans, ensures the survival of paternalistic forms of racism (in humor, language, gesture), and limits the organization's cultural references and, therefore, its ability to galvanize the broadest possible African American community.

That said, the implications of the 1965 expulsion go beyond the simple rejection of older organizational and political models and into profound issues surrounding institutionalized political movements, the articulation and revision of critical standards, and the strengthening or crossing of cultural boundaries. This lattermost issue, culture—that complicated, fluid, contradictory medium in which individuals and communities produce both themselves and their understandings of self—is the one that demands closest attention. The writers continue, "Too long have we allowed white people to interpret the importance and meaning of the cultural aspects of our society. We have allowed them to tell us what was good about our Afro-American music art, and literature. How many black critics do we have on the 'jazz' scene? How can a white person who is not part of the black psyche (except in the oppressor's role) interpret the meaning of the blues to us who are manifestations of the songs themselves?" They conclude, "We reject the American dream as defined by white people and must work to construct an American reality defined by Afro-Americans" (123). SNCC indicates with these comments that the organization was moving well beyond mere "ideological critique"; it was embracing new forms of political action oriented toward the specific cultural practices of "Afro-America" (not the "Negro") and against the modes of social and political interpretation they saw as hardwired into older leadership and strategic methods and organizations. What we see here isn't just the replacement of liberalism by a more radical political perspective (i.e., nationalism); the very notion of ideology and critique are being reformulated. The organizational shake-up of SNCC is emblematic of how countercultural communities sparked fundamental crises in the modes, methods, and categories of radical activism—and did so through new forms of cultural production. It is this dynamic relationship among methodological and categorical crisis, historical revisionism, and cultural production that will receive the bulk of attention in the case studies that follow.

The Counterculture and the Dialectics of Performance

Despite its inherent diversity and contradictoriness, and despite the presence of the kinds of firm boundaries of experience recognized and exploited by SNCC, there are shared structures that can give the critic and scholar some kind of through-line to follow, and perhaps help us to map general features of the social, cultural, and economic matrix in which the counterculture developed. Thinking about the counterculture in such a fashion—that is, recognizing both its plurality and its structural unity—takes one close to the project described by Fredric Jameson. He urges scholars and critics to assess the fact that the 1960s was an era that introduced innovative forms of oppression as well as unprecedented tactics of liberation, "a moment in which the enlargement of capitalism on a global scale simultaneously produced an immense freeing or unbinding of social movements, a prodigious release of untheorized new forces." Jameson suggests that a "unified field theory" of the 1960s is possible only if we engage in "a properly dialectical process in which 'liberation' and domination are inextricably combined."[15]

One of the sites in which this kind of process can be seen in action is *performance*. It is difficult to overestimate the importance of performance to the development of the counterculture; in fact, it is often asserted (incorrectly) that the 1960s marked the birth of performance as a cultural dominant. Certainly, it is true that performance practices reflected a general concern with tactics as opposed to strategy (that is to say, with local action as the ground for a wider address of larger global issues). At the same time, performance was a method that enabled radicals to devise actions that could address simultaneously the structures of language, economics, politics, social institutions, cultural history, and the body. As both practice and discourse, countercultural performance addressed the need (1) to identify and disrupt existing social, cultural, and economic boundaries, (2) to systematically challenge existing discourses of experience, everyday life, and the politics of culture, (3) to produce new ways of thinking and acting that effectively valued aspects of experience, everyday life, and culture systematically excluded from the mainstream, and (4) to ground all of this in specific social and cultural situations. The Living Theatre, Happenings and Fluxus, and the artists and audiences of the Black Arts Movement—to name only the countercultures studied in the case studies that follow—founded their visions of social, cultural, economic, and historical transformation on a dialectical vision of performance that allows us to comprehend plurality and structure and disables us from welding them together into some kind of static, dialectically synthetic unity.

While many countercultural communities viewed performance in exactly this way—as a unifying, even universal, activity—they did so for distinct, essentially incomparable reasons and in order to address situated concerns. For Julian Beck and Judith Malina's Living Theatre, for example, the moment of performance cleared a conceptual and affective space in the claustrophobic market halls of imperialist capitalism. Despite their efforts to instigate a global anarchist revolution, their efforts to clear that space always depended on the specific audiences for which they performed, even as they absorbed greater and greater numbers of performance practices and traditions into their repertoire. Happenings and Fluxus events also privileged performance as the grounds for global community, but unlike the Living

Theatre, the artists and audiences of early performance art utilized performance not so much to destroy capitalism and capitalist bureaucracy as to divert, exploit, and ironize it. In events such as Allan Kaprow's *Eighteen Happenings in Six Parts* (1959), performance enabled a radical individualization of art by empowering the spectator as an active maker of the art event and by calling into question the ability of any one spectator to create sensible, coherent accounts of it. Performance was also highly valued as a unifying, global cultural practice and critical mode by the Black Arts Movement, the third case study herein, a movement indebted to the pan-African negritude and transnational anticolonial movements of the 1950s and 1960s. However, just as performance addressed for Black artists a range of political, economic, and cultural needs that were very different from those of the Living Theatre and performance artists (not least of which being the desire to radically challenge the Euro-American aesthetic tradition that gave rise to those groups), it also enabled Black artists to articulate a specifically African *American* ethos, an ethos anchored to the traditions, tones, and trickery of African American urban and rural neighborhoods.

Thus, we see both a unifying principle (performance) and a pluralistic basis (the local) when we comparatively examine cultural production among such groups. However, to further complicate matters, we must take account of the terminological issues surrounding performance, which seems to resist any unifying or totalizing definition. Thus, taking account of such practices may complicate Jameson's assertion that a "unified theory" of the counterculture can be achieved—except on a purely terminological level (which may be no small accomplishment). Countercultural cultural producers not only performed the cultural, political, and economic crises of the 1960s, they inaugurated a form of political activity that even to this day— and despite the efforts of dozens of performance theorists—has yet to be sufficiently described; it can never be fully "marked," to recall Peggy Phelan.[16] As French Happenings artist Jean-Jacques Lebel put it in an essay he hurriedly scrambled together during the 1968 occupation of the Odéon Théâtre de France, "Something has changed."[17] The tantalizing vagueness of Lebel's claim isn't just the consequence of the perennial difficulty caused when one analyzes a situation in process; rather, it is the consequence of a more dialectical process, one that demands metaphors such as Karl Marx's "vague immensity," Pleynet's "all," Shattuck's "unmapped continent," or the "fragmentary thought" advocated by the intellectuals surrounding the French journal *Arguments* (1956–62). Countercultural performance trends such as the Living Theatre, early U.S. performance art, and the Black Arts Movement (again, to name only those specific cases I discuss in these pages) inaugurated what might be termed a "performance crisis," an explosion of staged activity that has permanently altered certain aspects of American culture and politics, constituted retroactively a cultural history that had previously existed only on the margins, and produced forms of cultural practice that can never securely enter critical and scholarly discourse. Countercultural performance highlights the limits of criticism.

One of the lessons the scholar and theorist of the avant-garde as a performance tradition must learn is that any theory of the avant-garde is, like Jarry's pataphysics, "the law that governs exceptions."[18] Such exceptions—such performative singularities—catalyze the productive failure of academic efforts to make sense of radical subject matter, but also open efforts to think about the avant-garde to new, more robust forms of diversity and difference. The American counterculture's revolt against bourgeois-liberal society, its singularly diverse matrix of performative events, is particularly hard to systematize. Stiles is therefore correct to "want to describe avant-gardes as plural, existing simultaneously, working in different media synchronistically in local, national, and international settings (each dependent on the context of their practices and politics), and functioning in different social configurations, at different times and for different purposes."[19]

The Limits of Criticism, Liberal Society, and the Performative Avant-Garde

Performance has been a long-lived tradition for the avant-garde, as RoseLee Goldberg demonstrated in 1979, the year the first edition of her pathblazing *Performance: Live Art 1909 to the Present* was published. But performance took on a fundamentally new and more extensive role during the first two decades of the Cold War; specifically, it challenged a vision of the avant-garde that focused on the art object and the objective standards advocated by formalist critics such as Clement Greenberg. The embrace of performance by the Cold War avant-gardes not only challenged critical standards, it compelled a rethinking—a critical remembering, if you will—of the avant-garde tradition as a whole, a rethinking of the basic concepts used to define it, and a rethinking of the methods needed to comprehend it. Goldberg writes, "It is interesting that performance, until that time [1979], had been consistently left out in the process of evaluating artistic development, especially in the modern period, more on account of the difficulty of placing it in the history of art than of any deliberate omission."[20] One reason for this forgetting is that the avant-garde has tended not to honor the kinds of categorical and institutional boundaries respected by its critics and scholars.

Goldberg argues that performance has served regularly as a critical mode *within* avant-garde movements:

> Such a radical stance has made performance a catalyst in the history of twentieth-century art; whenever a certain school, be it Cubism, Minimalism or conceptual art, seemed to have reached an impasse, artists have turned to performance as a way of breaking down categories and indicating new directions. Moreover, within the history of the avant-garde—meaning those artists who led the field in breaking with each successive tradition—performance in the twentieth century has been at the forefront of such an activity: an avant avant-garde.[21]

The problems raised by the intrinsic challenge of avant-garde performance practices are complex and not easily summarized. Goldberg writes that performance history can only "pursue the development of a sensibility. . . . It can only hint at life off the pages."[22] The problems are conceptual in nature, but they're also practical problems, problems that involve various kinds of ontological dilemmas, political judgments, and institutional affiliations; in other words, who is writing, publishing, and reading the pages. An example of such contradictory conceptual and practical dilemmas can be found when we turn to the difficulty faced by audience members who participated in Kaprow's *Eighteen Happenings in Six Parts,* the event that introduced the term *Happening* to art-world discourse. Divided into four groups and separated by semiopaque, sheet plastic room divides; gently assaulted by seemingly random lighting, sound, and performance effects; and continually teased into proclaiming interpretations about what was so clearly a "significant" event, Kaprow's audience members had to confront the fact that they were part of a moment that could never be credibly theorized, adequately criticized, or fully remembered. This notion will be discussed at greater length in chapter 2.

The confrontation of critical scholarship and the specific artistic manifestations of the Cold War avant-garde inevitably and unpredictably throw us into a looping network of lateral connections, unexpected lines of consideration, secret histories, and obscure but substantial conceptual connections— what I will later call a "reticulated terrain." Intensely distrustful of political compromise, cultural radicals during the 1950s, 1960s, and 1970s created profoundly contextual, intensely singular social, cultural, and economic practices that were intended specifically to outwit the institutions and progressive thinkers of liberal-bourgeois society, even those institutions and thinkers sympathetic to their programs. Among those sympathetic institutions and progressive thinkers that I am most interested in were the institutions of higher learning and the scholars and critics enthusiastically shouldering the responsibilities of avant-garde revolt (e.g., the editorial boards of *Tel Quel* and *Partisan Review;* the chairs of art departments at Rutgers, NYU, Cal Tech, etc.; faculty advisers to radical campus groups; Black student unions and Black Studies collectives at Merritt College, San Francisco State University, Wayne State University, University of Massachusetts–Amherst; performers and scholars organizing performance studies groups; etc.).

Without in any way disparaging such activists, organizations, and institutions, it is vital that we be honest about the limits of action and vision. Even if scholars, critics, and teachers serve as a critical force within liberal democracy—whether for Right or Left—they were and are, in the end, no true friend of the avant-garde, which must be defined, in the end, as a radical, revolutionary cultural movement that works outside of parliamentary process and not merely an urge toward formal or conceptual experiment. Regardless of political belief, the scholars, critics, and teachers who study the avant-garde are, by and large, employees of higher education, academic publishing houses, and the system of galleries and auction houses that buy and sell the works of the avant-garde.

Again, the intent here is not to disparage scholars, critics, and teachers who actively engage with the avant-garde—the intent here is to criticize, not dismiss. Indeed, a history of the Cold War avant-garde can't be told without taking account of innovative educational institutions such as Black Mountain College, Antioch College, and the New School for Social Research, not to mention equally important programs within traditional institutions, of which the art department at Rutgers and the performance studies programs at NYU and Northwestern are perhaps the most significant. Just as surely, it would be impossible to write this book without the work of individuals who have challenged the institutions in which they work to secure a place for performance and performance studies in the humanities and social sciences (e.g. Richard Schechner, Lucy Lippard, Dwight Conquergood, Diana Taylor, Barbara Kirshenblatt-Gimblett, Craig Owens, Kristine Stiles, Jill Dolan). Nor are terms like "radical" and "revolutionary" used blithely. Rather, there must be recognition of certain limits and of the hazards of forgetting that there are always new historical, conceptual, and methodological possibilities.

The avant-garde is, by definition and for better *and* worse, an antiliberal, antiparliamentary trend, a trend rooted in the military tendencies of extreme ideological positions, positions that tend to be lumped crudely together in terms of "Left" and "Right." The avant-garde is a cultural trend born in the radical ideologies and radical social movements of the bourgeois West, particularly those that favored the use of violent, nonparliamentary means to achieve their political goals.[23] That said, bourgeois-liberal governments and entrepreneurs have demonstrated, from time to time, support of the avant-garde in its less overtly political manifestations. One might think, for examples, of Napoleon III's reorganization of the Ecole des Beaux-Arts and support for the Salon des Refusés against the royalist conservatives and academic traditionalists of mid-nineteenth-century France or publisher Henry Clare Luce's enthusiastic support for the American abstract expressionists during the 1950s. Though it has more often than not targeted the avant-garde as an enemy, bourgeois liberalism stands in a pretty fickle relationship to its radical wild child. In part, this is due to the quirky nature of liberalism. Liberalism is a tradition as fluid and flexible as it is hardy, a fact that inevitably complicates any effort to challenge it from Left or Right, inevitably pressing the challengers continually to take on new forms while maintaining, as best they can, some sense of historical continuity.

Anarchism, fascism, communism, mysticism, addiction, pacifism, religious revivalism, obscenity, and many other radical challenges have all played significant roles in the avant-garde's persistent, mutative attack on the cultural, social, political, and economic institutions of bourgeois-liberal society. The always-changing terrain upon which avant-gardes maneuver often pose individual groups against each other in interesting fashion—and occasionally against their own fundamental imperatives. For example, Abbie Hoffman and Jerry Rubin both viewed their Dadaesque guerrilla performances as a way of radicalizing—if not altogether destroying—what is often called (after Guy Debord) the "society of spectacle." For Hoffman and Rubin's mythical organization Yippie! the ubiquity and vacuity of the mass media created endless opportunities for improvisational scandal and symbolic gestures; for example, throwing ashes in the eyes of utilities executives, or throwing dollar bills onto the floor of the New York Stock Exchange and inciting a stampede. Yippie! was itself the kind of mythic, spectral threat often manufactured by the media to generate public support for the harassment of nonconformists. For Rubin, the very impossibility of controlling the ways that countercultural acts were depicted by news organizations, administration officials, and professors was less a curse than an opportunity for mass revolt and anarchist collectivism. As he put it, "I've never seen 'bad' coverage of a demonstration. It makes no difference what they say about us. The pictures are the story."[24]

While certainly struggling within and against the politics of mass-mediated spectacle, the Black Arts Movement theater collectives of Seattle, Chicago, Harlem, Miami, New Orleans, and other urban and academic centers addressed very different concerns from Yippie! and in very different ways—yet performance was part of the fabric of their revolt, too. Black artists and audiences were not interested in making spectacle for the sheer sake of spectacle (neither were they in anarchist collectivism); quite the contrary, they had goals in mind that were specific to their community, particularly the generation of empowering, radicalizing images of Blackness that could counter the racism of the mass media and the mainstream institutions of arts and cultural criticism. For the cultural nationalists who drew the theoretical and strategic map for the movement, performance enabled a critical blow against Euro-American understandings of politics, aesthetics, and community organization and was also a way of creating radical events that could effectively outmaneuver the "white eye" of the mass media. The need to create empowering representations and simultaneously control the interpretation of those representations separates the Black Arts Movement from the anarchist high-jinks of Yippie! The very notion of throwing away money would have deeply offended artists and audiences who had been systematically excluded from economic opportunity.

However, despite their differences, Yippie! and Black Arts performance both emblematize a general countercultural interest in local action and grassroots organizing; in other words, political activism outside the standard institutional structures and procedures of the bourgeois-liberal state. They share in what Rebecca Klatch has described as the counterculture's "common sense of generational mission and . . . shared revulsion . . . for the liberal managerial state."[25] Like their counterparts on the putatively less artistic terrain of political activism—one thinks of Rosa Parks's refusal to take her place on a bus or the right-wing Young Americans for Freedom rallying against centrist forces in the Republican Party—these groups utilized a range of new organizational, analytic, and communication methods both to address the failure of national and international organizations and to map the contours of local concern. In the case of the Black Arts Movement, for example, the effort to build theaters of, for, and by the African American community (1) stood in opposition to the systematic misunderstanding of that community by the white-controlled media and governmental and social service organizations, (2) refined a pan-African aesthetic that was already a significant presence in global culture, and (3) addressed in dramatic and theatrical form the specific legal, spiritual, and historical needs of the neighborhoods it served.

The necessity of tailoring oppositional action to local situations often compelled countercultural groups to significantly revise their own theory and practice. As a consequence, groups often had to demarcate their own work depending on the context in which it was manifested. This is no more clear than in the case of the Otrabanda company. In 1969, Diane Brown and David Dawkins, armed with a well-thumbed copy of Mark Twain's *Life on the Mississippi,* assembled a simple, self-propelled raft out of oil drums, a hundred dollars' worth of lumber, and a few odds and ends of camping gear, then floated it down the river, where they discovered the small, almost forgotten towns that pepper the banks between St. Louis and New Orleans. This trip impressed upon the two the possibility of experiencing life and art together in a truly revolutionary way, marking their journey as an adventure in populist aesthetics. The validity of this adventure was further ratified (and globalized) when, in that same year, the Flemish playwright and director Tone Brulin was invited to give workshops at the school that Brown and Dawkins attended: Antioch College, a small, progressive school located east of Dayton, Ohio, tucked close by the Wright-Patterson Air Force Base, and committed to cooperative education and participatory democracy. Brulin's work in the theater was deeply influenced by the "poor theater" of Jerzy Grotowski and Eugenio Barba, which attempted to purify the form of the techniques and traditions that undermined global brotherhood by stripping theater down to its bare essentials: the actor's body and the cleared performance space. Brulin's pared-down, technically rigorous, spiritually oriented techniques appeared to Brown, Dawkins, and the other members of the workshop to embody precisely what the impoverished communities along the Mississippi River needed. The troupe's commitment to the implementation of a true "people's theater" that would synthesize both the newest trends from Europe and the popular cultures of the river regions led quickly to some fairly significant critical success in Baltimore, Los Angeles, and New York.

The troupe was also led to some fairly unsettling conclusions about what constituted people's theater; specifically, that what counted as people's theater in Manhattan had a tough go on the banks of the Mississippi. In the summer of '73, the company decided to take their well-reviewed play *Stump Removal* to the river, supplemented by a preshow vaudeville act that would showcase the diverse talents of the members and serve to gather and warm up a crowd. Typically, the communities would be thrilled by the arrival of the raft and its sarong-clad, hippie-ish performers and show their usual, profound hospitality. However, when the preshow ended and the play began, audiences simply left, bored, befuddled, and usually offended. Otrabanda quickly dropped *Stump Removal* from the bill and were bereft of the most explicitly political aspect of their program.

Literally in midstream of their first river tour, the company had to reassess their notions of what the people wanted and needed as well as their own need to do work that was socially significant. Their solutions are worth noting. Compelled to radically alter the experimental theatricals applauded in major urban centers and to drop overtly political references from their *River Raft Revue,* Otrabanda had to, in Ellen Maddow's words, "realize that a lot of content existed in the event itself. Here was a group of people, at first labeled 'hippies,' who turned out to be hard-working and dedicated to providing good entertainment to the towns."[26] First, they expanded their vaudeville intro so that it referenced local political concerns but in a form familiar to their audiences. Second, they established workshops so that their audiences could see how they transformed from "normal" people to performers. Lastly, they invented a bagful of participatory performance techniques. Otrabanda member David Dawkins found the changes ultimately positive: "What we were made a much heavier impact than our avant-garde experiments. [The rural audiences] always said we were just college kids. But we showed them that this is what we do for a living. This is our life. And that really energized them."[27]

As a consequence, Otrabanda stood in a position of empowering (if occasionally frustrating) ambivalence as an avowedly avant-garde group. This in-between state enabled them to be critical of a broader range of American cultural traditions, but never all at the same time. In Manhattan and Los Angeles, where the avant-garde was a deeply rooted tradition, the troupe turned its attention against the assumptions of that tradition. Where Grotowski's practices and theories were in the ascendant, Otrabanda criticized them. As Lloyd Steele noted in regard to the production of *Stump Removal,* "They have none of Grotowski's obsessive concern with the actor's inner truth; nor do they search in such fine detail for physical equivalents of the various states of mind; nor do they directly involve the audience in their deliberately 'old-fashioned' proscenium staging. Theirs is a 'poor' theater, but what they do on stage is somewhere between a happening and a children's show: a uniquely American form that tries as hard to be entertaining as it does to be enlightening."[28] Where Grotowski's innovations were too alien and the avant-garde barely a rumor, they turned to the local traditions of circus, vaudeville, religious revival, and puppetry—but in a way that challenged the traditional definitions of "entertainment" by turning the entertainment event into a community event.

We can break down this notion of localized vanguardism even further. Their annual shows at the Menard Psychiatric Center were most significant for their postperformance workshops in makeup technique, the success of which led the company to expose the backstage areas of their tent during subsequent river tours. Demonstrating the ability to take on new identities and perform living in new ways constituted a significant intervention in the lives of the inmates. Otrabanda demonstrates to us the ways that performance's problematic synthesis of the local and the global renders even the individual counterculture mercurial, situational. Just as surely, we also see it pressuring individual countercultures to transform themselves in response to the distinct demands of context. As David Riley says, "The problem lies not with the performers' talents, which dazzle even befuddled spectators, but in their split ambition of wanting to be in both the vanguard of the people and the vanguard of their art."[29]

This long-lived dilemma of the avant-garde—to be advanced both technically and politically—was not a dilemma to be solved so much as a tension to be played within, resolved and dissolved, resolved again, and so on. Plurality, while not a universal within the counterculture, was a vital force within its avant-garde factions, trends, and communities. Often attacked, often derided, the commitment to and practice of plurality marks the counterculture as both an innovative, if late-born, trend within avant-garde history (the countercultural avant-garde as a "neo" avant-garde); but it also demonstrates a profound continuity with that history's often forgotten roots deep within the tradition of social activism and universalist pretense, an answer, however tentative and ephemeral, to the unanswered questions of liberty, love, and democracy that have been asked continually since the great bourgeois revolutions of the eighteenth century and that became all the more pressing during the two centuries of reaction that followed.

Performing Crisis

These unanswered questions have, in recent years, come to be asked in terms of performance and performativity. Clifford Geertz has described the diffusion of performance methods and concepts during the Cold War as "not just another redrawing of the cultural map—the moving of a few disputed borders, the marking of some more picturesque mountain lakes—but an alteration of the principles of mapping. Something is happening to the way we think about the way we think."[30] On a less sanguine note, Jon McKenzie argues that "performance will be to the 20th and 21st centuries what discipline was to the 18th and 19th, that is, an onto-historical formation of power and knowledge." Riffing off Michel Foucault's work on the development of penal systems in the liberal West, McKenzie argues that, like discipline, performance "produces a new subject of knowledge," one that is "constructed as fragmented rather than unified, decentered rather than centered, virtual as well as actual."[31] As demonstrated by scholars from a range of academic disciplines, the concepts and vocabulary that define collective notions of community almost always define us as performers; that is, as individuals simultaneously obligated and enabled by the rules of decorum and standards of visible truth that help to constitute our sense of historicity and belonging. Normally, these rules and standards are so commonsensical that their performative nature is obscured. However, when such rules and standards begin to seem insufficient or illegitimate—as happened in diverse sectors of American society during the Cold War—then our sense of self, community, and history loses its patina of logic and righteousness. How we perform culture is put to the stake. Society suffers a kind of "performing crisis." In the 1960s, this crisis catalyzed the development of the new subject of knowledge described by McKenzie, though that subject was not always envisioned as fragmented, decentered, or virtual.

During such crises, officially sanctioned forms of artistic performance, which are in essence idealized forms of social consciousness, lose a sense of motivation. Thus, the performing crisis is mediated—made concrete—by the performance arts. At such moments, alternative theaters, performance communities, subcultures, and innovative performing arts tend to arise, bringing with them new visions of self, community, and history. In terms of theater, dramatic form, acting technique, stage-audience relations, the use of props, the significance of movement, acceptable kinds of content, the performance space, and other elements of the performance dynamic are often put to question. When the Living Theatre confronted the burgeoning War on Drugs in *The Connection,* they were not merely revealing a hitherto mis- or underrepresented reality. *The Connection* is not just a Bebop bastardization of Maxim Gorky's *The Lower Depths* (1902). By utilizing improvisatory jazz and a self-deconstructing, hyperrealistic performance methodology, they were hinting at new forms of subjectivity, new ways of communicating, new rhythms of self-transformation, and new models of community organization—the new mode and subject of knowledge described by Geertz and McKenzie. In this sense, the Living Theatre explored the ground described by Geertz when he writes, "What connects [the various disciplinary uses of performance] is the view that human beings are less driven by forces than submissive to rules, that the rules are such as to suggest strategies, the strategies are such as to inspire actions, and the actions are such as to be self-rewarding" (26). At the same time, their extensive borrowing from jazz performance techniques, drug literature, and Pirandello reflects a concern described well by Hal Foster: "Indeed, such art often invokes different, even incommensurate models, but less to act them out in a hysterical pastiche (as in much art in the 1980s) than to work them through to a reflexive practice—to turn the very limitations of these models into a critical consciousness of history, artistic and otherwise."[32]

No account of performance can fully conceptualize the intensely experiential, contradictory qualities, the "what" and "where" that tend to trouble formal analysis. This is particularly true of performances that, as is the case in the three studies that follow, establish and cross multiple lines of demarcation, lines that, in Foster's words, press on us the crucial "question of avant-garde causality, temporality, and narrativity."[33] One of our more useful inheritances from the "hermeneutics of suspicion" (to recall Paul Ricoeur's description of the critical heritage of Marx, Freud, and Nietzsche)[34] is that it has impressed upon critics and scholars the fact that all aspects of culture can be considered political. Moreover, the specific political structures in question need not be easily ascertainable; rather the structures must be reconstructed via acts of interpretation—of critical performance. Of great importance to such suspicious ways of reading—of performing—the world as text is the idea that interpretations are always predetermined by the context in which interpretations occur. Scholars and critics perform within a "hermeneutic circle" that is very much like a theatrical stage, predisposed in specific, not always conscious ways toward the object of our concern, predispositions that profoundly shape our interpretations. As a consequence, the question of performance becomes increasingly important not only for avant-garde performers, but for the intellectual event of scholarship, criticism, and pedagogy. This was certainly recognized by Pleynet and Shattuck.

Foster also recognizes this dilemma when he acknowledges the weaknesses of the avant-garde model: "the ideology of progress, the presumption of originality, the elitist hermeticism, the historical exclusivity, the appropriation by the culture industry."[35] Yet he also points out that the avant-garde "remains a crucial coarticulation of artistic and political forms" demanding "new genealogies for the avant-garde that complicate its past and support its future."[36] This is a rich attitude to hold, all the more so when we turn to sites in which coarticulations and histories intersect in especially complicated ways. As Goldberg has demonstrated, a focus on performance is perhaps the single most effective way to produce complications in theory and practice. Performance enables us to understand political struggle in useful, concrete ways—and yet it also underlines the gaps that continually open in our efforts to understand, the openness that thought must have to the situation of political activism.

Erwin Piscator, who along with Vsevelod Meyerhold and Bertolt Brecht can be tagged as a pioneer of self-consciously "political" theater, makes this point quite clearly when he describes the premiere of his 1924 production of *Flags*. The back projectors, the overtly didactic script, the strategic disjunctures of melodramatic form—all were, to use Piscator's metaphor, "shit."[37] Happily, the audience disagreed, finding the combination of proletarian hoopla and avant-garde shock both entertaining and energizing. This gap between Piscator and his audience's reactions will be a model throughout this book. As seen in the case of SNCC, Otrabanda, and the essays of Pleynet, Shattuck, and Roszak, it's difficult, if not impossible, to stabilize critical method and vocabulary in the face of the diverse communities that contribute to the performative event. In this sense, all theory can function as a form of forgetting, of bad memory (the irruption of hitherto unrecognizable genealogies), but potentially in a virtuous, productive way.

How can virtue be ensured? First, following Stiles, one must not utilize abstractions at the cost of the behavioral situations of the specific performance.[38] There are certain ways that text, performance, and theory play with and against each other in specific contexts, ways that necessarily result in the failure of explanation, historicization, and interpretation. Moments like these—Sade and surrealism both come to mind, but also such fleeting events as an exemplary performance of an otherwise desultory production of a play, a particularly apt inflection of a free-verse stanza, the *communitas* achieved during a fleeting minute of oratorical perfection, the mounting excitement of an jazz-jam finding new spaces in old standards, the high risk of a police line breaking, and even more individualistic moments like the taste of a madeleine soaked in linden tea or the particular conjunction of sights and sounds from a seat at a Happening—pull the scholar or critic forcefully into confrontation with a basic anxiety, as well as with an unparalleled opportunity to rethink how they think and how they relate experientially and intellectually to the subject of their analysis. Such moments enable one to reconsider the very act of scholarly consideration and its capacity to transform contradiction into platitude. Martin Heidegger noted that it is not when our tools work, but when they fail that the most far-reaching and self-critical analysis is enabled.[39] The failure of the tool is endemic to the moments with which this book is concerned.

One of the key functions of political performance, to recall Graham Holderness's *The Politics of Theatre and Drama,* is to identify the "political character of a cultural form," an identification that should trace "the politics of form—estranging, alienating, self-reflexive—and its politics of function—destabilizing the conventional relation between spectator and performance, disrupting traditional expectations of narrative and aesthetic coherence," and so on.[40] Holderness is working a Brechtian approach here, but he boils Brecht's theories down a bit too thickly and spreads them a little too thin. Theorists must be careful not to allow the important work of identifying the politics of a particular cultural form to devolve into what might be called the "technical fallacy," that is, the belief that formal innovation is political innovation. The technical fallacy tends to render abstract the singular relationships of form and content that are manifested in specific performance contexts. Holderness is himself guilty of this when he generalizes Brecht's theories, thereby forgetting the cultural, material, and historical determinations of form, content, and moment that were the foundation of Brecht's probing work. Theoretical approaches to the politics of cultural production are especially prone to this fallacy, given the general tendency to equate theory with deductive method. Theory is a form of technology, after all, and since technology is always and forever available for appropriation, unless critics and scholars focus on the particular contexts in which technology is put to use, they will lose sight of the crucial issues relating to context, the issues reflected in, say, the struggles of Otrabanda and SNCC to devise tactics to energize and activate their audiences. In the three case studies of this book, the relationship of form, content, and critical knowledge always engages the politics of theorization.

Such situational qualities in no way impede political efficacy nor the effective use of theory, though it does complicate analysis. For example, Black playwright Ron Milner's domestic melodrama *Who's Got His Own* (1967) was almost universally recognized by his Black Arts colleagues as a politically efficacious play, even by critics like Larry Neal who were well versed in (and suspicious of) the avant-garde, the modernist dramatic tradition, and Brecht's critique of melodrama. However, according to Holderness's theory of formal alienation, Milner's play could only be considered reactionary. It is a realistic domestic drama that follows an essentially Aristotelian dramatic line and relies on coherent characters and identifiable, progressively complicated conflicts. However, the critical edge of the play is found not in its form, but in the specific forms of sharing it sponsored between audience and actors in the specific contexts of its performances. Witnesses to the first production of Milner's play at the American Place Theatre relate that white and African American spectators perceived the play in distinct ways. Wynn Handman remembers the absolute silence of whites and the continual, self-recognizing laughter of African American viewers. Because American Place was a theater-in-the-round, the spectators were not only able to respond in highly communitarian fashion, but could also recognize the differences in community response.[41] They watched the play and they watched themselves watching the play, no doubt responding to both spectacles. It was the performance situation, not the form (character, dialogue, dramatic structure), that defined the politics of performance.

Herbert Blau has commented on the technical fallacy—particularly the tendency to use Brecht as a prop to such fallacious thinking—within academic studies. He notes that innovative, activizing performance techniques often begin as truly avant-garde only to be "sterilized or neutralized, coterminous with technocracy."[42] André Breton would agree: "It is not by 'mechanism' that the Western peoples can be saved . . . it is not here that they will escape the moral disease of which they are dying."[43] I'm not just rehearsing here the old argument on co-optation of the avant-garde; this is an issue of effective tools being carried beyond the contexts and situations for which they were devised.

Teresa de Lauretis has addressed this issue, too, arguing that even the most politically committed analyses tend to endanger concrete considerations of political action. Speaking to the dilemmas surrounding a theorization of feminist film, she writes,

> The questions of identification, self-definition, the modes or the very possibility of envisaging oneself as subject—which the male avant-garde artists and theorists have also been asking, on their part, for almost one hundred years, even as they work to subvert the dominant representations or to challenge their hegemony—are fundamental questions for feminism.[44]

But she refuses to conflate technical innovation with the complexities of reception and the singular dynamics of performance-in-context:

> To ask of these women's films: What formal, stylistic, or thematic markers point to a female presence behind the camera? And hence to generalize and universalize, to say: This is the look and sound of women's cinema, this is its language—finally only means complying, accepting a certain definition of art, cinema, and culture, and obligingly showing how women can and do "contribute," pay their tribute, to "society."[45]

De Lauretis finally refuses the question of form altogether, characterizing the form/content debate as "fundamentally a rhetorical question," and urges us instead to direct our critical gaze "toward the wider public sphere of cinema as a social technology" (134). Doing this, she argues, we can begin to understand the audience as possessing its own differences—for de Lauretis, "differences among women" and "differences *within* women."[46] De Lauretis pushes us to move beyond aesthetic questions to contextual issues, issues that may not possess any universal validity, but might be extremely potent. Stiles has also argued this point, warning us away from abstract consideration of radical*ism* to the description of radical acts.[47]

The courting of an audience and the establishment of situations for action were crucial concerns of most countercultural groups—an urge that places them at some distance from most pre–Cold War avant-gardes, which tended (with the exception of those affiliated with Popular Front organizations during the 1930s) to pursue an elitist line of development that is productively compared to the cenacle model that enjoyed widespread popularity in the late 1800s. Even if the cenacle model was rejected, more often than not the community for whom the avant-garde served as avant-garde (the working class, for example) was little more than a rhetorical mirage, a crutch for manifestos and aesthetic experiment. However, the counterculture tended to be profoundly committed to communication with the people they wished to help, not least because they were a part of that community. This kind of commitment and identity demanded new forms of avant-garde community and communication. Theodore Shank notes the impact of this concern on the organizational structure of one particular countercultural community, the theater troupe. He writes, "When an alternative culture and life-style began to take shape in the mid-1960s, another kind of producing organization came into being. In part it was a grassroots movement in that some of the participants did not come from the theatrical profession but were drawn to theater as a means of expression for their social and political commitment."[48] This kind of grassroots dynamic produced a number of unexpected problems for critics who wish to attend to the politics of form, problems that were hinted at by David Riley in his review of Otrabanda's first *River Raft Revue*.

The dilemma faced by the Cold War avant-garde—how to be in the forefront of art and the people—continues to be relevant for cultural activists in our own time. For example, Sue-Ellen Case has argued that the specific performance styles of Peggy Shaw and Lois Weaver and the specific formal qualities of one dramatic text enabled Holly Hughes's play *Dress Suits to Hire* (1987) to be a "lesbian text."[49] However, when that play was staged outside a "lesbian spectatorial community" in Ann Arbor in 1988, assimilation and co-optation occurred, according to Case, because of the demands of a more heterogeneous audience and its diverse "horizons of expectations."[50] As a consequence, Case argues, the political needs of lesbians were being transformed into mere themes for "presses, ivy league schools, and regional theaters . . . bedecking themselves with lesbian/gay themes and studies like wearing Liz Taylor's diamond."[51] Though sympathetic with Case's argument, Lynda Hart counters, "Depending upon whether a spectator is invested in the production of visible identities or whether she is looking at the performance and making identifications," the performance of lesbian subjectivity "is bound to be caught in the clash of conflicting desires."[52] Not unlike *Who's Got His Own*, *Dress Suits* is a lesbian text only in situation; taking a cue from Stanley Fish, one might argue that the "lesbian text" called *Dress Suits for Hire* does not *exist* at all.[53] Case's assertion is founded upon an a priori assumption of a particular, situational dynamic of performance and reception, a particular situation of text, performance, audience, and critic that she has hypostasized into a theoretical representation of the form/content relationship. In other words, she's committed the technical fallacy. As fallacious as it is, however, her criticism is no less worth attending to, even if we ultimately discover, following de Lauretis, that there are significant differences not only between the lesbian and nonlesbian audience, but also *within* the lesbian audience itself. In fact, Case acutely demonstrates how the critic can supply the language and concepts to describe how a group identity can be courted, reinforced, and transformed by a performance event carried out by a vanguard.

Like the "lesbian" text, the politics of countercultural performance are the creature of a situation. By "situation," I refer explicitly to the Situationist International's efforts to construct a political strategy adequate to the fact that all political analysis must ultimately answer to the singularities of practice, practice that occurs in a "unitary ensemble of behavior in time . . . composed of gestures contained in a transitory décor . . . a temporary field of activity favorable to . . . desires."[54] To the Situationists, the unity of theory and practice was inseparable from the "dynamization of elements" inhering in the specific context of activism. "Situation" also brings into play something along the lines of what Homi Bhabha calls the "third space," "which represents both the general conditions of language and the specific implication of the utterance in a performative and institutional strategy of which it cannot 'in itself' be conscious."[55] The effort toward such a third space can be detected in many countercultural performances, including those that, at first glance, seem to militate against the kind of instability and hybridity celebrated by Bhabha and other postmodernists.

One might cite the distinct political meanings of *Dutchman* when it was premiered in 1965 as an example of such a third space. The Cherry Lane Theatre production was a critical and financial hit; however, when the play was produced on Harlem street corners that summer as part of the Black

Arts Repertory Theatre/School's cultural offensive, it was deemed "racist" by the authorities and ultimately contributed to the reappropriation of the school's funding and, as a consequence, the school's demise. At the same time, the production enabled the self-identification of a community of African Americans who at one and the same time were appropriating the legacies of the Western Enlightenment and recapturing the history of the African diaspora.

Another example of a third space—this one more in line with the kind of decentered identity celebrated by postmodernists—would be drag queens such as Sylvia (Ray) Rivera, who played a significant role in the street fighting that broke out the night of Judy Garland's death, June 27, 1969, around Greenwich Village's Stonewall Inn. As Martin Duberman has it, "Sylvia didn't care much about definitions, which was precisely why she would emerge as a radical figure. She disliked any attempt to categorize her random, sometimes contradictory impulses, to make them seem more uniform and predictable than they were."[56] In the close confines of the Stonewall and the tangled Village streets surrounding it, such antipathy toward definition possessed enough explosive force to kick off the queer liberation movement.

Judith Butler, whose work affords one of the most complex and challenging articulations of performance (not to mention the "queer") as a critical mode and cultural practice, has much to say about the explosive force possessed by Rivera. It is precisely his/her problematization of gender (Duberman: "This was . . . why she decided against a sex change. She didn't want to be cast in *any* one mold")[57] that Butler would conceivably find most exciting, precisely because it refuses any stable relationship of form and content. Butler's writings persistently identify the conceptual instability introduced by performance into philosophy, political theory, and ethics. In *Gender Trouble*, Butler demonstrates that even the kinds of deeply rooted identities and experiences that motivated SNCC leaders to expel whites from the organization are ultimately strategic fictions. "From what strategic position in public discourse," she asks, "and for what reasons has the trope of interiority and the disjunctive binary of inner/outer taken hold? In what language is 'inner space' figured? . . . How does a body figure on its surface the very invisibility of its hidden depth?"[58] Butler's point is that a culture is composed of various kinds of institutionalized and socialized hermeneutic strategies, particular ways of interpreting or deciphering the body that congeal habitually, strategically, and behaviorally around certain pairings of signifier and signified, pairings that produce on our body's surfaces signs that produce, in turn, echoes of interiority. Performance precedes identity.

By conceiving objects, bodies, and institutions as always open to the disruptive potential of performance, she also acknowledges the deep gaps that can open between theory and performance. In a discussion of parody, Butler identifies a basic dilemma involved in any assertion that a particular performance technique is more or less radical than another.

> Parody by itself is not subversive, and there must be a way to understand what makes certain kinds of parodic repetitions effectively disruptive, truly troubling, and which repetitions become domesticated and recirculated as instruments of cultural hegemony. A typology of actions would clearly not suffice, for parodic displacement, indeed, parodic laughter, depends on a context and reception in which subversive confusions can be fostered. What performance where will invert the outer/inner distinction and compel a radical rethinking of the psychological presuppositions of gender identity and sexuality? What performance where will compel a reconsideration of the *place* and stability of the masculine and the feminine? And what kind of gender performance will enact and reveal the performativity of gender itself in a way that destabilizes the naturalized categories of identity and desire?[59]

Butler leaves these questions unanswered—and for good reason. That odd syntactical knot "what performance where" opens the deconstruction of culture and cultural signifiers to a different kind of critical activity, a criticism that searches out not only the place and time of subversion, but also the place and time of the critic-scholar, a place and time that stand in highly problematic relationship to the place and time of subversion. This different kind of critical activity demands a proficiency in the methodologically distinct fields of anthropology, historiography, sociology, economics, theater historiography, literary analysis, and psychology. By refusing the notion that a particular relationship of form and content is inevitably, virtuously radical, Butler compels us toward recognition of the site-specific nature of performative politics—something recognized by Marcelin Pleynet and Roger Shattuck.

A general theory of countercultural performance is impossible if, by theory, we mean a universally applicable, logically rigorous description that can bridge the gap between the general and the specific. The specific kinds of disruption, subversion, identification, and rebellion produced within the "what" and "where" of countercultural performance must be approached not only with a range of disciplinary methods, but also an acute consciousness of the "what" and "where" of the methodological application itself. If scholars, critics, and teachers wish to keep open the possibility of progressive aesthetic action, then the production, circulation, and reception of critical-scholarly work, the specific dynamic of power and knowledge in specific departments and educational institutions, and the larger social, economic, and cultural structures of our society must be recognized and, to whatever extent is useful, made part of the work itself. The technical fallacy should be identified in all its manifestations and counteracted by a properly performative perspective. It is precisely the failure to account for this perspective that doomed to failure that school of avant-garde scholarship and criticism which I've named the "Eulogist school."

The Strange Afterlife of the Eulogist School

Sarah Bey-Cheng reminded me once in conversation that everyone who writes about the avant-garde invents a new theory of the avant-garde, a theory that just so happens to perfectly explain the evidence and data that are cited and examined. Even admitting this kind of scholarly putting of wagon before horse, there are theories of the avant-garde that have proven pretty solvent: Lenin's theory of the revolutionary party, Butler's take on performativity, Bürger's institutional self-subversion, Maoist cultural revolution, the critical ethnography of the surrealists, Foucault's theory of the specific intellectual. These are all acute and effective descriptions of cultural radicalism in and against the West, descriptions that can work to unify avant-garde history in a way that is not totalizing or incapable of self-criticism, but nevertheless possess a degree of discursive coherence. The representation of the avant-garde that can ultimately be derived from the three case studies that follow is framed in and occasionally against these models and focuses particularly on how the avant-garde event exists not just in its moment, but occasionally as an ongoing crisis in thought, language, and institutions. In other words, it keeps in mind how a six-foot steel cube, a twenty-foot-tall puppet looming over an antiwar demonstration, or a five-bar moment of transformative jazz improvisation constitutes a situation or third space, an environment in which certain kinds of thinking, arguing, and acting take shape. Response to these kinds of events—whether in the moment of performance or in the performative writing of that moment—is itself part of that cultural situation, one that extends through time and space well beyond the original performance.

If we date the origins of the concept of the avant-garde somewhere between its proclamation by Henri de Saint-Simon in 1825 and the rise of "bohemia" in the 1830s and 1840s, we realize at one and the same time how young the concept is and how hardy and adaptable it has proven as a set of concepts, strategies, and tactics poised against various trends within post-bourgeois societies. The avant-garde's peculiar variety of *probity* has proven pretty hardy, despite the voices and forces weighed against it.[60] True, the continuing vitality of the avant-garde is due to the fact that it has played, in Manfredo Tafuri's phrase, the role of "ideological prefiguration" for ideo-logical and bureaucratic recuperation, giving its enemy both the imaginary and technical means necessary for it to overcome the immanent social, cul-tural, and economic crisis figured by the avant-garde.[61] However, I do not accept Tafuri's tacit assertion that, as prefiguration, the avant-garde is essen-tially dysfunctional. The interdisciplinary artistic works, theoretical pro-nouncements, and political acts of radical-minded painters, poets, perform-ers, dancers, playwrights, sculptors, impresarios, hangers-on, fellow travelers, art dealers, museum curators, collectors, composers, and musicians have no doubt changed the way postbourgeois societies and subjects think and enact themselves, for better *and* worse. The vitality of the avant-garde concept, at a new peak marked by 9/11, speaks to the avant-garde's contra-dictory capacity to catalyze progressive or reactionary movement within the core principles of the modern era: freedom of expression and cultural, polit-ical, and economic self-determination.

As Paul Mann has demonstrated, the writing of the avant-garde's death always brings into play *theory,* which can be defined, following Daniel Her-witz, as a way of thinking that, "in the weak sense," describes how practice is "prefigured by complex beliefs of all kinds, ranging from religious beliefs to beliefs about science, theory of color, method, craft, and social welfare"; or, in a stronger sense, "are designed to engender thought about the con-cepts, expectations, and desires a viewer inevitably brings to the art encounter."[62] In this stronger sense, theory doesn't just settle accounts with the artwork; rather, it can open up new kinds of questions and new direc-tions for artistic experiment and activism, or, on the other hand, close down such possibilities. Mann and Herwitz draw our attention to the necessary relationship of the avant-garde to the systematic, speculative abstractions that relate it not merely to the languages and issues of art, but to broader questions of philosophy, ethics, and politics. At the same time, they note that theory tends to foreclose on certain aspects of the avant-garde chal-lenge. The avant-garde work, Herwitz explains, has traditionally been viewed as the illustration of a specific avant-garde theory, whether that the-ory is named naturalism, Orphism, *lettrisme,* COBRA, or something else. This dynamic of theory and work can be viewed as functioning within a distinctly Western tradition that views art as "demonstrat[ing] to the world through its formal perfection the fact that extreme and ancient philosophical truths can and will be embodied in the world" (8).

This is no doubt a significant accomplishment, not one to be dismissed. Avant-gardes can be read in precisely such a fashion—and viewed as significant for embodying their truth. In fact, most eulogies of the avant-garde are ultimately eulogies for the unity of truth and art embodied, supposedly, by a specific moment or movement in avant-garde history. Yet there are, as Herwitz notes, other ways of viewing the avant-garde that can retain the logical rigor of theory but also take account of the concrete specificity of the avant-garde artwork. He wonders why we "find it crucial to contextualize artistic styles, to grasp who the princely recipients of such styles were, and whom such styles helped to marginalize. . . . Yet if we are rightly mistrustful of the veil of beauty, we are not equivalently mistrustful about the ease with which our theories explain what lies under the veil."[63] Herwitz explores the limits inherent to the urge to make theory and artwork fit clearly (an urge apotheosized in the conceptual art movement launched in the late 1960s) and wonders what remains after the work of theory has processed and pasteurized the challenge of the work: "[I]s there another dimension to the art, another set of intentions in it or ways of receiving the art which resist, ignore, overcome, or call into question the philosophical voice. . . ? The avant-garde is a mosaic of voices that exist in tension and partial contradiction. It is the specific configuration of voices that exist in tension and partial contradiction. It is the specific configuration of voices, rather than any one, which defines the richness, difficulty, intensity, and character of an avant-garde work."[64] The temptations of the "the" (as in "*the* avant-garde" or "*the* counterculture"), that definite article which propels thought into the thin air of abstraction, have proven very heady, drawing such notable scholars, critics, and avant-gardists as Irving Howe, Geörgy Lukács, Richard Schechner, Rosalind Krauss, Clement Greenberg, Robert Hughes, Irving Kristol, and Leslie Fiedler.

Critics, scholars, and (especially) teachers should never abandon the pursuit of concrete answers to the profound questions posed by avant-garde groups and texts. And it is appropriate at this point to qualify what might appear to the reader as an uncritical advocacy of plurality in the vein of popular understandings of postmodernism and difference that became current in the 1990s. The concept of the avant-garde is evacuated if it can't be used as a tool for critical debate oriented toward concrete issues, as a source for experimental thought, and as a standard by which to judge the political and aesthetic accomplishments of radical movements. Fred Orton and Griselda Pollock have noted just this, asserting that, as a "catch-all label," the avant-garde has regularly served the role of a normative standard by which art and art criticism can be judged.[65] Stiles extends Orton and Pollock's argument to make sense of why avant-garde criticism and scholarship possess such a consistently utopian flavor; in other words, why critics have felt the need to use the avant-garde as a vehicle for their own social, political, and cultural ideals.

Even so, Herwitz's point about losing the specificity of the artistic encounter should not be dismissed. Thus, we are brought to perhaps the most important conceptual quandary of our day: How to commit to plurality without losing the ability to judge. Stiles has little patience with this kind of indirect idealism often manifested in work on the avant-garde, idealism she views as consistently erasing the specific qualities of the avant-garde artwork. Moreover, theories of the avant-garde have a tendency to "[deprive] multiple and simultaneous avant-gardes of their real contributions to (and in) real cultural, social, and political contexts, and [fail] to acknowledge their effective alterations of conventional ways of seeing and reenvisioning life."[66] Such oversights, Stiles continues, "account for some of the reasons that it has been so easy, so often, to proclaim the death of both *an* avant-garde and *the* avant-garde. Both views equally consign multiple avant-gardes to failure, either by constructing a fantasy of transformation within a utopic discourse of reform or—as in the case of Orton and Pollock's argument—by limiting radical observation and practice to narrowly defined 'new discursive frameworks'" (267).

I agree with Stiles that abstraction (the distinction she marks between radical*ism* and the radical) is a common cause of the repeated and repeatedly incorrect proclamations of the avant-garde's death. The specific problems the avant-garde poses to critical analysis (particularly in its performative manifestations) cannot be solved through abstraction, but only through rigorous examination of the specific "behavioral situations" that are left behind by historiography and critical theory.[67] It's not by coincidence that avant-garde artists and their communities embraced performance at the same moment that the critical establishments with which they engaged started writing eulogies. At the moment when the avant-garde dropped its pretensions to universality; stopped trying to make perfect objects for sale; embraced profoundly local dimensions of political, cultural, economic, and social subversion (i.e., performance); and instituted the critical demarcations I have described, critical establishments have tended to cordon it off and declare it dead. This was nowhere more true than in the 1950s and 1960s. Despite the often clear-and-present plurality of avant-garde action (and the reasonable assumption of less clear, less present vanguards), critics and scholars were in virtually unanimous agreement that the concept of the avant-garde was dead. This unanimity in the face of growing plurality is itself worth investigating. What does it mean that high-ranking critics, scholars, and artists from left, center, and right should all come to agreement on such a problematic, challenging, inherently provocative topic—and why were they all drawn to writing obituaries of the avant-garde?

Matei Calinescu has argued that the avant-garde is at once a critical concept, an aesthetic (or counteraesthetic) practice, and a sociopolitical force. This well-rounded definition (one found also in the work of Susan Suleiman)[68] is one the case studies will stick close to, since it enables me to address simultaneously theoretical questions, situated sociopolitical struggle, and the concrete particularity of the avant-garde performance. More importantly, the definition allows these studies to incisively reflect on the unanimity of the Eulogists as the consequence of a shared set of critical and scholarly limits. Calinescu asserts that an avant-garde movement must maneuver on three fronts simultaneously: the theoretical, the political, and the material. This definition is, thankfully, responsive to the avant-garde's military and revolutionary origins, origins often forgotten (and with them, the notion of commitment to bettering the lot of the oppressed, marginalized, or disadvantaged), origins that compel us to consider theoretical questions inseparably from political and material questions.

The inseparability of those questions shouldn't be accepted uncritically, however; the inseparability itself demands careful theorization and the most determined, sensitive, and inductive consideration of the specific case. Calinescu asserts two principles that he believes encompass the theoretical, political, and material challenge of specific avant-gardes, but also enable him to retain the notion of the avant-garde as a unified tradition. The first assumption is sociopolitical, the latter basically metaphysical, and both are the heritage of a contradictory tendency within modernity. Firstly, the avant-garde is an innovative mode of *social antagonism* (this idea is taken in part from Poggioli's *Theory of the Avant-Garde*); in other words, it is a cultural force that struggles by cultural means to achieve in unprecedented ways specific social, economic, and political goals, goals that tend to be oriented in opposition to certain social groups and in support of others. Second, the avant-garde is a mode of cultural critique that redefines, both conceptually and experientially, basic concepts and cultural practices of *time,* particularly those associated with futurity (and its advent in the present) or with the present (and its representation as a temporal quality). In short, the avant-garde functions as a force that reshapes the very way we think about and produce history.

The implications of considering the avant-garde as a subversive social and philosophical mode of historical production should be explored at greater length by scholars and critics, who have, by and large, characterized the avant-garde's historical vision in fairly simplistic ways. As an example of how scholars might contend simultaneously with questions of social antagonism and historiographical production, we should turn to Walter Kalaidjian's *American Culture between the Wars: Revisionary Modernism and Postmodern Critique.* There, Kalaidjian writes that "criticism exploits historical framing to prop up disciplinary authority, institutional force, and canonical power."[69] It does this not so much through explicit commentary on a historical moment, the situational limits of critical knowledge, or through critiques of philosophies of history underwriting criticism and scholarship, but through reliance upon the technical fallacy, the freezing of subversive praxis into a limited set of specific techniques and critical standards. In his critique of scholarship on this crucial period in U.S. avant-gardism, Kalaidjian refers to the work of Cary Nelson, who convincingly argues that the history of American poetry during the period 1900–1950 as it has been written by critics and scholars is dominated by the standards and assumptions of formalism, a history that has effectively obscured the contentious reality of that period through "such reigning tropes [as] individual talent [that] have served to fix, regulate, and police modernism's unsettled social text, crosscut as it is by a plurality of transnational, racial, sexual, and class representations."[70] Kalaidjian demonstrates that the restoration of this unsettled, crosscut quality not only enriches our understanding of the politics of the avant-garde in general, but also restores the situation of specific avant-garde movements. Without such a restoration, critical and scholarly work ultimately mortgages the politics of the avant-garde to silence, obscures connections among avant-garde artists and movements of diverse place and time, and disables critical consideration of the institutions of criticism, scholarship, and teaching. In sum, a more situated understanding of social antagonism breaks open new possibilities for historical imagining.

Which brings us, again, to the Eulogist School, a critical trend that peaked in the 1950s and 1960s, but has remained a critical touchstone ever since. The debate concerning the supposed "death" of the avant-garde was carried on within some of the most prestigious journals and university departments in the United States, Germany, and France. Hilton Kramer, Hans Magnus Enzensberger, Leslie Fiedler, Roland Barthes, and the so-called New York Intellectuals (Daniel Bell, in particular) all agreed that the avant-garde was dead as a social force and bankrupt as an agent of progressive action. One rarely finds such an ideologically diverse group of critics agreeing on any topic. So why such unanimity? The question of historical imagination is at the heart of this trend.

The specific arguments of the Eulogist School differ in details and goals, but the conclusions of are surprisingly consistent with each other:

1. The avant-garde as a leading cultural antagonist is neutralized by the affluence-inspired tolerance of the post–World War II Western middle and upper middle classes (as Kramer argues),[71] which view the avant-garde not as shocking or subversive, but rather as a style, one among many. Complementing the flytrap insidiousness of the middle classes was the scandal of Stalinism, viewed by many as the logical outcome of Leninist vanguardism if not vanguardism tout court. This latter point was pressed by the so-called New York Intellectuals.[72] The chic middle class, the Moscow Trials, and haute couture cast the avant-garde tradition into disrepute and compelled avant-garde artists such as Mark Rothko and Jackson Pollock into an aesthetic radicalism divorced from any but the most general, humanistic sociopolitical critiques.

2. The avant-garde as an historical force is fatally wounded by the weakening or co-optation of traditional social agents of historical progressivism with whom the avant-garde had allied itself and by the loss of critical criteria that could firmly establish the "advanced" nature of a particular trend. In other words, the avant-garde as the promise of futurity, of an enriched and cataclysmic temporality, is lost when it enters the Sargasso Sea of the Eisenhower era.

Needless to say, the argument that the avant-garde was dead was (and is) bound to culturally and historically specific understandings of historical transformation and social struggle and a disguised or unconscious utopianism of the sort Stiles has criticized.

Moreover, this situated, parochial utopianism was contingent on specific changes in the status of critics and scholars who were committed to the possibility of progressive cultural and social action after the war. In the case of the eulogists, the intellectual framework that had directed the great bourgeois revolutions and counterrevolutions of the eighteenth and nineteenth centuries and the political divisions that dominated the industrial era until around World War II seemed to falter irredeemably, casting not only the Left into jeopardy, but also the authority of the critic. The utopianism of the Eulogist School should be viewed, therefore, not simply as a misreading of the avant-garde, but as the consequence of a larger anxiety about the fate of the working class as a progressive agent of history, the shape of history itself, and the possibility of critical perspective in a burgeoning, increasingly corporation-sponsored system of higher education. The announcement of the "end of ideology" and "the end of history" by Daniel Bell was the most explicit statement of the underlying ideological presuppositions of the Eulogists.[73]

The inseparability of theoretical questions from political and material circumstances is where we must turn our attention. Alan Wald has carefully charted the shifting fortunes of the vanguard model among progressive intellectuals in the United States. In his discussion of the politics of literary criticism during the 1940s and 1950s, Wald notes that the ideological movement of many formerly radical intellectuals into anticommunist liberalism was intimately connected to a series of significant changes in the structure of American higher education, changes that carried with them new understandings of intellectual leadership and critical authority. He notes that "the unprecedented economic prosperity of postwar America had provided enormous opportunities for them to pursue careers in the universities and in publishing, especially with the impeccable anticommunist credentials that they had earned through their activities in the American Committee for Cultural Freedom."[74] Wald further argues that this movement of radical intellectuals—former believers in the vanguard theories of Lenin and Trotsky—toward the political center was fundamental to the "taming" of the avant-garde tradition, a movement away from a "perception of [the avant-garde] as a means of sweeping aside bourgeois falsehood and hypocrisy in alliance with the proletarian revolution" and toward a basically ironic individualism.[75]

While irony was certainly a major part of this critical trend, the question of critical standards and critical authority was approached in a decidedly unironic fashion. Philip Rahv, in "American Intellectuals in the Postwar Situation" (1952), argues that intellectuals of his time were no longer committed to dissidence and revolt because of the exposure of Stalinism, the absorption of the avant-garde by the rapidly developing museum culture of the United States, the intellectual enervation of Europe, the rise of universities and think tanks, and material wealth. However, this lack of commitment to dissidence and revolt was not simply a symptom of ideological defeat or full pockets; quite the contrary, the "embourgeoisement of the American intelligentsia" made all the more important the revitalization of the avant-garde, not so much as a method to maintain the "shock of the new" (as Robert Hughes would later put it),[76] but rather as a way of staking out a place from which to develop critical norms and standards that stood in explicit opposition to a range of political and cultural trends in the West (qtd. in Wald 110).

This effort to devise critical standards was complicated by the fact that the "embourgeoisement of the American intelligentsia" coincided with the embourgeoisement of the forward-looking American artist. Diana Crane notes that, during the Cold War, "the artistic role underwent a major transformation. While the organizational infrastructure for avant-garde art was changing, so was the social and occupational role of the artist."[77] Crane quotes Stewart Buettner, who asserts that, as early as the 1960s, the social function of the progressive artist made him "at home among the upper-middle class because they were members of the same class."[78] Artists became members of the American academic system and also benefited from the increasingly "large, varied, and complex" art world enabled by the rapid increase in the number of museums, corporate art collections, the population of art collectors, graduates from art schools, galleries exhibiting avant-garde work, and other kinds of art centers.[79]

What Rahv, Crane, and Buettner overlook is the fact that many intellectuals and artists did not—either by choice or by necessity—become members of the middle class nor enjoy the fruits of the expanding art world and its matrix of galleries, classrooms, editorial rooms, and cocktail parties. Women, minorities, and political radicals generally did not enjoy the benefits of the Cold War art boom nor the embourgeoisement that ensured artists and critics at least a minimal level of comfort and security. This hardly doomed them—though it did ensure that their work rarely would be seen by the elite audiences of the formalist avant-garde. If we entertain the fairly reasonable notion that the nature of social struggle and the socialized time of both production and historical imagination changed after World War II as a consequence of shifts in capitalist production techniques, new understandings of leisure, the infrastructural pressures of globalization, the diffusion of hitherto obscured ethnic and regional aesthetic and philosophical traditions (especially Tibet, Japan, and West Africa), and the partial absorption of the avant-garde by a rapidly expanding art market,[80] then the death-of-the-vanguard debate can be viewed (*should* be viewed) as the moment when the avant-garde tradition bifurcated, one wing entering into long-term détente with the burgeoning museum, gallery, and academic network in the guise of a theoretically radical modernism, the other disappearing from the field of vision opened by the critical, scholarly, and curatorial possibilities of that network. This bifurcation of the avant-garde into a theoretically accessible, institutionally commodious, nevertheless challenging, difficult modernism and a theoretically inaccessible, institutionally self-critical trend marks a crucial turn in avant-garde history. Out of the latter trend emerged the leaders, theorists, and participants of the new social movements of the counterculture, movements that could not be adequately described, to recall Roszak again, by older modes of ideological critique.

In sum, some cultural activists, excluded from an art world and an academic discourse in which a particular tendency of the avant-garde enjoyed the fruits of Cold War prosperity, countered both the theoretical and the political assumptions of art world and academia and sought out new aesthetic forms, new social content, and new ways to produce, distribute, and consume art. While they accurately assessed the fate of one trend of the avant-garde, the eulogists ultimately did not consider the idea that an avant-garde could retain the sociopolitical and temporal responsibilities of older vanguards while stepping beyond the Christian, technophilic, and bourgeois understandings of social struggle and time that were the hallmark of such vanguards and the critical establishment that gathered around their corpses during the 1950s and 1960s.

There's a temptation here just to counter the Eulogists à la Samuel Johnson and kick an empirical stone across the floor. And there are plenty of stones to find scattered around the feet of the eulogists: El Teatro Campesino, Otrabanda, the Diggers, the San Francisco Mime Troupe, Women's Experimental Theatre, the Destruction-in-Art movement, the Black Arts Movement, Yippie!, the Living Theatre, the minimalists—these are only a few of the progressive communities that fought for political, economic, and social change during the 1960s and fought for such change in terms that reflected the unique conditions and lessons of the Cold War era. Such groups challenged the theoretical, sociopolitical, and material-aesthetic assumptions of their times and places, but also produced innovative methods for addressing these assumptions, methods that were cognizant of the critique of vanguard thought mounted by the liberal intelligentsia. However, relying on empirical evidence—and empirical methods—isn't going to get scholars very far since that would imply that they can simply overcome failure through an improvement in method. In fact, empiricism only raises the chances of new kinds of critical blindness since it inevitably papers over the critical limits defined by Pleynet and Shattuck: contradiction and emotional implication. Taking these limits into account, studies of the avant-garde can do something a bit a more subtle: view the Cold War avant-garde as a pluralistic tendency, part of which moved beyond the conceptual categories with which the critical establishment could identify, critique, and summarize. By doing this, avant-garde studies can avoid repeating an error first identified by Herwitz in *Making Theory/Constructing Art:*

"the belief that there exists a transparent relationship between theory and [the art object] it defines or explains."[81]

The belief in transparency is, to say the least, hardly useful for understanding the counterculture, which continually demarcated lines of vision and blindness both within and against the tradition of the avant-garde. Again, if avant-garde studies do not wish to consign the pluralistic, contradictory, contentious nature of politics and the problematic qualities of philosophical-historical speculation to the dustbin, then it needs to move beyond the isolated question of form and, instead, contend with the social and economic strategies of specific countercultures. For example, even the supposedly simplistic, broad-stroke style of agitation-propaganda drama—the very apotheosis of the mimetic tradition of art that was so roundly scourged by critics during the Cold War—was, during the 1960s, staged in social and economic situations that redefined the very form of "propaganda."

Such a redefinition of an older form by the pressures of a specific performance context is effectively demonstrated by Yolanda Broyles-González in her history of El Teatro Campesino, a book that not only considers the social, cultural, and historical contexts of the group's performances, but also systematically challenges the reception of that group's work by the American critical establishment, a reception that is, according to Broyles-González, "chronological, text-centered, and male-centered."[82] By revealing the Teatro's work as a "multifaceted cultural renaissance" that affirmed "an alternative social vision that relied on a distinctly Chicana/o aesthetic," she is able to dislodge the Teatro from a critical framework that has read *actos* such as *Las tres uvas* (1966) as simplistic repetitions of theatrical techniques perfected by European radicals (xi, 3). Focusing on communal creation and the oral traditions of Mexican working-class culture, Broyles-González challenges the received interpretations of the empirical theatrical and textual evidence. Rather than just repeating the techniques of Proletcult and Blue-Blouse (and yet without rejecting them), the Teatro *actos* reference a rich, complex tradition of clowning, oral performance, and historical consciousness among the Mexican working classes.

Broyles-González's book addresses two kinds of scholarly failure; first, the persistence of prejudicial views; second, the failure to perceive the complexity of the topic's situation. Ideally, scholars and critics of the avant-garde should be able to avoid both prejudice and oversimplification. However, the vanguards explored here seem to push precisely into such limited perspectives, into the politics of demarcation, a strategy upheld by radical groups around the globe at the time, groups that utilized symbolic actions to press their enemies into revealing the bases of their power. Calinescu helps clarify the nature of this strategy and the tricks it plays on scholars. While Calinescu is a card-carrying member of the Eulogist School, the particular conceptual "blocks" in his work are different from his colleagues'. According to Calinescu, the avant-garde has always been a mode of modern cultural production that can never move beyond its own crisis. If the avant-garde has "died," it is the consequence of a postmodern age that seems enamored, if not downright addicted, to crisis; the crisis that is the avant-garde can no longer claim to be innovative nor antagonistic. Calinescu makes a decisive move here; the avant-garde reveals its fundamental form only at the moment of its death, and that death is not a disappearance or death, but a *crisis*.

Calinescu is not unaware of the avant-garde's bias against critics and academics—again, he spends a good deal of time discussing the avant-garde as a creature and cultivator of "crisis." And indeed, "crisis" is an appropriate term to use, if one remains attentive to the fact that a crisis is not a crisis if one can simply step outside of it and judge it from afar. A crisis is no crisis if it can be made easy sense of. A crisis is an imminent movement that marks, after the requisite unsettling and reconfiguring of social institutions, language, aesthetics, and so forth, the birth of new criteria. What happened to the avant-garde in the 1950s was an example of the avant-garde's noncontemporaneity with the present. In other words, the Cold War avant-gardes represent a categorical and practical critique that challenged the institutional and conceptual conditions that allowed recognition of their work among scholars, critics, gallery owners, and the like. What died in the 1950s and 1960s (keeping in mind that critical and aesthetic traditions never really "die," but rather become "historical") was not the avant-garde, but a theory of the avant-garde developed within (and indebted to) the social, economic, and political upheavals in French middle-class society during the 1870s that profoundly altered the nature of the modern European bourgeois democracy.

The renovation of the practical and metaphysical tendencies of the avant-garde in the late 1950s does not, however, render moot the categories; rather, it compels critics and scholars to think dialectically, to question the *particular* limits of supposedly *general* categories of antagonism (progressive politics) and time (historical philosophy). This is one of the peculiarities of human thought; though its content may be emptied out, the form of a thought can persist. In this sense, we might consider the crisis of the avant-garde as an illustration of the notion that the conceptual problems of an earlier age can return at a later stage of historical development, thus revealing the inadequacy of answers that had seemed sufficient to an intervening age. Contradictions have a way of coming back when least expected. Though the theoretical and practical situation of the avant-garde will change, we can still hold onto certain concepts, certain problems, certain kinds of probity.

In the avant-garde movements that developed outside the formalist mainstream during the first three decades of the Cold War, the rejuvenation of antagonism and progressivism came as a consequence of intensive debate concerning the very nature of social antagonism and historical imagination. For example, in certain separatist feminist vanguards in the late 1960s, the refusal to distinguish particular men from patriarchy in general opened a range of tactical actions hitherto unrealized as well as a set of representational principles with which to guide and critique such actions. In addition, the new avant-gardes carried on internal debates concerning time as a critical category that could undermine or destroy dominant temporal structures. For example, the Christian eschaton and the ahistoricality of American commodity culture were favored targets of the Muntu group that helped pave the way for the Black Arts Movement. In other words, though radical feminist organizations and the Muntu group—to cite just two examples— would not agree on a common antagonist nor on a common understanding of time and history, they would absolutely agree that those were the right subjects of theory, criticism, and action. The models differ, but the concerns are largely the same.

In fact, the tools needed to conceptualize the new avant-gardes were being forged even as the Eulogists were tapping nails into their coffin. The avant-garde in the late 1950s was not lacking in critical self-appraisal and self-justification—the vanguards of the period are notable for their impressive theoretical range and acuity—but such appraisal and justification were not wholly from within the world of art and letters. In a sense, the Cold War vanguards simply continued a classic avant-garde tradition. As Herwitz writes, the avant-garde "has been obsessed with its own theoretical self-formulation" (1). If subsequent generations of artists and scholars are "the inheritors of the avant-garde's theoretical norms" (1), then surely they may entertain the possibility of rejecting such norms; in the most simple terms, the avant-garde has always rejected norms. This was certainly the case in the United States in the 1950s and 1960s. The philosophical, aesthetic, and sociological grounds for the revision of the avant-garde had been prepared by rebellious sociologists such as C. Wright Mills and Betty Friedan; politically committed writers of prose and poetry such as Norman Mailer, Allen Ginsberg, and Gwendolyn Brooks; and performers such as Allan Kaprow, the dancers and choreographers of Judson Church, and the Living Theatre, all of whom had been systematically excluded from the prosperity of the Cold War art scene.

All of these patiently and courageously confronted the failure of the avant-garde theory that had worked so well prior to the Cold War—but without losing sight of the continued necessity of vanguard action. And all confronted the ambiguities, uncertainties, and political failures of their own disciplines. Mills's resuscitation of utopian critique in *The Causes of World War III* and "Letter to the New Left"; Friedan's analysis of patriarchy (the "problem without a name" that Friedan would christen "The Feminine Mystique") as organized around maintaining the ignorance of the disempowered; Mailer's "The White Negro" and its scandalous analysis of the role of sex, violence, and racial stereotypes in social subversion; Ginsberg's use of sexuality as the grounds for the self-identification of a community and its counterhistorical project in *Howl;* Brooks's unraveling of traditional poetic modes as a lever against racism (most notably in "A Bronzeville Mother Loiters. Meanwhile, a Mississippi Mother Burns Bacon"); the Judson Church's exploration of everyday gesture and antinarratival dance; Kaprow's simultaneous embrace of Deweyan pragmatism and Pollock-inspired exploration of the limits of spontaneous gesture; and the Living Theatre's 1959 production of Jack Gelber's *The Connection*—all of these exorcised the spirit of the avant-garde from the body that had trapped it after the war. Or, to use Marx's metaphor, all of these helped the kernel of innovative antagonism to burst out of its conceptual and sociopolitical husk. New content filled an old category.

One significant innovation: the avant-garde perished as a *general* category and entered a phase of intensive *particularity* in order to maintain its efficacy as an antagonistic cultural force that could withstand an increasingly flexible, increasingly "hip," anti-Stalinist capitalism—as well as a critical establishment that, under the impact of decades of modernist experiment, had grown to understand the avant-garde as essentially no more than a stylistic choice (to do otherwise was to become complicit with Leninism and, according to the logic of the time, Stalinism). In this sense, these new avant-gardes were part of a more general shift in the role of the intellectual that Michel Foucault has described as a shift to the "specific" intellectual (who possess "a much more immediate and concrete awareness of struggles")[83] from the older notion of the "universal" intellectual. This bifurcation of the avant-garde marks a crucial turn in avant-garde history. These same individuals and communities became the leaders, theorists, and participants of the new social movements of the counterculture, movements that could not be adequately described by older modes of ideological critique.

The Theory Death of the Theory Death of the Avant-Garde

It is Paul Mann who has drawn the most focus to this challenge and made it clear that unless scholars and critics of the avant-garde confront such limits—such "pataphysical" exceptions—their work is necessarily incomplete if not downright naive. *The Theory Death of the Avant-Garde* has received little to no attention in publications on the avant-garde. For example, Mann's book receives no mention in Arnold Aronson's *American Avant-Garde Theatre,* one of the more recent publications on cultural radicalism in the United States. This is a significant oversight in what I find to be an otherwise interesting and useful book, an oversight that ultimately undermines Aronson's effort to theorize and historicize concepts that are fundamental to the avant-garde: aesthetic antagonism, broadened cultural participation, and political progressivis.n.[84] Much as is the case with Bürger's *Theory of the Avant-Garde,* the book that first drew critical attention to the question of the avant-garde's relationship with the institutions of art and the categories of critical appraisal, no scholarly book on the avant-garde can proceed responsibly without addressing itself to the problems articulated by Mann.[85] *Theory Death* has initiated a Copernican revolution in avant-garde studies, dislodging the scholar from his supposedly unmoving position in the center of avant-garde history. After Mann, no critic can assert that the avant-garde is defunct without pursuing the most rigorously self-critical analysis of his or her own critical terms, categories, and methods. A discussion of the possibilities and limitations of Mann's book will allow me to describe the specific methods I'll be using in the case studies that follow.

Mann's book begins with a discussion of the strategies that the aesthetic-avant-garde has used throughout its century-and-a-half-long history to present itself to its various audiences: critics, art collectors, the general public, the communities they wish to empower. This focus on rhetorical strategy allows Mann to move in two unexpected directions: (1) toward the economics of avant-garde subversion and (2) toward its discursive structures. This move demands more than a simplistic understanding of the economic or of institutional discourse; the economics of his analysis concerns more than the production, distribution, and circulation of objects; specifically, it concerns the larger question of *value* and how value comes to be ascribed to and understood by producers and consumers. One crucial aspect of the avant-garde's challenge to value is its polemical intervention in the discourses of art, politics, and history.

Thus, the question of discourse—and discursive intervention—allows Mann to overcome the gaps among politics, economics, and culture, the very gaps that hamper Calinescu's analysis and demarcate Pleynet and Shat-tuck's. Why, he asks, have the avant-garde and its critics been so obsessed with death? To address this continuing obsession, Mann describes the key terms and rhetorical structures of avant-garde discourse—and the gaps that exist within the terms and structures. He asserts that the avant-garde is the center of a discursive economy of "reviewing exhibition, appraisal, repro-duction, academic, analysis, gossip, retrospection" (5–6). This "will to dis-course" inevitably mortgages the challenge of the avant-garde to the stable, mutually agreeable standards of discourse itself. He concludes that "the tele-ology of the avant-garde can no longer be reduced to a thematics of success or failure, of revolt or complicity, of truth or illusion, of sincerity or hoax, of existence or non-existence" (3).

However, though we can't reduce the avant-garde to success or failure, we can address "whether the avant-garde has left anything vital behind; whether there is something vital about the death itself."[86] At the same time, we can attempt to trace "the hypothetical totality of such exchanges, will-ing or unwilling, voluntary or conscripted, voiced or even suppressed" of the discourses surrounding a specific avant-garde.[87] This tracing would allow us to see not only how the challenge of the avant-garde entered into the discourses of bourgeois-liberal society, but also address the ways that such discourses marginalized or attempted to erase aspects of that challenge. "In the end, one will also find that something is always missing from dis-course, always omitted, denied, concealed, lost, skipped over, ignored. Per-haps only in this missing residuum is the death of the avant-garde belied."[88] This crucial step in Mann's analysis presses him to engage in a different kind of critical writing, to understand that "the problem of the avant-garde is . . . essentially a critical one: how to enter its field without falling . . . into every trap of representation: how to write without merely manufacturing another or even better theory for circulation, another history for exchange" (93). This is achieved in part by the consciousness that something has been left out, perhaps the most vital aspect of the avant-garde

How Mann makes sense of this "residuum" is what I find most intrigu-ing but also most frustrating about his book. Mann convincingly argues that "there is no such thing as an extrinsic study of the avant-garde: all studies operate within a common if manifold discursive field, all share that field with their subject, and all must therefore represent their own sites within it" (8). Since it is impossible to step outside the discursive economy of the avant-garde, any attempt to map that field will necessarily be "anamorphic," a mapping that is distorted in the interests of the mapmaker.[89] This places the work of the critically minded scholar in an in-between state, at once a producer of discourse and a product of discourse. Mann articulates this state in terms that will be familiar to those versed in the strategies of deconstruction:

> Those for whom there is no satisfactory answer to the first and last question posed by this essay: what is the status of your own text in the white economy of discourse? Here the history of the avant-garde has been above all the genealogy of that question. . . . Only those willing to remain in the death of the avant-garde, those who cease trying to drown out death's silence with the noise of neocritical production, will ever have a hope of hearing what that death articulates. (141)

There are "two deaths then"—one circumscribed by critical talk and writing, the other disengaged; "after death one should go up in smoke or go underground" (143).

How does one hear what the death of the avant-garde articulates if it is only articulated in a "residuum," in the faded remnants of smoke or invisibility? This is not a question that can be answered by Mann due to the limits of his book; specifically, its dogged pursuit of deconstructive readings of critical discourse. However, political art can do more than simply dissipate or disappear and this can be made sense of without falling into the trap of separating practice from theory or radicalism from discourse.

Mann is honest about the limits of his analysis, noting that he is not concerned "with testing the objective, historical accuracy or inaccuracy of any given taxonomical set so much as with exploring the complex dialectical relations that obtain between event and comprehension, movement and definition, action and representation" (9). In other words, *Theory Death* is neither an aesthetic nor a sociological study; rather it is an exploration of critical discourse and its economies (5–6). And this is why he cannot answer the question he asks, because the relations between an event and its comprehension is itself an event and the perspective of discourse is not the only perspective from which to assess events. As Mann notes, there are "no neutral histories; in fact [there is nothing but] a history of resistance to such histories" (9). The trope of death is not "precisely a critical phenomenon but a crisis induced by the disruption of operational relations and differences between [the avant-garde and criticism], the absorption of each by the other and of both by the economy that once maintained them" (32–33).

The limits of Mann's book are, in brief, wrapped up with the fact that it is a *theory* of theory death; thus, it too necessarily suffers a theory death. Though the kind of absolute resistance symbolized by the silences, smokes,

cf

mckenzie

and undergrounds in *Theory Death* is a crucial, vital strategy of the avant-garde, there are other ways to carry the responsibilities of the avant-garde tradition. Moreover, there are ways to tell the story of the death of the avant-garde that can enable us to understand the contours of a specific avant-garde situation without dominating that situation or stifling the challenge of the specific avant-garde. How so? Certainly not by attempting to reconstitute the conceptually defunct distinctions between theory and practice. A brief summary of the methods that can add a bit of color to the "white economy" should be instructive.

First, we can turn to performance history and attempt to articulate the specific gaps (the "what" and "where" of performance) that open among the various participants in the performative moment of the avant-garde event. This approach is the dominant one in my case studies. As the reader will discover, a pluralistic methodology is at work in the case studies that follow, one that blends a variety of approaches, but always within specific contexts and concrete encounters of audiences and art. Though a wide range of theories are used, these theories are always utilized in an inductive fashion. Rather than impose a theory on the work deductively, the attempt is to draw connections and contextualize the ways that various printed texts (plays, theoretical explanations, newspaper reviews, memoirs, scholarly studies, etc.) made (and continue to make) sense of avant-garde events that occurred during the Cold War. A crucial part of this approach is the careful mapping of critical/scholarly limits, constitutional gaps in our ability to write history.

Not unlike the approach of the New Historicist, the case studies attempt to address "the writing and reading of texts, as well as the processes by which they are circulated and categorized, analyzed and taught, are . . . reconstrued as historically determined and determining modes of cultural work," and so on.[90] Concurrently, attention will be paid to the "theoretical indeterminacy of the signifying process and the historical specificity of discursive practices—acts of speaking, writing, and interpreting."[91] Exemplary of this is my approach to Happenings and Fluxus events. The processes by which early American performance art was transformed into a historical and theoretical object were consciously and continuously interrogated by the artists themselves and incorporated into the aesthetic event, as is described in relation to Kaprow's *Eighteen Happenings in Six Parts*.[92] As a consequence of this incorporation of criticism into the event itself, any attempt to historicize or theorize such events immediately and irresistibly enters into forms of discourse that challenge basic critical standards, forms that embrace edgy emotional states such as fetishism or demand infantile modes of subject-object interaction.

A second way that the limits of Mann's book can be overcome is by anchoring the discursive economy of a specific avant-garde in the particular social and material contexts in which books, journals, and other texts about the movement were produced, distributed, and consumed. In this respect, Mann's analysis of the avant-garde's discursive economy is ultimately too abstract, a theoretical white economy rather than a material, multicultural economy. By attending to the specific contours of specific economies as they obtained in specific times and places, we can make better sense of how the interrelated social, economic, and aesthetic struggle was waged. In the second half of the case study of the Black Arts Movement, for example, the editorial work of Ed Bullins is examined in order to understand how this emblematic Black Nationalist articulated a Black aesthetic in a range of writing and reading economies (i.e., radical political collectives, prestigious academic journals, national and little magazines, theater programs, etc.). The concrete limits and possibilities of such an articulation available to Bullins concretely impacted the theoretical articulation and practical enactment of the Black Arts. Such economic constraints and potentials demanded a high degree of irony from anyone who attempted to make "Blackness" visible; in the case of Bullins's editorial work, we witness rhetorical forms of double consciousness that allow him to make use of a radical aesthetic, ethical, and cultural system that shares in no way with the Euro-American tradition of philosophy or aesthetics yet depends fundamentally upon the technological and linguistic foundations of Euro-American power in order to survive. There is a residuum here, without a doubt, but it is a very specific residuum related to very specific ways of reading.

Lastly, we can recognize that discursive economies, like all economies, are hierarchical and based on the differential inclusion and acceptance of various producers, distributors, and consumers. There is a troubling tendency in Mann's book to portray the discursive economy as a unified, centered economy, a "white economy," to recall Mann's own metaphor. We should note that Mann himself states that he intentionally refuses to "explore heterologies of gender, class, ethnicity, etc." (141); however, some heterologies can't be easily included in the discursive logic of "theory death" that dominates the field of avant-garde studies and the limited avant-garde it has supported and critiqued. As self-conscious as *Theory Death* is, it ultimately relies on a definition of economics that separates out the concrete political nature of economic life, including the situational nature of production, exchange, and consumption. That which doesn't enter into discourse isn't doomed to silence, smoke, or the underground. In fact, by writing fairly traditional (read "empirical") counterhistories, scholars and critics can create a place in existing histories, curricula, syllabi, and the like for the formerly ignored or forgotten—can, in short, move beyond the "hypothetical totality" of discursive exchanges toward a more concrete sense of how such exchanges intersect or fail to intersect with other exchange systems. Rather than equate the avant-garde with silence (what exists outside discourse but silence, except maybe the wordless cry of Brecht's Mother Courage?), we can explore how, in Kalaidjian's words, "reigning tropes . . . have served to fix, regulate, and police modernism's unsettled social text, crossed as it is by a plurality of transnational, racial, sexual, and class representations."[93]

Readers will find this kind of counterhistory throughout the case studies. The obscured history of the War on Drugs surfaces in the discussion of Artaud, theatrical cruelty, and jazz. The Black Art Movement's uneasy relationships with the avant-garde tradition shed light on aspects of the history of Black radicalism systematically excluded from existing histories of radical culture. The "white economy" of critical and scholarly discourse is white not only in the sense that it flattens out and homogenizes difference, transforming plurality into the even conceptual planes of book and journal pages. When attention is focused on the poetics of drug experience, the destabilizing forms of memory and desire inspired by early American performance art, or the West African aesthetic of *muntu,* crucial forms of subversion can be discovered that don't fit into such an economy in part because the languages at our disposal are oriented to very different kinds of values. In such cases, the exclusion from discourse is homologous to other forms of exclusion and is, therefore, hardly to be celebrated in terms of smoke and invisibility.

To conclude, Mann's book signals a crucial development in avant-garde scholarship and criticism, a development that can push us beyond the stale dichotomies of the Eulogist School. His recognition of the primacy of discourse in the struggle of the avant-garde advances on the work of theorists such as Bürger, Poggioli, Calinescu, and Suleiman by addressing the economy of theory itself. However, this economy can never be addressed in the abstract; as those who suffer from the depredations of economic exploitation know, economy is never abstract. As I hope to demonstrate in these case studies, the limits of criticism must always be tracked to specific social, economic, and cultural situations in which the avant-garde and the theorist encounter one another. This situation-oriented approach enables a better understanding of avant-garde criticism, scholarship, and pedagogy's ambiguous role in the culture wars born in the great bourgeois and colonial revolutions of the seventeenth and eighteenth centuries and persisting through the globalization crises of our own fin de siècle. The failure of theory—and with it, the failure of other aspects of scholarly method, including the discovery of credible evidence, objective argument, clear criteria, and so on—is a sign that the object of theory may have evaded our grasp, but in doing so signaled to us the limits of our imaginations and the unconscious elitism of our institutional positions.

CASE 1 *THE CONNECTION*
Cruelty, Jazz, and Drug War, 1959–1963

And the least foolish, intrepid lovers of disorder,
Fleeing the herd restrained by Destiny,
Take refuge in Opium's vastness!
    —Charles Baudelaire, "The Voyage"

We are Europe's defeatists . . . We shall waken everywhere the seeds
of confusion and discomfort. We are the mind's agitators . . .
And let the drug-merchants fling themselves upon our terrified nations!
Let distant America's white buildings crumble among her
ridiculous prohibitions. Rise, O world! . . . We are the ones
who always hold out a hand to the enemy . . .
    —Louis Aragon, *Fragments of a Lecture Given at Madrid*

Hello there! I'm the nineteenth century and I'm producing the twentieth.
    —"Solly," in Jack Gelber's *The Connection*

1. Cruelty and the Cold War

The Migrations of the Avant-Garde

Cruelty landed on American shores in the spring of 1958 and premiered to mixed reviews the next summer. Like so many other immigrants, it relied on the sympathy and assistance of natives; in this case, the cosmopolitan bohemians of Greenwich Village. In April of '58, Julian Beck and Judith Malina, he a frustrated abstract expressionist painter but increasingly self-assured stage designer, she a poet, student of radical theater worker Erwin Piscator, and increasingly inventive director, both founders of the eleven-year-old, perpetually struggling Living Theatre, attended a soiree at Anaïs Nin's apartment. During the course of that evening, potter, poet, and Black Mountain College faculty member Mary Caroline Richards mentioned to Beck a translation project she was near completing. The book was Antonin Artaud's *The Theater and Its Double* and was to be published by Grove Press later that year. This kind of relatively banal occurrence—three artists discussing art and the avant-garde over drinks—would prove to have a profound impact on subsequent theater history. Beck has commented that, after receiving a prepublication copy of the translation, "The ghost of Artaud became our mentor."[1] Their conversation would affect much more than just their own work; it would permanently alter the terrain of political strategy in the United States and abroad. Sally Banes writes, "Throughout the 60s, the Living Theatre would be a model for political theater groups internationally."[2] She's right—and Artaud was a big part of their success as activists.

That said, it's likely that the techniques of cruelty would have influenced the counterculture regardless of Richards or the Becks having a drink together. After all, 1958 was the year an economic "hiccup" threw six million people out of work and severely trimmed the already lean audiences for off-Broadway theater. Artaud writes of the plague, "Beneath such a scourge, all social forms disintegrate."[3] The economic downturn, complemented by increasingly authoritarian responses to left-wing critique, pressed artists like the Becks even farther "off" in search of an ideal spectator and farther off from the standards and conventions of mainstream art and criticism. The desire for a more authentic form of theater was growing among this disaffected community; the Becks moved toward Asian art and religion, renegade forms of American popular culture, and more deeply into their own community's piecemeal rituals of selfhood. *The Theater and Its Double* couldn't have found more receptive readers. And Richards's translation wasn't a lark; John Cage had been talking up the renegade surrealist for years, having brought back a copy of the book from France in 1948. Cage's interest in Artaud was part of a larger trend; the theatrical "cruelty" advocated by Artaud enjoyed a sudden rise in fortune during the 1950s as he and his work were rediscovered by a younger generation of artists and intellectuals eager to renew the intransigence of the prewar avant-garde but unwilling to accept the leadership of its surviving members. After all, Artaud had been kicked out of the surrealist group by no less than André Breton himself. He was a consummate left-tendency vanguardist, a rebel among rebels who also, conveniently, rejected the traditional languages and subjects of politics—a nice plus for those unwilling to accept any more the organizational mandates of the Old Left.

True to the spirit of Artaud, his rescue by a younger generation did not result in any specifiable "school of Artaud," no "masterpieces" of the kind he despised. As Susan Sontag points out, the work of those most influenced by Artaud "shows there is no way to use Artaud that stays true to him."[4] As a consequence of relying on specific theater spaces, specific performers' bodies, and specific audiences to manifest the harrowing experience of what he believed to be true, essential theater, Artaudian cruelty is inevitably a highly *situational* mode of performance, one that is difficult to define and describe with any certainty of not being contradicted by a future "cruel" performance taking place in its own singular context. Artaud is often cited for his distaste for repetition: "Let us leave textual criticism to graduate students, formal criticism to esthetes, and recognize that what has been said is not still to be said; that an expression does not have the same value twice, does not live two lives; that all words, once spoken, are dead and function only at the moment when they are uttered, that a form, once it has served, cannot be used again . . . [T]he theater is the only place in the world where a gesture, once made, can never be made the same way twice."[5] Artaud's claim has proven notoriously difficult to sustain in practice. This may be due to the peculiarly fragmented nature of Artaudian theater. David Graver has convincingly asserted that Artaud's work "cultivates multiple sources of authority as much as possible without disrupting the powers of the theatrical event," that "we need to understand what Artaud wants done with three distinct and in some ways inimical centers of authority in the theatrical performance": specifically, text, spectacle, and somatic effect.[6] This affinity for singular contexts and intrasymbolic conflict is, perhaps, one of the reasons why his star was on the rise a decade into the Cold War, influencing not only the Living Theatre, but also the Black Arts (see Amiri Baraka's "The Revolutionary Theatre") and guerrilla theater movements.

The reasons for the differences among "cruel theaters" are as various as there are performance contexts and specific constellations of text, spectacle, and somatic effect, but there are some specific, generally underdiscussed, culture-centered concerns that I wish to pause over in preparation for this chapter's exploration of the Living Theatre's use of cruelty in their groundbreaking 1959 production of *The Connection*. The first of these concerns is drug use and its relationship to aesthetic radicalism, social control, and national autonomy. Artaud is a linchpin of this relationship, though hardly the only one. John D. Lyon notes that Artaud's "vehement and repeated calls for a new theatre, a 'theatre of cruelty,' and his fascination with the culture of peyote and opium are often considered two separate facets of his existence, one creative, the other anecdotal. Yet the particular urgency of his appeals for a reconsideration of the communicative process in Western culture is closely linked to his frequent description of the effects of various intoxicants."[7]

In the 1950s, the intersection of criminal drug use with various kinds of purposefully scandalous cultural expression was becoming an increasingly important presence on the American scene. By the late 1960s, drug use and the refusal of the mainstream would be virtually synonymous. Though the counterculture was not only about drugs, drug experience and drug culture were basic factors in the development and destruction of many countercultural communities. Taking a moment to map the intersection between drug use and cultural resistance will help to prepare the ground for a more localized exploration of the Living Theatre's production of a play about drug use and a deeper analysis of how drugs and drug experience were politicized by various kinds of performance practices during the 1960s. Cruelty, in this case, was a question of body freedom and body expression.

Psychedelic drugs are the most noted of those used within countercultural communities; Roszak writes, "At the bohemian fringe of our disaffected youth culture, all roads lead to psychedelia."[8] However, there was much more than psychedelia involved with the counterculture; just as strong a presence could be claimed for nicotine, alcohol, and marijuana, as

well as harder drugs like amphetamines, barbiturates, and heroin. Intoxication and aesthetic antagonism were one and the same for many countercultures. Roszak quotes from a fairly sympathetic series on the Haight-Ashbury
drug economy published in the *Washington Post* in 1967 that declared the
hippies "the biggest crime story since prohibition" (163). Drug experience
was often the first step a young person took toward becoming that fearful
"other" of American Cold War culture: the "hippie radical." However,
drug use was not just a characteristic of the counterculture; in fact, drug use
within the affiliated subcultures of the Left was symptomatic of the culture
as a whole. Roszak reports that during the same year, 1967, Americans of all
political stripes consumed over eight hundred thousand pounds of barbiturates. One out of four adult Americans used tranquilizers at some time (170).
The World Psychiatric Association reported that in Great Britain from 1964
to 1967 over forty-three million prescriptions were given for psychotropic
drugs (170). As had been the case since the middle nineteenth century (with
the exception of the period immediately following World War I), the
majority of Western drug users, whether casual or addicted, were white,
middle-class, middle-aged women—a community not often associated with
avant-garde antagonism, rarely mentioned by War on Drugs hawks, and
strangely absent from the Living Theatre's production of *The Connection*.[9]

The War on Drugs, officially initiated by the U.S. government in the
1920s following the repeal of alcohol prohibition, but unofficially pursued
for almost a half century prior, was, in the 1950s and 1960s, a complex
sociopolitical dynamic comprised of odd alliances, absurd antipathies,
quixotic strategies, inglorious defeats, systematic falsehoods, and blatant
hypocrisy. Always about much more than the illegal sale and use of intoxicants, it was, and remains, a war over the form and significance of community and communication, both within and outside the United States. Little
wonder, then, that one of the first avant-garde counteroffensives in the War
on Drugs occurred in a theatrical production that utilized performance
techniques that emphasized the crossing of borders: media borders, bodily
borders, the borders separating avant-garde movements, the borders
between textual sign, theatrical image, and somatic effect. Cruelty, as it
functions in *The Connection,* was about how the body can signal through the
flames of experiential, cultural, and legal *extremis*.

Though drug use is a major concern of this chapter—it's hard to imagine
either cruelty or the Living Theatre without drugs—I also need to bring
into play another issue. Any consideration of the avant-garde's ability to
resist or subvert bourgeois capitalist culture, as Mann has convincingly
argued, is bound up with institutions and the languages, analytical methods,

and concepts that help such institutions function; other words, discourse. As discussed in the introduction, Mann has convincingly demonstrated that these languages, methods, and concepts are of special importance when we're thinking about the history of the avant-garde and judging its successes or failures. Mann shows us that the avant-garde is about more than art; it is about the creation of critical discourses that help to situate and justify the avant-garde's challenge, often in explicit opposition to academic scholarship, criticism, and pedagogy.

To recall another point from my introduction, the death-of-the-avant-garde debate hinged on the idea that the avant-garde had been fully absorbed and negated by innovative sectors of bourgeois culture such as advertising, pop culture, and legal reformations—become, in sum, an organ of the bourgeois body politic. However, such co-optation did not take a single form throughout the West, a point not considered by Mann. In France, for example, the tradition of avant-garde outrage and experimental writing (Artaud playing a significant role in both) enjoyed a relative hardiness at the highest levels of society, due in part to the prestige enjoyed among the intelligentsia by writers like James Joyce, Louis Aragon, and Samuel Beckett and in part due to the entrenchment of the Left within the institutions of French civil society. The broad distrust of authority that was the legacy of the Vichy regime, the Resistance, and periodicals such as *Combat* helped keep the root system robust for the avant-garde as both an aesthetic and political tendency. The legitimacy of the avant-garde meant that broad and influential segments of the post–World War II French technical and educational classes were fully informed about and largely sympathetic with the avant-garde, especially the long-lived vanguard belief that social progress was best advanced through acts of public cultural criticism. "Co-optation" in France occurred most significantly in the late 1960s at the top levels of culture among leading leftist public intellectuals, intellectuals who played a key role in public policy, cultural production, and fashion.

The semiofficial presence of the avant-garde in French intellectual discourse was not unknown in the United States during the 1950s, thanks to the stalwarts at *Partisan Review,* the geriatric avant-gardists in the social circles surrounding Peggy Guggenheim, the faculty of experimental educational institutions such as Black Mountain College and the New School for Social Research, less radical institutions such as Rutgers, and the rapidly expanding gallery and museum system.[10] However, unlike France, where the avant-garde played a significant role in the revitalization of the Left, producing such significant journals as *Tel Quel* and *Socialisme ou Barbarie,* in the United States the avant-garde met a rather different fate due to the less substantial presence of the avant-garde at the top levels of labor and policy organizations and the less rooted tradition of radical public intellectualism. It's certainly true that during the Cold War, the avant-garde, in Serge Guilbaut's words, had been accorded by top-level American officials a "position of paramount importance," particularly in cultural exchanges with ideologically opposed nations.[11] However, this position was occupied, as I've demonstrated and Guilbaut admits, by only a very few avant-garde trends.

This is where things get interesting—and the situated nature of cruelty more clear. The embrace of the avant-garde by some sectors of the U.S. system of higher education and by a handful of public intellectuals occurred simultaneously with the development of rebellious, truly popular cultural trends that were, for at least a time, beyond the possibility of absorption. A kind of native tradition of cruelty sprouted among rock 'n' rollers like Elvis Presley, Little Richard, and Jerry Lee Lewis; actors like Marlon Brando, Rod Steiger, Montgomery Clift, and James Dean; stand-up comedians such as Lenny Bruce and Mort Sahl; and jazz musicians like Charlie Parker and Oscar Peterson. Though none of these artists was familiar with Artaud, each of them explored aspects of expression that should strike us now as distinctly "Artaudian": the use of the irrational, the refusal of complete fidelity to text, the belief in the overwhelming necessity of full and honest expression, the seeking of intense somatic responses from the audience as a consequence of intense feeling on the part of the performer and the liberal use of drugs, and a rethinking of the body as both a medium and subject of art.

Not simply the cultural creations, but the social settings that surrounded these popular trends linked them to Artaud and his intransigent vanguard attitude in a way not unlike what evolutionary scientists call "parallel development." In the case of rock 'n' roll, method acting, sick comedy, and jazz, the social settings themselves were seedbeds for native cruelty, many of them reminiscent of the kind of "total" or "environmental" theater advocated by the Frenchman. As a consequence of the extremity of gesture developed in these kinds of performance situations, these subcultures were under continual attack by authorities. Artistic content and drug use were coincident targets of harassment. Lenny Bruce, for example, was prosecuted not only for the sinister perfection of his satire but also for his use of drugs. The coincidence of censorship and antidrug prosecution wasn't new in the 1950s. Radical aesthetics in the capitalist West have often coincided with the illegal marketing or excessive use of drugs. Likewise, conservative attacks on radical aesthetic positions have often coincided with attacks on the cultural forms surrounding aesthetic production, cultural forms that often celebrated the use of drugs. Opium, opiates, and nicotine in the later periods of French and British romanticism; nicotine, cocaine, alcohol, and peyote for the one-man vanguard movement Stanislaw Witkiewicz; alcohol in the Lost Generation; nicotine and caffeine in the existentialist movement; alcohol, Benzedrine, and marijuana among the Beats; ecstasy in Rave culture—the socioeconomic history of substance abuse is entangled with the history of subversive aesthetics, and both are intertwined with the history of the law. The discourses of aesthetics, social control, and drugs have long been tangled in a tight, unruly knot. We're still untangling that knot today—and, from all appearances, we appear to be getting all the more tangled in it.

Cruelty and Historiography

A bit like grass, avant-gardes tend to appear greener on the other side. Such verdant visions of cultural intransigence tend to be fairly selective in representing the complex negotiations that have to be performed when the avant-garde migrates, as was the case with Artaud and the Living Theatre, both of whom led significant lives simultaneously in Europe and the United States.[12] A good example of this green-eyed vision is Guy Scarpetta's, in his provocative 1977 article, first published in *Tel Quel,* about Artaud and French avant-garde theater. Scarpetta puts together an argument based on a limited representation of the Living Theatre, its social context, and its impact on the counterculture and, ultimately, the contemporary French intellectual scene. It's worth exploring at length if we wish to understand the relationship among Artaud, Cold War politics, and the limits of criticism.

Scarpetta rues the "co-optation" of Artaud by the French intelligentsia. He writes that "there is no sign whatsoever of any engagement" with the real radicalism of Artaud in France (that is to say, with its *écriture,* or purposeful identification and disruption of conceptual and syntactical structures); rather, the rule is "outdated conventions, academicism, formalism, pedagogical treatment of 'classics,' hyper-inhibited or hyper-hysterical bodies, uninspired texts, uninteresting spaces, a general lack of invention and imagination."[13] It is in the work of Meredith Monk, Robert Wilson, and Richard Foreman in United States during the 1970s that Scarpetta sees Artaud's most radical and vital legacy. Attempting to define the distinction between French and American cruelty, he digs for a root:

Let us go back, therefore, to the beginning of the "sixties": what seems most clearly symptomatic of course, is the Living Theatre. . . . In the Living Theatre we can see Artaud's influence . . . with the emphasis placed on the physical concrete character of the directorial code, the escape from its "illustrative" function, the rehabilitation of the body and of gesture, the mistrust of rationality, the exploration of theatrical space through its mobile, organic dimension. An aesthetic of excess, of the scream. (218)

Scarpetta accurately identifies the heroic role the Becks played in the vitalization of radical performance in the United States in the late 1950s and the catalyzing of the counterculture, particularly through its innovative and precocious use of Artaudian theory. He wasn't the first. The French recognized early on the importance of the Living Theatre, awarding it three first prizes at the Théâtre des Nations in 1961 (for a triple bill that included Brecht's *In the Jungle of Cities,* William Carlos Williams's *Many Loves,* and *The Connection,* with Martin Sheen in the role of Ernie), a gesture that affirmed the Living's rightful place alongside the Berliner Ensemble and the Piccolo Teatro della Città di Milano. However, Scarpetta's representation of the Living is based on a limited sense of their work and its roots in U.S. Cold War culture. In fact, if we look beyond these limits, we can identify aspects of the avant-garde's unsuccessful battle with bourgeois capitalism that may not have been noticed before, characteristics that could help arts activists in our own time evade certain kinds of co-optation.

Most likely, Scarpetta is recalling *Paradise Now,* which toured Europe during the late 1960s and carried the Living into the streets of Paris's Latin Quarter during the events of May 1968. Perhaps the Living's best-known collective creation, it reflected the furthest extreme of their efforts to integrate their work as theater people with their lives as activists and promoters of pacifist ideology. The production also reflected the hard-edged cosmopolitanism earned by their long years on European tour and the kind of lateral, nonlinear, associative thinking promoted by their chronic use of marijuana and LSD. The text of the production, written cooperatively by the thirty-six members of the mercurial, nomadic community, was not so much a script as a set of performance actions structured by a complex, syncretistic spiritual map, a map that combined the *I Ching,* kabbalistic guides to language-body unity, guerrilla warfare theory, the acutely polemical political debate culture in Western Europe, and their own collective efforts to define the pathway from action and emergency to the permanent revolution.

Scarpetta may also be remembering the leading role the Living played in the ill-conceived takeover of the Odéon Théâtre de France during the explosive spring of 1968. The takeover is exemplary of the quirky shape that the co-optation of the older avant-gardes took in France and how the fight against co-optation often turned against the avant-garde itself. The Odéon was no bastion of conservatism; quite the contrary, it was a resolutely anti-bourgeois theater directed by Artaud's friend and disciple, the avant-garde veteran Jean-Louis Barrault. The attack on the theater and Barrault was, as James Harding acutely describes it, an allegory of the avant-garde's conflicted attitudes toward the politics of radical aesthetics, of its tendency to divide its own ranks.[14]

Whatever specific performance Scarpetta has in mind, there's no doubt that he views the Living as an avant-garde that brooks no compromise with co-opted vanguardism. Their integration of art, community, and politics and their attack on the Odéon and Barrault dovetail with Scarpetta's cry for radical intransigence in French intellectual and theatrical life, not least in the language and concepts with which radical intransigence is made sensible. But there's a danger to Scarpetta's celebration of the Living as an emblem of the 1960s: the danger of inadequate contextualization and historicization. Every act of resistance is conditioned by the force that it resists, and every act of resistance recasts the history of resistance. The longevity, extremity, and revolutionary resolution of the Becks' work in theater, performance, and political activism can lure the scholar into viewing them as a transhistorical, transgeographical presence, remaining fixed despite their constant travels and continual shifts in organizational structure and aesthetic concern. And this is where Scarpetta's invocation of the Living Theatre as the root of truly radical performance finds its limits.

The Living's performance politics actively cultivated contradiction. We should remember that the Becks were well versed in forms of political theater that did not necessitate synthesis and resolution. They knew Brecht and Piscator like the backs of their hands. They knew the surrealists; as a student at Yale, Beck had attended a lecture by André Breton. As an artist in Manhattan, he was part of a volatile mix of exiled vanguardists, marginalized identities (artist, bisexual, Jew), and advocates of expressive modernism. We should also remember that the Becks developed their most far-reaching work coincidentally with other kinds of Cold War excess, excesses that they hoped to defeat with their own modes of excessive politics. The Living Theatre's Artaudian screams mingled with those of sports stadiums and movie fan clubs, not to mention the more savage cries inspired among reactionaries by the peace and civil rights movements. They mingled with the excesses of jazz clubs where edge-bending music was played and heard in a creative cocktail of legal and illegal intoxicants, cross-racial mingling, and various kinds of delinquency.[15] It is for this reason that this chapter is devoted to the production that put Beck and Malina on the theater-historical map, a production in which the dominant metaphors and dramaturgical influences were jazz and heroin.

The Connection proves on careful examination to be an act of theatrical resistance that was situated, conscious of the theatrical and textual trends that enabled it, and profoundly concerned with the role the avant-garde was inadvertently playing in the strengthening of the capitalist system. Occurring almost a decade before *Paradise Now* and a decade after the company's founding, *The Connection* evidences both the radicalism and the necessary compromises of the Living's paradoxical position. It is a midpoint work in the trajectory the Living traveled from experimental art to the revolutionary acts celebrated by Scarpetta.

The geographical and historical situation of the work is key. Scholars should understand that the radicalism of *Paradise Now* and the Odéon takeover were rooted in the American 1950s, in an age of skyrocketing affluence, vibrant (if convulsively anticommunist) liberal progressivism, rapidly spreading civil unrest, unprecedented injustice and ignorance, and the systematic destruction of the Old Left—all aided and abetted (though not necessarily by intention) by a number of prominent pre–World War II avant-gardes. It was necessary, therefore, that the Living Theatre find a way to shoulder the burden of the avant-garde while shedding the baggage of its co-optation by Madison Avenue and the CIA.[16] Their movement toward more and more extreme, yet more and more situated, forms of revolutionary performance was first evidenced in an experimental theatrical piece haunted by the ghost of Artaud and fundamentally structured by (1) the cutting-edge jazz produced in Manhattan by the likes of Dizzy Gillespie, Charlie Parker, Charles Mingus, Miles Davis, and Max Roach, and (2) the equivocal politics of drug use, drug culture, and Drug War.

In the Belly of the Beast

It's hard to imagine a more situated attack on bourgeois capitalism than the Living Theatre's. Incapable of affording the costs of lawyers to obtain tax-exempt status as a nonprofit organization and incapable of proving to private foundations that their theater could turn a profit on the repertory system, the Living had to enter the politically unpredictable demilitarized zone between radicalism and entrepreneurialism. Given the need to sell tickets or go out of existence, Beck and Malina had to place their repertory theater in the belly of the beast. As if out of some guilty reflex, this paradoxical position in the financially constrained, aesthetically conservative Manhattan theater market had pressed the LT before 1959 toward acutely self-conscious productions, productions that made themes out of theater itself. On more than one occasion prior to their chat with Richards about the Artaud translation, the LT had produced self-referential treatments of the hidden power games of performance, whether the performance of theater (Gertrude Stein's *Doctor Faustus Lights the Lights* [1951] and Pirandello's *Tonight, We Improvise* [staged in 1955]), the performance of everyday life (T. S. Eliot's *The Cocktail Party* [performed as a monologue by Julian Sawyer in the Becks' living room in 1951]), or the self-conscious, dialectical modes of Brechtian politics-as-performance, learned by Malina as a directing student of Erwin Piscator's at the New School for Social Research.

It would be fair to say that the Becks were finding their position increasingly untenable, in both aesthetic and political terms. Their involvement with the burgeoning antinuclear movement led by anticapitalist, anticommunist Dorothy Day had led to their arrest and imprisonment in 1957 (the second time for Malina, who had been jailed for ten days the previous year). Their thirty days behind bars made palpable the deep penetration of oppression into American society. Their offense? Refusing to report to a fallout shelter after the sounding of an air-raid alarm. The politicization of everyday life that was the consequence of Cold War security needs had pressed upon them the need for a more flexible, more wide-ranging political-theatrical method. Pirandello needed radicalizing and Artaud's writings seemed to provide a way to do that.

The contradictions of that position fed directly into the directorial, design, and performance decisions of *The Connection,* a production about nothing so much as the cruelty of contradiction; specifically, the contradictions of theater market, drug experience and addiction, and jazz. Richards's translation of *The Theater and Its Double* preceded by only a few months the Becks' receipt of a good working draft of a script written by an unknown playwright, a script that possessed a keen understanding of the problem of revolutionary excess in an affluent society. Around the same time as the party where the Becks first heard about Artaud's book, Jack Gelber, living on his wife's secretary salary and his own unemployment insurance, presented the Becks with a paradoxically unabashed yet masochistically guilt-ridden exploitation play based on his experiences with a small community of heroin addicts, an experience that had led to arrest and brief incarceration, but whose dramatization emphasized less the "dramatic adventure" of addiction and illegality than its profoundly dangerous boredom.

Interestingly, Gelber later wrote an acute analysis of the Living Theatre's negotiations of the capitalist theater system. In "Julian Beck, Businessman,"

Gelber describes and critiques the burden of financial management on the theatrical work of the company. Gelber identifies the fundamental contradiction of Beck's four decades of work as the Living's principal administrator: "Half of Julian worked to eliminate cash as the enemy of the good life, while the other half made dozens of day-to-day decisions about the green stuff. . . . How to live with irreconcilables was a pill Julian took more than once a day."[17] That last concern stuck with the LT throughout its career. For even though, as Beck put it, this was not "the first nor last time the middle class had subsidized a revolution" (6), the honest word that the Living attempted to sound could not escape the structural limits of such subsidization. As a consequence, the word echoed with the evil tones of the "blood-money system, man-barter system, the war-system" (6).

On the eve of its first European tour, Malina told the troupe, "Every single move I make is a slave gesture to the system."[18] Much of the Living's work during the 1960s and 1970s was an explicit attempt to purify theater and drama of the resinous sediment of evil. Beck, recognizing the paradox of such an effort, described the relations of his troupe to its society as basically an economic one that directly impacted creative expression. The theater was, in all ways, "in all its parts," a struggle with the "structures of Mammon."[19] In their hearts anarcho-pacifists, at times transcendentalists, Beck and Malina were de facto materialists, and the clash between their political goals and their economic realities echoed in every theater they occupied, none more so than the Fourteenth Street theater in which *The Connection* premiered. As Beck put it, "If we were always working for [Mammon's] withering away, he never removed from us the yoke" (43). For Malina, that yoke threatened a deep and irrevocable fissuring of self and community. She described her personal situation in 1968: "I am torn, but not in half."[20] This sense of inner division had been felt long before 1968, particularly during the two years prior to the premiere of *The Connection*.

Torn, but not in half—the Living, Beck and Malina freely admitted, was a theater of contradiction. What else, they might have asked, could it be in such a deeply contradictory society, a society whose worst depredations sprang from the same soil as its most heady ideals? As I explore the relationship of jazz, heroin, cruelty, and community in *The Connection,* it behooves me to keep in mind a question asked by the Living and left unanswered to our own times, one that is also rooted in contradiction: Can a new world be figured utilizing the materials of this one? As *The Connection* suggests, the yoke of Mammon is as irrevocable as the junkie's craving for the drug, both a burden and a lever. This is a decidedly unromantic vision of political theater, one that must be kept constantly in mind as we explore the more utopian aspects of the Living's material-minded work. "Art is revolt," Beck writes. "It is the revolt that fails" (95).

Gelber wasn't familiar enough with the Becks in 1958 to understand just how intolerable living with irreconcilables was becoming for them. And I don't suspect the Becks were thinking all that much about economics when they finished their first reading of *The Connection*. What first struck the pair was the play's use of jazz—not just jazz music, but jazz musicians playing themselves and not just adding incidental music or authentic atmosphere. Even more fetching was what they saw in the play's dramatic structure: jazz functioned as a compositional principle of the piece as a whole; conflict and character were syncopated with one of the most formally interesting and potentially subversive artistic developments in American Cold War culture.

The Becks also appreciated the script's acute insights into the hypocrisy and absurdity of American drug policy, which they viewed as simply a handmaiden to the Establishment's larger geopolitical goals. Did the Becks know Artaud was a multiple-drug addict? Did they know that his struggle to describe and liberate the "implacable necessity" that led "things to their ineluctable end at whatever cost" was a struggle concretely related to his experiences with the brutalizing anguish of drug addiction and repeatedly failed withdrawal efforts?[21] Most likely not; however, they were sensitive readers, very conscious of the complex relationship of text and performance in the modern theater, and well aware, through personal experience, of the basic relationship of the body to the social management policies of the War on Drugs. Their decision to use Artaudian theatrical techniques demonstrates their acute sensitivity to the multiple political implications of Artaud's work, implications that led them to include Artaud's "The Theater and Culture" in the program for their play about "jazz and junk." They were all too aware that the experiences of community and communication they had discovered in Manhattan during the 1950s pressed the authorities into acts of "legislative interpretation" intended to destroy the fragile social structure forming in the ruins of the Old Left and the co-opted vanguards of the prewar era.

Jailed for thirty days in 1957, Malina and Beck got to know a great many prisoners, the majority of whom were addicts and prostitutes. This encounter of radical anarcho-pacifists with the inhabitants of the lower depths of the American pleasure market inspired the Becks to investigate and criticize the political structures and attitudes that could bring such seemingly disparate communities together under a common oppression. Surely, such a connection wasn't just a coincidence, but evidence of a shared necessity. This crucial moment in the Becks' political education

ratified for them a lesson first taught to them by Allen Ginsberg: artistic revolution was inseparable from bodily revolution. The use of drugs, the
expression of sexuality, acts of civil resistance, and poetic extremism all were
targets of the authorities. Gelber's script, with its hipster didacticism, acute
sense of the politics and economics of pleasure in the United States, and
Pirandello-esque jabs at the audience, was just the thing the LT needed.
The decision to dedicate the production to the prisoners of the Women's
House of Detention underlines the fact that *The Connection* represented a
crucial forward step in the LT's linking of aesthetic, social, and political
antagonism.

The fact that the Becks were able to see Gelber's play as a perfect vehicle for Artaudian performance principles is evidence of their acute
encounter with the notoriously elliptical, vertiginously metaphorical *The
Theater and Its Double*. The Becks had not read any of Artaud's other works
by that time, but their reading of Richards's translation was sensitive
enough to bring to mind other works, especially those that struggle with the
politics of drug experience. I find some curious parallels between the reticular imagery and political equivocality of *The Connection* and the description
of the anguish of opium addiction in a letter written by Artaud in 1925 to
the "Legislator of the Law on Narcotics":

> [T]he anguish of opium has another hue, it does not have this metaphys-
> ical flavor, this marvelous imperfection of tone [that normal anguish pos-
> sesses]. I imagine it as full of echoes, caves, labyrinths, and turns; full of
> speaking tongues of fire, of mental eyes in action, and of the clapping of
> a thunder that is dark and full of reason.
>
> But I imagine the soul under opium as well centered and yet infinitely
> divisible, and transportable, like a thing which exists. I imagine the soul
> as feeling, I see it struggle and consent at the same time, and turn its
> tongues in all directions, multiply its sex—and kill itself.
>
> . . . The void of opium contains as it were the shape of a brow that
> thinks, that has located the position of the black pit.[22]

Malina and Beck found in Gelber's play a similarly grotesque, reticular
anguish and a similarly equivocal attitude toward the politics of drugs and
drug addiction. Although the Becks weren't quite ready to abandon the
"masterpieces" of dramatic literature that so incensed Artaud, they were
more than prepared to take the theater into the kinds of physical extremity
that would one day lead them far away from literature.

Syncopating Politics

One key step was jazz. As an emotionally intense and formally daring performance form, jazz, especially the veering moods and modes of Bebop, was close in spirit to the attack on the text and celebration of "pure expression" that were so important to Artaud.[23] Bebop's use of ambiguity and discontinuity, its expressive manipulation of time, and the heightened attention it demanded of its listeners intersected with some of the more esoteric aspects of Artaudian cruelty. Jazz was also an extremely significant presence in the Manhattan bohemian/avant-garde scene of the 1940s and 1950s, a lingua franca of the fragmented subcultures of the Left.[24] It was a presence that the Becks recognized and respected. A decade or so after *The Connection's* premiere, Beck wrote that jazz "bends the mind. So that you think differently. It changes the understanding of reality, it projects different images, it has nothing to do with politics, but it changes politics. We are in a revolution. It began to bud a few hundred years ago, this lotus. Jazz is one of its petals."[25]

An ambivalent attitude toward dramatic text is evident in earlier LT productions—and certainly the Becks were fluent in the antitextual bias of the avant-garde long before *The Connection*—but jazz and cruelty were the levers the Becks needed to move beyond the merely thematic use of antitextuality in their productions of Pirandello's *Tonight We Improvise* (1955) and William Carlos Williams's *Many Loves,* which opened in 1959. Like Pirandello, they felt that improvisation was one of the keys that could open a morbidly textual theater to the protean chaos of everyday life and the epistemological uncertainties of modernity. In fact, Gelber's play possesses distinct echoes of *Six Characters in Search of an Author,* especially its repetitive plunging from self-consciously clever hyperrealism into melodramatic anguish. But *The Connection* afforded them more than just a dramatic meditation on the relationship of art and life, more than simply a theme. Beck notes that Malina's directorial style was immediately changed by the improvisational themes and opportunities of Gelber's script:

> She began to let the actors design their movements, creating a remarkable atmosphere in which the company became more and more free to bring in its own ideas. . . . The careful directing books we had used at the beginning were by now quite gone. She began to suggest rather than tell, and the company began to find a style that was not superimposed but rose out of their own sensitivities.[26]

The shift in Malina's directorial style marks a crucial moment in the development of the Living Theatre, a key preparatory moment toward the exploration of improvisatory, collaboratively created works such as *Paradise Now* and *Mysteries* (1964) and a crucial moment in the shift from a theater troupe to a revolutionary community. In sum, with the help of *The Connection* and the Freddie Redd Quartet, the Living Theatre began to view itself as a jazz ensemble.

At least primarily as a jazz ensemble. As I will demonstrate in more detail in the second half of this case study, the new organizational model Malina instituted in rehearsals for the production was implicitly modeled on not one but *two* marginalized, innovative, police-patrolled, and subversive communities: the jazz ensemble and the opium den. Each of these communities supplied the Becks with innovative understandings of communication and community and both suggested specific but distinct ways to contend with the perennially problematic text-performance dynamic. Each synthesized, produced, and disrupted sociotemporal rhythms in very specific ways. Most importantly, each supplied the Becks with the models they needed to explore organizational innovation and, thus, bring their artistic product in line with their artistic process. With such models, the Becks began to consciously and thoroughly conceptualize the theater troupe itself as an emblematic community and as home base for effective political activism. The jazz ensemble and the opium den enabled the Becks to begin intensive exploration of how the form and content of the plays they produced interrelated with the social structure of the troupe as a whole as well as audience-performer relations.

Their increasingly acute understanding of the changing, more and more intimate techniques of social management during the Cold War and of their own place among the grass-roots of the Cold War avant-garde virtually guaranteed that *The Connection* would prove to be an extremely significant event not just in the history of the Living Theatre, but in American theater history and countercultural politics. It was, from many accounts, a first-rate, even life-changing show. Lillian Hellman remarked that *The Connection* was "the only play [she'd] been able to sit through for years."[27] Tennessee Williams had exactly the opposite reaction, pacing back and forth in the rear aisle of the Cherry Lane Theatre throughout most of the two acts, too excited to stay seated (160). It was attended by the cream of Manhattan social life: John Tytell lists Leonard Bernstein, Charles Ludlam, John Gielgud, Anita Loos, Lauren Bacall, Langston Hughes, John Huston, Salvador Dalí, United Nations secretary Dag Hammarskjöld, publisher and riddler Bennett Cerf, the New York City commissioner of prisons (whose office would grow increasingly familiar with the Becks), and Kenneth Tynan (160–61).

But the audiences who were most affected by the production were hardly mainstream or elite, particularly in the interregnum between opening night and critical acclaim. As Gelber describes it, the early audiences for the production were "a mixture of working-class blacks along with middle-class black and white jazz lovers. . . . It was a raucous and responsive audience unlike any I've ever seen. Untrained in the etiquette of the theater, they talked back to the actors and often asked their neighbor to save their seat during intermission" (15). In this audience was Ed Bullins, a young fiction writer at the time, future founding member of the Black Panther Party for Self-Defense, and crucial figure in the Black drama movement, who incorporated elements of *The Connection* into plays such as *It Bees Dat Way, The Corner, Death List,* and *We Righteous Bombers.* Though this cult audience would not last and would eventually be diluted by a white, middle-class, more polite kind of ticket holder, it marks *The Connection* as a precociously countercultural event, one Beck protected by not allowing the play to be moved to Broadway (a gutsy choice considering that the Fourteenth Street theater held 162 people and the LT was operating in the red). For these less glorious spectators, *The Connection* showed new visions of community and communication and let loose innovative rhythms of historical transformation.

This revelation was sparked through the careful manipulation of one of the theater's most volatile materials: time. As James Schevill notes, pace is among the more difficult aspects of theater to describe and criticize; however, it is an emphatically influential one, "the central mystery in drama" and one of particular importance to the countercultural theaters his book explores.[28] In *From Ritual to Theatre,* Victor Turner argues that all ritual performances must include a rite "which changes the quality of time . . . or constructs a cultural realm which is defined as 'out of time,' i.e., beyond or outside the time which measures secular processes and routines."[29] Turner notes that the temporal distinctiveness of performance has changed in the West as Western society has shifted from an agrarian to an industrial-capitalist basis. For agrarian societies, the time of ritual inevitably supported the continuity of the culture. However, in industrial-capitalist societies, the secularization and diffusion of such rites makes getting beyond or outside the time-standards of work and everyday life a peculiarly complicated activity. As a consequence, the manipulation of time by performance can potentially serve as "a kind of institutional capsule or pocket which contains the germ of future social developments, of societal change, in a way that the central tendencies of a social system can never quite succeed in being" (45). Turner therefore sees a close relationship between theater revolutions and political revolutions. Political crises, "whether violent or non-violent, may be the totalizing . . . phases for which . . . tribal rites de passage were merely fore-shadowings or premonitions" (45). History has proven Turner right. Not only has theater helped to inspire and model political action, it has often supplied the specific understandings of personal, social, and historical time that underwrite such action. The relationship between theater and revolution is a rhythmic relationship.

The Connection supplied the bohemias and cenacles of the counterculture with a richly varied understanding of time as a critical concept and a revolutionary practice that could catalyze the creation of flexible political strategies. Though they weren't the first in the postbourgeois history of theater to reject the implicit philosophies of time and history through which the postbourgeois theatrical mainstream flows, Beck as designer and Malina as director wove around Gelber's script a dense layering of sonic, imagistic, and linguistic rhythms that was as significant, as innovative, and as complex as any time-art prior to 1959. Their theatrical revolution for better *and* worse, supplied a model for other, larger revolutions. Jazz is one of the keys to understanding this revolutionary rethinking of time.

However, the use of jazz compositional principles and their self-transformation into what was, in essence, the social-organizational equivalent of the jazz jam was prepared by long acquaintance with another avant-gardist with an interest in jazz and time. Gertrude Stein was idolized by Beck, read constantly by Beck and Malina during their courtship in the mid-1940s, and produced by the LT on two occasions (*Ladies Voices,* in the Becks' living room, and *Doctor Faustus Lights the Lights,* the first public Living Theatre production, both staged in 1951). Mama Dada's (as Sarah Bey-Cheng has named her) influence on the Becks can't be overestimated, particularly the lessons she taught them concerning the polyvalent nature of theatrical time. The Becks were especially attracted to Stein's notion of theater as a "landscape," explained by Bonnie Marranca as a dramaturgical principle that replaces dramatic action with pictorial composition. As a consequence, "Whatever you find in it depends on your own way of looking."[30]

The dramatic flatness and centerless dramaturgy of Stein's plays enabled the Living to explore many kinds of theatrical time, especially the highly manipulable dynamic of performer, text, and audience. Stein writes in "Plays" that as a girl she encountered a "fundamental thing about plays," "a combination and not a contradiction."[31] "The thing," she writes, "that is fundamental about plays is that the scene as depicted on the stage is more

often than not one might say it is almost always in syncopated time in relation to the emotion of anybody in the audience" (xxix). Three elements are
"syncopated" in theater, Stein continues: the thing that happens on stage,
the thing that happens in the audience's mind, and the thing that happens in
the performer's mind (xxxi). Stein felt distinctly "nervous" about this syncopation of happenings, this slight, seductive mismatch of rhythmic experiences: "that the thing and the thing felt about the thing seen not going on
at the same tempo is what makes the being at the theatre something that
makes anybody nervous" (xxx).

Stein's works explore and exploit this mismatch, often for purposes that
we call now "deconstructive." Stein, however, knew that there were other
ways to make use of theatrical nervousness. She points out that jazz is closely
related in form to her own efforts as a writer.

> The jazz bands made of this thing, the thing that makes you nervous at
> the theatre, they made of this thing an end in itself. They made of this
> different tempo a something that was nothing but a difference in tempo
> between anybody and everybody including all those doing it and all
> those hearing and seeing it. In the theatre of course this difference in
> tempo is less violent but still it is there and it does make anybody ner-
> vous. (xxx)

The syncopated experiences of performers, scores, and audiences were an
increasingly important concern for the fragmented artistic subcultures of
the United States. Daniel Belgrad has thoroughly explored the ways that
such syncopation (which he calls "spontaneity") enabled artists of the
1940s and 1950s to find alternatives to the progress model of Western history, to escape the cultural boundaries of corporate liberalism, and to challenge the domination of the Anglo-American cultural elite.[32] Jazz was
fundamental to this shift into what Belgrad calls the "culture of spontaneity." The ambiguous experience of syncopation, called by Stein "nervousness," was (to recall Aldous Huxley) a doorway of perception for
those locked in the staid, all-too-regular rhythms and emotion-tones of
Cold War capitalism.

Jazz was the lingua franca of the marginalized and alienated subcultures
of post–World War II America. The most significant performers and composers of the Becks' generation (Charles Mingus, Charlie Parker, Thelonious Monk, John Coltrane, Miles Davis, Dizzie Gillespie, Max Roach,
etc.) traveled with ease among these communities, sharing ideas, experiences, and formal innovations. Cecil Taylor, for example, ran the mimeo-

graph machine for LeRoi Jones and Diane Di Prima's journal *The Floating Bear*. Jackie McLean, another member of this fragmented cultural scene and the anchor member of the Freddie Redd Quartet during its four-year collaboration with the LT, avidly explored painting, literature, and nonjazz musical forms while in Manhattan. His association with the painter Harvey Cropper introduced him to the music of Bartók and the paintings of Cézanne and Hieronymous Bosch (the latter's broiling, centerless paintings communicated a vision of horror that "opened another world" for McLean).[33] His acquaintance with Jones and the Becks introduced him to much more, especially the kinds of links between art and politics that could be forged through performance, links that had long been apparent to him as a musician.[34] Like McLean, Charlie Parker was a polymath, actively interested in all the developments happening in the arts, sciences, and ideologies of his time. Like so many other jazz musicians of his generation, McLean and Parker took pride in absorbing these influences and constructing musical forms to express and relate them. In fact, one could go further and claim that the improvisational, flexible modes of jazz weren't just influential, they were a ubiquitous way of thinking that would allow the counterculture to respond effectively to the complexities and contradictions of their historical, artistic, social, and political situation.

It's the syncopated complexity of *The Connection,* a complexity made manageable by the continually varying structures of Bebop's emotionally intense experiments with musical form, that I will most strongly emphasize as I continue to work my way into the equivocal politics of the production's cruelty. Unlike the dramaturgical austerity of their productions of Stein, Auden, Eliot, and Paul Goodman during the 1950s, this one was supersaturated with symbols, traces of precursor texts, allusions to art and literature (high, middle, and lowbrow), aesthetic styles, and rhythms. The production reflects the Becks' search for a mode of cultural production and expression that could lead them out of the Cold War conceptual do-si-do of capitalism and communism, a rigidly structured dance they felt strictly curtailed social criticism, activism, and experience. *The Connection* was a baroque monstrosity that reflected the ever-more-inclusive nature of the Becks' political perspective, an inclusiveness that was the result of their cosmopolitanism, their struggle to find a workable ideology, their increasing affection for the lateral associative qualities of marijuana, and their enthusiastic move into jazz epistemology.

This inclusiveness is reflected in Julian's writings on politics, which, as we've seen already, compare the radical political traditions of the West to a lotus blossom: "Psychoanalysis. Pacifism. Petals. Trotsky. Louise Michel.

The 18th century's struggle to create conditions that would protect freedom of press, speech, religious worship, public assembly, creed. Petals" (129). One can find all of these traditions in the final version of Gelber's script—in addition to theoretical physics, abstract expressionism, oblique stabs at historical consciousness, and radical Buddhist theology. The synthetic nature of the production—its absorption, revision, and cobbling-together of so many of the modes of past and present avant-gardes—opened a door for the Living that would lead to literal stage monstrosities like *Frankenstein* (1965), in which discursive sources, rapid-fire allusion, and decentered, nonlinear action stretch the dialogue and dramatic structure to the breaking point, like the monster's skin in Mary Shelley's novel. As with McLean and Parker, the Becks and Gelber struggled to find the form to contain the complexity of their experience, desires, and knowledge.

A Note on *Frankenstein* and *Communitas*

As part of their continuing efforts to unify the diverse experiences, desires, and discourses of the fragmented Left, the Living relied more and more after 1959 on theatrical forms of collage and montage to formally manage the many suggestions, rehearsal developments, interesting ideas culled from wide-ranging reading and social interaction, individual obsessions, and meandering debates encountered during their long, interminable hours of group creation, self-criticism, and artistic revision. The result of this participatory and associative approach to intellectual synthesis was intense moments of multiply layered visual and sonic effects arranged in complicated, coexisting temporal sequences. This principle is much more apparent (though no more important) in later productions such as *Frankenstein, Mysteries and Smaller Pieces,* and *Paradise Now* than it is in *The Connection,* so it can help us to look at an older piece to get a better sense of how it functioned in the earlier work.

Pierre Biner's description of the action that occurred on the top level of the multistory, anthropomorphic set of *Frankenstein* is illustrative:

[A]n actor who seems to be a fugitive from Chaplin's *Modern Times* is executing a series of mechanical gestures. Three others . . . wave portraits of Marx and Lenin along with a placard reading "To each / his need / from each / his power." They march on the narrow gangplanks while declaiming Marxist maxims in jerky, broken tones of voice. From the control booth . . . an actor wrapped in a black hood is introduced as the spokesman of "international industries," and proceeds to read in monotones, amplified by loudspeakers, capitalist slogans consisting of typical phrases taken from books on economics. (The texts recited in this scene have been arranged as a collage. Besides Mao and Whitman, passages have been drawn from *The Age of Automation* by Sir Leon Bargrit and Bertrand Russell's *Power*. The total effect is that of an unmilitant discussion among electronic machines, each being given equal importance. On the other hand, the voice at the control booth explains that automation will provide an altogether higher level of civilization.) (120)

Frankenstein surrounds its source text with the din of the industrial, bourgeois, and romantic revolutions, simultaneously restoring historical context to Shelley's novel while at the same time threatening to overwhelm the viewer with contextual information. The densely layered textual and performance moment described by Biner gives a pretty good sense of the LT's belief that any social advance must be wrested from the aesthetic, philosophical, and ideological wreckage of industrial culture. Whatever insights a viewer culled from this performance had to be stitched together from the dismembered corpse of the century-and-a-half history of bourgeois culture. There is a truth filtering out from the age of Shelley's novel, the production suggests, but the production implies that we lack the body (both the physical body and the "body politic") to speak it.

If, as Phelan writes, "[t]he living performing body is the center of semiotic crossings, which allows one to perceive, interpret, and document the performance event," it is equally true that this body is often tormented by such crossings.[35] Significance is the cross that must be borne by the performer's body. The spatial complexity of *Frankenstein*'s set, composed of bodies and itself a body (i.e., a giant head), the simultaneity of the production's multiple textual sources (many of which deal explicitly with questions of time), the layered significance of the performers' sequential gestures—these all challenge the viewer's capacity to organize and conceptualize. In short, there is, on this stage, a contradiction between the play's materials—all of which cohere around a notion of time that is progressive, linear, orderly—and the play's form, which purposefully disables viewer's ability to achieve the promise of the play's materials. The enormous head on the stage makes manifest the very confusion that is going on in the viewer's head: a cacophonous, stunning simultaneity of futurological visions. The time of the future is, quite literally, *monstrous,* a body deforming under the pressure of immanent significance.

Monstrosity, however, does not preclude utopia. In fact, if we investigate older meanings of the word *monster,* we find it related to the idea that a future crisis manifests itself in the deformation of objects in the present (the calf with birth defects as marker of war to come). To Chaucer, for example, a monster was a marvel, a prodigy of something to come. However, such monstrosity was always manifested in a physical abnormality (a calf with severe birth defects, for example). I find this older meaning sympathetic with the tortured bodies so often featured on the Living's stages. The monstrosity of social crisis and spiritual communication is mirrored in concrete, anguished transformations of the performer's body and in the "other times" of performance described by Turner. Utopia is revealed in the anguish of the transformed body and the singular time of performance. The LT's *Frankenstein* played in the novel's own striping paradoxes; most notably, the belief that the virtuous future of the compromised bourgeois revolutions of the eighteenth century could be articulated only in monstrous, lighting-struck flashes of insight and bodily deformation. Beck characterized the production's design as follows: "*Frankenstein* not only menaces the public, it is the public. The Creature simultaneously menaces civilization and is civilization, it is civilization menacing itself . . . within us is the creature who raises his arms and breathes, conspicuously changing and transforming, and praying for the next development in humanity" (3). The actors performing within the multitiered, headlike stage embodied the alternative to such a menace, the embodied, concretely aesthetic, communitarian, utopian manifestation of the text's contradictions.

Manifestation, not solution. If the politicizing effects of the Living were ultimately directed toward the "authentic body" of the blessed community (i.e., the utopian body politic, that perfect, yogic achievement of mind-body balance), this did not by any means guarantee the acceptance of that body in the larger social field outside the theater in which that body manifested itself. In other words, given the LT's increasing distrust of words and bourgeois rationality, the representation of the blessed future could only be confusing, equivocal, fragmented, and *cruel*. The body, on their stage was "effervescent," to recall Banes's representation of the volatile physicality of American avant-garde performance in the early 1960s.[36] In other words, the body often served as the vehicle for communicating or mediating the peculiar time signatures of politically attuned art. Such body-centered, temporally antagonistic art often flummoxed the ability of critics to make sense of it.

Michael Smith was flummoxed when he attempted to criticize the production for the *Village Voice*. Having toured with the troupe for months, he realized that a "review" of *Frankenstein* was simply impossible. "I am already too far into the Living Theatre to write a 'review,'" he writes.[37] It is possible to view Smith's incapacity in two ways. First, it can reflect a failure on the part of the Living to successfully create a theatrical correlative to its total revolt against bourgeois society. The equivocality and ambiguity of a production like *Frankenstein* is the mark of a failure to work through the problems that motivated the production in the first place. On the other hand, we could also see this failure as the understandable inability of an initiate to find the language to encompass the mysteries to which he has been exposed. Smith, an initiate of the LT's communal consciousness, nevertheless attempts to work his way toward some kind of language that would capture the singularity of his experience:

> In spite of everything, what they have managed to do in *Frankenstein*— as a result of being forced to make do . . .—is a more or less evolved technique of play—acting, performance, total idea of what the theatre is—which perhaps is better in the long run than any single finished production.
>
> And this effort to me could be described as: the concerted effort of an ensemble to develop the articulation of ideas and values through mime and gesture and coincidence which leads into situations which are meant to involve the audience not so much through a conscious following of a sequence, but rather through being plunged into a total frame of reference in which they must feel forced to acclimatize themselves. This process of acclimatization is the new means of sequence. (160)

Smith's description of the experience of *Frankenstein* is similar to the experience of religious initiates who find themselves in the unenviable position of possessing an understanding of something that surpasses language. It is not that references are lacking, to use Smith's term; it is that the references are arranged according to an innovative mode of symbolic organization, a "total frame" that appears monstrous to the uninitiated.

Turner has observed that the problem with such totalizing experiences like Smith's among the Living and the audience's in *Frankenstein* is directly related to their equivocal role in the constitution of the community. He writes that the key problem

> is to keep this intuition [of performance *communitas*] alive—regular drugging won't do it, repeated sexual union won't do it, constant immersion in great literature won't do it, initiation seclusion must sooner or later come to an end. We thus encounter the paradox that the *experience* of *communitas* becomes the *memory* of *communitas,* with the result that *com-*

munitas itself in striving to replicate itself historically develops a social structure, in which initially free and innovative relationships between individuals are converted into norm-governed relationships between social *personae*.

However, Turner is guilty of a bit of romanticism here. Any intuition of *communitas* necessarily takes place within a cultural frame. Such *communitas* may be unmeasurable by the standards of the cultural frame that produced it, but that does not mean that it is simply beyond culture.

Radical sociology may supply a more precise insight into the relationship of intuition and cultural context. In his pioneering essay on drug experience among British hippies and bikers (originally published in 1976 as a working paper for Birmingham's Center for Contemporary Social Studies), Paul E. Willis argues that there tends to be a "fit" between the life and values of social groups, the things they do, the uses they make of things (including drugs), and the music they enjoy.[38] Willis notes that such groups used drugs not simply to produce abnormal, symbol-producing mental and physical states, but were themselves *symbols, symbolic states of altered experience.* Specifically, drugs were themselves a symbol of "a fundamental ontological change from the sense of feeling oneself as an autonomous determining agent, to feeling oneself, in part, as a determined variable in the world. And that sense for the cultural drug user was not confined to drug experience only. The economy, politics, society, industry, pollution, the police, upbringing, all became determining variables on the individual's consciousness" (109). Willis also notes that, for such community-oriented users, "One could be 'high' without the use of drugs, and the quality of normal experience, apart from drug experience, was changed." Drugs as symbols and as chemicals abet "the passage through the symbolic barrier" that separates the in-group from the out-group. The consequences for sociology are fairly serious: "[T]he symbolic barrier separating the 'straight' from the 'hip' presents us with a classic faith paradox. Either you understand or you do not, and there is no way of bridging the gap with logical argument. Nor could the presence of this symbolic world be proved to a disbeliever, especially a disbeliever who has already decided that you are 'sick'" (113).

What Smith doesn't address in his nonreview is the fact that this problem—the problem described by Turner and Willis of replicating the intense experience of the initiated without devolving into empty representations of that experience—is a thematic focus of *Frankenstein*, which, like other LT productions, directed audience attention toward the compositional principles and phenomenological data of the theatrical experience itself. This focus on composition and perception is the link noted by Scarpetta between the Living Theatre and Cunningham, Wilson, and Foreman. It was a concern that had grown so profoundly interwoven into the LT's work, community, and politics that it may have been obvious to Smith and therefore not worth commentary. The relationship of form and content is one of the things struggled with by *Frankenstein*'s spectators.

When the audience first entered the theater, an odd spectacle met them. The performers were seated on the stage in a circle, a young woman in the center. The program for the production explained the reason for this: the performers were meditating and "if the concentration is intense enough and the purity of the participants deep enough," the young woman at stage center will levitate into the air.[39] The program further explained that if such levitation were to occur, the performance would end then and there.

The program note, I imagine, was as frantically grasped as the proverbial straw, because the circle of performers remained in meditative silence for a full half-hour after the audience arrived, as if actively refusing to engage in the forward progress of dramatic form, as if deliberately compelling the audience to disrupt the ritual and initiate some kind of conflict, some kind of real drama. If the spectator wasn't "hip," then he or she was going to experience one of the most boring performances of their lives. If and only if the meditation failed, whether by virtue of distraction, the spiritual impurities of metropolitan life, or the sharp bark of a bored viewer, the drama would begin. If it failed, and it always did, the meditation would end and the performance would enter the second phase, which Beck named "victimization," in which the young woman would be pursued by the former mediators, now transformed into a fundamentalist mob. With the failure of transcendent community, drama begins.

The density of textual reference, the fluctuating frames of reference (the set is a stage for a drama, the body of the monster, a concrete illustration of yogic philosophical tenets, a diagram of the human mind), the fluid transformations of the performers (simultaneously characters, props, and shamans), the sheer length and intensity of the piece (over three hours of ritual and legend shot through with screams, groans, and strobe lights), guaranteed that it would physically, emotionally, and intellectually exhaust performer and audience alike. But this complexity was necessitated only because the performers and audience had failed to achieve the goal of unity and transcendence. In sum, dramatic movement was the price exacted by the failure to enter the "paradise now" of the blessed community.

Though the set design and script for *The Connection* weren't as explicitly monstrous as *Frankenstein*'s, it did exhibit both the same dense layers of signification that would become typical of the Living's stages and the same kind of play with the composition of the work itself. On the upstage wall of the set was a crudely painted pyramid against a Magritte-esque sky, a revivalist motto ("Heaven or Hell: Which road are you on?"), a large eye, and a bare green lightbulb. On the table, a pineapple; against the wall, a hula hoop; over there, a group of musicians warming up; here, the mouthpiece of a trumpet. Over the years, the walls of the set turned into a kind of palimpsest as actors visually improvised on available drawing and writing surfaces. Simply on the level of design, *The Connection* was semiotically overwhelming. The density of rhythms and allusions, the layering of improvisational association, and the sudden linking of seemingly distinct ideas was a clear indication of the Living's obsessive effort to encompass their culture's multiplex, headlong rush into the future in a single, explosive theatrical gesture. On the level of dialogue and music, this density of significance approaches cruelty, threatening, quite literally, to overwhelm performer and audience.

Like *Frankenstein*'s monster, *The Connection* tore its own dramatic structure to pieces as it attempted to stage the politically equivocal quality of community and communication in an America dearly addicted to the rugged, standardized individualism of an expanding entertainment market and a waxing military-industrial complex. In *The Connection,* this tension is most visible between the urge for community and the painful need for heroin. The intermingling of *communitas* and the selfish pleasure of heroin deforms the play's language, props, and gestures. The junkies seem perfectly aware of this equivocality; they rather matter-of-factly discuss the symbols that encrust their living space—the hula hoop is a symbol of cosmos, eternity, and death; the green lightbulb is a symbol of enlightenment—while at the same time they coyly deny their audiences any kind of stable interpretive framework with which to decode those symbols and connect them to each other. The language, props, and gestures of the play mirror the onstage community, which is both a group of initiates and a petulant mob of brutally selfish individualists.

As in *Frankenstein, The Connection* manifests its contradictory political impulses in an onstage body, a semiotically crossed body, a body manifesting clearly symbolic but ultimately indecipherable physical and emotional experiences. The labyrinthine, temporally swerving, topically local, and concretely embodied nature of the production, which blended together so many distinct rhythms, historical referents, and cultural fragments, marks the production as a uniquely intense, critically unmanageable event in the history of avant-garde performance, a kind of theatrical monstrosity. In fact,

The Connection's monstrous qualities enable us to get a hand on how the experience of time shifted in the late 1950s under the weight of economic innovation, geopolitical politics, and the devastation of older understandings of the relationship between radical activity and social progress. Careful, critical exploration of the production may enable us to respond to the imperative identified by Louis Althusser: "[W]e cannot be satisfied, as the best historians so often are today, by observing the existence of different times and rhythms, without relating them to the concept of their difference . . . we must also think these differences in rhythm and punctuation in their foundation, in the type of articulation, displacement, and torsion which harmonizes these different times with one another" (100). However, rather than search for "harmony" or "counterpoint" (metaphors derived from classical European music), I'll search for the common themes and the most effective theoretical approaches that give us insight into the kind of syncopation, improvisation, and cruelty that would make *The Connection* such a significant event in avant-garde history. *The Connection* isn't about harmony or counterpoint; it's a play, as the ads in the *Village Voice* told its readers back in 1959, about "junk" (i.e., heroin) and "jazz," about sudden, overwhelming associations and fluid, open-ended articulation of formal relations.

There is no harmony among the elements of the production, no stable rhythmic relationship. The musical model for the production was "new jazz," what has been called "Hard Bop," the most stringent trend in jazz during the late 1950s—harsh, honest, aggressive, sometimes blindingly fast, sometimes meditative, always shifting and moving in conscious appraisal of musical form, situational need, the frustrating limits of musical expression, and audience expectation. Moreover, the ability to listen effectively to such music demanded, as I will show, very specific physical adjustments on the part of the spectator, a very specific performance of listening that identified one as "hip" rather than "square."

Heroin, on the other hand, supplied its own performance meanings and modes. Willis notes that, for the counterculture, the "meaning of 'H' seemed mainly to be in a symbolic extension of its supposed physical irreversibility. To get on to heroin was not just to pass through the symbolic barrier dividing the 'straight' from the 'hip,' it was the unanswerable closure of relations with the straight world" (117). Willis concludes, "In one way this made 'H' the supreme expression of drug culture meanings. It was an expression of loyalty to beyond-the-barrier meanings that the straight could never begin to understand, and which straight society could never bring you back from" (117). But there's a difference in this drug that is worth noting. Heroin is unique, he claims (not altogether correctly), for the fact that its cultural and pharmacological significance agree: "[T]he final cost of its use is death" (117).

Boredom and Danger

Before moving further into the syncopations of the production's time signature with its literary, theatrical, and cultural precursors, it's worth spending a few moments thinking about *boredom,* a characteristic of the production noted by more than a few viewers, though not always pejoratively. Very little happens in *The Connection.* The junkies are *bored,* stuck in that enervated no-man's-land between the need to do something and the complete incapacity to imagine a reason for doing anything at all. This kind of nervousness wasn't just the junkies'; the production attempted to instill this nervousness in audience members, too. As in the long introductory meditation of *Frankenstein,* boredom in *The Connection* was intended to cultivate critical perspective, a syncopated interruption of audience expectation and narrative development, a manipulation of performance time. As such, the production fits within an extremely interesting trend of its time: boring art. In the 1950s, boredom served artists as a way to effectively resist the highly seductive forms of entertainment undermining the place of serious theater in American culture: movies, blockbuster spectacles, television, and pop radio. In a world so focused on fun, boredom was the most interesting thing going. This lesson was brought home for Beck during his incarceration in the summer of 1957. As Tytell notes, "Working every day as a dishwasher, sometimes for up to thirteen hours at a stretch, [Beck] found the real problem was monotony" (135). However, Beck had encountered boredom long before his incarceration for civil disobedience; after all, he had been a friend of John Cage's since 1951.

Cage's work exemplifies boring art and makes clear that just because something is boring, it is not necessarily insignificant. Boredom, after all, is an emotional state notable for its high degree of self-consciousness and -awareness. The bored possess a kind of totalizing consciousness in petulant repose. As is insisted upon by the bored, absolutely nothing can inspire interest—it's hard to imagine a more totalizing belief. Yet this failure to imagine doesn't bring with it despair. The bored persist in their nervous, unproductive quest for something to entertain and can become, as any parent in the company of a bored child understands, quite disruptive. Perhaps it is this that so attracted Cage, an anarchist, to boredom. In his essay "Boredom and Danger" (1969), Dick Higgins discusses Cage's *4'33"* (1952), in which a performer does *not* produce sound from her instrument for a precisely measured period of time. "Boredom," Higgins writes, "was, until recently, one of the qualities an artist tried most to avoid. Yet today it appears that artists are deliberately trying to make their work boring."[40] In the 1940s and 1950s, Cage began exploring the tradition of monotonous outrage pioneered by Erik Satie (Higgins: "[T]here is a certain bravura about asking a pianist to play the same eight beats 380 times" [116]) and Arnold Schoenberg. But Cage was seeking more than simply the rewards of formal experiment: "Cage was the first to try to emphasize in his work and his teaching a dialectic between boredom and intensity" (116).

This notion of boredom as intensity and intensity as boredom perfectly captures the physically symbolic qualities of the heroin high as it was staged in *The Connection*. Like *4'33"* but a great deal more noisily, *The Connection* frustrates but also affords the opportunity for unprecedented insight into theater, everyday life, and one's own fidgeting body. It also neatly emblematizes one of the unique conditions of avant-garde opposition in Cold War Manhattan, an environment redolent with increasingly intense forms of popular entertainment (football, pro wrestling, rock 'n' roll) and a burgeoning market in formally intense avant-garde art. It was crucial that such intensity be wrested from the seductive wiles of fun capitalism. Higgins writes that "the most intense art is necessarily involved with these things, boredom and danger, not as a new mode, but because they are implicit in the new mentality of our time. This mentality is one in which total success is impossible, total victory inconceivable and relativism axiomatic" (116).

The boredom of *The Connection,* a counterpoint to its "electrical ripples of tension and latent violence,"[41] reflects a basic struggle in the play between the old conceptual standbys of the avant-garde: life and art. Jaybird, the onstage author of the play, tells the audience, "Remember: for one night this scene swings. But as a life it's a damn bore. When all the changes have been played, we'll all be back where we started" (19). What he doesn't suspect in this early moment of the play is that the scene won't swing that night at all, at least not the way he expects it to. Rather, the time of addiction will be brought into syncopated relationship with the rhythms of the entertainment industry. It turns out that the production is hardly under the control of its author—it veers wildly between moments of intense, gut-rendering agony and long stretches of mumbling banality, a veering course determined more by the mercurial moods and alliances in Leach's pad than it is by the needs of dramatic structure.

The Becks were well aware of the ways that the avant-garde was being used by advertisers; after all, Madison Avenue was virtually around the corner. As part of its effort to turn exploitative entertainment into revolutionary boredom, the play (and its production by the Living) strives at times to be intentionally *bad*. In part, this is due to a very traditional strategy of the avant-garde: to identify those who are allied to the group by being "deep" and rejecting any appeal to mainstream assumptions and expectations. In addition, there is the tradition of stone-faced irony, the *blague* and *fumisterie* of the Parisian decadents. There are more than a few moments of self-conscious deepness in Gelber's script, but they are almost always parodied or undermined by the characters. But again, the self-conscious "badness" of the production is an act of resistance to expectations of entertainment and the seductive rhythms of mass culture.

The junkies continually point out the poor quality of the entertainment being provided and its failure to adequately communicate a moral. It gets to be a little much for the author; Jaybird erupts after the performers stop performing for more than two minutes to listen to an old vinyl LP of Charlie Parker. Very much aware of exactly how long two minutes without action is in a theater (i.e., *very* long), he interrupts the production, sounding more like a film director than a playwright: "Cut it! Cut it! What are you doing? Let's go over it again. You're to give the whole plot in the first act. So far not one of you has carried out his dramatic assignment" (33). Photographs of the production show many of the characters to be dropping their assignments and either actively antagonizing audience members or intentionally ignoring them. Kenneth Tynan, writing in the *New Yorker,* characterized the actors as drifting about the stage, murmuring, or staring at the audience "in a way that is oddly chilling, remote, and empty of human concern."[42] Louis Calta, theater critic for the *New York Times,* was driven to distraction by the play's intentionally slow, meandering, downright petulant pace. Though he recognized the play's debts to *Waiting for Lefty* (1935), *Waiting for Godot* (1953), and *The Iceman Cometh* (1946), he characterized it as a "farrago of dirt, small-time philosophy, empty talk, and extended runs of 'cool' music.'"[43] These periods of extended philosophical and musical improvisation were particularly maddening to him, "as frustrating as looking through a peephole into a darkened room" (30). When the play opened in London in the winter of 1961, the audience was so frustrated by the mumbling, stumbling pace of the show that they refused to allow it to go on. Judith Crist, in an ill-tempered review that cruelly parodied the American production's hipster attitudes, summed up by claiming "if the drugs don't get them first, these junkies will bore themselves to death."[44] Jerry Tallmer, in a positive assessment for the *Village Voice,* characterized the play as a "tired knowing endless deep-freeze of detumescence and utter hopelessness." Robert Brustein, in the *New Republic,* praised the jazz, but damned that hopeless pace: "Nothing, in fact, is happening, and you wait for boredom to release you from the need to care."[45]

Frankly, it's hard to imagine a better way to represent the often squalid, nervous, generally boring life of an addict than through a dangerously boring couple of hours spent in a stifling little off-off-Broadway theater in middle summer. Though, as Tallmer points out, the production suffered from too much talk about heroin and a bit too much self-consciousness, it did possess a precisely hewn slice-of-life quality and an aggressively mercurial pace. To summarize: the play concerns a group of junkies who have gathered to wait for their "connection," a man named Cowboy who will supply them with heroin. In the meantime, they soliloquize, dialogue, and digress about various topics in a fashion not unlike the insomniacs in Chekhov's plays, but with a great deal less charm, elegance, and attention to the rigors of the well-made play. There's not much more to it than this.

The intent of this tasteless, shapeless, meandering performance was not simply to rehearse the dusty antientertainment provocation of Dada shtick. In fact, the Dada comparison is absurd—Dada was everything but boring. Boredom mapped the boundaries of a blessed community manifesting itself monstrously in a situation distinct from those met by the Dadas in Berlin, Cologne, Paris, Zurich, and elsewhere. The linking of illegality, the myth of the American frontier (Cowboy), edge-mapping improvisational poetry and music, and intentional tastelessness places the play squarely within a hard-to-pin-down, antihierarchical, politically oppositional trend of utopian performance practice common among the avant-gardes of the late nineteenth century, avant-gardes like the international symbolist movement that were in battle against boulevard entertainment and in close relationship to the illegal markets, heretical ideologies, and deviant attitudes of the drug subculture (and whose theatrical productions were also criticized for being boring). *The Connection*'s slow and shifting pace makes clear that the avant-gardes it most identifies with were the very avant-gardes rejected by the fascist futurists and their descendants, the anti-Fascist trends whose exemplar is surrealism. *The Connection* is a symbolist play set in the society of spectacle—and it was boring as hell (at least to some).

2. Jazz and Drug War

The Jazz Jam as Social Organization

Though *The Connection* was a "boring" play, its boredom shouldn't be overemphasized at the cost of its most compelling, innovative, and immediately engaging contribution to the counterculture. Gelber called *The Connection* a "jazz play," and that's a fair assessment: Jazz was played on its stage, it structured the play as a whole, and it modeled a utopian community based on new principles of composition and communication, a community fully conscious of its singular place in the no-man's-land between entertainment and the avant-garde. Each of these issues will be dealt with in more detail. The production would be notable if only for its use of jazz, let alone the more esoteric extrapolation and amplification of jazz principles that would influence political movements throughout the 1960s. Tallmer notes that

> [t]his is the first production of any sort (not just theatre) in which I have seen (heard?) modern jazz used organically and dynamically to further the dramatic action rather than merely decorate or sabotage it; the music by Freddie Redd and his quartet (written by Mr. Redd) puts a highly charged contrapuntal beat under and against all the misery and stasis and permanent total crisis.

Tynan admitted, "How they contrive to play so well, so spontaneously, and yet in such perfect coordination with the demands of dramatic timing is a matter I can never hope to fathom."[46] Tallmer and Tynan's comments pinpoint the excellence of the Freddie Redd Quartet's performance as musicians and as a dramaturgical force capable of customizing their sound—and by extension, the dramatic pace—to each performance of *The Connection*. (It's been reported to me by several audience members that on at least one occasion, the quartet didn't stop playing for several hours, neatly foreclosing dramatic process and having fun while doing so.) However, jazz was more than just a performance principle for the LT—and not merely a bit of set decoration for this one production. Like LeRoi Jones, Beck and Malina were discovering much social, aesthetic, and ethical significance in the vanguard African American music scene of Manhattan. In *The Connection,* the relationship among the music, the dialogue, the movement of the characters, the give-and-take of audience and actor, the dramatic structure, and so on is a *jazz* relationship. It is a composition composing itself before our eyes and ears.

It's impossible to overestimate the importance of jazz to the Cold War avant-garde scene, though more often critics have limited their consideration of jazz to very local circumstances and the limited notion of influence. Bigsby, for one, makes the acute comment that, in *The Connection,* jazz "is itself a powerful image of the way in which spontaneous individual freedoms can be merged into a form which is generated rather than imposed" (77). Noting that Gelber is rather more tentative in his affirmation of this idea, Bigsby nonetheless links Gelber's play to Ralph Ellison's remark that jazz is "a marvel of social organization" (77). Lorenzo Thomas, in a discussion of jazz and the myth of redemption in Beat and Black Arts Movement poetry, writes that the jazz musician was, for these writers, "the custodian of authentic folk culture[,] . . . the leader of rebellion against postwar conformity, and the spiritual agent of the politically powerless."[47]

The relationship of jazz to the post–World War II American avant-garde has only just now begun to receive the kind of sustained attention it deserves, most notably in Jacques Attali's *Noise,* Daniel Belgrad's *The Culture of Spontaneity,* which devotes an entire chapter to the so-called Bebop movement of the 1940s and 1950s, and Lewis MacAdams's *The Birth of Cool: Beat, Bebop, and the American Avant-Garde.*[48] As Belgrad points out, the new jazz trends of the period "shared the disposition of other spontaneous art movements at mid-century [such as abstract expressionism and projective verse] to develop an alternative to corporate-liberal culture rooted in intersubjectivity and body-mind holism" (179). Though I am uncomfortable with the notion that jazz shared with these other movements "belief in the value of the unconscious mind," I do find extremely interesting Belgrad's discussion of improvisation as a performance mode that created a "locus of possibilities denied legitimacy" within the dominant cultural and aesthetic norms of the time. Belgrad's argument is supported by Allen Ginsberg, who writes that jazz

> was a model for the dadaists and it was a model for the surrealists and it was a model for Kerouac and a model for me and a model for almost

everybody, in the sense that it was partly a model and partly experiment in free form. The development of poetics, as well as jazz and painting, seems to be chronologically parallel, which is to say you have fixed form, which then evolves toward more free form where you get loose from this specific repeated rhythm and improvise the rhythms even, where you don't have a fixed rhythm, as in Bebop the drum became more of a soloist in it too.[49]

Inspired by Lester Young's legendary performance of seventy choruses of "Lady Be Good," artist-activists like Ginsberg discovered new understandings of how form, content, and context related to each other. Aesthetically, socially, economically, strategically, the jazz composer-musicians of the 1940s and 1950s supplied much to the performance-based, innovatively organized countercultures that would explode on the scene shortly after the premiere of *The Connection*.

In fact, rather than influencing the avant-garde, jazz *was* the avant-garde.

Though Ginsberg is correct to note the *formal* impact of Bebop, we must also take care to recognize its *social* impact, which was also broad. The sudden rise to prominence of Bebop in the middle 1940s as a consequence of being featured in predominantly white clubs in cities such as New York, Los Angeles, and St. Louis has been perceived by many as an early moment in the civil rights movement. Belgrad quotes Dexter Gordon, who calls it "the start of the revolution. . . . This is all the young generation, a new generation at that time. And they're not satisfied with the shit that's going down. Because they know there should be changes being made. . . . It was a time of great flux. And it was a time of change, and the music was reflecting this. And we were putting our voice into what we thought was about to be the thing" (181–82). We shouldn't let Gordon's comments tempt us into hyperbole. Eric Lott notes that the relationship of Bebop's formal revolutions to the political revolutions of the time was "intimate" but "indirect": "Militancy and music were undergirded by the same social facts; the music attempted to resolve at the level of style what the militancy combated in the streets."[50] Scott DeVeaux agrees. Bebop musicians' "relationship to politics was oblique at best, and certainly very different from that of their counterparts on the street corners," where one was much more likely to hear rhythm and blues, "the soundtrack for the urban black experience of the late 1940s and 1950s."[51]

That said, there are three aspects of Bebop that are easily linked with the activist politics of the Cold War avant-garde and that contradict Lott's and DeVeaux's assessment. First, Bebop musicians laid out a number of older avant-garde concerns for revision, remodeling, and rethinking, especially the struggle for expressive freedom in a society dominated by market logic (and it should be noted that many musicians were affiliated with Old Left organizations, contra DeVeaux and Lott). Second, Bebop as a musical form was anchored in an innovative social form; specifically, the "jazz jam," which I will discuss at length below. Lastly, Bebop established the formal, social, and aesthetic boundaries for the far more radical "Free Jazz" movement. This latter movement, Attali notes, was created in affiliation with the Black Power movements that proliferated after Malcolm X's assassination in 1965 and constituted a distinctly *local* response to the standardization of musical production in the United States. Free Jazz, Attali concludes, enabled a genuine "takeover of power in a repetitive society" (139–40).

In other words, Bebop recast certain basic elements of social and political life (new ideas, new ways of behaving in public, new ways of thinking the relationship of one's work to one's politics) in terms of music. Lott and DeVeaux say as much, but their understandings of politics are too traditional to allow them to admit it. DeVeaux characterizes Bebop as simultaneously an artistic, racial, and commercial endeavor. He writes, "The revolutionary qualities of bop are situated not within but outside the jazz tradition, in the collision between jazz as an artistic endeavor and the social forces of commerce and race" (4). Bebop musicians were "improvisers in the marketplace"—a decidedly political role. DeVeaux demonstrates that Black jazz musicians had long come to feel that "mass-market capitalism was not a prison from which the true artist is duty-bound to escape. It was a system of transactions that defined music as a profession and thereby made their achievements possible" (8, 16). Nevertheless, the Bebop generation defined its relations to the market in a fashion designed to outmaneuver the entertainment model of music. It was a separatist movement that lacked only the ideology—and the institutions—to make it truly revolutionary.

Coleman Hawkins was among the first composer-performer to reject the "long, honorable tradition of clowning in black performing" (as Lionel Hampton called it),[52] a tradition forced upon, but exploited and slyly deconstructed by, the likes of Duke Ellington, Billie Holiday, Louis Armstrong, Cab Calloway, and Bessie Smith. Instead, Hawkins "drew almost by default on the obvious model of the European concert tradition . . . an air of total concentration on the matter at hand" (89). Charlie Parker expressed a similar distaste for clowning; Ellison writes, "No jazzman, not even Miles Davis, struggled harder to escape the entertainer's role."[53] Jackie McLean told Nat Hentoff, in an interview that occurred while McLean was performing in *The Connection*, that "Bebop was a social statement as well as music because the whole thing evolved and changed. I mean the generation that was before mine absorbed the pain and humiliation of the fact that they had to be buffoons. They made it possible for my generation to get over on pure virtuosity and ability."[54] For the Bebop generation, the rejection of the codes of jazz entertainment was a revolutionary gesture in terms of economics, intersubjective relations among the musicians, and their relationship to their audience.

However, this struggle to escape the codified performance patterns of musical entertainment was riddled with irony. Though Dizzie Gillespie comported himself as the model 1950s hip intellectual in opposition to the supposed kowtowing of Armstrong, Calloway, and Ellington, his escape was a *staged* escape, a *performed* escape. Bebop, an innovative model of social organization that deeply influenced the counterculture, is striped by this contradiction, as we see when we explore the modes and codes of performance favored by its musicians and fans, a subculture well aware of its difference from the older, big-band community. DeVeaux writes, "In place of the often tawdry transactions between artists and audience summed up by the words *entertainment* and *showmanship,* Bebop offered the spectacle of musicians playing for their own enjoyment, capturing some of the dignity and autonomy of the concert stage without losing the informal atmosphere that tied jazz to a vernacular social context" (202). This "informal atmosphere" is the jam session, the characteristic form of musical communication, exploration, and competition for the Bebop generation.

Ben Sidran calls the jam session "perhaps the most important aspect" of the Bebop revolution. Sidran notes that "these sessions would take place informally," and often "last for days, literally," allowing artists to escape the restrictions of big-band format, union membership, and vinyl recording.[55] The jams were explicitly and rigorously set apart from the often brutal market conditions in which African American musicians worked. Sidran writes that the jam "provided a basis for the black musician to establish himself, once more, as one individual who was saying and doing what he pleased—outside the pale of white economics—and getting the support of his peer group. The fact that white society was bidding for his services only enhanced his self-imposed isolation" (88–89). DeVeaux argues that the jam session "underlies all claims for the legitimacy of Bebop—not simply as a jazz idiom, but as the decisive step toward jazz as art" (202–3).

Nonetheless, this decisive step was taken *on stage,* an oddly theatrical revolution considering that the jazz jams were "never intended to be public spectacles" (Ibid, 202). As a consequence, some of the distinct performance features of the jam would play a role in the more public, less predictable arenas of countercultural resistance and revolution that borrowed from it. This translation of private, community-oriented experience into a public, extracommunal performance carried many ironies with it. As a form of performance by and for musicians, the jam session, DeVeaux writes,

> offers few clues to the uncontexted outsider. There is little or no written music in evidence, and certainly no rehearsal. . . . There is no frame for the performance, no spoken introductions or attention-getting silences. . . . Everybody seems to know what to do without being told. The listener is left face to face with the mystery of improvisation—an alchemy that creates music out of nothingness. It is creativity without artifice. (Ibid., 203)

However, this lack of artifice is classic theatrical illusion. Any number of codes—from the repertory, to the order of solos, to the conventional signals that mark transitions and endings, to the ritualized expression of approval and disapproval—regulate the jazz-jam performance. Bebop musicians performed in public the initiation ceremonies and subcultural rituals that enabled it to come into existence—and thereby hoped to discipline its audience into a particular way of experiencing the performance. Rather than lacking a frame of reference (a logical impossibility for any cultural expression), the jazz jam functioned more like Smith's description of *Frankenstein:* as a "total frame of reference" in which the player-participants acclimated themselves to new sequences of cognition and creation. In a sense, jazz musicians attempted to solve the problem identified by Victor Turner: how to maintain *communitas* in contexts of repetition, irony, and misunderstanding.

DeVeaux describes the jam session's energy as "focused inward" both in terms of the staging of the musical performance (musicians clustered rather than ranged across the bandstand), the relation to the audience (composed originally only of musicians), and the concerns of the players, whether interpersonally (competition, one-upmanship) or formally (the esoterics of harmonics, tones, and key changes). As a consequence of the insider/outsider dynamic being carried into entertainment contexts for which it was not created, these implicit rules came to be perceived, by audience and performer alike, as evidence of a truer, more "authentic" form of community, a jazz relationship that modeled a marvelous form of organization available even to nonmusicians. The difference between the "hip" and the "square" was the difference between somebody who absorbed and followed the unstated rules of the jam and somebody who didn't. Another difference: the hipster believed in the virtue of such rules, believed them rooted in the authentic body of the elect. Such rules were, like Willis's description of heroin, "symbolically physical."

The use of the body as a symbolically physical theatrical element was a significant aspect of the jazz jam's translation into engaging but nonentertaining public performance. The translation onto the club stage of the jazz jam's typically clustered arrangement of musicians is one example: the arrangement of the musicians in the jam implicitly signals to performer and spectator alike the hermetic, closed-circuit aspect of the performance and the fact that it is the *musicians,* not the *audience,* who are the ultimate judges of the performance. The arrangement of performer bodies on stage also signals the importance of *listening* as opposed to *seeing.* There is no doubt that looking good was still important to the new-wave jazz musician— Miles Davis was one of the arbiters and innovators of fashion style across the Western hemisphere in the 1950s and 1960s. Nevertheless, like the musical performance, the appearance of the jazz musician was designed mainly for the in-crowd, one more shibboleth to separate the non- from the elect. Davis didn't just dress well, he dressed *hip,* a particularly understated, minimalist form of dress entirely different from the splashy accoutrements of a Calloway or Ellington. Hip appearance on the Bebop stage signaled the priority of perfectly executed expression, especially musical expression. His appearance signaled, paradoxically, that the viewer should ignore appearance.

This paradox extended into the performance strategies of *The Connection.* Carl Lee, who played Cowboy, is recalled by Gelber as "the epitome of cool,"[56] an impression supported by the Cowboy-esque character Lee plays in Shirley Clarke's groundbreaking film about alienated youth, gang life, and gun culture, *The Cool World* (1964). To supplement his acting career, Lee worked as maître d' at the Café Bohemia, where he became an acquaintance of Davis, who was a regular performer there. In an interview with MacAdams, Garry Goodrow, who played Ernie, stated that "Cowboy was Carl Lee's conscious attempt to emulate Miles's style" (206). Not just Miles was being emulated here; Lee invited a successful Harlem heroin dealer to a performance to offer constructive critique (206). MacAdams writes,

In *The Connection,* everybody wants to be cooler. The white junkies want to be as cool as the black junkies, and all the junkies want to be as cool as the musicians, who never seem to lose their cool. Freddie Redd is so cool, so completely unadorned and understatedly dressed as he plays his chunky chords, a cigarette dangling out of one corner of his mouth,

that he could pass by on the street like a phantom, like an old-time par-
adigm of cool, flying beneath the radar. The one person who never loses
his cool, even when he's so stoned that he falls off his stool, is Jackie
McLean. (207–8)

The performance of cool is a profoundly paradoxical performance; to put
oneself purposefully on display in order to demonstrate one's supreme lack
of concern for such display. In Bebop, the arrangement of the stage and the
priority of listening versus seeing marked a basic change in the relationship
of performance to audience, a theatrical innovation that prepared the Bebop
spectator (and, eventually, the spectator of countercultural theater) for the
rigors of the musical experience. Belgrad writes, "The polyrhythmic complexity and irregular phrasings that characterize Bebop jazz are signals that it
is a music meant for listening and not for dancing" (187).

This change in the relationship of spectator and performer runs deep;
there is a physiological shift in the nature of jazz spectatorship marked by the
arrival of Bebop, a palpable demand for a different kind of audience body.
This was noted by commentators of the time. Belgrad quotes Miles Templar, who, in an article defending Bebop to readers of *Partisan Review* in
1948, wrote, "The bopper's enthusiasm is a quiet thing. He wants to dig
everything that's being done and he knows that distractions will cause him
to miss the thread of whatever the musician is building. You see this enthusiasm on all hands and on all faces during a bop concert or session" (187).
The job of the listener becomes all the more difficult in such a situation.
Unlike the large swing bands of the 1930s and 1940s, there were no gregarious performance routines like those of Calloway to attract and guide the
viewer's attention, no glittering lights to entertain the eye, no conventional
movement of performers to signal a solo or section break. Bebop theatrics—
among which we must include the performance of the in-crowd audience—were primarily concerned with the *appearance of listening,* with the
gestures, clothing, and conversation that would indicate that the spectator,
like the musician, was "digging" the performance. Templar notes that this
change brought with it a distinctly physical burden; the casual, entertainment-minded audience had to abandon their regressive listening habits and
"pitch their attention at a high level of nervous excitement" to follow and
adequately appreciate Bebop anthems such as "KoKo" (187).

This new performance of listening was intertwined with Bebop's highly
intersubjective performer interactions, interactions that placed an emphasis
on the personality of the performer as an entity that was rebelliously independent of the performance situation. Due to the great respect shown for an

individual musician's technical and intellectual innovations, participants in
the jam enthusiastically explored the obsessions introduced by individual
members, particularly if such obsessions enabled them to increase skills or
toy around with the artist's formal experiments. Miles Davis captures this
celebration of personality and technique in a description of a remarkably
staffed 1957 performance:

> Because of the chemistry and the way people were playing off each
> other, everybody started playing above what they knew almost from the
> beginning. [Coltrane] would play some weird, great shit, and Cannon-
> ball [Adderly] would take it in the other direction, and I would put my
> sound right down the middle or float over it, or whatever.[57]

I have used the term "jazz relationship" to characterize the interaction of
characters, the form of dialogue/monologue, the syncopation of spectacle
and spectator, and the equivocal symbolism of *The Connection.* Davis captures this idea perfectly, helping us keep in mind the ephemeral, "effervescent" nature of these very communal collaborations. Davis elaborates on the
personal chemistry of Bebop performance and the way it can affect the performance as a whole: "One voice can change the entire way a band hears
itself, can change the whole rhythm, the whole timing of a band, even if
everyone else had been playing together forever. It's a whole new thing
when you add or take away a voice" (188). I will discuss this conversational,
personality-centered performance mode below.

The connection between Artaud and the "cruelty" of jazz of the early
Cold War years is evidenced in the nerve-tingling, audience-antagonizing
theatrical innovations of Bebop performance that were not so much borrowed by *The Connection* as transplanted directly from one stage to another.
However, deeper connections can be discovered in the tones and structure
of the music itself. Specifically, these connections can be sighted in the trend
that developed in response to the "cooling" of Bebop by Davis, Stan Getz,
and other West Coast jazz composer-performers. David Rosenthal argues
that the key to this reaction, the source of Bebop's emotional rebirth in
Hard Bop, was increasing interest among boppers in the "soundtrack of the
black urban experience": Rhythm and Blues. Though R & B was limited
in the formal virtues it offered the modernist-minded, it did supply musicians such as Davis (typically, both a creator and a reactor), Clifford Brown,
Sonny Rollins, Horace Silver, Art Blakey, and others, including Jackie
McLean, with "a new, more emotionally expressive and more formally
flexible style" (27). Favoring the minor mode and characterized by a ten-

dency to wring maximum expressive potential from every note, Hard Bop also found formal possibility in a more raw, less intellectually self-conscious sound (35). The cruelty of Bebop—the high-pitched nervousness it caused in audience members such as Templar—was both a theatrical and a structural effect caused by the form, emotional intensity, and timbre of the music.

No one better exemplified this increase in jazz's "cruelty" than McLean, who played alto saxophone during the four-year run of *The Connection*. Rosenthal comments on a performance of McLean's that occurred some years prior to his stint with the Living: "His solo is stiff, full of meaningless runs, strange pauses as though he were trying to think of what to play next. . . . And yet, there's something about his time, his timbre, his way of attacking a note that is riveting. A true cry from the heart, piercing and ragged, McLean's tone has always been his strong point" (22). Though he hadn't yet developed his trademark emotional dexterity and depth, McLean's ability to create *moods* is appreciated by Rosenthal (120). Even at this early stage, McLean is clearly struggling to produce a musical cognate for his emotional experience, an experience that included heroin addiction profound enough to cost him his club license in the late 1950s, and give him good reason to accept a long-term gig with the Living.

An important step in McLean's development was his rediscovery, after working with Charles Mingus, of gospel music. According to Rosenthal, this rediscovery brought back memories of the Pentecostal Baptist churches McLean attended as a child. McLean told Rosenthal that these churches

> got into the heavy aspects of the rhythm and the people passing out, feeling the spirit and the whole thing, so I saw that as a child, and I never really put that in place again and put it into my music . . . till Mingus's band, which gave me a kind of resurgence of that, because he used to like to shout and play shout music and music that was closely related to the church. (71)

The "heavy blues feeling" characteristic of McLean's work immediately after his stint with the legendary bass player, work that was developed nightly during *The Connection*'s run, sought, as he put it, a "sanctified feeling to it mixed with all the other ingredients that Bird [Coltrane], Bud [Powell], Thelonious [Monk] gave us" (71). McLean's emotionally raw saxophone style attempted to wed the formal complexity of Bebop to the anguish of situation; the result was a distinctly "hard" form of an already notoriously hard form of jazz. Like Ernie in the play, McLean rarely was in possession of his horn during the 1950s; it was nearly always in the pawn-shop, left for cash to buy heroin. Lacking the ability to practice, McLean had to focus on the conceptual content of his music: the anguish of addiction and the struggle to define himself as an artist.

Rosenthal notes that McLean's years with the Living widened his interests and enabled him to develop as a musician; that much is clear. Though the "fierce enunciation" and "trenchant attack" of his early style got him through the years prior to signing on with the Living,[58] it was not until working with them that he began to acquire, first, the "structural coherency" that would bring him a fair measure of critical attention and, second, fierce enunciation and fluent articulation of it.[59] McLean remembers the Living with fondness:

> I thought they were great people. I thought they were people who were looking far into the future, for a better way. You had to love them to be with them, because the Living Theatre was like a big commune. Mostly everybody lived together, ate together, and were together working out each person's problems. I didn't live with them because I had my wife and kids, but I was part of it because certainly I lived with them when we left New York, when we went to Europe.[60]

Rosenthal argues that the intensity of this communal experience translated into his work as a musician, enabling him to transform from what one critic called the most rhythmically vital but least disciplined musician into the "brilliant experimentalist" heard on records such as *Let Freedom Ring* and *Evolution,* albums pressed in the early 1960s. Just as his exposure to Bosch gave him a new approach to musical form, so did his experience with the community organized by the Becks. McLean recalls the departure of the LT for its first European tour in 1961. He remembers in particular the fact that, due to a snow emergency, the LT had to travel in a phalanx of ambulances to the dock where the *Queen Elizabeth* was moored. Riffing metaphorically on the incident, McLean settles on the metaphor of the "sick group . . . but when I say 'sick,' I mean sick in terms of having a better understanding of what life is supposed to be about. They were very hip people, Judith and Julian and the whole crowd."[61]

Bebop and the Dramatic Structure of *The Connection*

Jazz was not used incidentally in *The Connection.* The organic role McLean, his music, and the rest of the quartet played in the production and in the lives of their fellow Living demonstrate that Bebop served as a formal and intellectual crucible for the LT and, by extension, the U.S. avant-garde in general, enabling the invention of new aesthetic, social, and ideological languages. These forms would take the LT from repertory to revolution and fundamentally impact an entire generation of American performers and activists attempting to create the aesthetic form that might capture the unprecedented possibilities they were encountering. Jazz functions *within* the play's dramatic structure. Jazz also works as a *structural* principle in the play and in the production, affording the actors a polyrhythmic, polytonal, densely imagistic matrix with which to weave together their leaping thoughts and bridge their own monologues with the monologues of the other actors.

Much like the participants in a jam, both the characters in the script and the performers on this stage continually form and reform the dramatic line, treating the script like a score in order to assert personality and prerogative. A good example of this kind of social jamming is the series of monologues that occur in the latter half of the first act. Like musicians awaiting and performing their solos, each tantalized and antagonized by the previous, the junkies deliver their lines against an ensemble background of snide comments, audible signs of agreement or disagreement, onstage business, and the like, supplied by those who have already performed their solos or who wait their turn. Each of the soloists presents his or her character, a particular repertoire of gestures and tones, the character's concerns (thereby building a fabric of conflict and alliance), and the shifting metaphors with which they attempt to comprehend their anguish.

Solly initiates the dramatic jam: "Hello there! I'm the nineteenth century and I'm producing the twentieth. Unfortunately, the twentieth century has developed anti-social habits." In the mercurial fashion characteristic both of monologue and dialogue in Gelber's script, Solly moves from here to his concept of an ideal audience, then to the dilemmas of modern education, the junkie's love of death, and transcendental philosophy. Finally, much as a musician might signal through a conventional set of gestures—say, returning to the base melody or key—that his solo is coming to a close, Solly signals to the next soloist that it's time to play but carries on a little longer to allow for spot shifts. "Sam, someone, say something. Say something to the customers. . . . Pay your dues. Pay your dues."

Sam stands and asks, "But who's to say? Who's there to squeeze the ball into his own shape and tell me this is right? You know that. What does Jaybird want? A soft shoe dance? I don't need any burnt cork, you know." Sam shifts his attention to Leach, and shifts the monologue from minstrelsy to a bit of clumsy, but thematically significant comments on gender. Leach, the African American Sam tells us, "is a queer without being queer. He thinks like a chick." Then he moves to Cowboy, then to Solly. The performer (originally, John McCurry) is given the opportunity to reiterate, in his own vocal and gestural style, the exposition and themes that preceded his monologue as well as establish new themes, images, exposition, and relationships to be picked up by the next soloist (especially Leach's ambiguous sexuality, developed in detail in Ernie's section). He swoops to another theme, picking up a hula hoop to riff on symbols of death in Roman, African, and Navajo mythology. Then, like Solly, Sam asks Ernie to stand, telling the audience that his own confessional is about to conclude. Giving the next performer a few moments to prepare, he brings up Ernie's many foibles, then closes, claiming apologetically that he's "got some powerful stories in me when that shit flows in my veins." Ernie stands and picks up a thread of Sam's monologue, "Trust me? Man, I don't care one way or the other." Like Sam, Ernie moves quickly from topic to topic, weaving together themes, some of which have appeared before (the exploitation of performers, Solly's sagacity, Leach's sexuality) some of which are introduced to be picked up by the next section of the performance, which breaks into the give-and-take of dialogue (39–49).

This quartet of monologues shows the clear influence of Bebop aesthetics: the ensemble approach taken to the nth degree—and perfectly in line with the jam structure. It confirms the fluid, equivocal nature of the junkies' community and communication, doing so in a fashion that establishes a shared dramatic situation (the lack of heroin) while giving each character (and each performer) a maximum of freedom to develop within that situation. Belgrad notes that Bebop "often substituted the dissonances of extended chords . . . for the simple consonances of the popular standards from which they were derived."[62] Soloists would often end their runs on these tones in defiance of the European convention of tonal resolution, but do that within well-known standards. As a consequence, chords "using these extended harmonies blurred the line between harmony and dissonance, creating 'polytonality'" (183). It's difficult to imagine a better metaphor for the ambivalent feelings the junkies have for each other: a polytonal community.

The formal consonance of the four monologues (their similar lengths, themes, and expository material) is set against dissonant interpersonal elements built around character and performance elements. Arpeggios of loathing, rapid-fire allusions to prior trespasses, and sudden shifts from person to person are not unlike the McLean performance described by Rosenthal:

Over [the] driving beat, he mixes growls, penetrating cries, and edgily throaty outbursts with flatter [i.e., more "meditative" or "introspective"], Coltrane-like inflections. Melodically, the solo is chaotic. At times McLean's ideas flow smoothly, but at others they seem both banal and disconnected. Yet somehow this heightens the emotional pitch, as though he had so much to *express* and tried to convert raw feeling so directly into music that he didn't have time to think.[63]

Attempting to account for the oddly disconcerting simultaneity of Bebop polyrhythmic structure, DeVeaux notes that Bebop shared with the Blues an "elusive, floating rhythmic quality." The "expressive manipulation of time" in Bebop occurs most notably when one rhythmic layer momentarily suspends its movement while, on another, "the steady foundation pulse is rigorously maintained . . . so that one experiences the expressive time-stretch and the unchanging framework" at the same time (81). Bebop's compositional principles open up the linear structure of the traditional social-problem play to other time signatures and less emphatic tones. But this linearity doesn't dissolve; in *The Connection* there is insistent movement toward ecstasy and overdose despite the stalled-out moments of boredom and the intense pleasures of the music and monologues.

Another interesting moment occurs just after the play's characters and themes are introduced. Driven to distraction by all the seemingly mindless chatter, Ernie explodes, "Will you stop talking about it? You cats are a drag. It's getting on my nerves. I've got a job tonight and I've got to get straight. *(Blows his mouthpiece)* Why doesn't that bastard get here? He probably took all our money and burned us" (32). Gelber uses Ernie, the most physically distressed and inarticulate of the junkies (his horn is in hock), to interrupt the accumulation of imagery, allusion, and discourse established since the start of the performance. At that moment, a knock is heard and Harry McNulty enters. McNulty has no lines. Gelber's script tells us that Harry walks in, looks around, plugs in a portable vinyl record player, and plays a Charlie Parker record. The record plays for at least two minutes.

Following the explosive climax of Ernie's outburst, the theater stumbles uncomfortably into silence as McNulty wanders about greeting the other characters. This is followed by two minutes of recorded music, played while "everyone assumes an intense pose of listening," this followed in turn by another silence while McNulty packs up and leaves. Another "long pause" after the door closes. Then the musicians start playing, "cementing their feelings" for "about one minute." This is an astonishing theatrical moment, a sudden halt to the veering dramatic progress of the play. Five minutes of silence shot through with the canned sounds of a cheap vinyl record player—an eternity in stage time and an audacious use of sound to underline the themes of absence and presence that will dominate the play's second act. The rebellion from drama is more short-lived here than it would be in *Frankenstein*: Director Jaybird bursts from the audience, shouting, "Cut it! Cut it! You are murdering the play. What are you doing? Let's go over it again. You're to give the whole plot in the first act. So far not one of you has carried out his dramatic assignment. . . . Do you think you are doing a slice of life?" Solly responds in outrage, "Stop!? Stop the action!? Why did you seek out dope addicts?" (32).

With McNulty's entrance, itself introduced by Ernie's anguish, the forward progress of plot and dialogue is held in suspension across an agonizingly long period of performance time punctuated by the exquisite but canned agony of Parker's music. The junkies' hunger is momentarily forgotten by character and spectator; however, it continues to pulse beneath the apparent stillness, as is made clear to the spectator by the occasional fidgets and tics of the performers. Meanwhile, the varied experiences of the listeners (on stage and in the auditorium) are allowed to develop as vinyl recording and live musicians play and the actors assume conventional postures of "hip" attention (as evidenced by the Clarke film).

A new kind of dramatic arrangement is necessitated by the multiple desires, experiences, memories, and knowledge of the characters, as well as by the critical syncopation of performance time. Bebop is the model for such arrangement. To recall Ellison again, Bebop as both a social and a formal organization functioned for the Cold War avant-garde as an innovative model of community and communication. In *The Connection*, it serves to tenuously bind the petulant members of the addict community in a relationship that blurs the distinction between harmony and dissonance. This is a "polytonal" community of a piece with the egalitarian individualism underwriting the anarchist worldview. Bigsby notes the close connection between jazz and junk in the production: "There are moments of consonance in which the ironies of [egotistical community] are momentarily annihilated and those moments, embodied in the harmonies and orchestrated dissonances of jazz, are crucial" (78). Stories of shared experience pepper the monologues and dialogues as densely as accusations of betrayals, unpaid debts, and ulterior motives. Likewise, the relationship between performer and spectator is equivocal, both seductive and aggressive. The production possesses a highly ambivalent attitude toward community, as if it were at odds concerning the bases upon which a truly egalitarian, honest, embodied community might be built—and courageous enough to admit it.

The tangled utopian/dystopian qualities of the production mark it as a paralytically thorough reflection on that most mythical of communities, the avant-garde, and its absorption as imagined by so much of the Left during the Cold War. The following dialogue, one that occurs early in the play, illustrates this tangled, claustrophobic sensibility. In it, some of the newest avant-garde modes (i.e., intermedia) and some of the oldest (montage) are brought together under the umbrella of profit:

> *Jim:* All right, junkies. During our trip we will incorporate an allied art—the motion picture.
> *Jaybird: (from the audience)* What?
> *Jim:* This is the ad lib part. Don't worry. Money! And, if everything goes right, you will be able to see the film version of this play. It was the only hip thing to do.
> *2nd Musician:* You're hip, my ass!
> *Leach: (To Jim)* Will you stop this cornball stuff?
> *Ernie:* I knew they would pull something like this. I told you I didn't trust this cat!
> *Jim:* Come on Jaybird. This can't go on like this.
> *Jaybird:* So far, so good. Don't worry. Conflict!
> *Jim:* It just means more money. For you and for me. Besides, we aren't going Hollywood. They're making an avant-garde movie. The photographers know something about Griffith and Eisenstein.
> *Leach:* You sure have to mention the right names.
> *Solly:* Leave him be.
> *Jim:* Okay, you cats ought to smoke pot instead of using junk. It would make you more agreeable. *(Exit)*
> *Ernie: (To 1st Photographer)* How much they paying you man? . . . What are you getting out of this, man? (23–25)

Here, the traditional avant-garde urge for the new maneuvers a tortuous path between excess and exploitation, between the "true" avant-garde and the "false" avant-garde of Cold War capitalism and its innovative cliques. No one believes Jim's high-art pretensions; they know he's just out to make a buck. The Becks were just as aware that their audience was hip and jaded, able to use the wicked tongue needed in highly competitive art markets, and conscious of the significance of names like Griffith and Eisenstein and techniques like intermedia. As in their attack on the Odéon, an attack that earned the plaudits of Scarpetta and the editorial board of *Tel Quel, The Connection* shows the Living launching barbs at the audiences and impresarios of the avant-garde, being as vicious to its audience as the junkies are to each other. This was a tactic often used by the Living; as Gelber points out, the LT "could anger and outrage audiences of all political stripes" (21). Banes comments, "Even within the Movement they were controversial for their anarchism. But their political dramaturgy was as much in the vanguard in the 60s as their earlier work in the poets' theater had been in the 50s."[64]

It's impossible to understand *The Connection* without understanding the very specific way it framed, exploited, and basically *dramatized* the relationship of performer and spectator (a concern, as I pointed out in my discussion of *Frankenstein,* that would increasingly exercise the LT's interest). Having cut their teeth on Stein and Cage, having logged countless hours with jazz, the Living understood how this relationship could serve as an interesting, engaging compositional principle, both aesthetically and socially. This is not just a concern of the LT; the relationship of artist and audience has long been the linch pin of the avant-garde's attack on bourgeois culture, part of its long-standing effort to bring about, as Jonathan Crary describes it, "a fundamental reorganization of the subject, . . . the construction of an observer who was a precondition for the transformation of everyday life."[65]

Modernity as Drug: Performance and Text

The Connection's dramatic representation of junk and jazz is intertwined with the history and modes of modern literature, theater, visual art, and social control. For example, in its use of the box-office-for-drugs plot, the play indirectly references one of the more sordid sectors of American performance history: addiction tourism. Barbara Hodgson, in her history of opiate culture, describes how, after the first wave of Asian immigration in 1849–50 and the establishment of Chinatown in San Francisco, opium use—and addiction—became alluring enough to good white folks to incite official concern and spectatorial curiosity. Tours of opium dens became a must-do among the fashionable, a fad sampled by the likes of Rudyard Kipling and Mark Twain.[66]

The stereotype of the "threateningly exotic" Asian male was a strong flavor in this subcultural chop suey, a flavor that kept public opinion concerning addiction centered on visibly identifiable immigrant groups rather than the "unmarked" middle-class, white, female, medically administered addict—the same addict who constituted a solid majority until 1914, taking the lead again in the late 1950s with the rise of chemical psychiatry. The threatening but irresistible allure of alien ethnicity would, in time, infect many people's feelings about the class divisions that were causing such widespread trouble in the United States.

In his history of opiate addiction prior to World War II, David Courtwright shows that the seductive allure and knee-jerk moralizing of the performances in which Kipling and Twain participated were not just limited to situations in which ethnic differences predominated (as was the case in the predominantly Chinese opium subculture of San Francisco). After the Harrison Act in 1914 forced addicts to seek help from public institutions, upper- and middle-class opium and heroin addicts (most of whom had become addicted through medical prescription) were able to maintain anonymity by relying on highly paid, private, discreet medical help. However, the "nonmedical users" who queued up to register at the New York City clinic "were regularly harassed by sightseeing buses, replete with gawking tourists and blaring megaphones."[67] Such performances cemented for spectators the connection between drug use and low-class, delinquent populations, a connection that enabled upper-class addicts to remain beyond view, unmarked. Such tours were revived in the late 1960s to feature places such as the infamous Haight-Ashbury district of San Francisco, whose streets were not only traveled by LSD-dropping hippies but also by busloads of sightseers out for a look at LSD-dropping hippies. As with clinic tours, such countercultural sightseeing cemented the connection between drugs and the counterculture, generally at the expense of the counterculture's more significant goals and achievements.

It's interesting to note that addiction tourism has bequeathed to performance studies some of its most challenging and complex problems. Umberto Eco, in his 1977 essay "Semiotics of Theatrical Performance," cites Charles Peirce's lengthy analysis of a long-lived tradition in addiction performance: public drunkards forcibly exposed in a public place to communicate specific messages about the evils of drink. To Peirce, these performances created all kinds of problems for a theoretical explanation of signs and communication. Though the drunkard communicates, his message is not intended nor even necessarily recognized by the performer who is typically soused; rather it is the framing of his condition that enables the communication of the moral message. Attempting to work his way through the in- and oversights of Peirce's analysis as an early example of performance theory, Eco makes the point that the "performance" of addiction is not at all the choice of the performer in such cases.

Building on the work of semiotician Charles Morris, Eco notes that communication in such a context is the province of the interpreter, not the performer. As a consequence, Eco suggests that performance theorists take full account not simply of the actions of the performer and the assumptions of the viewer, but also the entire range of framing devices that surround the performer and audience.[68] As Marvin Carlson puts it in his discussion of Eco's essay, "When the performer may be quite unaware of the implications of his display, the agency of the production apparatus takes over these responsibilities."[69] As these moments in theater history and performance history reveal, the War on Drugs has been fought, at least in part, on the theatrical front, a front that can be dizzyingly mercurial.

This clash between addicts and spectator (better said, tourists) is an explicit theme of *The Connection,* as if the play is charting the slow, agonized birth of avant-garde consciousness in an era of increasing performance consciousness. Solly, the most educated, articulate, and politically and historically minded of the junkies, reveals in the first act that his choice to perform for Jaybird and Jim was made not just because it would allow him to make his connection and maintain his addiction; he also realized that here was an excellent opportunity to win a tactical victory in a long-running, wide-ranging, and decidedly theatrical war. The nature of this victory isn't clear at this point in the play; however, it is clarified before the performance concludes. Late in the play, after having taken heroin for the first time, Jaybird notes something has changed: "Mmph. I'm here and you're here. Just like a couple of months ago. Something happened in between. Maybe the idea of an audience. But . . . *(He touches Solly's shoulder)*" (91). Solly, who is also searching for an audience likewise notes the change: "You look like the Jaybird I first met" (91). What's been restored between the two is the communication that they shared before the decision to perform before a paying audience, the level of intimate communication that had nothing to do with drugs or money, a kind of romantically pure *communitas.* But this restoration comes at a price: Jaybird becomes an addict. And it carries its own quirky ambivalence: Solly realizes that the Jaybird he first met was only *acting* like a junkie. As we'll see, Jaybird is a model for audience transformation, an emblem of political change. On the other hand, Solly, the most introspective and articulate of the characters, is a model for a peculiarly small-scale form of countercultural militancy.

Though the role of theater in the War on Drugs is an important part of *The Connection*'s attack on the audience and promotion of anarchist communitarianism, there are other histories that manifest themselves on the tortured skins of the performers, histories that add even more ambivalence to the politics of this community-focused gesture of theatrical antagonism. To recall Phelan again, the performing body is the center of semiotic crossings; history lives in the reiterated gestures and language of the performer. If Gelber is compelled to confront the theatricalized suffering of addicts in order to identify important obstacles and way stations on the path toward the blessed community, he must also deal with the *literary* history of addiction, a tradition intertwined with many of the utopian sociopolitical trends identified by Beck in his description of the many-petaled lotus of the Revolution. *The Connection*'s representation of heroin addiction in fact owes much to the high-art, pulp, and avant-garde traditions of drug literature, traditions that obsessively concern themselves with the immorality of the drug experience. In this respect, the production reflects an irony noted by Christopher Innes: that many of the supposedly antitextual performances of countercultural theaters such as the LT, the Open Theatre, and the Performance Group in fact tacitly depended on text to articulate their antitextual biases.[70]

We see in such literature, first of all, a theme shared with addiction tourism: the *exotic*. Traditionally, literary representations of addiction have made it out to be the purview of the outsider, the languorous exile from the world of work, rulership, and procreation. Homer's lotus eaters and Shakespeare's drunks are early examples of the literary use of drugs and addiction that would come to dominate the modern mind: the intoxicated as threat to or respite from order and progress, especially the orderly progress of narrative toward dramatic, formal, and moral conclusion. Baudelaire's opium eaters exemplify a more sustained and supportive exploration of this threat; his "intrepid lovers of disorder" step outside of the constraints of Destiny and find in the vast spaces of opium intoxication experiences and language to resist the banal order of the bourgeoisie. The cosmic paranoids of William Burroughs's *The Naked Lunch* (1959) also find themselves thrown beyond order and progress, exposed to the cybernetic horror-factory of modern capitalist society. Ginsberg's *Howl* (1956) counts addicts among its "holy holy holy" angelic hosts. The addict-messiahs of Frank Herbert's *Dune* series (the first volume premiering in 1965) take command not only of a transgalactic society dependent on the spice "mélange," but also, through the exploration of drug experience and addiction anguish, discover insights into memory, history, creation, and historical transformation. These are simply a few of the many examples that demonstrate that the addict and the skewed, singular view enabled by intoxication and addiction have suggested to modern writers a way to creatively justify otherworldly, alien, and (at least on occasion) profoundly *critical* artistic representations. In all of these cases, literary representations of drug experience and addiction show both the drug and the addict as the source of compelling language, as if drug and addiction were a pair of muses, transcendence and concretion. In short, the literary drug user and addict signify the old Romantic idea that poetic language is *compulsive*.

The compulsion of modernist literature has many links to the compulsion of addiction. The alternately ravishing and devastating image of modernity so characteristic of a world in which "all that is solid melts into air" (to recall Marshall Berman recalling Marx)[71] is well captured by the intense, transient, anguished experience of narcotics and narcotic addiction, especially opium and opiates like heroin. This is one reason why modernist literature so often flirts with states of intense, dangerous intoxication. The creator of Papa and Mama Ubu, Alfred Jarry, writes in "L'Opium" of a journey on a train that passes through a landscape of collapsing walls, floating cathedral vaults, and sprouting columns.[72] Jean Cocteau, an opium addict long before his 1928 residence at the Saint Cloud clinic, captured the close connection of modernist composition and addiction in his book *Opium: The Diary of a Cure* (1930):

> The work which exploits me needed opium; it needed me to leave opium; once more, I will be taken in. And I was wondering, shall I take opium or not? . . . I will take it if my work wants me to.
> And if opium wants me to.[73]

Both Jarry and Cocteau—and Witkiewicz, too—are cognizant of the uncanny relationship of intoxication and addiction to work and industriousness, not so much as an escape from work (as Homer's lotus eaters do) as a revisioning of the very processes of intensive literary production, processes vital to the creation and sustenance of a literary career.

The repetitive, tragic coincidence of heroin addiction and artistic accomplishment should draw our attention to the fact that many artists used drug experience to open up the text (in this case, the musical score) to innovation. This was particularly true in the 1950s and 1960s. Leonard Feather notes that, in 1960, "of the 23 individuals listed as winners in a recent *Down Beat* poll, at least nine were known narcotics users, five of them with a record of arrest and conviction. The proportion is even greater among proponents of certain types of jazz, notably 'Hard Bop,' whose principal soloists include an alarmingly high percentage with police records as heroin addicts."[74] Nat Hentoff, in *The Jazz Life* (1961), attempts to capture the mystery at the heart of the close relationship of jazz and heroin in the Cold War era. He quotes one musician comparing the taking of heroin to "going into a closet. It lets you concentrate and takes you away from everything. Heroin is a working drug, like the doctor who took it because he had a full schedule so he could work better. It lets me concentrate on my sound."[75] Ben Sidran argues that heroin "alters aural perception in the user." He notes, "Although [Parker] himself said that anybody who claimed to play better under the influence of any drug was 'a plain straight liar,' the empirical evidence, as Art Blakey has said, is that 'although you do not play better with heroin, you do hear better.'"[76] Concerning Parker, Blakey said that he "wanted to kick the habit so that he could tell people what he heard. It was something like a neurotic. While he is suffering, he cannot produce; but reflecting about his pain, he can create. Musicians who have been junkies and then rid themselves of the habit have sometimes really then come into their own musically."[77]

Jarry, Cocteau, and Witkiewicz's literary personae are cousins to Parker, as are Leach, Sam, and Solly, who likewise find themselves pressed to produce in an anguished creative situation, a situation in which text and antitext coexist in an uneasy, but nevertheless productive dynamic. Jarry's and Cocteau's texts, with their carefully carved meters and shocking extremity of imagery, are genetic sharers with the monologues and jazz jams of *The Connection*. Gelber's addicts, whether they are musicians or monologians (or, as is the case with Ernie, both), stubbornly persist in and continually fail at the creation of a language that can adequately communicate the singularity of their experience. Leach, for example, runs through metaphors like a chain smoker through cigarettes, discussing rapidly Jacob's ladder, the theory of relativity, optics, and the battle of the sexes as ways to capture his experience. Sam is a bit more concrete in his choices, generally transforming the commonplaces of heroin subculture and Leach's apartment into spiritual metaphors ("I am the man as much as anyone. Listen, I am your man if you come to me. You are my man if I come to you" [36]) or improvising, after seeing Leach riff on a lightbulb, with props like a hula hoop.

Leach and Sam, compelled by their situation to produce interesting, engaging dramatic language and situations, are like Cocteau himself, poets *with,* not in spite of, their addiction to the opiate commodity. They are addicted to work. Sam sees it clearly; discussing his struggle with addiction, he notes that he's always running. But so is most of the audience:

> I used to think that the people who walk the streets, the people who work every day, the people who worry so much about the next dollar, the next new coat, the chlorophyll addicts, the aspirin addicts, the vitamin addicts, those people are hooked worse than me. Worse than me. Hooked. (31)

Spoken to earn his heroin, spoken as he jogs rapidly in place toward exhaustion, this hard-breathing diatribe is more than a little ironic. The compulsion to language and the capacity to recognize capitalism as a fundamentally addictive form of economics—both are the product of an intensive, body-centered form of work. Sam works for heroin and the heroin allows him to work.

The Connection seduces its audience with promises of uncut poetry, promises as empty as a dealer's promises of uncut drug. As Sam puts it, "I got some powerful stories in me when that shit flows in my veins" (43). However, the promise doesn't really pay off—the stories are tired and clichéd. After taking the drug and watching Solly collapse, Sam advises the others to forget about literary decorum, "You got to let yourself go. When you feel it inside, just let yourself go and wail." Solly can't do it. "Man, I feel it inside, but I can't move. I'm stoned. *(Sits at window)*" (62). The close connection between poetic performance and intoxication is made clear repeatedly by Gelber earlier in the play but is not allowed its dramatic pay-off in the second act. Is this exploitation or liberation, poetry or commodity, textual repetition or performance innovation? Jaybird asks, "Solly, where is the philosophy I put into your mouth?" Solly answers, "It went up in smoke before the show" (33). The exotic muse of drug and addiction is, perhaps, conducive to the junkies' spontaneous, philosophical riffing. The muse of drug and addiction may, perhaps, through those word-and-sound compositions, seduce the audience, tempting them to cross the line that separates the moralizing, but distant viewer traditionally associated with bourgeois theater[78] from the modernist poet-performer-participant traditionally associated with the antibourgeois avant-garde. Or it might just bore us to death.

This compelling, equivocally liberating poetry, entrained with the Redd quartet's performance, fulfills something called for by Paul Goodman in 1949 and pursued enthusiastically by the Living Theatre: "the physical re-establishment of community."[79] As Bigsby points out, plays like *The Connection* and *The Brig* (Kenneth Brown, 1963) enabled the LT to explore the nature of poetic language as a *transformative* theatrical force, a force that could produce and cement the revolutionary community through its potent combination of sound and movement (79). Bigsby writes, "Beck had learnt from these productions that precision of language and of rhythm was itself a primary mechanism, a necessary underpinning to analogical inference" (79). Bigsby's comment is grounded in a strong, accurate sense of the LT's increasingly physical but nevertheless poetic productions of the 1960s. The "authenticity of the body," Bigsby argues, was accessed at this stage of the LT's development not simply through nonverbal performance (as was the case after their reading of *The Theater and Its Double*), but through the careful crafting of sensibility-shifting language and the insightful anchoring of that language to the concrete elements of theatrical performance (81). As David Graver puts it, "Spectatorship always has its somatic consequences."[80] But the Theater of Cruelty's consequences are, at least theoretically, severe, even life-changing. As Lyon puts it, "Artaud's new dramatic language belongs to a vision in which signs, incantation, magic, the actor, and the material world are fused. . . . Man thus becomes himself both an object and a sign in the new symbolism of the world."

Cruelty marks a fundamental challenge to the calcified relationship of text and performance upheld by hawks in the War on Drugs. *The Connection* attacks the melodramatic heritage of and, by extension, the embedded racism of that war. In drug-addiction melodrama, we typically find a rehash of the Puritans' captivity narrative, though the innocent is seduced away from the community by drugs, not Indians and paganism. Even so, race and racialized cultural performances are as vital an issue in the opium captivity narrative as it was for the Puritans, as it is in *The Connection*. The importance of racial difference is vital to addiction culture in general, as I mentioned in regard to the addiction tours taken by Kipling and Twain and to the afterlife of the "exotic Asian" stereotype in modernist literature. The revisioning of the addiction captivity narrative coincides with the first influx of Chinese immigrants into the United States during the 1840s and the race panic that partly motivated the first opium-smoking bans in the late 1870s. Relatively late examples of the opium captivity narrative, such as the film *The Dividend* (1916), made their mark by focusing popular anxieties about racial miscegenation around the figure of the young, white, female opium den habitué. John Colton's play *The Shanghai Gesture* (1926) makes racist sexual anxiety a central concern, naming its Chinese villain "Mother God Damn," its ingénue heroine "Poppy," and choosing as its dramatic conflict a bit of sexual betrayal between Mother and the hero, "Sir Guy Charteris" of the "British China Trading Co." Perhaps the most interesting of these captivity tales is Thomas Burke's story "The Chink and the Child" (1917), which features at least a slightly more sympathetic vision of the Asian opium subculture. In the story, twelve-year-old Lucy has fallen both into the depths of opium addiction and into the hatred of her violent father, Battling Burrows.[81] Though the story features a Chinese character as hero, the story doesn't allow the lovers to remain together. Lucy is beaten to death by her father, and Cheng is captured and tried for killing Battling in revenge.

The Connection references the captivity narrative, but acknowledges its racist aspects obliquely, preferring instead to characterize the savages as part of a postethnic chemical class:

Solly: Hello there! I'm the nineteenth century and I'm producing the twentieth. Unfortunately, the twentieth century has developed anti-social habits. There isn't a day that goes by without some item in the daily papers involving insanity. We've gone out and bribed a few natives. Actually, I'm the only white man the natives trust. If we can start a small opium war—I always wanted to start a war. (39).

The War on Drugs is, for Solly, explicitly connected to the idea of an audience. Sam describes Solly as a kind of shaman-sage, "dancing on the street. Yeah, dancing down through the people. Sometimes yelling, sometimes whispering to people. Always with a book" (41). Solly is a kind of chemical savage, offering rambling excursions on the "fascinating and repellant" aspects of seeking death, on limbo, the history of the Salvation Army. But he also stops himself at times, catching himself in moments of hypocrisy: "I hate oversimplification" (40). The innocent caught in minuet with Solly-the-savage are the two photographers that record the performance, photographers who find spectatorial distance too weak to withstand the seductive assault of the sordid avant-garde on the other side of their lenses. In the second act, one of the photographers and Jaybird are taken into the bathroom to "try a little taste."

As in the Puritanical version of the captivity narrative, questions of order, ethics, and metaphysics are important to *The Connection*. Jim tells the spectators not to patronize the panhandling junkies they might meet during intermission: "No matter what they tell you they will be turned on a scientifically accurate amount of heroin in the next act. And that is their payment for the performance, excluding the money made on the money" (53–54). The atmosphere of paranoia created during the performance (sudden knocks on the door, Ernie turning manic, the inhuman stares of the performers) was intended to infuse the entire performance context, not merely the actions on stage, with the paranoia of an outpost settlement. A typical moment: Jim enters from the audience, muttering, "I'm getting panicked. I'm getting panicked. There's a rumor the fuzz are coming. The fuzz are coming. We're going to get busted. Busted" (92). The hyperrealism of the production (and recall that the cops did show up one night) compelled the audience into the same state of exotic allure as the junkies. The "opium war" called for by Solly is a war on the audience, avant-garde and otherwise; this war is a war *for* an audience, a war of dancing, yelling, and whispering, a war that uses the tongues of poetic fire called for by Artaud in his letter to the French legislator (39).

Composition and Community

Though the intertextual connections to drug literature are important to note, there are also subcultural connections that must be examined, connections that help us understand the conflicted attitudes toward community and textuality evidenced in the production. The notion that drug experience, poetic composition, intense reading, and compulsive creation are closely intertwined with resistant, marginalized, and subversive communities is also a fairly long-lived one in literature, going back at least as far as Thomas De Quincey's foundational *Confessions of an English Opium-Eater* (1821), many of whose scenes feature prostitutes, immigrants, and criminals. Drug use supplied to postrevolutionary French and British poets a potent antidote to the Christianized Greek notion of poetic inspiration, an antidote that found itself in the hands of adepts at the center of the burgeoning, international decadence movement, a movement that coincided with the first significant opium imports onto European shores. Drugs—especially opium and alcohol—were the physically symbolic stuff of the *poète damné,* that emblematic figure of Parisian café life in the 1870s, described by Laurence Senelick as "the artist self-dramatized as outcast and alcoholic and epitomized by Verlaine."[82]

The body-mind extremity of opiates would influence Samuel Taylor Coleridge, William Wordsworth, and Mary Shelley, as well as the ill-tempered monologues delivered "between clenched teeth" of Yvette Guilbert and the brothers Frank and Donald Wedekind.[83] It would also influence the production of innovative forms of social organization. This is especially true after the concept of the avant-garde began to acquire currency among the scattered subcultures on the fringe of French political culture. In France in the mid-1800s, Gérard de Nerval helped found the Club de Haschichins, a club that, as its name implies, (1) systematically explored opium and hash experience, understood as a "mystical" process that countered the utilitarian and moralist imperatives of Christian capitalism, (2) recalled the original order of Haschichins in their belief that all was possible (at least in literary, social, and imaginative matters), (3) included painters and writers who would profoundly influence the course of modernism (Théophile Gautier, Honoré de Balzac, Charles Baudelaire, Eugène Delacroix, and Honoré Daumier—the vanguard of the *l'art pour l'art* movement), and (4) served as a crucible for the production of new forms of collaboration, communication, and fellowship. The Haschichins is only the most elite and remembered of the many intensity-seeking communities of Parisian bohemia and haute society, communities that also sought intensity in its political life. Typical of the extremes of this quest was Félix Fénéon, an art critic and close friend of the neoimpressionists who was later accused of abetting Emile Henry, bomber of the Café Terminus in 1894. Fénéon was one of those rounded up for the "Trial of Thirty" (a group that included many opium and alcohol addicts and prostitutes), a show trial whose response to the bombing of the Terminus effectively ended anarchism as a going ideology in France until the 1960s.

Though Gelber didn't know Drug War history in any great detail, his representation of that war is extremely acute, particularly his anachronisms. For one, *The Connection* sets the junkies into a dramatic situation that is more reminiscent of the opium den than the isolated, alienated realities of post–World War II heroin subculture. As Courtwright describes it, unlike the often brutal, profit-driven relations among heroin buyers and dealers, "opium smoking was a social enterprise, carried on in a communal place," an enterprise characterized "by a rigid code of honor. . . : smokers would not take advantage of other smokers or tolerate those who did" while in the "inner sanctum" of the opium den (64, 73). Thus, though the opium den became "the matrix of a deviant subculture, a tightly knit group of outsiders whose primary relations were restricted to themselves," this subculture possessed many of the attributes of the anarchist community, if only in the den itself, and if only for the duration of the opium high (74). That said, it is worth noting that people of different races, classes, sexes, and sexualities freely mixed while within it. This blend of far-out ideas, *outré* behavior, cross-cultural mingling, and mind-expanding experience was one of the strongest attractions for artist-activists like Gautier and Baudelaire, artist-activists who sought not merely the modern in art, but the modern in *living*.

Such deviancy, which has proven on more than one occasion to result in innovative political developments (see, for example, surrealism, situationism, and Yippie!), forced administrative and legal officials in New York and San Francisco to take the War on Drugs onto the subcultural front.[84] The banning of opium smoking in these cities in the late 1870s was designed explicitly to break up these libertarian communities; there was little effort to ban the importing of the drug by pharmaceutical companies and physicians with "private" clients. However, as often happens, the ban actually enticed many into deviancy who might have otherwise avoided it. In 1882, one commentator noted that "many who would not otherwise have indulged to seek out the low dens and patronize them" did, and those who already did "found additional pleasure in continuing that about which there was a spice of danger" (qtd. in Courtwright, 79).

The breaking up of this growing, now illegal subculture—a subculture that was a seedbed for modernist literature and performance—became a central concern for authorities, who viewed the policing of deviant social groups and their gathering places as part and parcel of an effective response to larger global issues. Elihu Root, secretary of state at the time of the opium smoking ban, viewed the offensive as a way "to save our face" at the Shanghai Opium Commission meeting (qtd. in Courtwright, 830). Hamilton Wright, one of the architects of the law that also banned the nonmedical use of cocaine, "believed that in order to assume moral and diplomatic leadership on the world question, the United States must itself possess exemplary narcotic laws" (Courtwright, 28). Courtwright notes that Wright and others "especially stressed the danger to white women posed by Black[s]," a bias that also worked against Chinese immigrants, gamblers, and prostitutes (28, 83).

As we have already seen, Gelber's aware of the close relationship between the economic, aesthetic, and political exploitation of addicts and the larger concerns of authority. The explicit if equivocal call for community by Leach, Jaybird, and Sam; the formal relationship of dissonance and harmony among the various performers; and the implicit if equivocal desire for community expressed by the play's textual memories of opium and modernist-poetic *communitas* serve to critically offset the play's debts to the exploitative representations of addiction peddled by the entertainment industry. Offset, but not eliminate. The positive aspects of the production shouldn't be so emphatically stressed that they keep us from recognizing the contradictions of this production's representation of the vanguard community: Leach's apartment houses a community more or less forced by police harassment and shared hunger to cohere. And the nature of its commitment is based not in ideology or ethics, but in simple gut-need. The coherence of this blessed community is tenuous, for sure; the characters continually remind each other of differences, betrayals, annoyances. The contradictory basis of this community—compelled into community by their enslavement to a brutalizing commodity—is obvious to the Becks, to Gelber, and to their characters.

As in *Frankenstein,* this contradictory basis doesn't preclude visions of utopia. Sidran writes, "The use of heroin inasmuch as it was overtly deviant in terms of established conventions carried with it political overtones, albeit on a broad, cultural wavelength" (121). During the 1950s, many members of the jazz community were either forced or convinced to become patients at the Lexington Narcotics Hospital, a federal project administered by the U.S. Public Health Service. Inmates of the hospital held weekly jazz jams in the hospital's central courtyard, entertaining the other patients and developing the "chops" to challenge their peers and Anglo-American musical hegemony.[85] If heroin was, in DeVeaux's words, the "endemic curse of the jazz profession," affecting the likes of Parker, Blakey, Rollins, Davis, and McLean, then it was also, without doubt, a source of intense experience that revealed the contours of an oppressive society as well as a physically symbolic cognate to an all-too-real but often elusive sense of totalizing oppression. In "The Theater and Culture," featured in the program for *The Connection,* Artaud writes that "if it is important for us to eat first of all, it is even more important for us not to waste in the sole concern for eating our simple power of being hungry" (7). This power, which anchored addicts to the commodity in a brutal chain of habit, also led to the constructing new forms—both aesthetic and social—to achieve the technical and emotional insights given to them by the drug.

The monstrous deformation of the blessed body politic by the paradoxes of Cold War capitalism threatens to overwhelm the orderly, entertaining, moralizing progress of the plot as it is described by Jim and Jaybird, those entertainment-minded, decidedly co-opted vanguardists. Such deformation also occurs on the level of stage language. For example, in the first of many conceptually incoherent but rhythmically dexterous monologues, Leach complains:

> I'm hungry. This is my place, why shouldn't I eat? These people never eat. Don't they know it's nutritious? Oh, this boil. Dream world. Narcotics. I live comfortable. I'm not a Bowery bum. Look at my room. It's clean. Except for the people who come here and call themselves my friends. My friends? Huh! They come here with a little money and they expect me to use my hard earned connections to supply them with heroin. And when I take a little for myself they cry, they scream. The bastards.[86]

The stuttering, parataxic structure of Leach's monologue reflects on the level of the individual character the struggle of the larger community to find a common experience of satisfaction, a common body defined by a shifting set of tensions, and a common language. His thoughts leap as suddenly as his emotions, moving through a series of changes not unlike those gone through by the Freddie Redd Quartet throughout the evening. "Oh, this boil. Dream world. Narcotics. I live comfortable"—Leach's monologue is clearly struggling to organize its elements into some kind of orderly form. But the body, the dream of futurity, the commitment to the way of life, and the banal creature comfort mentioned in the monologue don't cohere, though perhaps they do as a performance, as a kind of sound poem. If there is coherence here, Leach finds it in the performative rhythms of jazzy scatting, an improvisation-tinged word-collage—in composition, not content.

Gelber and Malina's repeated reduction of dramatic language to a sonic element of the mise-en-scène, a reduction of language to sound caused by the pressure of hunger, pain, desire, and fear, is one of the clearest signs of Artaud's influence on the Living and their vision of vanguard community and communication as they transformed into a counterculture. In "The Theater and Culture," Artaud writes, "If confusion is a sign of the times, I see at the root of this confusion a rupture between things and words, between things and the ideas and signs that are their representation."[87] For Artaud, the cause of this rupture is "our superstitious valuation of texts and written poetry" (78). Therefore, the text must be reduced to simply one of many, equally significant elements of the theatrical spectacle in order that its physical power be restored to it. In this way, the "simple power of hunger" will not be mistaken for the satisfactions of eating (78).

Along these lines, Sontag notes that Artaud's role in the "movement to disestablish the 'author'" was based in new understandings of the performer's body.[88] "Artaud's theater," she writes, "is a reaction against the state of underdevelopment in which the bodies (and the voices, apart from talking) of Western actors have remained for generations, as have the arts of spectacle" (xxxii). However, unlike Artaud's rejection of text and concept, the Living (at least at this point in their development toward total revolutionary theater) chose to *dramatize* the rejection, creating what we would now call a deconstructive performance that troubles the distinction between text and performance. The script supplied by Gelber is a conceptual and sonic framework within which the performers find expressive posture, affective timbre, and compelling syncopation; in other words, they find the specific performance modes that will manifest the history of this underdevelopment, a history shared with jazz musicians, drug addicts, and avant-garde poets. But the script is also a thematic element, an object of struggle among the junkies and the so-called producer and writer of the play.

With typical insight, Malina saw the potent, if ambivalent, strengths of the Living Theatre's situation:

This time is a revolutionary period just because we are so constantly put in this fix: Not only we, of course, but everyone is constantly forced to act on decisions based on difficult, conscious moral judgments.

All of us are, by the nature of the times, put up against the line we have drawn, and if we stumble against it, we find ourselves retreating backward, and it's not a line, but a wall we're up against.[89]

The revolutionary lotus described by Beck, the ten-thousand-petal flower, takes root in similarly contradictory soil. Beck writes, "But look . . . it is dying . . . while it's maturing . . . can you wait? . . . how long?" (129).

The most scandalous moment in this production was surely the moment when actor Warren Finnerty, playing Leach, inserted a hypodermic needle into his arm. From reports, this decidedly cruel performance overwhelmed quite a few spectators, sending them crashing to the floor. The extremity of Finnerty's gesture is evidence of the Living's increased consciousness of their political situation and the increasing sense that language, even the most poetic, could no longer achieve the ends of communication. The excessiveness of that gesture marks a tragic development; the movement away from the text is a movement full of physical anguish for all involved—performer, character, spectator.

In his theories of theater, Artaud explored and exploited what he correctly saw as (1) the inextricable relationship among the form of a theatrical representation (i.e., staging, dramatic structure, audience/actor relations), (2) the role of the spectator's body in experiencing that representation, and (3) the potential transformation of the community participating in that representation. Each of these threatens to press the communication experience beyond rational judgment and beyond the text toward what Artaud described as "physical knowledge."[90] Artaud writes of

the need to abolish the idea,
the idea and its myth,
and to enthrone in its place
the thundering manifestation
of this explosive necessity;
to dilate the body of my internal night,

the internal nothingness
of my self

which is night,
nothingness,

thoughtlessness,

but which is explosive affirmation
that there is something
to make room for:

my body.[91]

The poet asserts that this explosive affirmation, this violent, embodied opening up of a space for feeling and expression in the claustrophobic architecture of language, is a key to "being in touch with oneself at every moment . . . not ceasing for a single moment to feel oneself in one's inmost being, in the unformulated mass of one's life, in the substance of one's reality; . . . not feeling in oneself an enormous hole, a crucial absence" (70). For Artaud, such explosive affirmation was best created in the theater, which he viewed as an art of "immediate gratuitousness provoking acts without use or profit."[92] The Theater of Cruelty "is a formidable call to the forces that impel the mind by example to the source of its conflict" (30).

In *The Connection*, Beck and Malina confronted the difficulty of creating contact through body and language, contact they hoped would help the mind toward its conflicting sources. Though the production was only the first step, they were no doubt pleased to discover that the golden path to blessed community remained available to the avant-garde despite its oft-reported demise. However, the kind of communication necessitated by their contradictory position in capitalist culture demanded the performer's body undergo a series of rigorous deformations and extreme gestures, deformations as anguished for the performer as they were for the audience. Like everything else on *The Connection*'s stage, the metaphors of flesh expand, encompassing a range of meanings and motivating a varied series of effective theatrical gestures. From the incessant scratching of the sick and lousy addicts, to the exploration of racial and sexual politics, to the scandalous onstage injection, the presence of flesh and bodies on this stage was a complex and troubled one. Leach emblematizes this troublesome body politic. His junk sickness, suppurating flesh, and ambiguous sexuality exhibit the violence contradictions of a community born of and situated in a society that it needed to destroy. White, middle-aged, "always trying to be so hip . . . [but] still just a petty conniving businessman" (44), Leach figures the violent tearing apart, the *sparagmos,* of the blessed community coming to self-consciousness and material being on the morning of postmodernism.

The one who offers food and shelter to his fellows at the start of the play and the one who devolves into a writhing, poetry-vomiting body at its end, Leach serves as the carrier of the play's lean, metabolic dramatic structure and is the emblem of its contradictions. Leach is compelled to negotiate the warring principles of visibility and invisibility, principles key to the theater as an art form and key to Artaud's theory of cruelty. Visibility, light, and the spiritual are explicitly—if ironically—linked by Leach early in the play. Sick from lack of heroin, his head held rigidly due to the painful boil on his neck, compelled by Jaybird to perform, Leach squints up at the bare lightbulb hanging above his kitchen table and wonders out loud why humans aren't killed by the incessant bombardment of sunlight. He concludes, "Man is transparent. You know what I mean? Man is transparent. Yes, transparent. That's why the light goes through him and doesn't hurt me or you" (26). This speech is more than lightly ironic: spoken by an addict, punctuated by the bursting of a ripening boil, and crosslit by the roaming cameramen, Leach's body is hardly transparent. Quite the contrary, the body in this production is not unlike Thebes in the LT's 1968 *Antigone*. As described by Michael Smith, the body politic of Thebes, represented by the massed bodies of the performers, "shakes until it destroys itself."[93] Leach's body does just this; at the moment it has acquired its maximum significance, a significance built up over the course of two acts' worth of dialogue, monologue, conflict, compromise, symbolic gesture, and expressive manipulation of time, he goes into a writhing overdose, spontaneous poetry oozing from his mouth like cold smoke.

Living as we do two centuries after romanticism, we're fairly used to the notion that art, theater, music, even daily life can express intensely mysterious forces. Whether such forces are viewed as spiritual, economic, racial, unconscious, or simply "other," it is not an uncommon belief that things are not what they appear to be. It's hard to imagine a work of theater that does not subscribe to this view in some way, even if only pragmatically (i.e., the systematic disguising of the production process). Beck and Malina definitely believed in invisible forces and, following *The Connection,* attempted to bring them together at all levels of theater, from production to performance. For example, the "plot chart" for *Paradise Now* maps a revolution that is bodily, spiritual, and political. The references to Bolivia, Jerusalem, Paris, Capetown, Birmingham (Alabama), Hanoi, and Saigon are not simply decorative elements in a composition composed mostly of hexagrams from the *I Ching,* kabbalistic body philosophy, a diagram of the chakras, and yogic breathing symbols. Rather, the politics are nested in an interlocking composition, a composition that will be performed much like a jazz jam per-

forms a popular standard—always with an eye to the expressive manipulation of time and "infinite plasticity" of form achievable in moments of
intense, collaborative performance.[94]

That said, the chart clearly focuses on the body, both the individual's and
the body politic. The map, woven from half a dozen hermetic systems of
thought, marks the Living Theatre's trajectory from the precision of language and image Bigsby views as the central focus of their work with poets'
theater to the densely layered, syncopated gestures of *Paradise Now*. The key
stage in this trajectory was *The Connection*. Its invocation of the opium den,
the jazz jam, the avant-garde poetic community, and drug experience is evidence of their struggle to find models of community and communication
that could both confront and evade the police, the military, the entertainment industry, and the critic.

At this point, we need to recall that the opium den was an influential
model on avant-garde communities such as the Club de Haschichins. This
in part because of den's mix of intense, hallucinatory personal experience
and rigid behavioral codes, in part because the physically symbolic nature of
drug experience enabled artists to track exits from the claustrophobia of
bourgeois capitalist aesthetics, and in part because the *outré* nature of such
communities put some glamour and grit into anarchist utopian speculation.
Symbolists read their De Quincy with care and knew by experience the
internationalist implications of drug experience. Though not all symbolists
smoked opium—most never touched it—the experience of the drug was
significant enough as symbol and legend to inspire British decadents like
Oscar Wilde (an avowed and active anarchist), Ernest Dowson, Arthur
Symons, and Aubrey Beardsley to attempt to represent it in a fashion that
could simultaneously bind together the community while enabling it to
move beyond the instrumental rationalism of bourgeois capitalist authorities. *L'art pour l'art,* so often deemed politically evasive and ineffective, was,
on the contrary, one of the early fronts of the War on Drugs.

The hermetic nature of symbolist poetry, dramaturgy, and visual art predicted to some degree the performance strategies of Bebop and its reliance
on "hip" spectators to keep alive the closed-circuit feel of the jazz jam. The
result is an irony noted by Edward Lucie-Smith. While, on the one hand,
the symbolists rejected bourgeois moralism and rationalism, protested
against naturalism and the novel, and retreated from the historical crises of
the Paris Commune into the ivory tower, their hermeticism "could also
lead straight to Socialism" (54). Gustave Moreau, pioneer of symbolist
painting, writes that the symbolist work established a new relationship to its

spectators, "giving no message at all to one, an inadequate conception to another, the full significance of the artist's own mind to a third, and telling their story to all, without any help or interpretation from the painter, as would be the case if he were dead."[95] Odilon Redon writes that the "sense of mystery" so dear to symbolists "is a matter of being all the time amid the equivocal, in double and triple aspects, and hints of aspects (images within images), forms which are coming to birth, or which will come to birth according to the state of mind of the observer."[96]

However, much like the jazz jam, the symbolists often found themselves trapped in such equivocality. On the one hand, their work was intended for the initiated; on the other hand, their leftist leanings demanded the public exposure of the mysteries. If, in critic Alfred Vallette's words, "[t]he issue . . . is not to be human but to suggest humanity,"[97] then the question is how one can suggest humanity while avoiding the cozy clichés of the humanist. This is one of the reasons the symbolists distrusted the theater, an art form that depends on the concrete and the perceivable. Understanding how the symbolists negotiated the borderlands separating antitheatrical theatrics, egalitarian community, and the restrictions of police, censorship, and the market can help us understand the Living Theatre's efforts to do likewise— and also introduce us to what appears to be a perennial dilemma surrounding the War on Drugs and efforts to render that war as just and fair as possible. As Solly tells us, the twentieth century is born from the nineteenth; the struggle for the new is mired in the old.

Symbolist theater artists such as Maurice Maeterlinck and Aurélien-François Lugné-Poë attempted to find compromise between the visual bias of theater and the antivisual bias of symbolism by utilizing texts considered unstageable and presenting them in a fashion that would remain mindful of the gap between representation and referent. As I've made clear, the public-oriented forms of Bebop retained their credibility by retaining the specific staging techniques, behavioral codes, and formal devices of the jazz jam in order to discipline the spectator into the appropriate performance of listening. Likewise, symbolist theater took the intense introspectiveness of the movement's texts—as well as the theatrical codes of proper reading, reaction, and discourse described by Frantisek Deak—and attempted to translate them into effective public events, events that would emulate the individual act of reading on a mass scale. Needless to say, this was an arduous process, a process acutely represented in Deak's work on symbolist theater. The result was a complicated transformational logic that she feels is typical of most avant-gardes:

Historically, the development [of the techniques to adequately discipline the spectator's perception] moves from a situation in which the audience perceives the production mainly as a realization of particular conceptual, aesthetic, and ideological propositions to a situation in which concepts are experienced through their perceptual properties, but without the loss of a sense of discourse which is fundamental to any avant-garde enterprise. (183)

Likewise, Bebop performance for the public attempted to translate the difficult formal and technical aspects of the music into physically compelling presentational modes. DeVeaux writes that jazz musicians played in the belief that "[i]n the heat of live performance, the boundaries between abstract musical logic and the physical spectacle of entertainment melt away" (75).

The scandalous intersection of composition, community, and communication has proved a perennially hot topic for bourgeois authorities. The symbolists, like vanguard jazz players, were tagged by French authorities as criminal deviants to be carefully monitored. *Deviancy* isn't the most historically grounded term—*decadent* is the preferred one. Virtually a synonym for symbolism, decadence was of a piece with psychological theories of degeneration applied to opium and opiate addicts. Decadence was not just a term that expressed anxiety about a threatening subculture; it expressed fear that the very possibility of historical progress was being undermined. It was defined as "a morbid deviation from the normal human type," to recall the words of drug hawk Benedict Augustin Morel, "transmissible by heredity and subject to progressive deterioration across generations."[98] Morel links cultural hygiene to historical progress—and to anxieties about a new class of knowledge workers produced by capitalism, a class with a disturbing tendency to disrupt the boundaries among class, ethnic, and sexual identities, a tendency it shared with capitalism.

Jon Curtiss has demonstrated that U.S. social policy in the 1950s concerning addiction was linked tropologically to jazz, homosexuality, and communism, each of which represented putatively similar communitarian desires and *outré* styles of communication. "The Addict Psychology" (1957) makes much of the "erotic pleasure" addicts supposedly derived from scratching themselves. It argues that such autoerotic behavior is a sign of "polymorphously perverse" sexuality, which, "[l]ike the 'cool' jazz solos with which it is popularly associated, . . . seldom reaches a climax."[99] Likewise, this author continues, addicts are rather like schizophrenics, who "select other means of expression for their basic [Oedipal] conflicts: Thus, the family constellation and personality of the addict are often not only similar to the schizophrenic's, but they are also similar to those of some members of the American Communist party" (Ibid.). The author of *What We Must Know About Communism* (1958) writes, "It would make any one of us feel queer to know that he was being sized up by a Communist as a target for the Party line" (Ibid.). The problem is that the Communist "does not always advertise his presence; nor, even when he is working with non-Communists in a united front, does he always advertise his mental processes" (Ibid.). The text is laughable only as long as we ignore the fact that aides and ideologues working for McCarthy and the House Un-American Activities Committee took this kind of nonsense seriously. U.S. Senate publications such as the 81st Congress's "Employment of Homosexuals and Other Sex Perverts in Government" (1950) extolled precisely the same logic evinced by these anticommunist Drug War hawks, advising rigorous screening for homosexuals and drug addicts due to their "psychological" affinities to subversive ideologies like pacifism and communism (Ibid.). Julian Beck—an anarcho-pacifist; a bisexual; a lover of jazz and other improvisational, collaborative art forms; a regular consumer of nicotine, alcohol, marijuana, and other drugs; and a Jew—would have found such language hardly humorous at all.

The lunacy of such metaphoric play doesn't need commentary, except to note that it might have been avoided had a more sophisticated understanding of theater and performance (any at all, in fact) been available to the American intelligentsia and political class. What we see in the writings of anticommunists, drug war hawks, aesthetic conservatives, and homophobes is a shared desire to define a stable, identifying principle that would allow the categorization and control of people, communities, and texts that threatened, in one way or another, the status quo because they were "theatrical." The policy papers, editorial columns, and habits of speech reveal that, when the institutions, discourses, social circles, and entertainers of the Establishment purged themselves of dissent and dissenters during the first decade of the Cold War, the cultural Left bifurcated. One wing began the long march through the institutions, a march that, some would argue, left it high and dry in gallery and university. One wing became a theatrical plague.

Artaud asserts that his theater is a fatal, terrible sickness and that his epidemic can never be fully delineated by the authorities; searchers for the cause will always be thrown back onto the shifting ground of metaphor, metonymic "morbid entities," and theatricality: "Although there exists no concept of an actual morbid entity, there are some forms upon which the mind can provisionally agree as characterizing certain phenomena, and it seems that the mind can agree to a plague described in the following manner" (i.e., as an "unprecedented organic upheaval") (19). Artaud's mercurial approach reflects the nature of his object: the Theater of Cruelty, which functions as a kind of sign-always-to-be-deciphered, a hieroglyph that changes like a mutative virus. John D. Lyon has explored the lack of systematicity in Artaud's theater works, and nevertheless notes that "[d]espite the absence of a rigorously defined semiotic or of a lexicon and syntax in which light and sound, space and gesture, rhythm and tone could combine to convey meaning, Artaud's work . . . clearly centers on the problem of the sign."[100]

The compulsion to identify the clear and present danger of aesthetic, sexual, and ideological perversity promotes metaphoric and metonymic invention. The Left was like the improvising jazz musician who circulated freely between formal and informal entertainment and economic scenes. The Left was like the homosexual, never quite appearing like the pervert he or she was, always infecting the behaviors of the straight with lavender suspicion. The Left was the addict, chained to his habit more tenaciously than to his country.

In his work on the policing of gay/lesbian bodies, Lee Edelman has directly addressed this tendency to turn behavioral signs into metonyms of lifestyle and, consequently, into metaphors of identity. The body becomes a sign: "Just as outing works to make visible a dimension of social reality effectively occluded by the assumptions of a heterosexist ideology, so that ideology, throughout the twentieth century, has insisted on the necessity of 'reading' the body as a signifier of sexual orientation."[101] But Edelman problematizes that position, since reading "a vast array of signifiers as evidence of what we now define as 'homosexual' desire" has enabled a dispersal of "perverse signifiers" across the cultural field (732). Edelman argues, in the vein of Judith Butler, that the consequence of such a dispersal is a disruption of the boundaries between straight and gay. However, following the logic of this disruption rigorously, Edelman also demonstrates that the effort to develop visible signs of "deviance" is no less problematic for those attempting to define a community-in-opposition. Thus, Edelman argues against the practice of outing gays and lesbian men who would otherwise keep their identities secret. He points out that outing mimics the efforts by homophobic authority to identify and ostracize the deviant. The signs of community formation are shared by police on both sides of the border.

Heroin, *The Connection*'s most obsessively discussed yet mercurial stage property, can be read as an effort to give some kind of dramatic form to this symbolic border dispute. It is Willis's physical symbol dramatized. And if it is drama, it is drama taken into the deconstructive, emphatic chambers of the jazz jam. Jacques Derrida, in "The Rhetoric of Drugs: An Interview," argues that drugs are many and shifting things: linguistic signifiers, catalysts of experience, commodities, and conceptual objects. They are also inherently destabilizing; like the other unstable "anticoncepts" in his writings (*différance, pharmakon, hymen*), drugs corrode a number of irreconcilable conceptual distinctions basic to the bourgeois sense of order. Thus, the discourses surrounding drug experience and addiction necessarily shoulder a "metaphysical burden and a history which we must never stop questioning."[102] Derrida argues that every effort to control and contain drugs inevitably reverts to masculinist, homophobic fantasies of bodily impermeability, fantasies that foreclose even the merest consideration of more communitarian forms of political organization and communication. The consequences of Drug War are, therefore, profound on both the social and philosophical level. "We have at stake here," Derrida concludes, "no less than the self, consciousness, reason, liberty, the responsible subject, alienation, one's own body or the foreign body, sexual difference, the unconscious, repression or suppression, the different 'parts' of the body, injection, introjection, incorporation (oral or not), the relationship to death (mourning and interiorization), idealization, sublimation, the real and the law, and I could go on" (14).

These issues are absolutely pertinent to avant-garde and scholarly-critical efforts to theorize progressive action in the context of the Sargasso Sea of the Cold War and its aftermath. Derrida's interviewer notes that interest in addiction and the Drug War should be natural to philosophers who share common concepts with addiction studies: dependency, liberty, pleasure, *jouissance* (1). For Derrida, a member of the intellectual class that helped institutionalize the avant-garde among the French intelligentsia, the "modernity" of drug addiction is at least partly rooted in the "intimidatingly intertwined history of the division between public and private" (5), a division that, in avant-garde discourse, has been viewed as a variation on that old saw of avant-garde studies, the distinction between "art" and "everyday life." In the simplest terms,

[d]rugs make us lose any sense of true reality. In the end, it is always, I think, under this charge that the prohibition is declared. We do not object to the drug user's pleasure *per se,* but we cannot abide the fact that his is a pleasure taken in an experience without truth. Pleasure and play (now still as with Plato) are not in themselves condemned unless they are inauthentic and void of truth. (7–8)

For Derrida, this condemnation implicates literature and, more broadly, writing. It also implicates theater, which Derrida fails to note. The War on Drugs, according to Derrida, is a war on pleasure without truth, precisely the damning sin of theater. This condemnation compels society into the unfathomable complexity of constructing laws that are "at once as broadly and as finely tuned as possible," "guided by a concern for the singularity of each individual experience" (10)–which sounds a bit like literary and theater criticism. The drug experience is, to Derrida, an experience that cannot be finally and firmly defined—and that is the source of its threat and the cause of its consistent misrepresentation by scholars, critics, and teachers. Rather, it is necessary to speak of "experiences," plural, "which are qualitatively highly nuanced, occasionally even for the same 'individual,' and which we cannot mention without multiplying qualifications and points of view" (13).

I've come to the point where the sociological insights of Paul E. Willis must be combined with the avant-garde provocations of drug-infused sub-cultures and with the critical insights of Derrida, Scarpetta, and other members of the *Tel Quel* group. If drugs are "physical symbols" for the subversive communities engaged in the War on Drugs, then heroin in *The Connection* is "physically symbolist," a set of performance cues and effects that put the spectator into a frame of theatrical experience in which, much like Moreau's paintings, some will experience bafflement, some insight, and others a complete transformation. In short, the Living Theatre's translation of heroin from mere prop into dramaturgy aims toward the construction of a peculiarly mercurial *social bond,* a social bond that challenges authority through the systematic disruption of conceptual categories, communication practices, and body boundaries.

Though by no means typical, the Living Theatre is emblematic of the possibilities and limitations of its moment. As such, it stands as a significant way station for the pre-World War II avant-garde's exodus into the American counterculture and the Cold War. Within the mercurial community sustained by Malina and Beck, the bohemian subcultures of New York City mingled with the most radical theatrical traditions of the European avant-gardes and engaged the most far-reaching thoughts about the relationship between aesthetic activism and social change. The consequences were explosive; rather like Baudelaire's "intrepid lovers of disorder," Beck and Malina attempted to produce a theatrical experience so grotesquely vast and physically intense that it rendered the sterile historical dreams of Cold War destiny moot. Nothing less than time itself was permanently transformed by *The Connection,* transformed from abstract measure and ideological a priori into a somatically compelling, physically symbolic experience that could be manipulated, disrupted, fractured, and gathered by the Bebop aesthetic. However, having rejected history, having rejected ideological certainty, having rejected language, the Living Theatre placed itself at the fulcrum point between embodied certainty and the anguish of addiction, between the manifestation of the blessed community and permanent exile in the prison house of language.

CASE 2 HAPPENINGS, FLUXUS, AND THE PRODUCTION OF MEMORY

And as in the game wherein the Japanese amuse themselves by filling a porcelain bowl with water and steeping in it little pieces of paper which until then are without character or form, but, the moment they become wet, stretch and twist and take on color and distinctive shape, become flowers or houses or people, solid and recognizable, so in that moment all the flowers in our garden and in M. Swann's park, and the water-lilies on the Vivonne and the good folk of the village and their little dwellings and the parish church and the whole of Combray and its surroundings, taking shape and solidity, sprang into being, town and garden alike, from my cup of tea.

    —Marcel Proust, *A la recherche du temps perdu*

Ambiguity is the manifest imaging of dialectic, the law of dialectics at a standstill. This standstill is utopia and the dialectical image, therefore, dream image. Such an image is afforded by the commodity per se: as fetish. . . . Such an image is the prostitute—seller and sold in one.

    —Walter Benjamin, *The Arcades Project*

3. Bad Memory

Memory, Pleasure, and Cold War Performance

Admittedly, the epigraph and introductory comments on a chapter devoted to the first wave of American performance art and its impact on the paradigm-shattering countercultural movements of the 1960s and 1970s are an odd place to find Proust's teacups and Benjamin's favorite Parisian shopping haunts, the crumbling, irresistibly passé arcades, and the prostitutes he found so irresistibly significant. However, memory, pleasure, accident, and critical creation are vital to any work of performance history and theory, and of particular importance to any work devoted to Happenings and Fluxus, this case study's topics.[1] Proust's novel and Benjamin's critical archaeology of the Paris arcades map an elaborately *reticular* terrain of desire and politics, a terrain that shifts under close inspection, and—most importantly—is quite similar to the one explored by the small community of artists, critics, and audiences that participated in early performance art events in Manhattan and other capitals of the United States, Southeast Asia, Europe, and South America from the early 1950s (with the advent of Yoko Ono's *Lighting Piece,* Anna Halprin's use of everyday actions and tasks in dance, and the untitled event staged by John Cage at Black Mountain College) to 1968, the end of the first wave of what we now call performance art.

There's been little discussion of the relationship between the avant-gardes of late-nineteenth-century France (especially its discourses about the status of progressive movements and radical conceptual systems) and the Cold War's vanguard communities. My discussion of the literary and performance roots of *The Connection* has already established a basic connection between the two. The connection is also in the early performance art community in the United States and—though in more problematic ways—the Black Arts Movement, which I'll discuss in the next chapter. Proust and Benjamin demonstrate in their writings that the past has a way of resurging unexpectedly, bringing with it things not even known to be lost until they were found. In both cases, the advent of a particular kind of consciousness (for Proust, authorship; for Benjamin, a future world of justice and equality impinging on the present) propels the individual into a state of "productive uncertainty," a state in which the crisis of the present ignites a wildfire in a society's "forest of symbols," a wildfire that threatens collective sense of history, individuality, community, or the lines between private and public.

With a similarly keen sense of the potent, productive ambiguities of events, George Maciunas, publisher, performer, and curmudgeonly master of ceremonies for the Fluxus community, attempted to map a genealogy of one particular kind of event: the *art events* favored by the folks with whom he associated. Even if a genealogy of event art includes, as it does in Maciunas's genealogy, only performance and poetry events and excludes or marginalizes the more expansive, collage-like "Happenings," the genealogy will quickly grow unmanageably complex, as is illustrated by the incomplete "Diagram of Historical Development of Fluxus and Other 4 Dimentional [*sic*], Aural, Optic, Olfactory, Epithelial, and Tactile Art Forms." Maciunas was wise enough to understand that any genealogy of art events—even of a single Fluxus performance—is an unfinished work, no matter how persistent, how obsessive the genealogist might be. He admits it on the document itself, on the byline. Events and histories of events have a way of shifting under the proddings of analysis. Every act of remembering is part recovery and part resurgence, both an act of objective historiographical reconstruction and a surprising discovery of pleasure and new memories. As I'll demonstrate, these kinds of events are inseparable from the changing conditions of avant-garde consciousness, the innovative practices of commodity culture, and the social status of the artist during the first half of the Cold War.

This brings me to the central question of this case study: How does one make sense of the Proustian qualities of the Happenings and Fluxus event either as an audience member or as a scholar attempting to approach the event through audience accounts and historical documents? Related to this question is one of more general concern: What is the place of forgetting and of the intensely individual sensation in historical memory and in the critical and historiographical processes by which history is made to reveal its forgotten children?

Maciunas's genealogy can be viewed as a kind of Mercator projection of performance history. Like the map drawn according to Gerardus Mercator's model, the genealogy visually emphasizes certain regions while de-emphasizing others, inflating some parts and condensing others in the interest of rationally eliminating the irregularities caused by representing a multi-

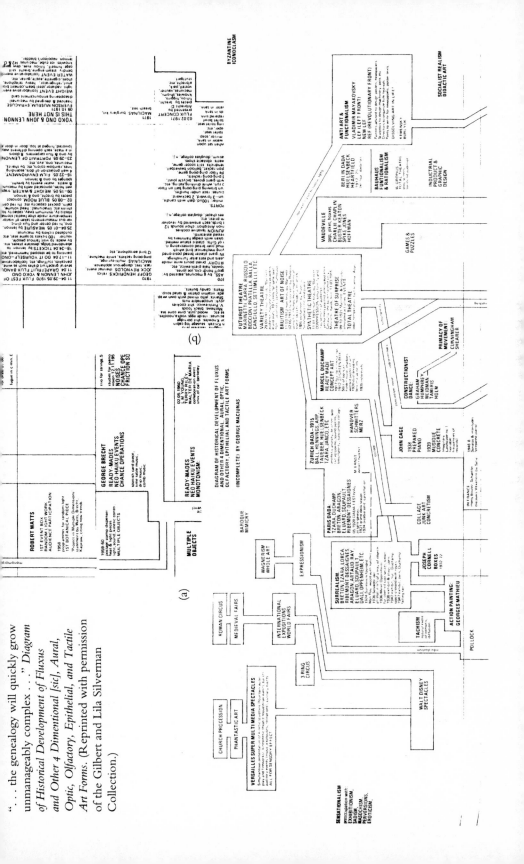

". . . the genealogy will quickly grow unmanageably complex . . ." *Diagram of Historical Development of Fluxus and Other 4 Dimentional [sic], Aural, Optic, Olfactory, Epithelial, and Tactile Art Forms.* (Reprinted with permission of the Gilbert and Lila Silverman Collection.)

dimensional object in only two dimensions. Thus, the history of performance prior to 1948 is compressed into a dense sedimentary layer, so dense
that, according to the map, multimedia spectacles held at Versailles during
the 1700s are more or less coincident with the ill-mannered *serrata* of the
Italian futurists and the almost gaseous "Byzantine Iconoclasm" that blurs
into "Baroque Mimicry." After 1948, things get a bit less dense, more
loamy, a kind of mushroom mulch as opposed to a petroleum-dense condensation of sedimentary rock. They also get a lot more roomy; individual
years are represented up to 1971, each enjoying about the same amount of
space. As a consequence, the odd quirks of pre-1948 are generally not
found. This movement from dense, tangled, unruly beginnings to more linear forms is a typical rhetorical strategy for Maciunas; we find it in his manifesto-advertisement-collage *Fluxiosity,* which I will explore later in this
chapter. Here, it reflects a couple of quirky, but not wholly atypical, avant-
garde notions. First, the performance art community is visually presented as
carrying an enormous historical burden, a characteristic of the avant-garde
first identified by Peter Bürger.[2] Second, the performance art community is
granted a solid, significant place in history—and an expansive one, too
(Yoko Ono and John Lennon's *This Is Not Here* of 1971 takes up almost
twice as much space as the surrealist movement).

In short, the Mercator logic of this performance genealogy reflects an
egoistic vision of history, an articulation that actually *produces* history by way
of the production of the map as an aesthetic event. This productive aesthetic
event is enabled by the multiplicitous choices given to the reader of the
map. To paraphrase Roland Barthes, the map pronounces the death of the
historian and the birth of the historical performer. Let me explain a bit
more, though I'd ask the reader to bear with the density of what follows—
I'll unpack it below: If the performance event is experienced with an eye
toward writing the genealogy of its form, content, and context, and if the
particular event is situated in the genealogical map as a kind of indexical
representation of the experience of the event, then the map can be read and
reread as the reader traces that experience's historical roots, a tracing guided
by his or her sense of relevant routes to trace or absences to note (where is
Yoko Ono in 1955?). The result of this readerly performance is a kind of
reticular, resurgent experience of memory and criticism, a historiographical
performance. This performance is *reticular* in the sense of being highly reticulated, like a paisley stocking, a tree in leaf, the human large intestine, or a
limestone cavern. This performance is full of highly complex linguistic,
conceptual, and affective structures, also full of cul-de-sacs and steep, slick
chutes. It is *resurgent* in the sense that connections occur serendipitously,
suddenly, and sometimes overwhelmingly.

Proust's narrator as a child marveled at this kind of productive, entangling resurgence when he tasted the "exquisite pleasure" of a morsel of *petite madeleine* soaked in linden tea, a toddy given him by his beloved mother to warm him on a cold day (41). But at the time he didn't recognize the resurgence as such—the event had manifested its past, but not consciousness of the relationship between event and history. Only years later, as an ambitious young novelist equipped with an aesthetic philosophy and a persistent writer's block, does he remember it. Proust's grown-up narrator drinks tea and cake once more as an adult and recalls, this time intentionally and with a tricked-out aesthetic philosophy, that oddly doubled moment in his mother's kitchen. In a moment of spontaneous composition, the narrator experiences a vertiginous convergence of the present with his multiple, refractory pasts. He suddenly realizes that the intense pleasure he experienced with his mother was due to a sudden, but unconscious, resurgence into his child's memory of the visits he had paid a few years earlier to the village of Combray and his grandmother, who fed him a similar treat.

This is the emblematic moment in Proust's novel, an unfurling of morsels, memories, and mothers—and the revitalization of the author's desire for writing. The narrator, lost in a momentary but voluptuous fragmenting and gathering up of the self, thrills at how the cake brings to life a past that had not existed, paradoxically, until it had been remembered in a moment of *glottal* pleasure, a moment that brings together the intimate spaces of the mouth and the public spaces of family, town, and shop. Like Maciunas when confronted with Fluxus events that were little more than the lighting of a match, the brushing of teeth, the eating of a tuna fish sandwich with a glass of buttermilk, asking for a friend's name, Proust's narrator is inspired to begin the meticulous, painstaking work of articulating the world in which the voluptuous thrills of the glottal had occurred. In other words, he begins writing.

Maciunas begins mapping, the critic tracing. The sound of dripping liquid in George Brecht's *Drip Music* (1959) can be traced to La Monte Young's *Long Tones* of 1957; to the vaudeville antics of Charlie Chaplin, Buster Keaton, and Spike Jones; to the tradition of games and puzzles; also to Berlin Dada, Bauhaus functionalism, industrial design, and the radical left-wing aesthetic weapons of Vladimir Mayakovsky. There's a kind of stoned staggering prompted by Maciunas's map; one gets caught up in details and odd cul-de-sacs (like Ben Vautier's readymades of 1959—signs, walls, war, continents, peace, words, famine, noise, end of world—and of 1960—illness, epidemics, death). Like the regular user of pot, the map remembers poorly; it's incomplete, often in ways uncomplimentary to Maciunas. (Where, once again, is Yoko Ono, who more or less invented the trademark Fluxus "event score" in 1955?) But that's to be expected; history in this region of the avant-garde succumbs to prejudice, bias, and oversight (accidental or otherwise).[3]

Compare these tightly reticular moments in Proust's novel and Maciunas's genealogy to George Brecht's Fluxus event score:

> *Tea Event*
> Preparing
> Empty Vessel
>   (1961)

Despite its textual minimalism, *Tea Event* is a baroque monstrosity when it comes to performance. Typical of most Fluxus scores, *Tea Event* is textually brief and, to use an oxymoron, *precisely imprecise*. One of the names Brecht called these kinds of texts was "performance haiku," and that can help us understand the underlying principles of these highly performative texts. Like haiku, the event score captures

> a sense of spontaneity in the act of composition, particularly in regards to the objects and processes represented by the text;
> careful selection of terms/signifiers so to enable a large number of interpretive choices on the part of the reader/performer;
> a blurring of the distinction between reading and performing ("preparing" can be the reading of the text, an "empty vessel" a written word);
> thus, an invitation to enactment, to the inevitable self-differentiation of the singular event of reading.[4]

I'm not interested in close-reading *Tea Event* or in specifying some authoritative connection between the event of "tea" (or of a "tea-ness" that doesn't necessarily have anything to do with leaves and water but plenty to do with awareness) and the performance elements named so "precisely imprecisely" in the text. Rather, I want to understand how to comprehend this event in its fullest sociohistorical and political significance. We might speculate, with the genealogical humor of Maciunas in mind, that Brecht is attempting to produce a textual version of Proust's teacake, the tasting of which will reveal, in an almost psychedelic moment of splintering completeness, the *event* of being, its self-differentiation from other events, other beings, and from the background noise and haze of postindustrial civilization. The tea that is prepared doesn't even need to be tea: it can be the preparation of consciousness, for example, the preparation of consciousness of vessels and emptiness, the preparation for a material substance that is, as in the Japanese tea service, incidental.

On the face of it, *Tea Event* has no real sociohistorical significance when compared to, say, the Blue Blouse troupe of the Russian Revolution; very few people outside of art and performance history have heard of Fluxus, let alone this specific work by this specific author. Granted, a good many people outside these fields have heard of Yoko Ono and know she does "weird" artistic things. But the event form itself doesn't invite significance in the ways that great "works" do, works like Picasso's *Guernica* or the original production of Hansberry's *Raisin in the Sun* that seek to make manifest their historical moment.

The question is partly about *value*. Hundreds of Fluxus events were composed by the "members" of this loosely aggregated association of nattily dressed intermedia artists; and hundreds more, "in the spirit of Fluxus," have been composed by my own students during the past several years as I've used the deceptively simple event genre to help them bridge the gap between historical and ethical understanding of the avant-garde. They pretty much fulfill the logic first identified by Marcel Duchamp, the inventor of the readymade: unless readymades are produced with great reluctance, they'll simply become a boring bit of aesthetic *shtick*. They're pretty easy to do, almost frustratingly so; any undergraduate can put together at least one spirited Fluxus event or pull off an interesting, fully committed performance of a Fluxus event score.

And that's precisely where things get complicated. The moment that value is undermined, history shivers apart. Like the movement itself, any Fluxus score such as *Tea Event* has both a history and a living, social existence as a text-always-being-read. Brecht believed that the performance of such events began with the very reading of the text—thus, a cluster of performances, of events, surround this spot in my own text (a congealed mass made up of my own readings of *Tea Event,* the readings of the event and my text by this book's readers, etc.). And such clusterings extend back to the event's compositional moment, itself a revisionary glance at the Japanese tea ceremony. Such clustered readings are characteristic, of course, of any text; all texts are a gathering up of readings and rereadings, every novel or poem or throwaway magazine is a tightly furled performance history. But not too many people really thought about such things before Fluxus came along, and few have really exploited their possibilities. And that's where things not only get complicated, they begin to get significant, too.

The banal miracle of Proust's soggy little cookie, the lighting of a match in a Fluxus performance, or Vautier's aestheticized illness is not to be found in the fact that they are so thoroughly possessed by the past, so soaked in memory. The notion that objects possess traces of persons and past events is an old and common one in many, if not all, cultures. But the madeleine is no haunted heirloom, it's no unsanctified bone whose owner wanders the boundaries of the village, it's no treasure guarded by cobras, no shard of a broken sword. It's a commonplace (a piece of a commonplace, actually); its riches are discovered completely by accident in banality, completely unintentionally, as if a thin crust of earth had suddenly fallen away under the narrator's feet and deposited him in the foyer of some damp, glittering limestone cavern. In his mind? Or in the world? Proust problematizes this distinction: Memories exist in the world. Despite having repeatedly passed the trays of little fluted cakes in the windows of bakeshops throughout Paris, despite having struggled interminably to remember his past and inaugurate the writing of his blocked novel, it is only when the narrator serendipitously falls into his past that the writing can begin. There is an animism to Proust's novel that is fairly sympathetic to the kind of work done by performance scholars, critics, and teachers.

Quite a cake! The past, the present, and voluptuous consciousness bloom like paper flowers in a porcelain bowl. And if not for a whim, the tea-and-cookie event might not have occurred at all. In the insomniac hours of early morning, when he struggled intentionally to remember the contours of Combray, the narrator could see "no more of it than this sort of luminous panel, sharply defined against a vague and shadowy background" (46). His efforts to remember foundered on the sensory limits of voluntary memory, "the memory of the intellect," when it attempts to recapture the qualities of a performative moment (47). It is utter serendipity (a word coined by Horace Walpole during the early days of bourgeois liberal society) that the indescribably soft morsel of cake dissolves on his tongue and a glittering grotto of involuntary memory opens itself to the writer's exploration.

Proust's novel—and this is the philosophical edge that would prove so sharp to writers like Benjamin and Beckett—gives preeminence to accident and to the priority of individual subjectivity in the recovery of a fully conscious and richly experiential time. "There is a large element of chance in these matters," Proust writes, "and a second chance occurrence, that of our own death, often prevents us from awaiting for any length of time the favors of the first" (47). The favors of the first—the inaugural sensory moment when the madeleine is first tasted, when the event is first experienced, but not as such—lie dormant, awaiting the accident of rebirth, the performative reiteration that establishes the memory itself, the chance meeting of the lover and the beloved. Proust doesn't mention the third occurrence in this passage: the adult's experience of a more replete, voluptuous consciousness and the inauguration of the act of writing. Nor does he mention the fourth: the reader's. Early American performance art was dominated by emphasis on accident, most likely due to the fact that it was a significant and energizing theme in John Cage's composition courses at the New School for Social Research as well as the various public lectures he delivered during the middle 1950s.

An interesting fact to be found on one of the many insignificant genealogical branches of Fluxus history not included in Maciunas's genealogy: When my students perform Fluxus events, invariably there are a number of them (roughly three out of twenty) who will choose to "perform" their own pasts, remembering some moment of their lives as if they had suddenly become their own spectator and their past been transformed into art. Fluxus performance is, for a few students, an act of remembrance and a potent invitation to writing. It's also profoundly annoying to some (about the same ratio, three of twenty), an endless inside joke that is just as endlessly boring. Those people are right, too. Fluxus is boring, and not always dangerously so.[5]

The ornately reticulated descriptions of Combray, the Parisian salon hierarchies, and the ambivalent passions of M. Swann are always, in *A la recherche perdu, grotesque* and in the apocryphal etymological sense of the term *grotesque:* "like a grotto," glittering, deeply shaded, gothic, suggesting shapes and analogies unavailable to the observer expecting the clean, functional lines of the factory or the book. The human figure, its languages, collections of souvenirs, and its dwellings are exquisitely distorted by the pressures of desire, power, and forgetting as they congeal in the singularity of performance, the conceptual black hole of the event. This baroque, densely reticulated deflection of perception can be perceived in the long sentences of Proust's novel. Those long, circuitous sentences mark the author's struggle to steer writing between the spirals of quasi-surrealist mad love (emblematized by Swann's masochistic devotion to the eternal coquette Odette, the fetishism of Charlus, by the crinoline femme fatale Albertine) and the stable, monumental, romantic lines of Hugo-esque realism (emblematized by the narrator's grandmother who, rather like the realistic novelist, sits at her window and observes, organizing everything within her gaze and her gossip's ear). Wavering between the decadent and the romantic-realistic, the ideological moorings of Proust's novel suffer erosion, sagging into involuntary memory. History turns into a paper flower or a limestone cavern, reticulated so densely as to challenge our ability to map its contours.

Brecht's event score is far more minimalist in form than Proust's novel.

The grottoes are there in the textual signifiers, certainly, but there are bigger surprises to be discovered in the event's performance history, in the variations of *Tea Event,* a history that extends to this very moment, the moment of this chapter's reading. The burden of Proust's novel is description; of Brecht's event the insatiable possibilities of performance. Maciunas's genealogy of event art proves to be a lot more unfinished than we might have thought at first.

The performance historian, confronted with the records and critiques of early American performance art, may find himself in sudden sympathy with Proust's narrator and think about turning to novel writing. Nowhere is this sympathy more strongly felt than when we begin to examine one of the signal events in the development of the Cold War avant-garde, Allan Kaprow's *Eighteen Happenings in Six Parts* (1959), a performance event that had its audience divided into three distinct groups and escorted to small rooms walled by floor-to-ceiling semitransparent panels made out of pine and plastic sheeting. At specified moments during the performance, the audiences would be moved from one section of the Reubens Gallery into another, where they would experience a different, if no less baffling, concatenation of sensory events. Though fragmentation of this kind is a well-worn modernist technique (going back to cabaret and futurist *serrata*), never before had the capacity to perceive the fragmented work of art as a whole been denied to the perceiver. Hannah Höch's collages cause unease, fitful laughter, perhaps occasional flashbacks, but they are small affairs physically—their frames are right there; these are little pictures. Pollock's twenty-foot-long splatter paintings challenge our ability to take them all in at once, push us toward dance, but ultimately they are paintings (one can explore at one's leisure any particular detail or overarching color-theme in the work), and it is no great feat to trace the edges of the grandiose canvas, even if it's tucked behind the wooden understructure.

Kaprow's viewer-spectator is displaced from spectatorial authority—he or she can't tell where the boundaries of the event are to be found. Don't the street noises penetrating the walls count as active elements in such performances? Don't sudden associations in the memory of the spectator? A cramp in the foot? Thoughts about a dying aunt? They all do, for better and worse. All synoptic perspective is lost by the spectator in a moment of grotesque, interactive, discursively unmanageable complexity. The individual's experience of *Eighteen Happenings* was inevitably partial, accidental, unverifiable. Just as the realistic novelist's love of the apposite detail was both revived and mortified by Proust's mad love for tea cakes and idealized women, transformed by Proust from the vehicle of ideological communication to the very end of writing, so had dialogue, props, and action been transformed by Kaprow into the ends of the performance event, so many exits from history. With *Eighteen Happenings,* the Copernican revolution in theater finally arrived on American shores. Not only had narrative structure been abandoned (a perennial trend in modern theater), but the coherence of the spectacle itself. At one blow both narrative structure and the centrality of the spectator was destroyed. Pushed from center to margin, the spectator was no longer the center of the universe. Worst of all, he couldn't tell anybody how it happened.

Bad Memory and Performance Historiography

Only one other avant-garde movement of the time went so far as to deny even the spectator his role in the comprehension and critique of theatrical events. A few years later, this same avant-garde, the Situationist International, launched an attack on the Happenings, evidence of the uncomfortable sharing of formal principles by ideologically distinct avant-garde subcultures. In Kaprow's event, none of the audience (including the author himself, who was also a "viewer-participant" in the rehearsed but aleatory event) could attain an overarching perspective of the event as a whole. Distracted by, say, a toy robot buzzing jerkily by her foot or the sudden mental association stimulated by a line of dialogue, the viewer found herself enmeshed in spirals of intention and accident. The elements of the theater no longer cohered in any orderly, rational fashion; everything was a morsel awaiting a beloved tongue.

The consequences of Kaprow's splintered, splintering event and its nomadic audience have been profound for both experimental performance and the work of performance scholarship. The luminous, tautly stretched plastic panels that structured the gallery's performance space, panels that were gradually covered by the opaque paint applied by a performer hiding on the other side or obscured by the sudden movement of a performer or prop, is the very figure of memory's fragmentation and performance history's breakdown. This becomes clear to us when we move away from memory aids like the script and production notes assembled by Michael Kirby in his groundbreaking anthology of Happenings;[6] that is to say, when we move beyond scholarly accounts of the performance that suggest a totality that was unavailable to the viewer-participants. Unlike personal accounts of Happenings and Fluxus events, which are inevitably partial, bemused, silly, even a touch bored at times, such totalizing accounts inevitably possess a goal of objective, totalizing description actively undermined by the event itself. Unlike such totalizing accounts, personal accounts of Kaprow's event demonstrate that a basic quality of all performance arts—their inability to be taken in all at once—is a formal, perhaps even ethical principle of the Happening or the Fluxus event. Occurring at a moment when Broadway and off-Broadway were dominated by realism and its well-made plots, *Eighteen Happenings in Six Parts* suggested that a basic capacity of narrative to make sense of history, interpersonal relations, work, play, had suddenly shorted out, a result of poor design and ineffective maintenance. History—that passionately loved myth of the avant-garde—entered the realm of the Proustian involuntary memory in the works of artists with such distinct formal, ethical, and ideological perspectives as Kaprow, Maciunas, and Brecht.

We can begin to understand the self-conscious significance of such complexity in the Happenings and Fluxus movements by looking at nontotalizing accounts by artists and their viewer-participants and taking seriously their meanderings. Kaprow himself understood the importance of such nontotalizing perspectives, unwaveringly avoiding broad theoretical generalizations when discussing his art. He once described the Happenings as "the myth of an art that is nearly unknown and, for all practical purposes, unknowable."[7] This unknowability is not the consequence of willed ignorance or egoistical gamesmanship; rather, unknowability is the insurmountable complexity of the event and a catalyst for discovery.

How did this kind of supersaturated "unknowability" in Happenings and Fluxus help shape and direct the counterculture and its splintering aftermath, so-called postmodernity? Or if we're less interested in the postmodern, then we can consider a more local question: what is the place of these kinds of events in the genealogy of the avant-garde as it maneuvered through its own death and became a generalized phenomenon of Western society?

In order to understand the peculiar, chaotic, critically petulant oppositionality of the event-art movement that developed in the shared margins of experimental painting and theater in Manhattan during the late 1950s and 1960s, we must understand how the phenomenological processes of remembering and forgetting were exploited by such events. Later, I will take a more economics-oriented approach to "being unknowable" in order to show how early performance art was aided and abetted by a politicization of memory within an American capitalist culture that was intensively marketing its products even as it was being undermined by productive developments inside itself (specifically, a looming environmental crisis, the advent of the leaner, meaner capitalist systems of Germany and Japan, and the beginnings of the high-tech revolution). Benjamin will be our guide in that part.

By considering the ways Happenings and Fluxus events challenge memory and critical judgment and open the Proustian dimensions of theatrical experience and theater criticism, we will be able to place the event-art movement within a genealogy of antitextualist, avant-garde performance that includes the likes of Alfred Jarry and Jacques Vaché; Elsa von Freytag-Loringhoven, Arthur Cravan, and Johannes Baader on the margins of Dada and surrealism; Neal Cassady among the Beats and the counterculture; Andy Kaufmann; and other artists of everyday life and small-time scandal known and unknown, studied or understudied. Such artists courted rebellion but refused any but the most ambiguous and shifting presence within the precincts of literary history, effectively exploding it by dragging it down into the eccentric, egoistic depths of the Warhol "superstar." These artists of everyday life challenged simultaneously the commodity status of art and the discursive economies of art and theater criticism and scholarship that Mann discusses in *The Theory Death of the Avant-Garde*. Like Freytag-Loringhoven and her compatriots, the event-art community made only fitful alliances with the literary text, traditional avenues of art and theater criticism, and the existing network of art dealers and buyers, preferring instead the more difficult, challenging, potentially damaging paths of the underground artist. Most event artists considered text, criticism, and the artistic commodity as just the pretext for more performance, which they viewed as a much more significant, social, and far less hierarchical form of social and artistic production. The formally and theoretically distinct work of Kaprow, Maciunas, Brecht, Claes Oldenburg, Emmett Williams, Jim Dine, Allison Knowles, Jill Johnston, and others compelled a similarly pleasurable, often ironic failure of memory and logical coherence, a falling away of reason into the grottoes of subjectivity.

Memory and coherence are the sine qua non of scholarship; thus, their failure cannot and should not be ignored (or glibly avoided) by the critic, scholar, and teacher. The avant-garde may suffer a theory death, to recall Mann again, but the critic is no better off. Happenings and Fluxus mark the limits of a certain kind of history of the avant-garde: a history that depends on a unitary text, shared critical standards, agreed-upon methodology, and linear models of history. Memory was both disrupted and goaded by the fragmented, decentered structure of the antitextual, spectacular Happenings and the intensely associative, pun-saturated texts and small-scale performances of Fluxus. Thus, no survey, no synopsis, either of the event-art movement as a whole or of individual events, is really possible or desirable. Faced with such events, the critic suddenly discovers that his office shares a wall with Proust's cork-lined writing room—or even more astonishingly, finds that office recorded in an infrequently traveled cul-de-sac in Maciunas's labyrinthine genealogy.

In his memoir of life in New York's East Village during the 1960s, *The Motion of Light on Water,* science-fiction writer Samuel Delaney describes his own experience as a "participant-member" in Kaprow's *Eighteen Happenings in Six Parts,* the event—part theater, part collage, part Dadaist provocation, part thought-experiment—that introduced the term *happening* into the American cultural stream. "The only truly clear memory I have of the performance proper," Delaney writes, "was that I wasn't very sure when, exactly, it began."[8] Delaney does remember, if less precisely, the tiny loft (recently become the "Reubens Gallery") divided into three distinct chambers by mostly opaque pine and plastic flats. He remembers a windup toy robot chattering and clicking around the floor and spends a few lines exploring its qualities. Most significantly, he remembers his unsatisfied desire to know what was going on on the other side of the flats. Typical of most Happenings, the performative gestures and stage properties of Kaprow's piece were not linked together in any logical or even systematically illogical way. They moved and transformed, as Kirby was to describe them a few years later, in an "a-logical" way.[9] Even though most of the Happenings were rehearsed and planned with great care, in the moment of performance, many things tended to "just happen" without conscious intention, and many of these without being noticed by the majority of attendants. As in Proust, the favors of experience and reminiscence are granted capriciously. Such favors can't be earned; they are discovered by accident, and only some will ever be discovered; even fewer will be incorporated into an act of textual memorialization as Proust's madeleine is.

There is a lot that doesn't make it into Delaney's account that one might find in other accounts—persons marching rigidly in single file, the malfunctioning slide show, the violins and ukuleles played badly, the fractured dialogue of two women muffled by the flats—but that is to be expected. Delaney might not have known they were there. As we recall, Kaprow split the audience up so that no spectator could achieve a synoptic perspective on the piece; moreover, he cluttered each "part" of the happening with a unique hodgepodge of sound and lighting effects, nonsensical gestures, and incongruous stage properties—all of which were prone to the improvisations and accidents of the performance. Delaney's rather fetishistic focus on the little robot couldn't be helped; one of the necessary effects of Kaprow's particular variety of Happenings is the pressure it put on the viewer's ability to organize, narrate, and, above all, to remember objectively.

Such "bad" or Proustian memory was not, however, intended to debilitate its audience (as was the case in the futurist *serratas*). As a devoted student of the pragmatic philosopher and educational theorist John Dewey, Kaprow for one viewed the decentering of the aesthetic experience and the individualization of history to be a vital corollary of his libertarian vision of the avant-garde, an opening of history to the kind of unfurling hyperdevelopment seen in Maciunas's genealogy. And in fact it could prove enormously empowering to individual expression and criticism. Delaney uses his poor memory of Kaprow's piece and his expertise in postmodernist theory to vitalize his understanding of his individual place as a gay writer within the complex dynamic of capitalism, memory, and the Greenwich Village community of the late 1950s.

Spinning and riffing off his memory of Kaprow's event—perhaps more like a jazz musician, a participant in a surrealist game of "Exquisite Corpse," or a Barthesian hedonist than a Proustian isolate—Delaney informs us that in 1956, two years before Kaprow's event, white-collar workers in the United States exceeded in number both blue-collar and agricultural workers combined, signaling a shift in the class structure of American culture and supplying a first indicator of the advent of a so-called postindustrial era (183) (I will return to Delaney's inflationary account later in this chapter). Though he does not specify how inflated milk prices and mass-transit tokens were related to his inability to criticize or remember Kaprow's Happening properly, he insists on their connection, relying on simple rhetorical conjunction to support his assertion. Recalling his feelings about the event, he writes,

I, of course, had expected the "six parts" to be chronologically successive, like acts in a play or parts in a novel—not spatially deployed, separate, and simultaneous, like rooms in a hotel or galleries in a museum. I'd expected a unified theatrical audience before some temporally bounded theatrical whole. But it was precisely in this subversion of expectations about the "proper" aesthetic employment of time, space, presence, absence, wholeness, and fragmentation, as well as the general locatability of "what happens," that made Kaprow's work signify: his happenings— clicking toys, burning candles, pounded drums, or whatever—were organized in that initial work very much like historical events. (189)

Likewise, the audience was organized very much like the massed but isolated individual of the Cold War, but experienced history more like the bourgeoisie of the nineteenth century experienced economic development, as a "giant international gambling house, where the bourgeois wins and loses capital in consequence of events which remain unknown to him."[10] The texture of Kaprow's Happening as a whole—if we still insist on total-izing perspectives—is actually an aggregate of the individual responses and partial views of the audience, an audience that includes ourselves, historians and critics five decades after the fact. These early manifestations of perfor-mance art function as a theatrical version of what Roland Barthes would, in 1968, call the "writerly" text, the text that foregrounds the desires of a reader invested with genuine authority to create and roam. Like the writerly text, Happenings and Fluxus events allowed themselves to be altered and reconfigured by the spectator, to be "put forth as a force" in the world.[11]

The individual elements and memories of Delaney's particular experi-ence in the audience behave as if they, like common commodities such as milk and tokens, had been subjected to a felt but ineffable inflationary pres-sure, as if words, gestures, and windup toys were transmogrifying, expand-ing under pressure of some deep and unsuspected shift in the cultural weather systems of self, community, and history. To adequately analyze a particular Happening, one would have to understand, among other factors, the particular community of participant-members that were in attendance and the glottal pleasures of personal remembrance.[12]

Like milk and subway tokens, the signifiers and acts of signification in Kaprow's Happening were torn from the associations that commonly sur-rounded them, were torn from their traditional conceptual and experiential matrices of subjectivity, sociality, and tradition, from the commonly held information structures of memory and value that are commonly known as "plot," "character," and "moral." Divorced—or "dematrixed," to use Michael Kirby's useful term[13]—from their traditional context by the aes-thetic hiatus of performance, a toy robot's connotative meanings (child-hood, ingenuity, science-fiction B-movies, automation, and the deluge of personal meanings possible) could be set wandering like displaced laborers, a few of which migrated close to Samuel Delaney and were critically "rein-vested" in a book about Greenwich Village, the 1960s, and Samuel Delaney published many years later (and discovered by myself some years after that, read and reread, returned to during revisions for this chapter, etc.).

Returning once more to an insignificant branch of Maciunas's geneal-ogy: it has been my experience that students, when they understand the elaborate series of accidents and intentions that led them to reading about and performing Happenings and Fluxus events, are flatly astonished and immediately conscious of the freedom this gives them to create their own events. The difficulty they face afterward is to understand how such freedom is anchored to the concrete elements and rhythms of performance in context. (I will return to this concern below in my discussion of Happenings and Fluxus as a "mode of production.")

Delaney understands this anchoring of freedom and object, and, therefore, I do not want to forget the generally positive implications of Delaney's critical performance as member-participant of Kaprow's Happening, nor how his experience dovetails with Barthes's description of the empowered reader, nor how his autobiography functions as a kind of reinvested memory. Nevertheless, I also don't want us to forget that the politics—the embodied and critical experience of self, community, and history—of the Happenings and Fluxus movements were inseparably tangled with the alienating, repressive dynamics of American capitalism in the late 1950s, to a larger feeling of hopelessness experienced by many Americans (not least of which were the left-leaning participants in the event-art movement), and to the dawning of a revolution in communication, social management, and production in the 1960s that Thomas Frank has appropriately named "The Conquest of Cool."[14] Empowered as Delaney and his fellow spectator-participants might have been in some regards, they faced the same kinds of conceptual difficulties most people experience within late capitalist culture, dominated as it is by the unprecedented dynamic of ignorance and forgetting sponsored by the culture industry and the capacity of capitalism to absorb concepts and practices of cultural opposition.

This puts the critic into a difficult position: How does one describe the dynamic ambiguity of the performative event without delving into self-serving, egoistical explorations of one's own subjectivity? How does one respond to intensely complex but highly determined events like these in a way that makes sense of the interrelationships of subjectivity and larger, more "objective" trends in economy and culture? I think that, even granting the Proustian effects of event art and the trapdoors of commodity culture, the critic may still effectively pursue the goal described by Susan Sontag in *Against Interpretation:* "[T]he aim of all commentary on art now should be to make works of art—and, by analogy, our own experience—more, rather than less, real to us. The function of criticism should be to show *how it is what it is,* even *that it is what it is,* rather than to show *what it means.*"[15] In the present case, though, showing how something like a Happening *is* is tantamount to abandoning interpretation altogether and simply indicating the mobile, voluptuous gaps performance opens in self and society. Making a Happening or Fluxus event more real is like jumping into a limestone grotto with a handful of matches.

Lighting Event
Light a match and watch it till it goes out
Yoko Ono (1955)

Delaney's experience of Kaprow's Happening was the consequence of an unpredictable dynamic of intensity and absence, of perception flashing for a moment, then flashing out, leaving only smoke. The intensity of personal experience (the proximity of objects, performers, sound sources, the involuntary personal associations stimulated by the various happenings) is inseparable from the intentionally structured absences in the event (the inability of the audience to see what is going on on the other side of the plastic barriers, the audible audience reactions and other sounds).

How does one make sense of such a thing either as an audience member or as a historian attempting to understand the event through the lens of audience accounts, historical documents, and critical theory? What is the place of forgetting and of the intensely individual sensation in historical memory and in the critical and historiographical processes by which history is made to admit its forgotten children?

These questions are not rhetorical; we must understand the anti-intellectual qualities of early performance art not simply as the consequence of an encrypted mysticism (as was the case with the international symbolist movement of the fin de siècle), but as evidence of a particular community's efforts to give value to a broader range of concerns, to reveal how fundamental to the experience and definition of culture such concerns were, how they served as an attenuated bulwark against the high-pressure, dehumanizing pressures of the Cold War. Though the ephemerality of performance is often the bane of performance historians, sometimes it is the necessary antidote to performance history.

Text and the Performance of Memory

Before moving into these broader concerns, though, I want to spend some time discussing the textual component of event art. In my account thus far, the text has served as something of a scapegoat, a fairly traditional role played by text in recent performance theory. But the Proustian qualities of performance history are not only discovered in performance, in the "behavioral situations" left behind in the inevitably reductionist, linear accounts of the events textualized by even well-meaning individuals such as Delaney and Kirby. They can also be discovered in the documents and textual objects left behind. Emmett Williams's *Let It Not Be Forgot* is a sodden, del-

" Don't let it be forgot
That there was once a spot
For one brief, shining moment
Called ~~Camelot~~."
FLUXUS

". . . a sodden, delicately flavored morsel of history, a paper flower waiting for its bowl." Emmett Williams, *Don't Let It Be Forgot.* (Reprinted with permission of the artist.)

icately flavored morsel of history, a paper flower waiting for its bowl. Like the performances themselves, documents such as Williams's possess a peculiar power to both disrupt and stimulate memory. In the case of the texts left to us by Fluxus artists such as Williams—who was always conscious of the inevitability of forgetting and the importance of letting personal concerns outweigh political ones—this power is simultaneously exploited and preserved. Thus, our readings of Fluxus texts empower and surprise the reader in a fashion Barthes would have appreciated.

The complex interconnections of intentional misremembering, avantgarde performance, and the text are exemplified by Williams's fascinating bit of graffito. It can be found on the Internet, downloaded, printed, and taped to the wall next to one's desk. In its original form, the graffito isn't all that impressive: a small sheet of paper with a machine-printed poem and a handwritten correction at its bottom. But when we examine the performative reading dynamic sponsored by the piece, we discover not only something significant about early performance art, but also something about ourselves (not in any humanist sense; rather, "ourselves" in the Proustian, personal sense) and the function of criticism. The thing's a virus, unfurling histories and associations like lines of useless computer code.

Williams is perhaps known best for his 1961 event *Duet for Performer and Audience:*

Performer waits silently on stage for audible reaction from audience which he imitates.

A very silly, fun, even spooky event, as student performers have shown me over the years. Williams is also remembered for his 1962 event *For La Monte Young:*

Performer asks if La Monte Young is in the audience.

Like these two events, events that rely on a close relation of artist and audience (or the recognition of the *lack* of relation) in the production of an essentially social aesthetic experience, *Let It Not Be Forgot* inspires an experience that is highly personal while remaining resolutely public, a characteristic virtue of text as a material object. Any laser-printed duplicate of Williams's little paean to the golden age of post–World War II American performance still retains this capacity to fascinate, to draw its reader into a reverie on history, performance, myth, and memory. It accomplishes this by defacing one of the more pernicious utopian myths of recent American history (the Kennedy "Camelot") with a highly personal, even petulant, mark or trace—the monument to the brutality of kitsch is marked with graffiti. Appropriating the myth of Camelot—what one might call the "Kennedy commodity"—Williams defaces it, at once undermining its monumentality and inflating the significance of his community's presence in the early 1960s. Williams's graffito is a historiographical and critical act of vandalism in perfect accord with the spirit of countercultural event art: it is a highly performative, petulant meditation on the relationship of memory, events, and texts.

A kind of performance disguising as documentary evidence, Williams's text compels its reader to perform the relationship of memory, valuable/antique commodity, and text. It presses us to abandon the clarity of concept and theory in favor of more personal forms of consideration similar to those that the performers, composers, and audiences of the original Happenings and Fluxus events attempted to inspire and experience.

Such nontraditional, but highly charged ways of conceiving the relationship of art and individual were put to effective use by Allison Knowles's Fluxus event *Proposition* ("Make a Salad," 1962); in that case, in the energetic if quiet dynamic of habitual actions (cutting greens for a salad), situated cravings (no radishes tonight, please, I had them for lunch), social concern (but does *she* want radishes?), brute necessity (if I don't eat soon, I'll suffer pangs), and dematrixed action (the quiet of the act itself that, if entered completely, may cause us to ignore realities such as the burning lasagna and the hushed conversation in the other room). By placing domestic labor and the banal pleasures of so-called private life literally at center stage, Knowles challenges our notions of both artistic significance and interior experience, deconstructing the lines between private and public. "Center stage" can be considered in its traditional sense (an actual brick-and-mortar structure) or in a more radical sense (the home as a place of performance, self-consciousness, and empowering sharing)—either way, the implications of *Proposition* are critically fruitful. Like Williams's act of vandalism, Knowles's proposition allows the situation of the performer to serve as a lever against critical assumptions concerning artistic excellence, aesthetic analysis, and timelessness.

Such nontraditional ways of conceiving performance often functioned effectively within and against specific readings of event-art texts, allowing the relations among the artists to serve as fodder for situational, performative criticism of the artistic community itself. Such criticism occurred in a performance of John Cage's *Music Walk*. Unlike the original 1958 performance, which featured Cage and David Tudor, the 1962 performance at the Manhattan YM-YWHA featured a "dancer," Jill Johnston. Cage characterized the piece as "a composition indeterminate of its performance." Johnston describes the performance as a high point in her career as a performer.[16] *Music Walk*, in this case modified into *Music Walk with Dancer*, was performed according to an arrangement of ten graphs whose randomly generated intersections determined the sounds and actions that would be performed in some fashion by the performers. Thus, as with Kaprow's *Eighteen Happenings, Music Walk with Dancer* exploited accident. Johnston recalls that she left her script at home (her stack of cards accidentally fell in a puddle on the way to the event, ruining them and forcing her to improvise). Rather than sticking to what she remembered about the script—in which she was to "do a slight dance action on stage, slow and vampy (wearing heels, a floppy hat, and red dress)"—she "went mainly as a Mother" (93).

Sometimes, accidents work out very well—it's easy to imagine Johnston's reaction to Cage's sexist directions and her relief when her script was ruined. As she puts it, she "took the 'life-art' equation seriously then." She writes, "I was a critic moonlighting as a mother of two small children, or vice versa. I chose a number of sound-action implements that I moved around my apartment every day: a frying pan and bacon, a Savarin coffee can, a broom, a baby bottle with brush, a pull-toy, vacuum cleaner, etc" (93). Surprisingly, her improvisations annoyed the usually equanimous Cage: "[A]fterwards, Cage reprimanded me for not 'giving up my ego,' meaning acting on my own, by choice, according to my likes and preferences [which, I assume that Cage assumed, involved vamping in high heels]. But of course, the carload of household equipment I brought with me, like his pianos and radios, already indicated plenty about choices we had made in our lives, whether 'preferences' or not" (94).

By insisting on the critical significance of her autobiographical experience (an increasingly important political gesture for women as the 1960s progressed) as fundamentally more important than any preexisting communicative or aesthetic structure and by exploiting the opportunities for critical performance in the script and the performance context, Johnston forced the event to answer to her needs, to her situation, to her own memories. What this demonstrates is that the accident of association need not simply be a response to pleasure or the unfolding of a previously unremembered element of subjectivity (as in Proust), but may be explicitly critical and oriented toward social concerns. Johnston utilized the potentially reticular structure of the event-art form against itself, ironically reminding Cage that despite the fact that certain artists and certain audiences were no longer making essential distinctions between art and nonart activities, the relations between art and nonart were no less in need of continued interrogation. In short, Johnston demonstrates that the line between art and life must be continually examined and continually subverted, and event art is especially good at promoting such continuity. As Kaprow wrote in "The Education of the Un-Artist, Part I," "The art-not-art dialectic is essential."[17]

As Johnston's critical opening of Cage's supposedly open-structured textual graphs suggests, the textual components of early performance art are essentially unstable and continually available for critical resituating. But unlike most texts, the textual remains of event art compel us to *perform* that instability and interrogation, compel us to spatialize and temporalize our readings, make them a part of the genealogy of event art. Because they compel a deconstruction of the distinctions between artist and audience, expert and amateur, public and private, the peculiar, hitherto private desires and fantasies (not to mention the personal politics) of the critic are invited onto the field of criticism.

Performance and Fetishism

However, it would be improper to separate the highly subjective aspects of early American performance art and these supposedly more "social" dimensions. That said, to bring the two together requires that we delve into dimensions of critical thought that are downright perverse. Claes Olden burg demonstrates one way that such individualistic—but also socially minded—criticism might function. Ruminating on the objects produced during the performances he staged at the Ray Gun Mfg Co, Oldenburg decided to call them "Love objects. respect objects. Objectivity high state of feeling."[18] As he diddled about his combination small business-gallery-performance space after his performances were over, he pondered the objects he had made and was suddenly responsible for, the "subordinated pieces which may be isolated, souvenirs, residual objects" (110). And he reminded himself that he must "be very careful about what is to be discarded and what still survives by itself. Slow study & respect for small things . . . Picking up after is creative" (110). The artist becomes his own scholar—like Benjamin's prostitutes, "seller and sold in one." Though the subjective opens space and time, it opens within the objective constraints of economy. Such constraints may be weakened, attenuated, or undermined by such openings, by the clustering categorical "holes" opened in the social by event art.

Oldenburg modeled a form of critically productive and productively critical activity explicitly linked to fetishism, both the sexual and commodity varieties. His personal desires and situation impact the ways he makes sense of the dynamic of performance, text, and prop. The results of the impact are densely anecdotal, taste-oriented, noninterpretive forms of critical consideration. They are synthetic, not analytic. Like the gloppy, glottal objects and language produced at Ray Gun, the text becomes a "love object," a "respect object"—a souvenir. Just as "Ray Gun" inverts "Nug Yar" (an infantile, glottal pronunciation of "New York"), the objects produced during performances at the factory were in-between things, half-chewed, slimy, fascinating. Performance, for Oldenburg, was a productive *social* process despite its flirtation with individualistic monomania. Chew toys left on the stage of history, crumbs on a saucer.

Performance was, in a sense, a genealogical event at Ray Gun as well as an act of critical self-analysis and gloppy, viscous self-expression. The art object that results from the event (say, a script or a Day-Glo ice-cream cone) turns out to be a highly unstable amalgam of commodity, memory, and critical-historiographical statement. The objects produced by these kinds of performative events compel new production of compelling objects in a highly subjective version of capitalist production, where commodities become raw material for other commodities and so on, each production step obliterating the previous one while opening new forms of individualistic pleasure. Take for example, a sculpture of an ice-cream cone; for Oldenburg, it is a combination text/art object/fetish that allows for a diverse variety of productive readerly performances:

> There is first the ice-cream cone as it is. This would be one imitation.
> Then begins a series of parallel representations which are not the ice-
> cream cone but nevertheless realistic or objective: f. ex. the ice-cream
> cone in a newspaper ad. The ice-cream cone or any other popular shape
> as a fetish object. The ice-cream cone in altered scale (giant). The ice-
> cream cone as a symbol etc. Only the created object—my parallel
> cone—will include and/or concentrate several of these. (48)

Such an ice-cream cone, as the objective, partly digested remainder of a
specific performance at Oldenburg's studio, is a complex condensation of
multiple meanings, emotions, histories, economies, and memories, at once
a script, a stage property, and a souvenir. Oldenburg's hope was that such
souvenirs would somehow retain the fundamentally "organic and psychological" (52) qualities of their production context. For Oldenburg, the art
event was a liberated production zone that the artist opened in the rifts
between the standardized, characterless objects of consumer culture and the
deeply contextual gesture of the hand, the mouth, the reticular genealogy,
the Proustian memory.

Such discomfiting, overly intimate, narratively unmanageable, but distinctly social entanglements of text, memory, and desire were aimed at by
Ben Vautier in his *Audience Variation No. 1* (date unknown):

> The audience is all tied up together using a long string. Performers in the
> aisles use balls of string, throwing string over the heads of the audience to
> opposite rows of performers. Balls are thrown until all the string is used
> up in creating a dense web over the audience. Enough string must be
> used to entangle the whole audience, tying them to each other, to their
> chairs, etc., making it difficult for them to leave. After this has been
> achieved, the performers leave the hall. The audience is left to untangle
> itself.

Like the participant-members of Vautier's event (an event that recalls futurist experiments with audience discomfort but lacks futurist antagonism
toward the audience), historical study of early performance art is inevitably
tangled up with an unruly, singular, but undeniably social hodgepodge of
competing interests, microscopic turf wars, and absent artists—many of
these exerting insistent pressures on scholarship. True, whatever perspective
can be shed on any experience of performance will be inevitably partial—
this is critical common sense among performance scholars and theorists. But
such partiality is more than simply a by-product of scholarly representation,

more than simply a lack to be acknowledged; rather, it is a formal principle of Happenings and Fluxus event art, a principle verging on the ethical.

Like the toy burro one might purchase on the rim of the Grand Canyon, any criticism of Vautier's event experiences the pressure to move into something personal, partial, petulant. Vautier seems to intend this; the significance of *Audience Variation* is precious, partial, perhaps too personal to be widely significant or *theoretical,* if by *theoretical* we mean some sort of generally exchangeable conceptual discourse that both describes and unveils the object it addresses. If there is a theory to be retrieved from the event, it is more a kind of souvenir of the performative moment or evidence of a genealogical branching that can serve as a key into, or a brief flash of light upon, other events.

Performance theory, here, shares a property line with a slovenly neighbor: the engineered obsolescence of the Cold War commodity. As Vautier's *Audience Variation* demonstrates, the more fragmented, alogical manifestations of early American performance art pressed their viewers to abandon the kinds of narrative and formal assumptions that operated within the mainstream; by extension, critics were and are pressed to abandon the historiographical, formal, and analytical procedures dominant in academia in favor of essentially anecdotal forms of "bad memory" or essentially partial and ephemeral varieties of theoretical consideration. The critic becomes, like Proust, a fetishist, a spelunker of the personal, plumbing the penumbral contours of memory's grotto, a grotto that goes on and on and on. But he does what he does tangled with others. There is no license for rugged individualism here; rather, individualism is pressed into play with the impersonal structures of language, economy, and politics.

This is not just true of performance. As W. B. Worthen reminds us, we must continually interrogate distinctions between text and performance in order to avoid facile generalizations.[19] Williams's *Let It Be Forgot,* like virtually all Fluxus and Happenings scripts and scores (and all the memoirs and treatises surrounding them), presses us into performative processes. In short, the text here is a fetish, manifestation of private pleasure negotiating public structures. Like Williams's text, event scores by Knowles or Brecht or Vautier are destructured by the text/performance distinction. Whatever stability can be discovered (through theater-historiographical research) or theorized around one pole of the binary is inevitably undermined by the other; likewise, whatever instability can be theorized or historicized will be inevitably stabilized around the other pole. Much like the crisis in memory and narrative sponsored by *Eighteen Happenings in Six Parts,* these event scores and textual souvenirs function like categorical crises in miniature.

They are memorially resurgent souvenirs of an event of social production lost in various ways to memory and analysis, objective correlatives of bad memory that demand performance and new events—new productions. The texts that have survived such events are purposefully tangled in myth, memory, and the scholar's own desires. And if they are not tangled, then the criticism is indecorous and off target, has lost track of the socially productive aspect of performance. The scholarly work of untangling the various meanings and chance meetings of the event should lead to more tangles: surprise coincidences, accidents that are disconcerting, perhaps seductive, chance events that need not be the intent of the artist (who has, after all, long since left the building). In any case, memories of the events and readings of the scripts should be hopelessly tangled in stuff that isn't supposed to make it into criticism and historiography (the bad breath of the stranger tied to one's leg, boredom, the hit-and-run spat with a spouse the event has somehow caused). If the critic ignores such aleatory materials, he will be missing the very spirit of the event.

More importantly, the critic will lose sight of a crucial aspect of performance as an avant-garde mode of the counterculture: economic antagonism/innovation. Returning to Williams's graffito, what is happening in that defaced text is complicated in terms of content (the historical references and emotional cues that saturate the piece, many of which are more or less "lost" to contemporary scholarship), form (its banal objecthood, its kitschiness, its apparent lack of artistic "seriousness," its simplicity, its nostalgia), the demands and authority it invests in the reader/performer (the lack of "instructions" as to how the thing is to be made meaningful, made to happen), and its value as an art object. Because it is a kitschy commodity, a trace of graffiti, and a valuable treasure, Williams's text threatens to break down the very narrative machine of history and criticism. It places at stake the very notion of value. What constitutes the value of such texts? This question is relevant both to the economics of art (i.e., the thing's worth to collectors, publishers, etc.) and to pedagogy (i.e., the thing's place in various classroom canons). But there may be a larger significance here concerning how value is generated and how we can pursue a genealogy of values.

The textual object is, like Benjamin's prostitutes, both seller and sold in one. As such, it subverts logic, linear notions of history, and value; it is "dialectics at a standstill." Williams's paean to the "golden age" of American Cold War politics and performance is a text and an occasion for a Happening, for a range of productive activities that conform to, subvert, and expand the processes of value production that support the larger mode of production in which we exist. As the spike heel functions for a certain breed of "pervert," Williams's text serves as a screen. I'm tempted to compare it to the luminous panels upon which Proust's narrator viewed the images from his magic lantern, a symbol of his blocked memory and writing—upon which the conflicting memories of trauma, production, and pleasure that constitute the matrix of self, community, and history are formally, if temporarily, resolved. Or the phantasmagoria that fascinated Benjamin. By compelling us into bad memory, involuntary associations, and petulance, Happenings and Fluxus events restore the full complexity of the exchange process, a process that, as Jean-Joseph Goux has thoroughly demonstrated, demands the systematic erasure of the full complexity of production itself, a process that involves not simply the creation of objects, but the creation of subjects and history itself and the systematic indifferentiation of matter and situation:

> The opposition between money and commodities (and, more generally, between the universal equivalent and its relative forms) pertains to all the philosophical oppositions that permeate the discourse of Western civilization: particular and universal, contingent and necessary, multiple and synthetic, terrestrial and heavenly, profane and divine, real and ideal, subordinated and sovereign, relative and absolute.[20]

Though I am discomfited by Goux's totalizing, occasionally loose historiography, his point is well taken and his audacity inspiring. It is precisely within this opposition of universal (money, concepts, canons) and relative values (usefulness, matter, situations, personal favorites) that a crisis can be described and, potentially, generalized. And as Goux argues, such a generalization impacts our very understandings of history, subjectivity, and communication.

As fetishes themselves or as events that sponsor the production of fetishes, Happenings and Fluxus events (whether past performances or present readings) catalyze such crises, which may explain their relative lack of worth in art and literary history. As Naomi Schor demonstrates, fetishes are both realistic and fantastic—they are, in short, phantasmagoric resolutions of the individual's desires and the social structures in which those desires are satisfied; recalling Goux, they are resolutions of the opposition of universal and specific. "Accurate in every detail," Schor writes, "[they] paradoxically conserve apparently indifferent events, while contemporaneous events of great importance . . . go seemingly unremembered, unrecorded."[21] For the fetishist confronted simultaneously with irrecoverable loss and, more importantly, the self-consciousness of productive power, the moment of confrontation with loss and power is often so intense that any attempt to narrate it is bound to failure. As a result, that which is lost is replaced by a precious souvenir, an object that helps the individual maintain the source of pleasure while simultaneously consigning it to a mythologized past in a pathological or touristic gesture of historicization. In other words, the memory is both retained and obliterated. As Susan Stewart puts it, "The souvenir seeks distance (the exotic in time and space), but it does so in order to transform and collapse distance into proximity to, or approximation with, the self. The souvenir therefore contracts the world in order to expand the personal."[22]

Can criticism make sense of such a thing? Or is criticism consigned to suffer the fate described by Roland Barthes in "From Work to Text"—to become a simple mediator of more or less interesting associations, filiations, and readerly meanderings?[23] If the avant-garde, in pursuit of its most radically democratic implications, becomes a general phenomenon, then what else would we expect to occur to the critic? The critic, as I've demonstrated, is a concern of the avant-garde. The success of the avant-garde depends on the failure of a contained kind of criticism. And such a failure is prompted by the various formal, experiential, and analytical blockages of the entire artistic production, circulation, and consumption process.

The vehicle for the generalization of the avant-garde project (i.e., the structure of that total process) will vary from one avant-garde subculture to another. For the Living Theatre, the pacifist-anarchist community spread like an addictive drug, relying on the covert, subversive circulation and consumption rituals specific to the jazz and heroin subcultures. For Larry Neal, the Black revolution would circulate through the existing folkways of the African American community, through the closed circuit of the jazz jam, the storefront church, the speaking of poetry in public. For the Happenings and Fluxus community, the generalization of the avant-garde would be catalyzed by bad memory and artistic overproduction.

The scripts and memoirs surrounding event art are oddly melancholy souvenirs, objects that invoke memory and inspire aesthetic production. Like the exquisitely sculpted shoe or scent, the script and scholarly account of early American performance art are, as Laura Mulvey has described the fetish, "always haunted by the fragility of the mechanisms that sustain it."[24] Thus, the event script, for example, can function as a thing of inflated value, a "memorial, marking the point of lack (for which it both masks and substitutes). . . . It is in this sense that the fetish [i.e., the textual component of event art] fails to lose touch with its original traumatic real and continues to refer back to the moment in time to which it bears witness, to its own historical dimension" (11).

The thing about these art events that makes them so fascinating—and so useful for all kinds of dissident performance in a postmodern era—is that they are a textual form of "bad memory" that is always available for new performances, morsels for the beloved's tongue. As scripts they continually allow the reader-performer to reconfigure the past for present purposes. As commodities that can be easily produced, reproduced, altered, and transmitted; they circulate freely and freely sponsor new fetishisms, new entanglements, the production of souvenirs, the falling into of grottoes. Like the clownish artist in Jim Dine's *The Smiling Workman* (1961) who drank from his can of paint before plunging through the text he had just painted, the critic of early performance art must necessarily interrogate the line between art and life in their own situation, plunge through text into very specific, local, "glottal" performances.

By intentionally challenging our ability to remember performance and mythologize the past while pressing us into various kinds of productive dynamics, this kind of American event art of the 1950s and 1960s compels us to use the signifiers and significatory activities of commodity culture as stage properties in our own critical improvisations, our own scholarly and teacherly Happenings. As John Cage explained to Richard Schechner and Kirby, "I think of past literature as material rather than as art. There are oodles of people who are going to think of the past as a museum and be faithful to it, but that's not my attitude. Now as material it can be put together with other things. They could be things that don't connect . . . as we conventionally understand it."[25] Art events—whether Happenings, Fluxus—are the myth of an art form that compels us away from the past and into our own localities, our own unknowables.

A productive, enticing, reticular gap exists in our ability to know event art; that much I think is clear. The politics and economics of these kinds of events highlight the politics of memory in late-capitalist culture; the materiality of the event, the desires of the moment are left behind like a well-thumbed promptbook, the sweat of a line-worker, a dirty spoon, burned-out match, placenta. The result of this alienation, oddly enough, is a strange kind of liberty for the events and their participant-members, a peculiarly unalienated existence in the wilds of historical memory and theory that is distinct from other vanguard movements of the 1960s. As Kristine Stiles has demonstrated, while political groups that shared theoretical ground with the communities that produced, criticized, and consumed Happenings and Fluxus—most notably the Situationist International—have seen their work virtually canonized by cultural studies, the supposedly less political Happenings and Fluxus events "remain outside critical discussion despite these artists' effort to create an aesthetic strategy that would *insert* their aims into the discourses of art and its history."[26] The entangled, situational, grotesque qualities of these art events remain unalienated by the academic industries of criticism and historiography. "Bad memory" marks the politics of event art as a politics of memory and aesthetic overproduction, a politics that works against academic commodification of performative dissidence.

4. The Avant-Garde Disappears

The Poverty of Performance Art

It is worth recalling—if with a healthy dose of irony—the criticism leveled at the Happenings by the now-canonized Situationist International, the ultravanguard that instigated the dematrixing of intellectual capital and the mass participation of Parisian students and workers during the events of 1968. In "The Avant-Garde of Presence," the SI argued that "the happening is an attempt to construct a situation . . . on a foundation of poverty. . . . In contrast, the situation defined by the SI can be constructed only on a foundation of material and spiritual riches."[27] The SI's specific concern is, ironically enough, the question of banalization and academic commodification of the participatory ventures of their own revolutionary activity and theory: "When these people draw on our theses in order to finally speak of some new problem (after having suppressed it as long as they could), they inevitably banalize it, eradicating its violence and its connection with the general subversion, defusing it and subjecting it to academic dissection or worse" (109). Though the SI does sympathize with the Happenings' utilization of memorially irrecoverable and theoretically problematic devices ("People urge us to present trivial projects that would be useful and convincing [and why should we be interested in convincing them?]; but if we were to oblige them they would immediately turn these projects against us" [110]), they find the retention of the "antiquated" distinction between art and life utterly despicable. Rather than superseding the idea of culture as a separate sphere, the Happenings maintain it, ensuring political and critical failure and, far worse, boredom. The criticism is right on the mark.

While early American performance art may have been founded on a basis of ideological "poverty," it is nonetheless true that Routledge has recently released a precise new edition of *Society of the Spectacle*. Meanwhile, despite the publication of Mariellen Sandford's excellent sourcebook, *Happenings and Other Acts* (Routledge, 1996), the original Happenings and Fluxus events remain strangely absent from our scene except as potential. Theory and script—like all commodities—can only tease us with memories of community and pleasure. Our absence from the events themselves ensure that such art events remain, to recall Kaprow once more, "the myth of an art that is nearly unknown and, for all practical purposes, unknowable."

That said, I do not wish to indulge my own Proustian associations, my own fetishistic pleasures, at the expense of politics. Nor do I wish to overestimate the political implications of the work of Kaprow, Maciunas, Knowles, Ono, and their colleagues. To write about the avant-garde without dealing explicitly and concretely with political struggle, however local and small-scale such struggle should prove to be, is to lose sight of the avant-garde's single most important legacy and responsibility. Certainly, autobiography and the hedonistic critical style of the late Barthes can result in insightful, significant critical work. But I prefer, instead, to map the gap across which traditional criticism cannot go without suffering the reticular deformations of bad memory and aesthetic overproduction. Happenings, Fluxus—these mark the boundaries of a distinct social and aesthetic logic, a situated solution to the conceptual and practical dilemmas of avant-garde activity during the Cold War. Just as the Living Theatre, in their production of *The Connection,* was able to dislocate critical judgment and enable a revised humanism through the use of jazz and Artaudian cruelty and thereby avoid the "critical gaze" of the Eulogist School, the fluid, nomadic communities that produced the earliest forms of American performance art also moved beyond the horizons of a certain form of historiography and criticism. Thus, Happenings and Fluxus fulfill one of the basic functions of any avant-garde movement: to transform concepts and practices of time and social production by introducing innovative performative modes into the dominant forms of production, circulation, and consumption of cultural goods.

To further specify the particular modes of performativity enabled by Happenings and Fluxus, we will leave the cork-lined room of Proust and walk slowly into the penumbral light of Benjamin's arcade. "Seller and sold in one"—Benjamin's prostitutes share much with performer-producers such as Oldenburg, Dine, Ono, Vautier, or Maciunas, who often made of the acts of producing, circulating, and purchasing art themes of the art object or art performance itself. To comprehend the ways that the highly ambivalent intermixing of accident, obsession, and opposition that constitutes the Proustian dimensions of Happenings and Fluxus can be considered as more than simply an individualistic, discursive form of play, we need to understand how such voluptuously confusing modes of temporal antagonism relate to the larger economic and cultural contexts in which these events occurred and continue to occur.

One place to start is with Friedrich Engels and Karl Marx: "The bourgeoisie," they write, "historically, has played a most revolutionary part."[28] The genius of *The Communist Manifesto*'s opening analytical move is its reminder to the European proletariat that revolutionary practice is not only available to the dispossessed, to the working class. The proletariat is lagging behind, in fact; it is their turn to take on the role of vanguard and take their place on the world-historical stage. Revolution, the manifesto demonstrates, is a complex process of borrowing, appropriation, destruction, and reconstruction enabled by shifts in the technology and social significance of production, circulation, and consumption. As the Marxists have it, the struggle of the working class is the struggle—a brutal, violent military struggle, but also a conceptual and critical one—to dematrix the productive potential of their own community and the productive technologies of their day and utilize them for full and liberating self-development. This is where revolutionary struggle intersects with the history of the avant-garde: appropriation of the means of production and development.

As was all too apparent to Engels and Marx, certain revolutionary communities could create unprecedented forms of oppression and alienation by dominating the processes of production and development in the spirit of self-interest. As they put it, "For exploitation, veiled by religious and political illusions, [the bourgeoisie] has substituted naked, shameless, direct, brutal exploitation" (15). But if we grant that certain revolutionary communities can create new techniques and disciplines for the exploitation of other communities, then it follows that such new forms will also inevitably result in new tactics of resistance, revolt, and critical inversion. This resistant, revolutionary, inversional criticism is the core of dialectical materialism. As Engels and Marx—as history itself—has demonstrated, the conservative tendencies of capitalist development can lead to unexpectedly radical results, particularly when those tendencies are appropriated and diverted by the disempowered for the disempowered.

Not unoften, the agents of such appropriation and diversion are from the oppressor's class or from classes whose place in the socioeconomic hierarchy is far from stable. Utopian-minded industrial designers and urban planners, rogue industrialists, style-mongers, chic bohemians, and class-abdicating intellectuals have repeatedly played a significant role in the unraveling of the fabric of tradition as they searched for new sources, techniques, and concepts of profit. This despite their lack of stable position within the social structure. The vanguard factions of the bourgeoisie and its marginalia often contest not only the techniques but also the social and political significance of production and consumption. These vanguard factions cannot be said to simply "oppose" or "promote" capitalism, bureaucracy, and brutality; rather they are the seedbed from which grow *both* liberating production techniques and the disciplinary methods that can harness those techniques for profit.

Until only about three decades ago, economically oriented radical movements such as communism and socialism have tended to have little patience with such avant-gardes (and equally little with the politics of everyday life), favoring instead the military model of vanguard leadership and an essentialist notion of revolutionary subjectivity. But beginning in the sixties, the Marxist assumption that alongside the technological development of capitalism would come an essential, ethical subject of history and an adequate form of critical thought began to prove profoundly problematic. Culture began to be viewed as more than simply propaganda, more than simply a local perturbation of universal history. Among many radicals, Henri Lefebvre's *Critique of Everyday Life* (volume 1, 1947) would prove decisive in the interest paid to the world outside the factory, to the world "off the clock."[29] Lefebvre's book was evidence of a general turn toward the theory of alienation, the critical construction of cultural experience, and toward a rethinking of the strategies and tactics of progressive transformation. As Lefebvre demonstrated, economics had for too long failed to take account of productive practices beyond factory and finance, thereby losing crucial ground to the anticapitalist struggle. Marxism, therefore, had to engage everyday life if it was to claim the status of critical theory. Lefebvre was not the only one to recognize this necessity. Betty Friedan defined the terrain of feminist resistance and criticism as the terrain of everyday life; particularly, the cluttered but empty homes of the American middle class, homes in which alienation opened up gaps, moments of discontinuity that feminist theory would enrich. Larry Neal celebrated the street culture of African American, urban neighborhoods as the core of any progressive movement in the African American community and founded a critical epistemology on that street culture's relationships to West African philosophy and aesthetics.

Fredric Jameson, attempting to dialectically assess this increasing focus by radical writers and movements on the world outside the factory, asserts that the rise of such locally minded, left-wing social groupings and the advent of an experiential, localized critique of political economy were the parcel of a capitalist system that had grown increasingly flexible, increasingly intrusive, and increasingly capable of fragmenting class solidarity among the increasingly numerous disempowered. For Jameson, the rise of new social movements during the 1960s and the theoretical turn of criticism after 1968 are inextricable from—though not entirely determined by—the ubiquity of advertisement, the exfoliation of smaller and smaller niche markets, the political and economic demands of colonized peoples, and the spectacular crisis management of decentralized capitalism. The maintenance of the system, Jameson argues, has demanded new forms of representation with which to shape consciousness. These new forms of social control have deeply problematized critical practice of all kinds while at the same time supplying it with a varied collection of oppositional tactics. Much like contemporary capitalist transformation, the techniques of resistance and analysis now extend "into the farthest reaches of the globe as well as the most minute configurations of local institutions."[30] I will return to Jameson's argument below in my discussion of Happenings and Fluxus as a mode of production.

In the meantime, I will attempt to complement my discussion of the subjective, Proustian aspects of early performance art with a more economically oriented analysis of the formal principles of Happening and Fluxus. Such an analysis will be no less troubled by the aporias of desire, memory, and crisis, which is why the work of Walter Benjamin will play a significant role. My aim is to understand how the unknowability of this avant-garde trend was related to the decade-long growth cycle of American capitalism prior to the social crisis of 1968 and the economic crisis of 1973. My assumption is that it was indeed related and that exploring such a relationship will teach us much about the nature of our socioeconomic system, particularly the way that postmodern capitalism depends upon highly individualized, subjective forms of aesthetic production and aestheticized exchange. To make sense of this mutual dependency of economy and aesthetics, I will explore the various ways that Happenings and Fluxus events articulated a highly mobile form of institutional critique (namely, of the increasingly bureaucratized Manhattan gallery system), artistic production and reception in a commodity-oriented art scene, and the concrete experiences of a particular community of vanguard artists that was at once alienated from and enriched by transformative capitalism. The reticular subjective experience of early American performance art will prove to be just as tangled and mercurial when criticism moves beyond the subjective into the putatively more objective level of economic history.

At the same time as I describe these reticularly aestheticized economic events, I will attempt to deconstruct the binary terms that are conventionally used to describe the relationship between avant-garde artistic production and capitalist commodification. Unlike the Situationist International, which in 1962 expelled members committed to the production of artistic works in order that the remaining core might liberate political practice from the realm of art-as-object and performance-as-spectacle, the artists and audiences of the Happenings and Fluxus events ironically embraced object and appearance in order to, if you will, "jam" the cultural logic of commodity production and circulation.[31] In this sense, they suggest an aesthetic version of the flexible control-and-command regime of accumulation that is commonly known as "post-Fordism." Some Happenings—*Eighteen Happenings* or Carolee Schneeman's *Meat Joy* (Judson Church, 1964) for example—seem almost like allegories of postmodernizing capitalism; they are highly productive, decentered landscapes of self-determining objects and flows of desire that are beyond the control of a single, central composer-director while always, ultimately, "owned" by that composer-director (thus, the continued presence of "Kaprow," "Schneeman," and "Vostell" in the stories we tell about Happenings), while remaining firmly beyond the comprehension of any single spectator, including the composer-director. This highly reticular, but incredibly productive aesthetic-economic landscape is the territory walked by Walter Benjamin's prostitutes, they who are both seller and sold, who add value and are value, who transform themselves in order to expand the spectator's titillation and multiply the opportunities for fluid, personal, petulant exchanges. The relationship between the avant-garde and capitalism in such a landscape is full of ambiguity, disguise, and mercenary flirtation.

The Vanguard in Disguise

Benjamin quotes a French writer explaining the rapid rise in the number of Parisian prostitutes in the 1830s:

> That the number of *filles publiques* at first seems very great is owing to a sort of phantasmagoria produced by the comings and goings of these women along a routine circuit, which has the effect of multiplying them to infinity. . . . Adding to this illusion is the fact that, on a single evening, the *fille publique* very often sports multiple disguises. With an eye just the least bit practiced, it is easy to convince oneself that the woman who at eight o'clock is dressed in a rich and elegant outfit is the same who appears as a cheap *grisette* at nine, and who will show herself at ten in a peasant dress. It is this way at all points in the capital to which prostitutes are habitually drawn.[32]

There seem to more of them than there really are; in actuality, it is not the number of prostitutes that is growing but the potential customers, attracted by the ever more varied, voluptuous range of objectified desires for rent. It's not the artists but the aesthetic itself that becomes expert at the theatrical quick change during the 1950s and 1960s, expanding its "market demographic," attracting more and more consumers to a more and more competitive artistic marketplace.

Seller and sold in one. The artist as commodity has long been a commonplace in American society, the creature of the Theatrical Syndicate of Charles Frohman, the Hollywood studio-system publicity mill, and the cult of personality. Significant to the project of performance history, such artistic commodities have tended to be a performer of some sort: a stage or film actor, a dancer, minstrel artist, singer or musician. But on occasion even a vanguard painter could achieve the celebrity of a Cary Grant or Bette Davis. Salvador Dalí and Picasso were among the first mass-market avant-gardists, featured as they were repeatedly in the middlebrow publications of Henry Luce. Warhol comes to mind as the apotheosis (though by no means the originator) of this brand of artist-commodity, actively collecting evidence of his own status as a valuable object. But is the artist-as-commodity the same thing as the artist-as-artwork, that other, far less popular form of aestheticized self-alienation? Alfred Jarry, Jacques Vaché, Elsa von Freytag-Loringhoven, Arthur Cravan, Johannes Baader, Neal Cassady, and Andy Kaufmann can be counted among the small community of artists who devoted themselves primarily to the construction of public personae and who paid an enormous price for their intensely individualistic, underground aesthetic existence. The artist-as-artwork should be considered distinct from the artist-as-commodity; otherwise, crucial historiographical, theoretical, and pedagogical elements of their work will be lost. If the artist-as-commodity courted celebrity in order to obtain visibility as such, the artist-as-artwork courted celebrity in order to advertise his or her own disappearance.

The two modes of the public artist—as suffering producer of art and as an embodied, petted, scandalous commodity—crossed circuits in the 1960s with the arrival on the scene of Happenings, Fluxus, and other "neo-Dadaist" artists and trends. The consequence of this crossing is a mode of performativity that enabled the mass marketing of the avant-garde concept. Like the Campbell's soup can in one's kitchen after one first sees Warhol's screen prints, Happenings and Fluxus events dematrix everyday life, rendering it into something *uncanny,* both familiar and unfamiliar, a fetish that is both sexual and economic in nature. The artist becomes, by virtue of the new status of the artist and the generalization of the techniques of artistic defamiliarization, simultaneously common as commercials while retaining the mysterious, occasionally threatening character of a von Freytag-Loringhoven or a Kaufmann. The artist-as-social-role became available to the general public in the 1950s and 1960s. This role is best described as a highly mobile performative mode that functions only in a widely dispersed production-circulation-consumption. The artist becomes both seller and sold in a fundamentally aestheticized economy.

Benjamin writes, "Ambiguity is the manifest imaging of dialectic, the law of dialectics at a standstill. This standstill is utopia and the dialectical image, therefore, dream image. Such an image is afforded by the commodity per se: as fetish."[33] As I hope to demonstrate in the following pages, the shifting role and social status of the artist in the 1950s and 1960s were coincident with a more widespread sensibility produced when older forms of social control were destroyed by American capitalism after 1945. Such destruction felt liberating, certainly, but also brought with it new kinds of uncertainty, paranoia, distressing cravings, self-doubts, and the like—exactly the kinds of ambiguities I have already described in the Proustian half of this case study. Such political ambivalence is at the heart of a new form of social practice and community organization developing by vanguard sectors of the counterculture. This innovative, performative mode was at once dispersed and innovatively productive and was less about freedom than about new, more profitable forms of social alliance, communication, and cooperation. Because of its general refusal of traditional elements of left-wing and art-historical criticism, these events are saturated with contradiction and resolutely incapable of supplying stable critical standards or clear representations of that most cherished of vanguard myths: the generalized movement into a substantially better future. History—one fundamental concern of the avant-garde—slows to a halt for the vanguard communities of the early U.S. performance art scene, overburdened by baggage and garbage.

The rhetorical slippage, aesthetic dispersal, and productive innovation of the Happenings and Fluxus communities make it difficult to firmly and finally define the critical edge of early performance art vis-à-vis capitalism—a characteristic that still holds true in broad segments of performance art since the 1960s; consider the odd phenomenon of Laurie Anderson and the Talking Heads during the 1980s. Focusing on everyday activity, antinarrativity, and destructive consumption, Happenings and Fluxus events seem to perfectly embody the kind of practical and conceptual innovation needed by an expanding, niche-seeking capitalist system. On the other hand, Happenings and Fluxus are not simply the dupes of transformative capitalism.

They model a critical, performative strategy that, limited in its effects as it may have been, enabled a form of community and communication that engaged and diverted the exploitative demands of an intensive capitalist market. In fact, given the presence of such significant figures as Kate Millett in the Fluxus group,[34] it can be reasonably argued (as Katie O'Dell has done) that the Happenings supplied much of value to feminism, queer liberation, and other social movements of the late 1960s.[35]

Andreas Huyssen affords a useful perspective on this kind of volatile ambivalence. As he demonstrates in *After the Great Divide,* the American avant-garde of the 1950s and 1960s "was up against bigger odds than futurism, Dada, or surrealism were in their time. The earlier avant-garde was confronted with the culture industry in its stage of inception, while postmodernism had to face a technologically and economically fully developed media culture which had mastered the high art of integrating, diffusing, and marketing even the most serious challenges."[36] It is in this highly ambivalent context that Claes Oldenburg's assertion that, in the early 1960s, "one could be anti-bourgeois by being bourgeois" finds resonance.[37] What outfit does the artist wear? What costume will afford the most customers? Does this explain all the narrow ties and sensible shoes we see in photographs of Happenings and Fluxperformances? How many artists are out there? What exactly is it that is being purchased?

In one door, out the other, never the same outfit twice—there is a necessary, dynamic, and performative relationship of capitalist development to the vanguard producers, middlemen, and consumers of the avant-garde. In his essay "Modernism and Mass Culture," which I will refer to throughout the rest of this chapter, Thomas Crow maps the origins and development of this performative relationship, beginning with a particular community of aesthetic producers, namely the early modernist painters, especially the ones with bad reputations, one of the first coherent avant-garde subcultures. According to Crow, the historical origins of a fully developed aesthetic vanguardism can be traced to the moment when the French middle classes divested themselves of political power during the crisis years of 1848–52. The takeover by Louis Bonaparte signaled not only the rise of a "law and order" regime uncannily similar to the Cold War United States, but also the start of a long-term political, psychological, *and perceptual* impact on social relations caused by the domestic re-entrenchment of capital following the defeat of Napoleon Bonaparte's army some years earlier. The fortunate offspring of this crisis were the impressionists, artists who capitalized (so to speak) on the new forms and sites of perception, expression, and leisure, forms and sites developed and patronized by the newly "domesticated"

French middle classes. As Crow argues, the parks, prostitutes, and cabarets so dear to the early impressionists enabled forms of expression and social exchange—forms of "radicalized leisure," we might say—that compensated for the middle class's forced sharing of political power with what we might call, if a little anachronistically, a "military-industrial complex."

The social and economic situation for artists in lower Manhattan a century later was uncannily similar to the experience of the impressionists during the regime of Louis Napoleon. Like Paris in the 1850s, the American 1950s were marked by insistent, innovative corporate and governmental efforts to enforce conformity in order to aid smooth, rapid economic expansion. In the United States such expansion was largely successful until the crisis in overproduction of 1957–58 (it was in 1959 that Kaprow coined the term *happening*). Also similar to the age of impressionism, the era of Happenings and Fluxus saw rapid market expansion buttressed by innovative institutional, managerial, and technological bureaucracies; in the case of the United States: (1) rapidly capitalizing television networks with close structural relations to the military-industrial complex, (2) the purging of communist (read: "critical") voices from all levels of the productive apparatus, particularly the mass media, (3) the selective cultivation and destruction of overseas markets, (4) the creation or heating up of military situations to support the tactical needs of the American economy, and (5) the intensive, saturational marketing of everyday life. The brand-new chrome-plated blender on the umber countertop of a New Jersey suburb was an object profoundly enmeshed in a social, political, cultural, and economic matrix.

However, unlike the impressionist community and their artistic works, both of which possessed the luxury of what still remained a relatively autonomous realm of leisure and representation, the Cold War artist's focus on everyday life and individual perception was deeply tangled in the tactics of capitalist intensity after the Second World War (i.e., the marketing of new objects and textures for the domestic space, the creation of sexually charged commodities such as rock 'n' roll, the saturation of daily life by advertisement, etc.). If, as Huyssen has argued, the American avant-garde of the 1950s and 1960s was faced with a fully developed media apparatus, it was also faced—*pace* Crow—with a fully articulated leisure industry.

Avant-Garde Investment Strategy: The Strange Case of Walter Gutman

Odd characters wandered across this wild terrain of resurgent memory and intensively contextual production. One such character was Walter Gutman, a former art critic who, as a consequence of acquiring responsibility for a sizable family fortune rattled by the stock-market crash of 1929, became a full-time investor, company report writer, and part-time painter-photographer and enjoyed great financial success basing his investment decisions on trends in modern art, poetry, and performance. (He also raised the funds—all from Wall Street investors—for the first underground film, Robert Frank and Alfred Leslie's *Pull My Daisy* [1959] and pioneered Andy Kaufmann's scandalous matches with female wrestlers.)[38] Many of the weekly market letters he wrote for Shields & Company can be examined in *The Gutman Letters,* published by Higgins's Something Else Press in 1969. In his introduction to the letters, Michael Benedikt notes that these letters indicate "that the entire structure of the arts in America has in recent years been engaged in a radial, critically accessible shift" concerning the role of "business, mathematics, engineering and so forth."[39] The letters marked a shift in approach for Gutman, who had, up to his first foray with Shields, taken a fairly traditional approach to theorizing trends in economic performance. In 1959, a year that saw the sudden end of the previous year's severe recession and a sudden increase in aesthetic productivity, Gutman began writing texts, according to Benedikt, "the like of which the stock-market had not seen before, has not seen since, and which it is not likely to see again in the foreseeable future."[40]

The basic message of the letters is that the filiations between the artistic vanguard and future-minded investors (what other kind of investor is there?) should be allowed to proliferate. One crucial aspect of such proliferating connections was theory. As Benedikt writes, "Gutman wishes to link the realms of art and business not just by association, but by philosophy; and according to an aesthetic."[41] The language and dynamic of this "philosophical aesthetic" is fundamentally connected to the bad memory and aesthetic overproductivity of the Happenings and Fluxus events. In "The Great Industry of the 1965–75 Decade and Thereafter is Chatter," Gutman advocates steady investment in telecommunications (smart advice, it turns out, until just a few years ago). "The point," he writes, "is that the greatest of all pleasures is communication—love is a communication—the body communication—the reason problems develop in love is that the body ceases to communicate—if chatter were the only basis of communication then there would be few problems—but it is the very fact that chatter is inadequate that makes its volume so necessary."[42] Gutman's focus on love, bodies, and the overproduction of information is not simply the rococo meanderings of a stock-investor taking a time-out; he wished to establish the means and methods by which capitalist economy could grow without reliance on military industry and expenditure. "With Telephone passing through 95 on the tape as I write this, it is obvious that there is a way to make money out of peace."[43] One of the ways to ensure profit is through diversification, "the accumulation of as various a portfolio of holdings as possible."[44] To do so, Gutman writes, is "to put ourselves in a position where death is possible" without it becoming a crippling burden.

As Benedikt notes, Gutman's favored gesture as a painter and prose writer was the arabesque, a form ideally suited for bringing together two objects, no matter how far distant they might seem from each other. Gutman's essays bring together fuel cells and Allen Ginsberg, the Courbet retrospective of 1960 and molecular electronics, Vicks VapoRub and Homeric aesthetics. He is, in short, a Proustian investor (a very successful one at that), keenly open to the sudden blossoming of futurological potential in everyday objects and activities. Like Vautier's *Audience Variation,* Gutman's letters explore the tangles, the quirky associations, the reticular grottoes pocketing the world of *homo economicus.*

The Avant-Garde of Absorption

Keeping an eye to both this tangling and to the larger crisis in conformity ignited by the six million people laid off work in 1957–58 and the sudden, meteoric rise in the stock market the next year caused by massive increases in defense spending, the art events I have been describing appear as an *ambivalent* response to a *contradictory* conjunction of (1) contestatory notions of play and consumption (e.g., rock 'n' roll, jazz, dancing, drug use, etc.), (2) the commodification of those forms of play and consumption by innovative sectors of American capitalism, (3) an unstable, inflationary economy, and (4) highly performative forms of representation inspired by the rediscovery of the European avant-garde by the American artistic establishment during the early 1950s. When, in 1960, Jim Dine dressed as a clown, drank paint, and plunged through a canvas upon which he had just painted the phrase "I LOVE WHAT IM [*sic*]," he was articulating a performative statement that conjoined a number of concerns, including the place of the artist in a capitalist system that was actively (if inconsistently) embracing the avant-garde, the possibility of avant-gardist rupture enabled by the unrepeatable gesture of artistic production, and the difficulty of assigning stable value to a one-time-only art event.

Given this complex intersection of formal, economic, subjective, and political concerns, it should not surprise us that event art is difficult to define as a genre; in fact, the artists who created Happenings and Fluxus events rig-

orously opposed the kinds of formalist, medium-oriented criticism dominant in art discourses of their time. Dick Higgins staked his own claim
against such discourses by characterizing event art as a form of "intermedia."
As he described them, such events "developed as an intermedium, an
uncharted land that lies between collage, music, and the theater. It is not
governed by rules; each work determines its own medium and form according to its needs. *The concept itself is better understood by what it is not, rather than
what it is.*"[45] Higgins's focus on continuity rather than compartmentalization
is usefully juxtaposed to Kaprow's seven axioms of Happenings. To
Kaprow, Happenings (1) kept the line between art and life "as fluid, and
perhaps as indistinct as possible," (2) derived "the source of themes, materials, and actions, and the relationship between them . . . from any place or
period *except* from their arts, their derivatives, and their milieu," (3) took
"place over several widely spaced, sometimes moving and changing
locales," (4) utilized a varied and discontinuous time signature, (5) "should
be performed once only," (6) tended to eliminate the traditional audience as
much as possible, and (7) compositionally "evolved as a collage of events in
certain spans of time and in certain spaces."[46] Following the kind of negative logic utilized by Higgins and Kaprow to define the practical and conceptual ambiguities of this formless form, Kristine Stiles has defined event
art less as a genre than as an ethos.[47]

This refusal to positively define the aesthetic-political event is not self-
serving egotism (as it could be among members of the self-obscuring symbolist movement) nor the mark of a less than fully developed theoretical
apparatus. These gaps or holes in the work of Kaprow and Higgins are
intentional and politically motivated. But what are the "politics" of this
refusal to be recognized? Is it simply a slightly oblique reflection of the old
liberal idea of negative freedom? Possibly. The traditional liberal notion that
freedom exists only in the absence of coercion is certainly a persistent presence among Happenings and Fluxus artists and audiences, especially the
U.S. contingent. But there is another presence in this particular avant-garde
subculture's attack on representation; specifically, a recognition that an
answer to certain long-standing dilemmas in avant-garde practice and theory were being formulated at the limits of rational, linear thought. Moreover, the answer that was found was compelling a rethinking of the questions of the avant-garde itself.

The very ambiguity of the event form, its capacity to enable a disengagement of specific performances from more abstract generalizations (a
capacity that extends, as I've shown, into the experience of the individual
viewer-participant and the scholar), and its focus on the momentary con-

junction of specific communities of viewers mark an important principle of event art as a subversive, not oppositional, social practice within both bourgeois and avant-garde community histories. The question is one of production—a question germane not only to innovative artistic practice during the Cold War, but to economic practice as well. Not only do the Happenings and Fluxus events generally refuse to produce valuable objects that can be disengaged from the performances themselves, they also deeply problematize representation, memory, and value. Such problematization of conceptual practices and categories was not merely the result of formal "choice." As Huyssen has asserted, the problem of capitalist cooptation of avant-garde art in the 1960s and 1970s "was compounded by the fact that experimental strategies and popular culture were no longer connected in a critical aesthetic and political project as they had been in the historical avant-garde."[48]

Both aesthetics and politics underwent a sea change in the late 1950s, partly as the consequence of the attention paid to everyday life by critics such as Lefebvre and Friedan and by artists such as Anna Halprin and Yoko Ono, partly as the consequence of a larger perception of radicals (on both left and right) that traditional political strategies (lobbying, strikes, demonstration) were no longer effective ways to affect implementation of governmental policy. The role of the avant-garde in creating innovative representational, organizational, and critical methods was vital in this sea change. As it has been defined by Peter Bürger, the litmus test of the avant-garde is whether the artists and art in question are merely uncritically replicating their relationship to capital or are actively resisting and revising the relationship of producer, middleman, and consumer. Happenings and Fluxus events intentionally problematize the links assumed by older avant-garde movements, such as Dada and surrealism, between aesthetics and politics. In other words, Huyssen's assertion that the new avant-gardes suffered from a disconnection between experimental strategy and popular culture is an assertion that fails to take into account that this disconnection was in fact a critical theme in Happenings and Fluxus. The gap between strategy and culture is the gap within which can develop the kinds of reticular productions I have been describing. By fully theorizing the generalization of artistic production first announced by the surrealists, by fully incorporating the institutionalized critic into their oppositional program, by identifying and exploiting a number of crucial links between aesthetics and economics not recognized by the older avant-gardes, and most importantly by overcoming a basic contradiction in the avant-garde (its "elitist populism"), the artists and audiences of Happenings and Fluxus events took the problem of aesthetics and politics onto the grotesque terrain of fetishism.

What I am pressing toward here is a concept of commodification (that is to say, of the valuable gap between production and reception) that can allow us to imagine the processes of social and economic alienation as a crucial site for innovative antagonism. Because it is enabled as both a coercive, external force for the exploiters but also as a self-motivating, internal force for the holders of productive potential, alienation is a perfect process for avant-garde experimentation. "Dematrixing" names the result of one avant-garde experiment. Such a concept of alienation as a catalyst for reticular social experience is crucial if we are to understand the innovative antagonism of the Cold War avant-gardes as they responded to the baroque development of capitalism within its most advanced sectors. Not surprisingly, such a concept also allows us one more vantage point on the general scorn and dismissal heaped on the "neo" avant-gardes by the Eulogist School. Relative to this question of productive alienation, Kristine Stiles has suggested that Fluxus events such as Allison Knowles and Philip Corner's *Identical Lunch* (a habitual lunch of tuna fish, buttermilk, and soup ordered daily by Knowles at a café around the corner from her and Corner's studio) afforded performers and affords us a densely layered cross section of the performance's sociopolitical moment. Exploring the ontological, epistemological, economic, ideological, and aesthetic dimensions of *Identical Lunch,* Stiles demonstrates that events such as these can actually broaden the field of aesthetic and political action and also serve as critical levers for opening up traditional notions of aesthetics and politics to innovative criticism. Fluxus serves as a kind of laboratory for social thought, a tool for mapping the reticular contours of an event's totality and identifying the potential for value.[49]

As performance-theory pioneer Erving Goffman describes it, the separation of "strips of experience" from their cultural frame enables both a repetition and a transformation of the experience and a possible reordering of the cultural frame itself. Goffman's description of cultural performances dovetails tightly with the notion of alienation I have been describing, a notion borrowed from Marxists such as Lefebvre and Guy Debord. The potential contained in these strips varies widely, a variance increased when we move from considering, say, the making of tea or the lighting of a match in the abstract to considering their effects within specific performance contexts. Performance theory has been dominated by the theory of alienation, though often without acknowledging it. As is commonly known, performance is both a doing and a judgment, a doing that is judged by others but also a doing that marks the persistent threat of a crisis in values. In short, it is the fulfillment of a standard practice but also a performative and, as a performative, the possibility of a rupture in a community's value structure.

Happenings and Fluxus events contain this contradictory potential, marking it as a source for ideological demystification not unlike that practiced by Benjamin in his studies of the Paris arcades and phantasmagoria. The dialectical standstill of these kinds of art events can be found in the logic Goffman describes for performance theory in general, a logic of alienation, transformation, and valorization that is structurally analogous to the logic of commodification, a logic articulated by Goffman in the first moments of capitalism's most significant and long-lived phase of innovative transformation. If we lose track of the simultaneous presence of potential pleasure and profound pain experienced by individuals and communities as they engage such a logic, we lose the possibility of understanding why such a claustrophobic form of aesthetic and political antagonism was so energizing to this small sector of the counterculture.

There is a masochistic tendency to this art that shouldn't be overlooked. Tomas Schmitt's *Zyklus für Wassereimer [oder Flaschen]* (Cycle for waterrhymes [or bottles]), in which the performer carefully pours water from one bottle into another (from ten to thirty in number as specified by the script) in clockwise direction until all the water disappears through accidental spillage and evaporation, is a physically punishing event. I performed it once for an hour and found it to be an unbearable experience. Schmitt performed the piece in 1962 on his knees in a tailored business suit for over eight hours. Students of mine who have performed variations on the event (standing, for example, in front of a table) have described the experience alternately as hallucinatory, mystical, and nauseating. One performer almost passed out and had to be helped to a chair.[50] Benjamin never forgets the dialectical force of such subjective experiences as pleasure, pain, intoxication, melancholy, or doubt, which is why he has played such a significant role in my exploration of early U.S. performance art's avant-garde antagonism. Capitalism's innovations often rest on the ambivalency of desire.

The ambivalent relations among innovative capitalism, desire, everyday life, and the avant-garde is figured in suggestive form by Maciunas in his combination manifesto-advertisement-collage *Fluxiosity*. Unlike earlier, formally similar pieces that utilized a more straightforwardly leftist rhetoric (and were, as a result, largely rejected by most of the American contingent of the group), *Fluxiosity* asserts a more poised, almost Proustian relationship to capital, as if inviting the avant-garde to become the self-consuming fetish of capitalism, or to draw the capitalist law of exchange into an endless reverie on ice-cream cones, tuna fish sandwiches, lighted matches, twine, silence, exits, madeleines.

The document begins with a highly ambivalent address, an address that

FLUXUS HQ P.O.BOX 180 NEW YORK 10013
FLUXSHOPS AND FLUXFESTS IN NEW YORK
AMSTERDAM NICE ROME MONTREAL TOKYO
V TRE-FLUXMACHINES-FLUXMUSICBOXES
FLUXKITS-FLUXAUTOMOBILES-FLUXPOST
FLUXMEDICINES-FLUXFILMS-FLUXMENUS
FLUXRADIOS - FLUXCARDS - FLUXPUZZLES
FLUXCLOTHES-FLUXORGANS-FLUXSHIRTS
FLUXBOXES-FLUXORCHESTRA-FLUXJOKES
FLUXGAMES-FLUXHOLES-FLUXHARDWARE
FLUXSUITCASES-FLUXCHESS-FLUXFLAGS
FLUXTOURS-FLUXWATER-FLUXCONCERTS
FLUXMYSTERIES-FLUXBOOKS-FLUXSIGNS
FLUXCLOCKS-FLUXCIRCUS-FLUXANIMALS
FLUXQUIZZES- FLUXROCKS -FLUXMEDALS
FLUXDUST - FLUXCANS -FLUXTABLECLOTH
FLUXVAUDEVILLE-FLUXTAPE-FLUXSPORT
BY ERIC ANDERSEN - AYO - JEFF BERNER
GEORGE BRECHT-GIUSEPPE CHIARI- ANT-
HONY COX - CHRISTO -WALTER DE MARIA
WILLEM DE RIDDER - ROBERT FILLIOU
ALBERT FINE-HI RED CENTER-JOE JONES
H.KAPPLOW-ALISON KNOWLES-JIRI KOLAR
ARTHUR KØPCKE-TAKEHISA KOSUGI-SHIGE-
KO KUBOTA-FREDRIC LIEBERMAN- GYORGI
LIGETI-GEORGE MACIUNAS-YOKO ONO-BEN-
JAMIN PATTERSON- JAMES RIDDLE- DITER
ROT-TAKAKO SAITO-TOMAS SCHMIT-CHIEKO
SHIOMI -DANIEL SPOERRI- STAN VANDER-
BEEK - BEN VAUTIER - ROBERT M. WATTS
EMMETT O. WILLIAMS - LA MONTE YOUNG
FLUX-ART-NONART-AMUSEMENT FORGOES
DISTINCTION BETWEEN ART AND NONART,
FORGOES ARTIST'S INDISPENSABILITY,
EXCLUSIVENESS, INDIVIDUALITY, AMBITION,
FORGOES ALL PRETENSION TOWARDS SIG-
NIFICANCE, RARITY, INSPIRATION, SKILL,
COMPLEXITY, PROFUNDITY, GREATNESS,
INSTITUTIONAL AND COMMODITY VALUE.
IT STRIVES FOR MONOSTRUCTURAL, NON-
THEATRICAL, NONBAROQUE, IMPERSONAL
QUALITIES OF A SIMPLE NATURAL EVENT,
AN OBJECT, A GAME, A PUZZLE OR A GAG.
IT IS A FUSION OF SPIKES JONES, GAGS,
GAMES, VAUDEVILLE, CAGE AND DUCHAMP

"The ambivalent relations among innovative capitalism, desire, everyday life, and the avant-garde . . ." George Maciunas, *Fluxiosity*. Reprinted with permission of the Gilbert and Lila Silverman Collection.

deconstructs the distinctions between the local and the global, performance and institution: the word "FLUXUS," the letters "HQ," and a post-office box address in New York City. This first line possesses a number of reticular ironies, not least being the parataxic linking of the decentered, international, precociously multicultural community in which Maciunas (himself a Lithuanian) participated, an imagined institutional center (the headquarters, with its connotations of efficiency and hierarchy—hardly traits one associates with the purposefully disorganized Fluxus community), and an official, state-sponsored location within the American geography of power and information circulation. This visual and syntactical linking of community ethos, organizational structure, and state power does not so much allow the things to stabilize for the reader as create a kind of conceptual *vibration,* rather like the *moiré* effect achieved in "op art," in which a two-dimensional pattern sets off a trembling effect in the vision of the viewer.[51] The Fluxus group opened a number of these Fluxshops, only one of which did all that well as a business, but wherever they were found (and they could be in New York, Amsterdam, and Nice), they attempted to mediate the same economies of performative flux, rule-and-command, and bureaucratic infrastructure described by the manifesto, hypothetically opening those economies to subversive and highly local appropriations and diversions. Like Oldenburg's Ray Gun Mfg Co, the manifesto and the Fluxshops challenged the distinction between process and product and sold the potentially infectious logics of play to the public in the form of highly inventive, seductive art objects.

Like Williams's *Let It Not Be Forgot,* Maciunas's document invites a performance by the viewer not merely on the syntactical level but also on the level of form. In other words, we have here a readerly performance not only of the object of the text ("Fluxus") but also a nonlinear, nonhierarchical sequence of possible relationships to that object. This is the force field in which the critical aesthetics of the dematrixed event function: between the object in flux and the knowing of that object in flux. *Fluxiosity,* like the "Diagram of Historical Development," is an aesthetic object and an object for sale. One particularly difficult turn in Maciunas's manifesto is the fourth line, where the text veers suddenly, and something like a bill of sale is announced, each commodity on the docket neatly punctuated by "FLUX," a sort of corporate imprimatur not unlike the "Mc" that monograms global sales of beef and potatoes. There's a bit of drama here, a flirting with apocalypse; at the moment when the flood of Fluxified goods threatens to overwhelm the reader, when even water ("FLUXWATER") and dust ("FLUXDUST") have fallen to commodity capitalism, faint tracks of individuality come into view. At the moment when even those standbys of avant-garde representation—play and leisure—are revealed as more things for sale ("FLUXSPORT"), a list of Fluxus members begins and one is reminded that this isn't about hamburgers at all, but art. The shift from commodity to community is sudden, a parataxic shift prepared for by the first lines of the document but no less shocking for that. The selling out of selves and communities threatened by the viral Fluxus trademark and the virulent, microscopic commodification processes the document alludes to, is put into a dynamic, trembling, conceptual waltz with the supposedly unique gesture of artistic production; namely, the signature.[52] The difference between the various FLUXCOMMODI-TIES and the FLUXARTISTS who follow is not immediately apparent. It can't be; the art object has for centuries been the medium with which the West has thought about the paradox of the human and its objects.

The next moments in Maciunas's manifesto works to define the difference. Attempting to move beyond the simple, formal linking of trademark and artistic signature (a movement not so much explained as insisted upon, the wrenching conceptual consequence of this parataxic text and the seemingly unrelated names and objects it arranges in a visually coherent composition), the stuttering list-structure of the document shifts into a more syntactical, more typically manifesto-like prose: "FLUX-ART-NONART-AMUSEMENT FORGOES DISTINCTION BETWEEN ART AND NONART." The previous objects of the text—geographical decenteredness, commodity saturation, and the artistic signature—give way here to a more "rational," linear description of the Fluxus ethos (should we say "FLUXETHOS"?), described here as "nontheatrical," "simple," "natural," "prankish." Maciunas's manifesto, which for all its performative demands might better be called a "script," blurs the supposed individuality and moral force of the unique artistic gesture (the great fetish of abstract expressionism) and the standardized products of mass-manufacture capitalism. As a manifesto, it describes not so much a movement or an ethos as a shared matrix of conceptual paradoxes and structural contradictions that individual artists might explore like aesthetic archaeologists or ideological spelunkers. The manifesto creates a theoretical, essentially performative space in a claustrophobic matrix of state power, bureaucratic stultification, and commodity saturation. It does not transcend the contradictions, nor does it ultimately define its theory or its performance structures in any stable way. Like Higgins and Kaprow, Maciunas defines Fluxus in negative fashion, as an event so volatile yet so ephemeral that it demands a Proustian sensibility to recover and labor over it. The object is in flux, the knowing of the object is in flux, and the spectator's relationship to the knowing of the object in flux is in flux.

A more positive, concrete manifestation of this negative, vertiginous performative space can be discovered by examining specific events; for example, Yoko Ono's *Lighting Piece* of 1955. The gesture in Ono's script plays within same the dynamic described by Maciunas, but is unhampered by the linearity of text and the conventions of manifesto prose; therefore, it is able to avoid the syntactical discontinuities that structure *Fluxiosity*. The collage-like composition of map-commodity-signature-ethos in *Fluxiosity* is kneaded into a self-consuming moment in *Lighting Piece*. Like all Fluxus events, the script is brief and disarmingly simple: "Light a match and watch it til it goes out." But the brevity and simplicity of the piece (a script that lacks both setting and character) ultimately opens onto a virtually infinite number of performance choices, many of which are stunning to experience as spectator or performer. In *Lighting Piece,* the gesture of the artist (reified and moralized in the work of the abstract expressionists and the New York School of poetry) is linked concretely with a common activity, a banal material component, and a specific location. And no matter where or when the match is lit, the artistic commodity is consumed at the very moment that the banal commodity is consumed and only to signal the end of a performance, the destruction of the performative frame, and the return to everyday life. Criticism burns, lacking only fuel to keep it going (the fuel of memory, reading, contemplation, action). Returning for a moment to the masochism of performance, it should be noted that performances of Ono's script often end in the burning of the performer's fingers. Unless the performer prepares for and withstands this pain, the script will not be fully performed.

As in Maciunas's text, the object (the match) is in flux; the knowing of the object, the relationship of the spectator to this knowing are also in flux. The tension between simplicity/commonality, the open-ended qualities of the script, and the specific temporal and spatial qualities of its performance suggests that avant-garde artists such as Ono perceived aesthetic perception as being closely associated with the commodity form itself and the vertiginously ambivalent processes of alienation (Ono's *Lighting Piece* can, therefore, be described as one of the earliest manifestations of the "Pop" aesthetic associated with Warhol's Factory). Aesthetic perception, such artists insist, can be inspired by a match, a can of Campbell's soup, a foot tangled in twine, a word on a page.

Thus, the hiatus of aesthetic perception—and the critical distance such perception enables and across which develops the reticular structures of fetishism—was, for Ono and others, itself a raw material to be labored over. No longer simply the goal of art, the gap or hiatus between aesthetic perception and the institutions that secure aesthetic perception was objectified by this vanguard subculture, reified, commodified, and aestheticized in performance texts structured by the performative principle of dematrixing (a principle I will discuss in detail soon). As a consequence, the gap itself was enabled to circulate, something like a portable hole, as easily as all the other kinds of mass-marketed mentalities and penetrate just as deeply into the American cultural consciousness, occasionally igniting Proustian reclamation of the time we all lose to exploitation and boredom. Given the portability of performance scripts such as Ono's (virtually anyone can light a match, virtually anyone can perform *Lighting Piece*), the holes produced by the event are like moth holes and dandelions—they seem to spring instantly from nowhere spreading everywhere—enabling an extremely varied repertoire of "resistant rituals."[53] Not only is this kind of microscopically corrosive perception enabled; the productive potential of aesthetic innovations also approaches a ubiquity comparable to that of, say, labor power in a fully developed, highly differentiated labor market no longer reliant on the production of material objects after the discovery of the profit to be gleaned from information and experience.

The ubiquity of the aesthetic gap as it appears in *Fluxiosity* and *Lighting Piece* is also evident in the "certificate of authenticity" created by Ben Vautier. As represented by Vautier's document, the activity of artistic production appears to be not so much the result of talent or skill as of "pretense," the "pretention" or distancing attitude enabled by certain linguistic, conceptual, and practical postures and gestures. Art is divorced by the certificate from the object and enabled to become a pure *potential,* a kind of *productive capacity* with no binding relationships to products, depending more on perception and the continual refreshment of perceptual astonishment than on technically adept manufacture, depending more on the concept than the tool. The certificate can be glued to anything. On the other hand, Vautier, much like Maciunas, doesn't fully abandon the artist's valuable uniqueness, and the authority (and the "authenticity") behind the gesture is left uncertain: "Your name here/I don't sign." The politics of the aesthetic event as figured in Maciunas's manifesto, Ono's script, and Vautier's document exist only as unarticulated potential, and only in the shifting, reticulated gaps among aesthetic framing, personalized gesture, and the self-alienating labor of artistic producers.

Surprisingly, such conceptual instability and productive potential has retained its capacity to challenge critical categories to this day (once more effecting the same strategy on both the subjective and objective levels of cultural production). Janet Jenkins has described the difficulties faced by modern curators attempting to catalog Fluxus works:

BY THE PRESENT CERTIFICATE

I BEN DECLARE AUTHENTIC

WORK OF ART . . . .

. . . .

. . . .

. . . .

DATE   (I DONT SIGN)

"The ubiquity of the aesthetic gap . . ." Ben Vautier, *By the Present Certificate.*
(Reprinted with permission of the artist.)

Attributing dates, dimensions, titles, and even authorship to Fluxus
works is often a tricky affair. For these works are the product of a great
number of artists living in a great many places, and they have been produced or performed in various incarnations over long periods of time. To
complicate the situation further, Fluxus gave license to a collective spirit
that encouraged free appropriation or interpretation of ideas among its
participants, and it produced works that more often than not defy traditional classification. Thus a number of perplexing questions are raised: If
an artist offers up the score of another artist as a part of his or her own
work, who is its author? If an object conceived in 1964 is produced in
varying form for more than a decade, how is it to be dated? If an artist
creates a score for a film that is not made until years later—and then as a
video—was the film "unrealized"? Careful consideration of such questions will yield conflicting opinions; many Fluxus artists would (and perhaps should) laugh at the exercise.[54]

By refusing to distinguish between concept, gesture, and object, by creating
objects that are literally dissolving such distinctions as we speak in the museums and commentaries that house them, by purposefully deconstructing the
boundaries among art, commodity, and critical category, Happenings and
Fluxus events allow the "pretension" of aesthetic perception and artistic
production to circulate freely throughout the cultural field—almost as a
kind of ur-commodity—enabling a particularly unstable form of liberty

within the constraints of a rapidly expanding, increasingly flexible, ever-more-seductive capitalism.

Kaprow explicitly linked such unstable forms of categorical and practical liberty with the expanding field of commodities available in the American urban space:

> Objects of every sort are materials for the new art: paint, chairs, food, electric and neon lights, smoke, water, old socks, a dog, movies, a thousand other things which will be discovered by the present generation of artists.[55]

Given this rapidly expanding field of potential artistic materials—compare the sudden discovery of Parisian leisure by the impressionists that Crow describes in his essay—the production of value seemed literally at hand, like manna from heaven. To Kaprow and his colleagues, the ability to add value to the raw materials of artistic production had become a gesture as powerful in its own right as that of the worker in an automated factory, a worker whose smallest gesture might initiate and manage a varied and powerful sequence of production processes toward the creation of an object more valuable than the sum of the elements and processes invested in it. As Kaprow described it, "Value, then, however relative, is taken for granted as the real goal. It is valuable just to make something. It is valuable just to point to something."[56] Happenings artist Al Hansen agreed: "To those who are tuned up, art seems to be going on everywhere."[57] Indeed, the ubiquity of the commodity form and the role of style in a highly competitive market[58] seemed to afford a kind of potent ubiquity both to the logic of art and to the artist him- or herself, as John Cage seems to suggest: "The trick is, without any apparent means of transportation, to suddenly appear at a different place."[59]

Though it is true that Schneeman's *Meat Joy* was in no direct way a meditation on Hegel's ruse of reason or the tactical limitations of working-class organization, it certainly confronted the paradoxical, potentially revolutionary, definitely transgressive desires exploited by the American "conquest of cool," that revolution in organizational and marketing theory described so well by Thomas Frank. The simultaneously titillating and repulsive "flesh celebration" of young performers writhing on the floor of the theater covered in the bloody scraps Schneeman had recovered from the small butcher's shop around the corner certainly reflects the vertiginous forms of alienation and liberty available in an age of McDonald's hamburgers, *Playboy,* abstract expressionism, and the early echoes of radical feminism and vegetarianism. Maciunas hated *Meat Joy;* in what appears to have been a consciously ironic repetition of surrealism founder André Breton's excommunication of colleagues, he unilaterally kicked Schneeman out, citing her work's operatic scale and expressionistic excesses. The other Fluxus artists didn't take the excommunication all that seriously, seeing Maciunas as simply parodying the dogmatism of earlier avant-garde movements. Maciunas, though, saw himself as being seriously engaged in ideological disputation *as well as* parodying earlier movements.

The rejection of the artist's traditional function as a producer of spiritually uplifting or financially worthwhile art objects, the courting of scandal, and the obliteration of critical perspective are traditional moves of the avant-garde artist. But unlike the Dadaists, who could count on the shock caused by the presence of garbage, kitsch, and obscenity in traditional art contexts such as galleries and museums, the Happenings participant-creators and Fluxartists had to work in a context in which seemingly *everything* was becoming a commodity, including the work of the Dadaists, newly rediscovered in the 1950s by Manhattan museums and collectors. Market expansion was based on a conceptual expansion; specifically, the expansion of the field of things that could be considered sellable. And in this regard, there appears to be a perfect homology between market expansion and avant-garde erasure of the line separating art and life. Just as anything could be art regardless of its status vis-à-vis high culture, low culture, or refuse, anything could be a *commodity,* notwithstanding the occasional complaint by public decency squads or ambitious politicians. In a sense, the formal principle of dematrixing "piggybacks" on the cultural logic of the highly capitalism dominant in the United States during the 1950s and 1960s, taking it beyond older, more rigid forms of political economy that no longer served the needs of capital. Doing so, event art deconstructed the distinctions between avant-garde artistic production and vanguard commodity production. Let me emphasize that I consider this to be a deconstruction, not the "false sublation" that Peter Bürger accuses the "neo-avant-garde" of abetting (e.g., a transference of aesthetic consciousness to the praxis of everyday life without substantial alteration of the institutional and economic foundations of everyday life).[60] Such deconstruction was intended not to pronounce the death of the avant-garde (a characteristic of much post-Pop art and the Eulogist School that promotes it), but rather to allow the techniques and imperatives of the historical avant-garde (particularly Dada) to diffuse into the economies of cultural production and reproduction as a whole. Rather than a false sublation, we have here a highly conscious effort to preserve the aesthetic imperative in the face of overwhelming power, an effort to ground that imperative in a theory and practice of community (the litmus test for Bürger).[61]

There's no doubt that the piggyback mentality of this community aided and abetted transformations in American capitalism during the 1950s and 1960s. Frank writes, "When business leaders cast their gaze onto the youth culture bubbling around them, they saw both a reflection of their own struggle against the stifling bureaucratic methods of the past and an affirmation of a new dynamic consumerism that must replace the old."[62] This struggle was waged not only against puritanical aversion to luxury and thriftlessness, Frank demonstrates, but also against notions of what was appropriate—or conceivable—to buy, sell, and circulate. Taking into account the vigor of capitalism during the era, with the exception of the breathtaking recession of 1957–58, the first decades of the Cold War prove, in retrospect, to be not only an era of political liberation, struggle, and the rise of new social movements, but also an era of unprecedented capitalist saturation, market expansion, and popular subversion. Frank captures this ambiguity when he demonstrates that the "meaning of 'the sixties' cannot be considered apart from the enthusiasm of ordinary, suburban Americans for cultural revolution," particularly those affiliated with innovative capitalist trends, such as advertising and youth.[63]

It was during this period that the notion of performativity that has proven so invaluable to queer liberation, feminism, and other oppositional movements found its initial theorization and implementation.[64] If, as Jameson has suggested, a "unified field theory" of the 1960s is possible—that is to say, a conceptual representation of "a properly dialectical process in which 'liberation' and domination are inextricably combined"—then we may find an early effort at such theorization in early U.S. performance art, a trend in art production, circulation, and reception that seems to have effectively exploited for the purposes of freedom "a moment in which the enlargement of capitalism on a global scale [as well as the saturation of capitalism on a local scale] simultaneously produced an immense freeing or unbinding of social movements, a prodigious release of untheorized new forces."[65] If Jameson is correct, then his notion that "the 60s were in that sense an immense and inflationary issuing of superstructural credit; a universal abandonment of the referential gold standard; an extraordinary printing up of ever more devalued signifiers" (208) suggests that Happenings and Fluxus events, for a very brief period, articulated a method of expropriating such energies from capitalism and putting them to use in the construction of new forms of community, communication, and critique. At the same time, these events also served (occasionally quite explicitly) as research-and-development labs for a hipper, gentler, more interesting capitalism.

Like the judo artist who uses the momentum of the enemy against that enemy, early U.S. performance art attempted to divert the invasive momentum of postwar capitalism. While the market attempted to exploit and control by way of an intensive saturation of daily life by the commodity form, the Happenings and Fluxus communities attempted to expand and liberate daily life as both a practice and a concept. They did this by appropriating the logic of the commodity for their own purposes; namely, the expansion of our concept of artistic merit and the rejection of tradition (except as a fund of materials to use and abuse at will). As Richard Schechner once put it, "A very interesting basic freedom is involved" in art that appropriates the degraded materials of Madison Avenue.[66] If fantasy and daily life could be commodified, the Happenings and Fluxus artists asked, then why don't we just start doing it ourselves and on our own terms and in such a way that only the participants themselves can possibly understand it? Schneeman's *Meat Joy,* which combined Artaud, Beat poetry, and the sensory assault of the meat-market dumpster, certainly embodied a profound ambivalence toward consumption and production. But there is something undeniably *sexy* about the event, something captured in the photographs of performers in a moment of paradoxically self-conscious, perhaps ironic *ekstasis.* As Delaney shows us in his memoir, the contradictory feelings evoked by the Happenings—in the case of *Meat Joy,* disgust and titillation—do not allow traditional kinds of history or criticism, only highly individualistic, paradoxical forms of hyperproductive "bad memory."

If Maciunas's *Fluxiosity* and Ono's *Lighting Piece* suggest a link between event art and the commodity form, and Vautier's certificate suggests a link between events and global regimes of production and circulation, then the work of Allison Knowles suggests a close relationship between the saturation of everyday life by the commodity form and the liberation of domestic labor. In the early 1960s, Knowles created a number of performance scripts designed, at least in part, to dissolve the boundaries between the public and the private, between a cosmopolitan, transnational realm of value and fame (the realm of the idealized and aestheticized form of capital known as art) and the banal rhythms and putatively "valueless" qualities of domestic labor. In works such as *Proposition* ("Make a Salad") and *Variation #1 on Proposition* ("Make a Soup"), the line between artistic production and domestic reproduction is blurred. As a result, distinctions between the serious and the nonserious as well as taste and beauty are also blurred. In these pieces, an op-art trembling occurs among the hiatus of aesthetic perception, the singular qualities of the performance, and the private pleasures and pains of the domestic space.

This tension is explicitly foregrounded in *Child Art Piece* of 1962: "The performer is a single child, two or three years old. One or both parents may be present to help him with a pail of water, a banana, etc. When the child leaves the stage, the performance is over." The presence of an untrained, potentially unruly performer in the charged and unsettling context of untraditional performance (1) challenges intentionality as well as the notion of artistic expertise, (2) compels recognition that performance is not alien to the work of child-rearing and labor reproduction, (3) suggests that the pressures of representational innovation and commodification are felt also in the domestic space (thereby threatening the "natural" relations of the family), and (4) opens up the supposedly private relations among parents and children to aesthetic perception and public display. And if we recall Jenkins's lesson about the tendency for authority to resurge even within supposedly "chance" relations and Vautier's suggestion that aesthetic value is ubiquitous, then we might be able to see Knowles's scripts as suggesting to us that a realm of commonality and oppositional production exists in the domestic space as such—that the domestic can serve as a kind of counterinstitution to divert patriarchal/capitalist control into a conceptual black hole, can compel the patriarch to cross the event horizon of the avant-garde and fall into the grotesque caverns of bad memory.

As Johnston puts it,

> *Anyone can do it.* During the 1960s, this idea swept through the art world like a brushfire. No special knowledge of John Cage or his thought or the Fluxus movement was necessary for artists to believe that anything was possible. The idea hung porously in the atmosphere. Artists made dances. Dancers made music. Composers made events. People at large performed in all these things, including critics, wives, and children. Dogs, turtles, and chickens made it, too.[67]

I find Johnston's comments simultaneously creepy and inspirational, as I do much of the rhetoric produced by these Cold War vanguardists. As the textual events engineered by Maciunas, Ono, Vautier, and Knowles suggest, Fluxus attempted to engage and exploit the simultaneously expansive and invasive momentum of American capitalism, the dialectic of "liberation" and oppression identified by Jameson and Frank as the dominant cultural logic of the 1960s. Doing so, they risked hanging themselves on its horns. In the case of Maciunas's *Fluxiosity,* the speed and discontinuity of the commodity form enable an innovative and deeply ironic vision of self and community. As Ono's *Lighting Piece* demonstrates, such a vision was quite literally tied to the temporalities—the flux or *différance*—of performance, temporalities that are often difficult to separate from those of commodity consumption and obsolescence. One experiences beauty without the possibility of possession. Vautier's certificate renders artistic production effectively ubiquitous while placing subjectivity and authority at radical, subversive risk. And in Knowles's domestic scripts, the abstracting logic of aesthetic perception compels recognition of the beauty, value, and contradictions of domestic labor, a conceptual gesture that would find ready acceptance among feminists later in the decade.

Dematrixing the Dematrixing of Experience

It is time to begin a circuitous return to the inflationary subjectivity of Proust and Delaney. To repeat the central question of this case study: How does one make sense of the Proustian qualities of the Happenings and Fluxus event either as an audience member or as a scholar attempting to approach the event through audience accounts and historical documents? And then the more general issue: What is the place of forgetting and of the intensely individual sensation in historical memory and in the critical and historiographical processes with which a society can be pushed to acknowledge its forgotten children? To answer these questions, we'll return again to Delaney's experience at *Eighteen Happenings in Six Parts.* As Delaney recalls, "No one in the audience—nor, possibly, the artist or any of his assistants—could have more than an inkling (at best a theory) of the relation of a textured and specific experiential fragment to any totalized whole."[68] Delaney makes just such a quirky connection, "at best a theory" (as he puts it), between *Eighteen Happenings* and its historical moment, helping to further reveal the complex relationship of capitalism and the Happenings.

As I have already mentioned, two years before the performance, in 1957, white-collar workers in the United States exceeded in number both blue-collar and agricultural workers combined, signaling a shift in the class structure of American culture and the first clear indicator of the advent of a so-called postindustrial society (183). Delaney cites this fact as well as the rise in cost of subway tokens and milk in New York in 1958 as a kind of epigraph to his memoir of Kaprow's fractured event. And though he does not mention the six million people put out of work in 1957 nor the conscious decision by the Eisenhower administration to orient the military-industrial complex toward "strategic readiness" as a way of consuming overstocked military goods and jump-starting economic growth, Delaney does connect his inability to derive a "totalized whole" from Kaprow's performance to what he sees as a historic shift in class relations and a sudden upward spike in inflation.

As we have already seen, Delaney's expectations of logical chronological succession were subverted by the spatial layout of Kaprow's piece, but he also enjoyed unprecedented authority as a spectator in an event enriched by the grace of bad or Proustian memory. While Kaprow certainly intended to subvert both the narrative form and synoptic perspective, he also intended that the spectator-participant play as significant a role as the artist in assembling the materials into a coherent—if partial and contingent—whole. The windup toys, burning candles, drums, and other elements of the eighteen happenings that do make it into Delaney's precociously postmodern experience of the performance appear to have expanded under some deep and uncanny shift in the systems of self, community, and history. Dematrixed from their customary context by the hiatus of aesthetic perception and the spontaneity of the performative moment, the connotative meanings surrounding the stage properties were set free to circulate like newly minted coins, allowing the spectator to collect them and critically "reinvest" them in his or her own lifeworld. The spectator-participant, as Delaney describes it, is a laborer—collage artist who adds value to the self-consuming art object.

To understand this vertiginous mixture of participatory production and inflationary desire, we can consult the work of Claes Oldenburg again. His lumpy, garish, essentially glottal commodity-sculptures and the performances that produced them also reflect the kinds of shifts in the relationship of individuals to objects and each other described by Delaney. According to Oldenburg, the objects he produced were the result of both individual and objective inflation: "Volume: Increased flatulence. Model: a balloon. Pressure from center out. From inside. Skin over matter straining out."[69] The performances and products of Ray Gun described in *Store Days* suggest an ambivalently liberatory linking of aesthetic performance, the creation of art objects, and everyday experience in an inflationary economy. The objective uselessness of immediately recognizable commodities as they appear in Oldenburg's art—underwear, socks, fast food, and so on—seems to assert both an empowering sense of productivity and a disconcerting fear of the ultimate consequences of overproduction. Even now, Oldenburg's oversized, misshapen commodities still possess the ability to shock, less for their monumentality than for their enormous gloppiness, their squishy massiveness, almost as if they were gigantic chew toys splattering the landscape with kilo-liters of slobber. The conceptual contradiction between the immediate obsolescence of the commodity form and the enduring bronze from which they are manufactured refuses to be resolved. As conceptual *moiré,* such art objects can only be negotiated, performed.

In the essay that first identified the technique common to Happenings and Fluxus events, Michael Kirby attempts to describe this sort of concep-tual conflict.[70] As Kirby puts it, the Happenings utilize objects, bodies, and language without regard to narrative logic or totalizing critical perspective. They are divorced from the matrix of common social, economic, and aes-thetic associations. They are "dematrixed." They therefore "liberate" cul-tural signifiers and social materiel from the fabric of tradition and taboo. In Kaprow's event, for example, the conversation of women, the playing of music, the splashing of paint, even the audience itself functioned as "things in themselves," available for any number of uses. In Ono's *Lighting Piece,* the everyday gesture of lighting a match is transformed into an art object and the art object consumed by time and the hungry gaze of the spectator-par-ticipant. By dematrixing objects, actions, and signifiers from their custom-ary social significance, Happenings and Fluxus events engaged the cultural logic of American capitalism, a logic that is more concerned with discover-ing new sources of value than sustaining old ones.

The commodity is itself a dematrixed object. As Marx demonstrated, the commodity has no intrinsic relationship to its context of consumption nor any necessary trace of its context of production. It is more than coincidence that, just around the corner from the neighborhoods in which these events were first performed, Madison Avenue advertising executives were saturat-ing the cultural field with engineered obsolescence. Kaprow insisted, I would note, that Happenings should be difficult to remember and impossi-ble to perform more than once. It's better to be eaten by zombies than to walk with them.

Like Kaprow and Maciunas, Oldenburg found it difficult to discover a stable place for the dissident artist in an era of innovative capitalism. As he put it, "[O]ne could be anti-bourgeois by being bourgeois. It got very com-plicated."[71] For the small, international community of performance artists, the commodity was more than metaphor; it was, terrifyingly, all there was. Dine's paint-drenched clown figures the terror of such ambivalent empti-ness, as does Vostell's concentration-camp-carnival *You* of 1964, Schnee-man's *Meat Joy,* and Kaprow's *Spring Event* (which sent a roaring lawn-mower toward the audience). This kind of simultaneous uneasy and euphoric performance is explicitly described by Oldenburg. He ruminates on it in an interview with Susan Hapgood:

> I was trying to think the other day where it all comes from. The idea is that the art object is a kind of corruption or perversion of a magic object. And that once upon a time in history the objects, everything, were endowed with a kind of mystical aura, and people lived in relation to that kind of perception. . . . It was a matter of where you found such objects and you could find them in a dime store as well as in an art museum. So there was an idea of the art object . . . that transcended its use as a commercial counter, as a thing to sit in museums and so on.[72]

Oldenburg blurs the line between the "aura" of the unique artistic object and the "mysticism" of the fetishized commodity.[73] Production becomes something grotesque, a process warped by the competing tensions of the fetish. This blurring—which, as I have been arguing, was at least partly due to the changing social status of one long-standing fetish of bourgeois society—the avant-garde artist—guaranteed Oldenburg no small amount of guilt, educated as he had been on the virtuous examples of Dada and surrealism. As Susan Hapgood describes them, Oldenburg's "slices of frosted cake, gloppy overstuffed pastries, giant hamburgers, fake TV dinners, and plaster underwear" pose a "humorous metacritique" that "disguise" art in order to "protect it from destructive forces like the bourgeoisie and commercialism."[74] I'd strike a more ambivalent note—I'm not entirely certain that Oldenburg's "antibourgeois" stance can be so easily differentiated from his "bourgeois" disguise. To recall Benjamin's *fille publique:* in one door, out the other.

Kaprow, for instance, firmly asserts that the social role of the avant-garde artist had shifted significantly after 1945 and that this shift created new opportunities just as surely as it guaranteed new kinds of alienation. Kaprow argues that it was impossible to separate the economic conditions of artistic production in the late 1950s and early 1960s from the philosophical or ethical underpinnings of the art itself. As Kaprow put it, "[I]f artists were in hell in 1946, now they are in business."[75] If Dada managed on occasion to capture the unavoidable paradox of commodified revolution in its collages and publications, the Fluxus and Happenings artists turned the paradox into an ethos, a way of life.

The traces of socioeconomic shifts that Delaney detects in *Eighteen Happenings* are by no means idiosyncratic. In a passage that describes a social scene uncannily similar to other kinds of intellectual workplaces that have developed since the 1960s, Kaprow asserts that the artist has become indistinguishable from the white-collar worker:

> Like anyone else, they are concerned with keeping the rooms warm in winter, with the children's education, with the rising cost of life insurance. But they are apt to keep quietly to themselves no matter where they live—in the suburbs or in the city—rather than enter into the neighborhood coffee break or the meetings of the PTA. . . . Their actual social life is usually elsewhere, with clients, fellow artists, and agents, an increasingly expedient social life for the sake of career rather than just for pleasure. And in this they resemble the personnel in other specialized disciplines and industries in America.[76]

Incapable of seriously entertaining the romantic isolation of a van Gogh, the notion of working-class affiliation (as left-wing artists did in the 1930s), or a fall from grace (as did the Beats), the avant-garde artist of the "American Era" went to work in a world where work and leisure had become indistinguishable, the status of the art object more a crisis than a status, and the old-school function of the avant-garde artist (to oppose capital) almost *but not quite* untenable. "Unfortunately," Kaprow writes, "there is nowhere else to go."[77]

Representational strategies would surely be affected by such basic life conditions. Unlike their avant-garde forebears, the experimental performance community did not have the luxury of autonomy, either as myth or reality—their places in the art world and the "real" world were equally precarious. The fully developed commodity spectacle described by Huyssen and the fully developed leisure industry hinted at by Crow had rendered work and leisure inseparable. Devoid of autonomy, artistic production entered the realm of work, as in Dick Higgins's score *Danger Music Number Twenty-Nine* (March 1963): "Get a job for its own sake."[78]

The urge among event artists to overcome the guilty terror and omnipresent uncertainty infusing the relations among commerce, art, and the everyday virtually guaranteed that Happenings and Fluxus events guaranteed them critical scorn from their contemporaries, particularly from those whose disapproval was indebted to a romantic insistence on art's lack of commerce with, well, commerce. In a letter to fellow former Dadaist Hans Richter, famed cross-dresser, ludic chess-player, and (via Cage) singular influence on Happenings and Fluxus Marcel Duchamp wrote, "When I discovered ready-mades, I thought to discourage aesthetics. In Neo-Dada they have taken my ready-mades and found aesthetic beauty in them. I threw the bottle-rack and urinal into their faces as a challenge and now they admire them for their aesthetic beauty."[79] This may well be true; however, Duchamp's comments beg the question of whether the concepts and institutions of the aesthetic and the avant-garde had shifted or transformed since Duchamp first entered his *Urinal* into a New York art exhibit and let loose the virus of conceptual art. Sad to say, but many of Duchamp's readymades *are* lovely objects, visually enticing in the most uncritical ways. We've learned Duchamp's lessons well. Duchamp begs the question: he may have in fact aided and abetted transformations in the aesthetic and the avant-garde—and in the commodity form with which it is locked in a wildly veering box step. Given Huyssen and Crow's comments concerning the growth of the culture and leisure industries during the twentieth century (and the development of industrial design, a field neither one considers), it may be more appropriate to ask whether the antiaesthetic gesture of Duchamp possessed any real institutional (as opposed to imaginative) strength by the early 1960s. Beauty is what escaped.

If such a shift has indeed occurred since the advent of the avant-garde (and it is difficult to argue otherwise given the convincing work of Bürger, Huyssen, Debord, and the Eulogist School on the subject), and if such a shift has been abetted in some fashion by the avant-garde itself and the institutions that govern the circulation and reception of avant-garde art, then it behooves the critic to follow the intentions of the event artists and recognize that, rather than a definable boundary or conceptual distinction, the line between art and nonart is fluid and negotiable, unspecifiable, inalienable. Such fluidity and negotiation were foregrounded in Ken Dewey's *City Scale* (1963), in which participants were led through the streets of New York and exposed to a variety of events (a woman undressing in a window, a tour of a cafeteria, a walk through a bookshop, an automobile "ballet" in a parking lot, etc.) in order to challenge their ability to delineate the intentional from the accidental, the aesthetic from the commodity. Like other FLUX-TOURS the intent of Dewey's piece was to *challenge* such distinctions, not conflate or synthesize, certainly not to construct boundaries of the sort described by Duchamp. As Kaprow argued in "The Education of the Un-Artist," "The art-not-art dialectic is essential."[80]

Crow has demonstrated that "[f]rom its beginning, the artistic avant-garde has discovered, renewed, or re-invented itself by identifying with marginal, 'non-artistic' forms of expressivity and display—forms improvised by other social groups out of the degraded materials of capitalist manufacture."[81] Modern artists have, Crow elaborates, depended on the apparent "aimlessness" of nonart activities such as leisure and consumption for its models of expressive and community autonomy. Dewey's event certainly functions in a context similar to that described by Crow. But Dewey's event is itself a marginal, nonartistic form of expressivity and display created within a social class that was itself marginalized. Arjun Appadurai argues that "[t]he diversion of commodities from specified [traditional, legal, or habitual] paths is always a sign of creativity or crisis, whether aesthetic or economic. . . . The diversion of commodities from their customary paths always carries a risky and morally ambiguous aura."[82] In fact, the attempt to regulate such paths is an inherently contradictory effort: "[T]he politics of enclaving [valued goods], far from being a guarantor of systemic stability, may constitute the Trojan horse of change."[83]

If we complement Appadurai's analysis with Kaprow's comments concerning the degraded social status of artists after 1945, we might usefully assert that, given the increasingly dubious distinction between artist and intellectual laborer in the 1950s and 1960s, Duchamp's distinction between aesthetic and nonaesthetic activities reflects the conceptual possibilities (and limitations) of the avant-garde as a mode of community and communication, possibilities that were not available to the subcultural formation that created event art during the first half of the Cold War. Appadurai's and Kaprow's commentaries suggest that one of the most effective ways to challenge existing social structures is to appropriate and divert its systems of value into "inappropriate" contexts and processes, as was the case with early American performance art's engagement with Cold War capitalism, an engagement that, like *Meat Joy,* was pleasurable, critical, shocking, and profoundly distasteful. Dewey's *City Scale* foregrounds the very act of voyeurism and borrowing upon which the avant-garde was founded and thereby foregrounds the social and institutional privileges of the artist, privileges that seemed increasingly dubious to the artists and audiences of such events.

Crow makes the important point that avant-garde formal experiment has tended to depend for its content on marginal forms of production, leisure, and consumption. Likewise, such dependency tends to put the critical dimensions of the art at risk once those forms of production, leisure, and consumption are brought in from the margins. But I am not so certain (as Crow seems to be) that the mainstreaming of subversive leisure and consumption is always or ultimately prone to strictly rational or utilitarian consideration. It, too, has its Proustian dimensions, dimensions that may afford an alteration or "perversion" of capitalist exchange. The history of capitalism is replete with moments when nonrational, nonutilitarian forms of leisure and consumption threatened to ruin the economic system as such.

One might recall the "Tulipomania" suffered by the Dutch at the beginning of the seventeenth century when a single bulb of *Semper Augustus* could claim a price equivalent to fifty thousand dollars today. When the "tulip bubble" burst, according to Charles Mackay, "Substantial merchants were reduced almost to beggary, and many a representative of a noble line saw the fortunes of his house ruined beyond redemption."[84] The Happenings and Fluxus events seem to exploit the unstable relationship between subversive leisure and capitalist rationalization as a way of protecting their own fragile social status from the threats of transformative, irrational capital. Appadurai would argue that such subversive forms, when linked with the ambiguous "liberties" of the market, tend to "combine the aesthetic impulse, the entrepreneurial link, and the touch of the morally shocking."[85]

In other words, if the avant-garde has been recuperated, then the forces of recuperation might have been altered, too. This is a logical and historically valid position as is demonstrated in Ernesto Laclau and Chantal Mouffe's *Hegemony and Socialist Strategy*. As they demonstrate in their genealogy of the concept of "hegemony," the increased interest in questions of cultural power during the twentieth century is due, at least in part, to a crisis in the relationship of vanguard and masses. Though their capsule explanation is a dense one, it bears careful reading:

> "Hegemony" will allude to an absent totality, and to the diverse attempts at recomposition and rearticulation which, in overcoming this original absence, made it possible for struggles to be given a meaning and for historical forces to be endowed with full positivity. The contexts in which the concept appear will be those of a fault (in the geological sense), of a fissure that had to be filled up, of a contingency that had to be overcome.[86]

As they discover in a careful examination of Rosa Luxemburg's concept of "spontaneity," "[t]he unity between the economic and the political struggle—that is to say, the very unity of the working class as a practical and theoretical tendency—is a consequence of the movement of feedback and interaction. But this movement in turn is nothing other than the process of revolution."[87] Any act of domination leaves a "hegemonic suture," a discursive force field that warps both dominator and dominated.[88] This is the central point of Laclau and Mouffe's book: Any act of domination alters both the dominator and the game of domination. The terrain of the contest is changed by the relative positions of the antagonists. In short, be careful what you eat because it might take a bite out of you.

Proust's sodden morsel of teacake has come back into view, now at the magnitude of an Oldenburg sculpture: the all-consuming consumable. The combination of aesthetics, entrepreneurialism, precious individualism, and shock that was fundamental to the Happenings and Fluxus community was recognized by Marx as a parcel of the commodity itself, which he famously described as a "very queer thing, abounding in metaphysical subtleties and theological niceties."[89] During much of the Cold War, one of the queerest of commodities was the art object, which enjoyed a fascinatingly speculative character.[90] Such fascination is certainly reflected in Oldenburg's *Store,* with its banal objects made fantastic by invisible pressures and excessive dreams (to recall Schneeman's description).[91] Likewise the painting in Dine's *The Smiling Workman:* its inscription ("I LOVE WHAT IM") blurs the line between labor, desire, and being and presages the literal consumption of artistic materials and the literal breaking of the representational frame. Likewise the objects that chattered about the Reubens Gallery in Kaprow's *Eighteen Happenings in Six Parts* and the salads and soups of Knowles's domestic scripts. Like these other artists, Oldenburg fetishized the fetish, selling broken-down fantasies of unlimited productivity and consumption by selling essentially unconsumable commodities, partly digested, unproductive products. *Store Days* marketed the loopy metaphysics of late-capitalist abundance, an abundance that no longer seemed to depend on enormous corporations and centralized states, but merely on the whims of the individual.

But this decentralized productivity also brought with it profound fears of the object itself as a threat to community coherence—not to mention fears that the party could end at any time with no advance notice. The dematrixed objects (whether quite literally objects—matches, cans of food or coffee, melting ice—or strips of "restored behavior") of Happenings and Fluxus events speak to an essential distance between the self and its world enabled by the transformative event. While a certain degree of power was granted the spectator-participant (as Delaney demonstrates in his insightful Proustian meditations on his partial view and as Knowles and Johnston demonstrate in their protofeminist performances), such power came only with the destruction of narrative and audience. Nevertheless, despite their deformation under the pressures of commodification, such events enabled an intensified individual productivity, community fame, and self-generating histories on par with the grandest fantasies of the country's most utopian technocrats.

The urge to engage the shifting lines between life, art, and the commodity underwrite an astonishing number of Happenings and Fluxus events. Thus they function as a mode of performative subversion that sought to reveal the inherently subversive nature of production and consumption in advanced, spectacular capitalism. And in this sense, the Happenings and Fluxus events may have fallen victim to their own deconstructive methods. Fluxus artist and critic Ina Blom describes the intricate conceptual maneuvers required to extricate Fluxus from the cultural logic of late capitalism; maneuvers that specifically concern the objective remains of the era:

> Inherent in most Fluxus work (I would perhaps call it a main characteristic) is the feeling that the work need not be a "work" at all: its true realization would be as an idea floating freely up in the spheres somewhere, and not in a platonic sense, either, since the boxes [in which Fluxus scripts and objects were commonly sold] do not relate to the concept as the shadow (or the shadow of a shadow) to the idea. In the true Americanized Zen-spirit of the Sixties, the concept is just the manifestation, and so the boxes, the objects, and the performances are, in the deepest sense, irrelevant; a side order arriving too late to be enjoyed with the main dish.[92]

The metaphor—the commodity—was the method. Blom warns the scholar not to be overly concerned with either the object or objectivity, not the text, not the memoir; but rather to be attuned to the "holistic silence" in which these fragmentary events now exist in the cultural memory. Her warning that the retroactive gaze of criticism inherently subverts the present-oriented nature of early event art is more than warranted, precisely because it identifies the fundamental liberalism motivating the early performance art subculture. Attempting to define their practice in the rapidly shrinking interstices of an expansive and intensive capitalism, the artists and audiences of these events attempted to have their cake and eat it, too.

Such cultivate-one's-own-garden attitudes were hotly scorned not only by Duchamp, but by another community that recognized and exploited the contradictory cultural logics of advanced capitalism: the Situationist International, which instigated the dematrixing of intellectual capital and the mass participation of students and workers in Paris during the events of May 1968. The links between the SI and the Happenings are extremely rich but much too complex to enumerate here. Both were part of a hot ferment of theory and practice surrounding the question of art's increasing inseparability from the commodity form, a ferment that manifested itself in diverse sites across the globe, including New York, Hanover, Tokyo, Mexico City, and São Paolo.[93]

Kristine Stiles has explored the historical and theoretical significance of the SI's exclusion of artists such as Asger Jorn, particularly as it relates to the "theory death" (to recall Mann) of Situationism in contemporary cultural studies. Stiles argues that "[t]he historical irony of the absorption of the SI in academia [particularly in cultural studies] is that artists whose social aims resembled theirs and with whom they contended in the 1960s still remain outside critical discussion despite these artists' efforts to create an aesthetic strategy that would *insert* their aims into the discourses of art and its history."[94] As a result, Situationism *as theory* has been stabilized "at the expense of the behavioral 'situations' themselves [and] . . . at the exclusion of the actual behavioral alteration of material conditions."[95] Stiles asserts that this simultaneous absorption and rejection is the result of a post-1968 split between direct action and critical representation engendered by, among other things, the rise of a postmodernist academy "in which 'plurality,' 'appropriation,' and 'simulacrum' are championed as deconstructive modes of counterattack on the 'society of the spectacle,'" and in which the question of radical action has become increasingly problematized."[96]

I would argue, contrary to Stiles, that the practical and conceptual split between action and representation can be sighted much earlier, not at the rise of "tenured radicals," officially sanctioned performance art, and post-Fordism at the end of the 1960s, but rather at its beginning. Once more, it was in 1962 that a left tendency within the Situationist International excluded those Situationists who still believed in the possibility of radical art. The coup led by Guy Debord and ratified by an intense period of theoretical production and publication instigated the SI's increasing reliance on *theory* and *text,* the two entities that, according to Stiles, have most contributed to the absorption of Situationism, the two entities that, according to Higgins and Kaprow, were most insistently rejected by the Happenings. The irony is profound: the activities of the excluded have been forgotten and in some sense remain un-co-opted; the theories of the vanguard have become critical commonplaces and, it would seem, co-opted. In a sense, both vanguards attempted to devise aesthetic and economic strategies to ensure their survival in an era of spectacular obsolescence.

As I've mentioned before, by 1968, the watershed year of the Situationist International, Happenings had more or less disappeared from the scene and Fluxus had gone underground. That said, their absence should not deceive us; their influence on subsequent theater and performance has been profound—as has their influence on subsequent political organizing and demonstration. Recognizing this, we can account for an anomaly on Maciunas's "Diagram of Historical Development": 1968 is a virtually empty horizontal band not because of the *absence* of performances that year, but because of their *overwhelmingly general presence.*

But, given the historical irony identified by Stiles, it may be worth recalling a moment in the shared history of the SI and the Happenings. In 1963,
a year after the exclusion of the artists, the SI published a critique of the
Happenings in an issue of their organization's journal devoted to criticism of
the trope of "nature," the "universality" of language, and the increasingly
counter-Situationist tendencies in art. The essay, "The Avant-Garde of
Presence," attempted to establish clear boundaries between Happenings and
"situations." The SI argues that "the happening is an attempt to construct a
situation . . . on a foundation of poverty . . . In contrast, the situation
defined by the SI can be constructed only on a foundation of material and
spiritual riches."[97] The question of wealth and poverty aside for a moment,
it is worth noting again that nearly one hundred years after Manet's crucial
avant-garde gesture, *Le Déjeuner sur l'Herbe,* the imagination of freedom by
Parisian students and workers in 1968 still depended on the cultivation of
scandalous desire, the looting of commodified pleasures, and the reappropriation of stolen time. In other words, the SI's program derived fundamentally from the same cultural logic as the historical avant-garde, and
derived from a social and methodological engagement with the putatively
oppositional practices of those marginalized by capitalist development and
bourgeois taste politics (the chronic unemployed, the professional student,
the drunk).

The SI's critique of the Happenings was based not on aesthetics (aesthetics were irrelevant to the question), but of the *location* and *use* of the event—
and of the crucial role to be played by an audience no longer content with
spectatorship: "[T]he first ventures in constructing situations must be the
work/play of the revolutionary avant-garde; people who are resigned in
one or another respect to political passivity, to metaphysical despair, and
even to being subjected to an artistic pure absence of creativity, are incapable of participating in them."[98] Given the close formal relationships
between the SI and the international performance art scene of the time, one
might wonder what would have "happened" had the SI not excluded its
artists in 1962, had not devoted itself to text and theory, but had attempted
to negotiate a "double front" of aesthetic and practical activity. What critical tactics might be available to cultural studies today if the split between
radical action and representation had not occurred in this particularly crucial
vanguard organization?

Considering the ways in which Happenings and Fluxus events have in
some sense evaded the critical gaze of the academy, leaving the events
themselves in a curiously unalienated state of potential, one might wonder
what would have "happened" had the performance art community

embraced a more coherent political program (a position maintained, for example, by Fluxartist Henry Flynt throughout the 1960s) while maintaining its complex engagement with the institutions and technologies of capitalist innovation. The futurist flirtation with Italian nationalism and the surrealist commitment to anarchist communism only confirm the historical irony marked by the split between the Happening and the Situationist International. The particular, ambivalent negotiation of the art/commodity divide that we call Happenings and Fluxus marks only a brief moment in a long history of lost chances. The avant-garde's engagement with capital-in-transformation has afforded new concepts, techniques, and sources of value. And if revolution is indeed a complex process of borrowing, appropriation, destruction, and reconstruction, then it may behoove the next vanguard to study those that have been left hanging on the horns of transformative capitalism.

5. Performance and the Mode of Production

Though it would be interesting to speculate about an alternative historical timeline or imaginary cul-de-sac in which the avant-garde managed to finally elude the horns of transformative capitalism, the implications of the richly productive mode of "temporal antagonism" apparent in Happenings and Fluxus events can be instructive. How might the tendencies of capitalism be diverted were its performative necessities enriched, diverted, complicated, and most importantly, generalized as in the aesthetic logics of the Happenings and Fluxus events? A utopian question of the first order, I think. By exploring this cul-de-sac a bit more, we can work through the critical permutations of early American performance art—particularly the extreme ones described thus far—to test the validity of the avant-garde's oppositional stance vis-à-vis capitalist growth and transformation. Louis Althusser writes that the "truth" of any particular mode of producing knowledge (and every theory is, for Althusser, a way of producing knowledge, a kind of technology that produces a peculiar kind of use and exchange value) "constitute[s] pertinent 'experiments' for the theory's reflection on itself and its internal development."[99]

Althusser tells us that this is as true of the failures of a particular experiment as it is of the successes, a considerable consolation to scholars of avant-garde history, a history whose failures far outnumber successes and whose successes tend more often than not to serve the Right rather than the Left. The avant-garde's long-running war within bourgeois capitalism can be understood, at least in part, as a war over the methods and social significance of production, circulation, and consumption; a war waged on the fluid, shocking, fractured front-line between the aesthetic and the nonaesthetic. The failure or success of a particular avant-garde antagonistic mode is ultimately irrelevant, because the avant-garde can be understood (at least in part) as a *mode of aesthetic production* that contains within it a vision of futurity, a vision of a better, more just, critically aestheticized society lurking within the ruins of the present society.[100] As such, it is capable of being rejuvenated, revised, resituated.

Maciunas's genealogy, in line with T. S. Eliot's "Tradition and the Individual Talent," demonstrates that every art event unfurls a history. It does this occasionally without the presence of great works of the kind associated with Michelangelo, Ibsen, Hansberry, or Picasso (or Eliot, for that matter). At a certain extreme, the avant-garde hardly allows itself to be seen, even by its own members. At that extreme, often a theory and a spare collection of moth-eaten objects are all that is passed down to descendants.

That said, disappearance is not the goal of Happenings or Fluxus; indeed, a theory and a spare collection are, as I've demonstrated, treasure. This Cold War avant-garde focused on performance not simply as a theoretical principle, but also as an activist lever, a kind of self-contained, paradoxically Walter Mittyish recipe for social action. Performance was a public, gregarious activity for these artists—not simply objects were produced, but objects in space, objects in relationships, objects in mediation. Happenings and Fluxus took the two aspects of performance—something that is both done and judged—into public space and into various forms of social hierarchy and communication and put them into a highly fluid dynamic. This unstable dynamic is the core of the productive processes of memory, aesthetic reception, and object creation. Two questions arise that define and bound this particular Cold War avant-garde: What was produced by Happenings and Fluxus? How was that production an example of the temporal antagonism of the avant-garde?

To begin answering these questions, a definition of "mode of production" is useful. Marx used the term to describe the basic social relations and material processes that dominated a society's understanding of value at a given time. For Marx, the most significant aspect of such relations was the division of labor, the separation and hierarchicization of a society in order to amplify the wealth and power of one or more groups in a society at the expense of others. In Marx, such relations are governed by a basic and brutal scarcity (either real or imagined); thus, social and material relations are organized in relations of *ownership* and *nonownership* to enable the success and survival of certain classes within society. The means of production—be it a machine for producing clock hands, a particular kind of literacy, or a paintbrush—are controlled to benefit certain classes of people. That benefit tends, by and large, to be protected both by military resources and by *philosophical* resources that defend the rights of differential ownership. However, under capitalism, Marx argues, the rapid growth of power enabled by technology, industry, and the massing of labor power in modern city enable a previously unimaginable event: the radical democratization of production relations enabled by the destruction of capitalist relations and the creation of a socialist society.

This potential compels (both consciously and unconsciously) the owners and their favored associates to develop methods of control and command that allow them both to harness whatever productive potential is available as well as manage the continual social crises caused by the unfolding of this potential. Following Antonio Gramsci's lead, Althusser divided these control-and-command methods into two kinds: "repressive state apparatuses" that use force and violence to suppress actions that might put in jeopardy fundamental relations of ownership; and "ideological state apparatuses" that use persuasion, seduction, and strategically truthful education to enable the most "productive" individual possible.[101] The latter apparatuses do not simply produce propagandistic messages to be received by drones; quite the contrary, as Althusser's student Michel Foucault demonstrates, not simply ideological messages are produced by such institutions, but individuals, subjects. And the history of these apparatuses demonstrates in its tangled genealogies that such production is both innovative and productive of oddities such as phrenology, mesmerism, or Dianetics. It is within such overlapping, variably permanent institutions that the individual acquires an identity that defines a productive relationship of the individual to the social structure and the basic methods of value creation.

Althusser stresses that this is an *imaginary* relationship; in other words, the individual works within a productive fiction, an "imaginary relationship of individuals to their real conditions of existence."[102] Given this tangled, grotesque relationship of subjectivity, representation, and basic material relations, what can the critic do? For Althusser, the project of Marxist criticism was the construction of a *science* (a knowledge free of the subject's historically and socially situated bias) that would describe the nature of ideological distortion and, thereby, enable a bias-free understanding of the material relations in which humans work and suffer. This puts him into a very difficult situation, as more than one critic has noted: "Now it is this knowledge that we have to reach . . . while speaking in ideology, and from within ideology we have to outline a discourse which tries to break with ideology, in order to dare to be the beginning of a scientific (i.e. subjectless) discourse on ideology."[103]

The importance of Althusser to the understanding of the interplay of economics, representation, and subjectivity in relationship to early American performance art is less due to this extremely problematic description of "science" and to his revision of Antonio Gramsci's theory of the relation-

ship of intellectuals to the civil state than to his welcome recognition that
the ideological state apparatuses are extremely varied, anchored to distinct
elements within the total social structure, and that (in a move that should
garner the sympathy of performance theorists) they penetrate the practices
of everyday life: "a small church, a funeral, a minor match at a sports' club,
a school day, a political party meeting," and, by extension, such situation-
specific gestures as "kneeling down . . . a gaze . . . a hand-shake," each of
which possesses a "materiality" dependent on the relative significance of the
ideological institution in question.[104]

It is at this level, the level of everyday life and everyday institutions,
where the lighting of a match might reveal imaginary relationships of selves,
bodies, gestures, and the banal objects that surround them, that the
significance of Happenings and Fluxus can be found in a way that is germane to their oppositional position within Cold War capitalism. Though it
is far from the "ultimately determining instance" of economics that grounds
Althusser's work in the Marxist tradition and keeps him just the other side
of a truly neo-Marxist analytic, the economically self-conscious, class-con-
scious, production-conscious nature of much early American performance
art nonetheless functions within a similar kind of "problematic": the liberating potential of capitalist development gravely threatened the Left's
enduring mission to link criticism, social agency, and productivity in progressive, democratic fashion.

Though hardly Marxist in tone or rhetoric, the Happenings and Fluxus
events are nonetheless tangled up with Althusser and with the Situationist
International, whose key text, *The Society of the Spectacle,* is one of the most
trenchant and influential of analyses of the threat posed to democratic revolution by the disciplinary innovations of capitalism.[105] Early American performance art is just that, art, and is able to defend itself by relying on a highly
situational aesthetic (the mere "pretense" of an aesthetic, to recall Vautier)
in order to outwit the rationalist demands of political analysis. As a consequence, though such art events lack the obvious political impact of the SI,
they have avoided the theory death suffered by the SI. Flexibility seems to
ensure survival (as does scuttling about close to the ground, as the earliest
forms of mammalian life learned to our collective benefit). The Situationists
were as fundamentalist as Althusser, believing, as Althusser did, in an ultimate ground for critical analysis (not science, however, but the free flow of
debate and organization exemplified by the ultrademocratic committee).
However, given the *fluxiosity* of objects, relations to objects, and relations to
relations to objects described earlier (the enigma within the frame within
the frame that is the aesthetic event), it is difficult to define specifically the

relationship of producers and consumers as well as the value that is produced within the art events and avant-garde subcultures analyzed in these pages, and this is a potent source of productive potential.

Thus, while I am uncomfortable with even the self-critical reliance on the category of "science" in Althusser's work, his theory is useful to this case study. It enables us to make sense not simply of the objects of avant-garde oppositionality (value production and social relations), but also the problem of how we *know* those objects given the fact that we live within an economic system, a system that we simply cannot step outside of, a system that biases our criticism, often in ways we cannot recognize. The resurgent nature of performance events couples with reticular critical effects to produce an object that simultaneously opposes capitalism and knowledge.

Even so, Althusser was profoundly committed to identifying and wrecking the illusions of critical theory. By exploring the way that Marx rejected the Hegelian notion that what we know is identical to the thing that we are attempting to know ("the real process [thus identified] with the knowledge process"),[106] Althusser was able to describe what he believed to be a truly Marxist apparatus of thought, one congenial to a post-Stalinist communism as well as a "neo" avant-garde. Such apparatuses of thought, like all forms of knowledge, are distinct modes of production. Althusser and Balibar explain that knowledge, "[a]s such, . . . is constituted by a structure which combines . . . the type of object (raw material) on which it labors, the theoretical means of production available (its theory, its method and its technique, experimental or otherwise) and the historical relations (both theoretical, ideological, and social) in which it produces."[107] Marxism is a perfect example of how a *critical* system functions as a mode of production; Marxism is a theoretical model that guides the development and implementation of an interlocking system of ethos, object, and social relationships.

Althusser's reading of Marx has been lurking in my analysis of the value of the object (the spasmic walk of a toy robot, the lighting of a match, the Fluxus movement), the relationship of the spectator-participant to the object in moments of performance, and the relationship to the relationship to the object as it survives in the many media utilized by the scholar to make sense of such events historically and critically. Again, the enigma within the frame within the frame that is early American performance art presents us with a very thorny historiographical and theoretical problem. By approaching the problem through the attitudes and methods of Proust, Benjamin, and (now) Althusser, I am trying to understand how Happenings and Fluxus events open up, by way of the process of dematrixing, a productive gap between objects and ways of knowing, a gap that mirrors Cold War capitalism's intensively alienating innovations, but in a kind of fun-house fashion. This swirling, reticular, grotesque gap, once opened, has two interesting effects: (1) self-critical tendencies in scholarship that can be characterized as Proustian or fetishistic, and (2) expansive and intensive kinds of "political" analysis, aspects of which I have explored in Benjaminian fashion in the experiences of Delaney, Johnston, Knowles, and my students.

Both Thomas Crow and Manfredo Tafuri (in his groundbreaking polemic, *Architecture and Utopia*) have mortally wounded the old myth of the avant-garde as a force external to the developmental history of capitalism.[108] However, the *myth* of the avant-garde remains vital, even among those such as Maciunas, Kaprow, and Ono who understood the hopelessly compromised position of the avant-garde artist. Early American performance art indeed reflects the structural limitations of the Cold War avant-garde, but does not admit defeat; rather, it devises a change in strategy in order to secure the responsibilities of the avant-garde, responsibilities whose enactment was surrounded by limits well known to the artists themselves. Indeed, these limits of the avant-garde were often manipulated in highly self-conscious ways in order to enable even a miniscule act of transgressive production.

Jack Burnham's essay "Problems of Criticism," first published in 1971, convincingly argues the untenability of the avant-garde as a futurological imperative, but without falling into the parochial cynicism of the Eulogist School. He does this by attempting, for perhaps the first time, to identify the linguistic and logical structure of the myth of the avant-garde, engaging in an analysis that falls very close to Althusser's in terms of its intellectual precursors (namely, Claude Lévi-Strauss's structuralist anthropology) and its critical intentions. Like Althusser, Burnham targets the unconscious, ideological notions of *time* that lurk at the center of the myth. Althusser criticizes classic political economy for imagining that anything can run ahead of its time. "The present," he and Balibar write, "constitutes the *absolute horizon* of all knowing, since all knowing can never be anything but the existence in knowing of the internal principle of the whole. . . . Even if [philosophy] takes wing at dusk, it still belongs to the day, to the today . . . tomorrow is in essence forbidden it."[109] Burnham argues that the avant-garde is a linguistic concept based on "transparently logical mechanisms" that sustain the idea of historical change.[110] "Being linguistic, art cannot evolve or progress; it can only define the parameters of linguistic expression allotted to it."[111] Even so, the myth survives. Why? Because, as Lévi-Strauss argues, we exist in a semihostile (at least) environment, and myths help mediate the boundaries between security and hostility. The myth of the avant-garde isn't a lux-

ury, it is a necessity rooted in the need to humanize technological and economic innovation and crisis.

It is the idea of *generalization,* of a radical decentralization of the avant-
garde project, that saves Burnham from becoming one more member of the
Eulogist School. Following Duchamp, Burnham suggests that artists "go
underground" (68). He writes, "The underground artist may well be a
housekeeper or a businessman, since these are professions where *naturaliza-
tion of the cultural and culturalization of the natural* can take place through ordinary skills" (68). Burnham makes a move here that is typical of structuralist
critics: having done away with the idea of *time,* he invests *space* with radical
potential. In this case, having done away with the idea of avant-garde futur-
ology, he invests the surrealist idea that art must be made by all with new
energy. Art, rather than being the lever of temporal transformation,
becomes the lever of antitemporal inertia. Time, no longer the measure of
progress from point A to point B in history, becomes simply material for an
art that brooks no social, geopolitical, or critical hierarchies. "Obviously,"
Burnham concludes, "it is no longer important who is or is not a good artist;
the only sensible question is—as is already grasped by some young people—
why isn't everybody an artist?"[112]

It's difficult to overestimate the importance of Burnham's question,
asked as it was during the interregnum between the first wave of performance art and the first wave of punk. Burnham's question is a poised
moment between the recognition of universal productivity and the
inflationary economic consequences of such productivity's implementation,
between the identification of a certain myth of history and degeneration
into cynical self-absorption and malaise. The coincidence of the Do-It-
Yourself aesthetic with the rejection of the idea of progressive, linear history
is not accidental. The development of a truly global market demands a
rethinking of both value and time. As local traditions experience the buffet
and impact of intensive marketing, local ideas about value and time must
achieve dominance, be defeated and incorporated, or admit relativism. Is it
accidental that performance studies is coincident with the intensive globalization of capital during the Cold War? Without at all forfeiting the critical
value of performance studies, we can nonetheless admit that avant-garde
performance was not the only place where dematrixing was occurring; it
was also occurring on a theoretical level in performance studies and on a
practical level in the innovative capitalist enclaves that gave us punk, hip-
hop, and camp.

Though coincident and even contributory to capitalist intensification,
performance studies marks out precisely the critical problem central to the

avant-garde: time. Performance bides its time, keeps it secure, submits to it, persists in it, commits to it. Avant-garde performance—here, the early American performance art scene—bides avant-garde time, securing it against various forms of expropriation. Perhaps early American performance art forms such as the Happening and the Fluxus event actually enabled the survival of the counterculture, provided escape routes and loopholes during the years of reaction that followed 1968. It supplied an opportunity to play with the kind of ontological awareness that spread throughout the Left during the 1970s, an awareness described by Antonio Negri as rooted in an "intolerable fickleness (that is, intolerable for whoever has aims which are exploitative or instrumental in nature)."[113] This awareness is, in short, the awareness of intellectual labor as labor and the "mobility and power" it enjoys and supplies to capitalism.[114]

For Negri, work has become generalized, "diffused throughout the entire society."[115] Thus, "Every subject of this productive complex is caught up in overpowering cooperative networks."[116] As a consequence of this generalization, value becomes diffuse: "The whole of society is placed at the disposal of profit . . . and the infinite temporal variations that compose society are arranged, set and made malleable in a unitary process." Negri therefore calls for the oppositional activities of cooperation and communication: "Work abandons the factory in order to find, precisely in the social, a place adequate to the functions of concentrating productive activity and transforming it into value."[117] The "judo throw" of performativity is, to Negri, both the product and the doom of capitalism: "This accumulation of potentialities and their appearance in an unmediated form is both a product of capitalist development and one of its residues. That is to say, the accumulation of potentialities is something which capital has produced but has not been able to exploit. It is something which falls outside the framework of capitalist production and which only socially liberated labor can put to use."[118]

The situational, reticular, fetishistic aesthetic of Happenings and Fluxus events modeled—and perhaps partly catalyzed—the highly mobile, acutely productive, intensely social work celebrated by Negri. But here's the rub: If performativity is generalized (and Negri is ultimately describing a performative vision of community and work), does it possess any real critical perspective? To shift the frame a bit, do such performative productions fulfill both aspects of performance, a something done and a *judging* of that doing? Do the two aspects exist in a dynamic that allows the one to reveal and critique the other? In other words, we must return to the question I raised before: What is produced by Happenings and Fluxus events, objects or relationships? However, I don't think that's a question that can be answered, not because it is too hard to answer, but because it's so frustratingly *easy*. And there are so many of them. The answers are so numerous that they boggle the ability to fully and comprehensively describe and judge them.

So another question: How was this situational, reticular, fetishistic, performative production aesthetic a functioning example of the temporal antagonism of the avant-garde? This is the question that leads me back to the start of this second case, to Proust and Benjamin. The answer is that it often *wasn't* a particularly functional example, but occasionally could be. Lacking an overarching sense of history, politics, and identity, the artists and audiences of early American performance art vanished into a landscape of dangerous boredom and sudden association. The unknowability of the form is the coy disguise worn by this seductively oppositional art to ensure its survival and mobility amid an increasingly dextrous, seductive, and intimate capitalism. The issue, then, is less whether or not this particular avant-garde disappeared into the trackless reticules of capitalist performativity (it surely has) than what will happen when it finds its way back out. The answer to this final question is one, I suspect, that will happen well beyond critical view and scholarly earshot.

CASE 3 THE BLACK ARTS MOVEMENT
Text, Performance, Blackness

Can you hear? Here
I am again. Your boy, dynamite. Can
You hear? My soul is moved. The soul
You gave me. I say, my soul, and it
Is moved. That soul
You gave me.
. . . .
I mean
Can you?
　　　　　—Amiri Baraka, "A Poem for Willie Best"

6. Blackness as Critical Practice

Soul: Textual, Performative, and Otherwise

In Ed Bullins's one-act play *Malcolm: '71, or Publishing Blackness* (1975), the reader discovers a highly self-reflexive, racially charged drama of (of all things) editorial negotiation. A drama about editing is rather odd find in a countercultural movement dedicated to the destruction of the West and its intellectual models. However, when we consider that avant-garde tradition has often focused on the textual object and its deep links to power, the drama might not seem quite so odd. Nevertheless, Bullins's play stands as a unique contribution within that tradition. In it, the textual object is literally dramatized—and dramatized in ways that deserve careful inspection given my concern with the ways that avant-garde drama, theater, and performance of the 1960s thematize and exploit the limits of scholarship and criticism.

First, we should look over the dramatic structure of the piece. It is austerely crafted, no doubt. The structure is straight to the point, a characteristic of the agit-prop plays Bullins calls "revolutionary commercials." The curtain opens on "Blackman" in his study. The phone rings and he answers it, "Black Aesthetics Limited."[1] On the other end of the line, we hear "Whitegirl," calling on the recommendation of Professor "Jack Hack," "the white professor who teaches poetry and aesthetics at the new Black Revolutionary Third World City university . . . the Black Students' victory for burning down the administration building during that dreadful hassle over Black Studies."[2] She explains the nature of Professor Hack's project, an anthology of "Radical/Protest/People's Poetry." Meanwhile, in the background, a dog barks. After discovering that said canine is named "Malcolm" (as in "Malcolm X"), Blackman "gently hangs the phone up." Curtain falls. Nothing too complicated, at first glance.

For certain, this isn't the traditional fare of revolutionary theater, which tends to favor large-scale events like the storming of winter palaces, sit-downs at textile factories, or the arrival of indefatigable leaders. Bullins's

217

play seems so *minor* when we compare it to his agit-prop contemporaries, say, the *actos* of El Teatro Campesino or the haunting parades and tableaux of the Bread and Puppet Theater. However, the dramatization of a seemingly minor aspect of a far-reaching cultural revolution is what makes the Black Arts Movement (or BAM) so fascinating. As will become clear as I explore the BAM's complex, at times contradictory relations with that tradition, with Western philosophy and aesthetics—with, in sum, the West, period, including its vanguard tradition—the "soul power" of this movement demands real subtlety and persistence on the part of the scholar and critic.

A closer, more persistent look at *Malcolm: '71* helps us to understand this troubled relationship of the BAM and the Western tradition of cultural radicalism. First, Blackman's initial greeting ("Black Aesthetics Limited . . . Go on . . . run it on down") puns on the tensions among revolutionary aesthetics, economic necessity, essentialist views of ethnic-racial being that were common in the Black Arts Movement, and what might be called "racial-sexual-textual" politics. "Limited" puns on corporate structure (one in which contributor liability is limited to capital contribution) and the existential boundaries of this one man's struggle. The colloquial "run it on down" identifies Blackman as a man of the people, but also comments on the "running down" of the Black Aesthetic, its wearing out, its supersession. Second, our status as viewer or reader is in play here. As readers, as watchers, as teachers and critics, too, we (and I'm conscious of the diversity of identities covered by that "we") are explicitly identified by the play as a limiting and/or radicalizing factor. Whether we are reading or watching the play, we're made immediately conscious of our role in the politics of the "Black text." That politics would seem fairly broadly defined: By breaking contact with the offstage representative of an even farther offstage (white) editor, Blackman evades inclusion in the (white) text and, by logical extension, doglike domestication in the (white) lineage of "anarchists, wobblies, nihilists, etc." that will structure the proposed collection's chapters.[3] The representatives of domesticating (white) textuality are evaded by the sage, macho, Black man who carries on the revolution with a simple flick of the wrist. Third, *Malcolm: '71* puts into effect a combination of theatrical and textual techniques that produce a volatile blend of the dramatic, the iconographic, the materialist, and the deconstructive. Blackman is an iconographic, almost social-realistic (better said, "soulful-realistic") representative of the Black Revolution. He loves his Blackness the way the strapping young Bolshevik of the Soviet social-realist tradition loves his trusty tractor. However, Bullins nests the play's agit-prop message and style in what might be called a "dramatized discursive situation" in which play the performances of the actors and the performances of the audience, including us, the readers of the text.

Much as Claes Oldenburg used his Ray Gun Factory as both a studio and a performance site, as a hybrid space to explore the contradictions of memory and imagination in a commodity-saturated culture, Blackman uses the site of scholarly consideration (the study) to initiate concrete acts of material activism (the theater). This is indicated when Blackman performs his independence from white judgment by cutting connections with white-controlled textual industries, including the university. But this is itself an odd gesture, given that *The Black Scholar* was founded in 1969, a direct outgrowth of the Black Studies movement initiated by Black artists and activists in 1965 at San Francisco State University. First written in 1971, the play was revised for publication in 1975. The years between composition and publication saw the devastation of many of the independent educational and theatrical cooperatives of the Black Arts, including the New Lafayette Theatre, Bullins's home for almost seven years. The profound economic crisis that began in 1973 and the systematic destruction of radical political organizations by the Nixon administration's Counter-Intelligence Program (aka COINTELPRO) radically altered the conditions of Blackman's independence. Equipped with this contextual knowledge, we find the play evoking contradictory emotions, expressing a kind of militant, future-oriented nostalgia for institutional and personal possibilities no longer available. The flick of the wrist is haunted by futures lost.

As we saw in *The Connection* and Maciunas's *Fluxiosity*, the counterculture's struggle against the institutions that enabled it to exist was often the theme of the artwork, and just as often incorporated into the structure of the text. For some critics, this turn to process marked the death of art. During these same years, a period that saw the rise of so-called minimalist art, critic Michael Fried repeatedly attacked what he viewed as the increasing theatricality of art. His anxieties about the corruption of the art object are instructive to our efforts to read Black Arts Movement drama, theater, and performance. Theatricality is an inherently degenerative force, Fried argues, that undermines the objective autonomy of the art object and the specificity of the visual arts as an artistic medium and philosophical concern; in sum, undermines the modernist project as described by Clement Greenberg. The six-foot steel cube of the minimalist throws art into a chaotic aesthetic, institutional, and conceptual environment in which "everything counts," including the bodies of museum- and gallery-goers and the strategies of artistic interpretation they've carried with them.[4] Like the austere cube placed strategically in an otherwise empty space, Bullins's apparently simple agit-prop drama transforms the space of consideration into significant space, into "discursively dramatized" space.

Consider the books lining Blackman's walls. The textual objects on stage and off are wickedly unstable elements in the "limited" nature of this drama of Black Aesthetics. First of all, those texts *on* stage are props and, therefore, have an ambiguously significant materiality, a kind of dialectical quality characteristic of all props, a fitful conceptual instability that never fully resolves itself. This is a typical quality of the stage prop. In a fascinating analysis of the handkerchief prop in Shakespeare's *Othello,* Andrew Sofer writes,

> [F]rom a phenomenological perspective, the peculiarity of stage proper-
> ties is that they both are and are not themselves. Oscillating between sign
> and thing, props are "felt absences" that draw our attention simultane-
> ously to their signifying function—Bianca's word "token" simply means
> a sign—and to their materiality ("felt" is of course a particular fabric).[5]

In the case of *Malcolm: '71,* the books and magazines on stage are "felt absences," at once recognizable as texts that communicate a specific ideology and as iconographic weapons for the cultural revolution. They are both useful things and signs.

Then there's the proposed anthology. This purely hypothetical publication is *voiced* by Whitegirl and represents, if Blackman's courage should falter, the possibility of his own objectification, a reduction to commodified text. Unlike the books on stage, the anthology is a purely acoustic and linguistic apparition, a signifier, a sequence of sounds—a materially significant utterance that doesn't yet have being but carries the weight of institutional power (the press and the academic department) and the erotic solidity of the theatrical voice. Again, we see the body in play—exactly the thing that concerns Fried. In the revised version of the play, the one published in *The Black Scholar,* Bullins gets rid of the split-stage approach we find in the first version. Whitegirl is no longer visible in her own space. In the revised version, her whiteness and her femininity is established through voice and, possibly, the visible impact of that voice on Blackman's posture, gestures, and voice. The anthology enjoys a solidity rather different from the books surrounding Blackman. In fact, one might say that there are two dramatic conflicts here: the obvious one, Blackman versus Whitegirl; then the less obvious one, the battle of books.

There's one more textual prop to consider: the copy of *Black Scholar* in my hands. To recall Sofer again, this real-world journal both is and is not itself. The journal copy is a thing that shifts beneath our hands as its material and social determinants come into view and the drama plays out. The journal issue brings into the theatrical composition its own institutional, social, and historical contexts. It dramatizes its own material conditionality, becoming a prop in a play whose proscenium and temporal boundaries wickedly expand, tugging centrifugally on the very writing of this case study. The reader is forced to decide which end of the line he's holding. In this sense, the play affirms Anna Scott's assertion that the embodied practices of the Black Arts Movement are not based in romantic notions of "blood memories" or "retentions," but are instead a practice of ciphering and deciphering codes, a practice carried out by the artist, her audience, and her students.

Scott's point is important, as it identifies the "black arts makers" as those who "identify the process at work rather than solidify the codes into a fixed 'read,' thereby destroying their potential to traverse time, space, language, and national boundaries."[6] Of particular significance is her assertion that "recollection is purposeful and productive" rather than merely conservative.[7] As I hope to show in the following pages, such purposeful, productive remembering is anchored to performing contexts that persistently bring into play the demand to perform and to recognize the limits of criticism. An unusual but not atypical Black Arts text, *Malcolm: '71* manages to be an agit-prop call to action, an opportunity for meditation about a very local but important concern for revolutionary Black writers, performers, and critics, and a performative object that continues to catalyze concrete forms of material and conceptual critique in our own times. The play is very much like the Bahia dances described by Scott, which continually ask, "Yes, we gotta 'move somethin',' but what will it be: records and tapes or liberated black bodies?"[8]

The diverse BAM community saw the struggle against slave consciousness as a struggle against cultural, economic, and political compromise in art and against the denigration of folkways and everyday life practices. Likewise, they created and exploited a broad range of artistic techniques and media in order to politicize these folkways and practices, doing so with the belief that they would prize the autonomy of the African American community away from the forces of compromise and secure it within a permanently revolutionary, resolutely soulful Blackness. Which brings me to this chapter's epigraph. In 1964, Amiri Baraka (LeRoi Jones at the time, on the verge of Black Nationalism and the second of three name changes) published "A Poem for Willie Best," a text that systematically, at times expressionistically, and always with a high degree of self-reflexive poetic urge explores the contours of a terrain not unlike Blackman's study. Baraka's rigorous examination of the interrelated questions of aesthetic form, the commodification of art, and the necessity of rejecting a society of mass-mediated racism is worth examining in detail now that we have seen the kind of whirling complications raised by even an austere text like *Malcolm: '71*. If Bullins's play teaches us that Blackness is determined by the spaces in which Blackness is considered, celebrated, and cultivated, "A Poem for Willie Best" forces upon its reader the realization that Blackness must occupy a dangerous but strategically significant middle ground between mass-mediated, racist, commodity culture and the deepest, (at the time) uncelebrated, most vital, and secret precincts of African American culture. Soul is critical practice, not metaphysical mumbo-jumbo.

"Willie Best" is anything but austere, rather like a topographic map of cultural contradiction. The poem's continually changing visual and rhythmic structures complement the dizzying shifts in narrative voice and implied audience that are sounded in the text. To help him in the mapping of this infernal terrain, Baraka follows the fate of two African American singers who, not unlike the damned Florentines in Dante's *Inferno,* lived public lives in their communities, lives that have materially and spiritually impacted those communities. The first singer is Willie Best (aka "Sleep 'n' Eat") who performed demeaning, stereotypical, but physically and expressively honed roles in Hollywood, on screen and off, during the 1930s and 1940s. The other singer is an anonymous, itinerant, blues musician who travels through the juke joints and crossroads of rural America. Their fates, the former infernal, the latter perhaps purgatorial, can be read as defining the two paths available to the Black singer seeking a soulful nation in a society of spectacle. Though Baraka indicates only briefly and metonymically a way out of this contradiction—that is, the leather jackets of a youth gang stenciled with the etymologically uncertain history of the word *jazz*—the poem clearly addresses an imperative acutely described by Larry Neal: to reevaluate "Western aesthetics, the traditional role of the writer, and the social function of art." Neal's call for reevaluation is intended to obliterate what W. E. B. DuBois identified in *The Souls of Black Folk* (1903) as "double consciousness," the fissuring of self and community caused by racism, the sense that one is both an independent self and a self on view.[9]

The poem suggests that to be heard as a Black poet, the Black poet must be *seen*—though, judging from the title, perhaps not *named*. As we know, enforced visibility can contribute to the categorization, commodification, and humiliation of cultural producers. African American artists have had to continually struggle against being seen as merely "entertainers." Bill "Bojangles" Robinson, Louis Armstrong, Best, Bessie Smith, Flava Flav of Public Enemy—all of these artists negotiate positions that enable them a language and space in which to express themselves. Yet, at the same time, they risk reduction to stereotype. The negotiation demanded by this condition of "hypervisibility" (to recall Saidiya V. Hartmann's term)[10] is complicated, and must be acutely attuned to the vacillating attentions of the culture industry, its audiences, and the ongoing transformations of African America. In the poem, Best is an emblem of failed negotiation: He is silenced, crucified, and degraded, a kitsch-encrusted, prime-time, knockoff Christ symbol. The untitled bluesman, on the other hand, negotiates another kind of terrain, follows a path that rejects the enervating gaze of white, middle-class society, and plays instead only to the "Blackest" members of the African American community. The bluesman plays to the "lowest" economic and cultural levels of the African American community— and never stays for long. But he enjoys a profoundly sympathetic relationship to his audience. So, unlike the passages about Best, the bluesman's are full of voices, the lines crowded with a montage of fragmented conversations, one-liners, confessions.

The bluesman's path certainly isn't portrayed by Baraka as any kind of sunny alternative to the mass-mediated vivisection of Best. The choices of both are determined by double consciousness, so though the bluesman is treated in a more sympathetic, if not downright heroic fashion, he nevertheless does not serve as a model of artistic virtue. That said, his impact is nevertheless palpable; he demands a distinct use of language. Baraka's poem is structured around the contrast between the two singers and their fates, a contrast framed by Baraka in terms of visibility and invisibility, the visual and the audible (with both senses merely evoked by the written text). The spotlight of the spectacle illuminates Best; the dark woods hide the bluesman and force us to use our ears to try to *hear* his memory. It's almost as if Baraka is rehearsing in poetic terms the conceptual "strobing" that he would later use in the ritual drama *Slave Ship* (1968), where strobe lights, spotlights, and long periods of darkness help the audience distinguish the revolutionaries from the lackeys. If Best's punishment takes place in full view and light, the bluesman's takes place on a back road, unwitnessed and unremembered except in flashes.

The dense symbolism, deliberate ambiguity, and free-form visual and metric structure of "Willie Best" reflect a contradictory desire to make "Blackness" visible but not allow it to be pinned down by a reactionary, "soulless" reader. In short, the poem attempts to devise a formal solution to the paradox of "double consciousness." Again, the answer is not found on either Best's or the bluesman's path. In fact, it's not found in the poem at all, which is where we begin to find connections between the poem and Bullins's one-act. The solution to the Best/bluesman riddle, the resolution of the paradox of double consciousness, has less to do with the poem's metaphoric and thematic structure than with the reader and his or her reading situation and subjective identifications. Much like Clay in *Dutchman* (1964), Baraka here divides his audience into "we" and "they," the initiated and the noninitiated, the soulful and the soulless, those who can hear and those who cannot. The poem crawls with innuendoes, puns, and allusions that demand a range of well-developed literacies, a high degree of "Black" knowledge: old jokes, iconographic situations, call-and-response, sexual double entendres and convoluted sexual insults, embedded blues rhythms, spurious etymologies, oral histories. Baraka's playing Bessie Smith here, explicitly telling his audiences, as Clay puts it, to "kiss his ass" as he expresses emotional and aesthetic contours that both refine and reject mainstream standards.[11] As the poem puts it, "A renegade / behind the mask. And even / the mask, a renegade disguise."[12] The mask doesn't disguise; it puts its rebellion right out in front of us, certain that it's going to be remorselessly commodified and consumed. The message is right there on the surface, but only those with "soul" can read the doubled signs, the meanings that flee as soon as the "white eyes" show up.

As in Dante, the damned souls are neither rejected as a moral model nor dehumanized; but they are brutally scorned. Best is represented in the poem with a truly Dantesque mixture of pathos and fundamentalist certainty. Though Baraka directs us to feel "nothing of pity / . . . Nothing / of sympathy"[13] for the sellout entertainer, he does so only after allowing us to see Best suffering intensely, a bleeding man in a pit whose walls are built out of televisions. Predicting his manifesto "The Revolutionary Theatre," Baraka seems to be placing Best and the bluesman into the "history of victims" that he views as a necessary ingredient in a revolutionary art that is both militarizing and memorial, a revolutionary art that views itself as a "differential" moment between past and future.[14] The experience of reading the poem makes us confront the fact that any refusal of pity and sympathy can only come through the most rigorous examination of self, society, and artistic form. Only then can Best be useful as an emblem for the revolution heating up across North and Latin America, Canada, the Caribbean, Africa, China, and on and on during the months the poem was being composed.

Baraka attempts to transform Best from travesty into an iconic object lesson for a transnational avant-garde of decolonization:

The top
of a head, seen from Christ's
heaven, stripped of history
or desire
Fixed perpendicular to shadow. (even speech, vertical,
leaves no trace. Born in to death
held fast to it, where
the lover spreads his arms, the line
he makes to threaten Gods with history.
The fingers stretch to emptiness. At
each point, after flesh, even light
is speculation. But an end, his end,
failing a beginning.[15]

The emphasis on history and cosmology, an emphasis anchored in a basically Christian metaphysics, is suddenly dislocated by way of an abrupt shift
in perspective. The second section of the poem begins with the cross being
laid on its side to become a "crossroads" at which "sits the player," the blues
traveler, not crucified, but definitely pinned down at a moment of choice
not unlike Blackman's. An icon is transformed into a site of choice by way
of a move from the vertical to the horizontal. Is the bluesman an Afrocentric Virgil who can restrain our pity and keep us moving? Or is he just one
of the nameless damned that falls outside the poet's social circle? Baraka
doesn't give us a clear answer. One reason for not giving us an answer is that
he's taken the poem and his readers to a highly symbolic site. The crossroads
is an iconic setting in Euro- and African American cultures. Specific to the
latter, it's the legendary place where, as tradition has it, the blues singer,
having rejected the European-tainted traditions of spiritual and classical
music, makes the devil's bargain for fame and fluency among the lowest of
black folk.

Very much like the reader of *Malcolm: '71*, the reader of Baraka's poem
finds him- or herself at this same crossroads: "One road is where *you* are
standing now."[16] DuBoisian double consciousness is suddenly revealed as
not only the content of the poem but the constitutional, primordially struc-
turing condition of all interpretation and perception of aesthetic and moral
form. The singer flees. Who's left? The reader and the poet. Are we fellow
travelers on a Virgilian quest? Or just long-term neighbors in Hell?

The passage immediately following this moment of readerly situating also
recalls Bullins's play and its paradoxical materiality. The bluesman runs, and
in his place there is a sack that contains much more than its mundane

appearance would suggest. At first glance, we see pig bits and cheap wine—the making of an impoverished but recognizably "soulful" feast. But on closer inspection, we find "holy saviours, / 300 men on horseback / 75 bibles / the quietness / of a field."[17] However, as it turns out, even closer inspection fooled us—we should have been *listening*. The evidence of our eyes is disproved by the evidence of the ears. Baraka writes, "*I said*, / 47 howitzers / 7 polished horses jaws / a few trees being waved / softly back under / the black night."[18] Like a blues singer continually shifting emotional registers within the simple structure of the blues ballad, like a jazz musician changing keys, like a reader suddenly recognizing the material conditions of her own reading, Baraka transforms words and objects into "multiaccentual signs," to recall a term coined by V. N. Vološinov to describe the way cultural struggle is often waged over the meaning of words, things, and experiences. The contents of the bag have an "inner dialectic quality" that reflects "times of social crisis or revolutionary change."[19] In this case, the crisis is the crisis of text, the crisis of a poet who's aware of readerly difference.

The bluesman disappears from view, but has left behind traces that would seem to be understood differently by those who do or do not have "soul." To stress this theme, Baraka plants a crucial pun to lead off the next section of the poem: "Can you hear? / Here / I am again."[20] This pun reflects Baraka's increasing concern with the shared borders of poetic language, audience identity, and community and the highly unstable relationship between written and spoken language. It's true that he's writing a poem that can be read by any textually literate person and appreciated by anyone with a modicum of experience reading difficult poetry. But he's breaking down that audience further by utilizing techniques and language that demarcate readings based on the reader's ethnic identity (understood here as a mode of literacy), cultural allegiance, and sensitivity to the complexity of language. The readerly situation is brought into focus; the reader must be with the poet ("here") to fully understand ("hear"). We must, in some sense, stand close to the singer to truly the hear the song.

Following the pun, we move through a rapid set of scene shifts, a kind of geographical variation on the trick with the paper bag, a spatiotemporal sleight-of-hand not unlike the dizzying, thrilling shift from cross to cross-roads. First, we find ourselves in a dark juke joint, then a village street where a fight between the bluesman and a "dumb white farmer" is about to turn bloody, then into the poem itself where we, as readers, find ourselves transformed from reader into the subject of the poem. Baraka follows this sequence of spatial dislocations with a carefully placed repetition of his refrain; the last line of the poem echoes the pun: "Hear?" To "get this," the reader has to both imaginatively listen to and read the poem. The line between the soulful and the soulless is the line, always shifting and troubling, between the written text and the contextual, multisensory nature of performance.

Malcolm: '71 and "A Poem for Willie Best" reveal the complexity of the blackness articulated by the Black Arts Movement. In distinct ways, they designate a "soulful materialism" to be cultivated by a struggle that is at once political, economic, and cultural. These texts demonstrate, too, that the struggle of the African American poet against Blackness-as-blackface and for a Blackness rooted in the history and culture of Africa and African America was rejuvenated and revisioned by the Black Arts Movement partly in response to the development of what we now call, following Debord and Situationist theory, the "society of spectacle.[21] The persistent presence of the minstrel-show format in the United States into the 1960s is only one piece of evidence to support the correctness of the movement's position about the inherent racism of Cold War capitalism.[22] However, there's more here than simply a blunt concern with selling out. The Black Art Movement's anxiety about the co-optation of the African American body and the African American tradition possesses a distinctly metaphysical and ethical hue. The Best/bluesman paradox in the poem is a concern both about poetry's place in a racist society of spectacle and about the enervating compulsion that alienates the Black artist from his or her community.

Understanding the complexity of Baraka's poem and Bullins's play only begins to open a set of questions and concerns that needs to be addressed if we are to understand the relationship of the Black Arts Movement both to the counterculture and to the avant-garde tradition. In both texts, the writer, activist, editor, and scholar are fixed in an unsettling but highly ordered—perhaps jazzy?—regress of theatrical and readerly frames that includes the writing and reading of this case study. In light of these text, it is therefore best to understand Blackness as a mode of performance that can account for both aesthetic events (a performance of a play, the encounter with a sculpture, the parsing of a revolutionary slogan) and material conditions. And this performance *swings*. There is an underlying rhythm to this philosophical and political process, a rhythm aptly described by Charlie Cobb:

4 July. Atlanta Stadium. Energy, Music, Motion. Twenty thousand blacks erupting into a finger popping of dance and rhythms.
"You don't mind if i do the

Boogaloo?"

WELL, ALL RIGHT

Feels so groovey

HEY

Ain't that a groove.

Only James Brown—"the hardest-working man in show business."
Soulful wrenching, "gonna jerk it out baby." Black motion. A dozen
kids spill over onto the top of the dugout.

White cops scramble after them. Their rhythm is "order." Their
motion is ugly brutal, and disjointed. They move as in fear of a black
voodoo.

"It's just the boogaloo."

feels so groovey

hey

Ain't that a groove.[23]

You bet it is. Cobb swings from mass-media critique to leadership theory to
the latest dance moves, modulates from oratorical stridency to anecdotal
account, from carefully objective analysis to improvisational fictionalizing
and performative realization. It is all groove—and it perfectly captures the
soul force of Black revolution, "the active tones of the community."[24]
"Whitecop jacked up is a real reason for doing the boogaloo. Look at us:
Dance, sing, and swing. Black rhythms. Watch out now (I'm into *my*
thing)." Note the limited presence of "Whitecop" in Cobb's paragraph:
he's a reason and the subject of the sentence. But then he's left behind in a
cascade of brief phrases, imperatives counterbalanced by an assertion of
presence, wrapped up with a swingy little rhyme. "Let's use it," he concludes, "Our sound. Ou[r] beat. Against the problem of the Local White
Motha-fuckers."[25]

The Black Arts Movement as a Performance Movement

To discuss the Being of Blackness less as an entity to be defined than as a
critical practice to be enacted, critics need to marry the methods of performance studies to a detailed assessment of the movement's social, political,
economic, and aesthetic sources, concerns, and confrontations. It requires a
great deal of theoretical "backfill" to accomplish this. Baraka, Neal, Haki
Madhubuti (aka Don Lee), Sonia Sanchez, Nikki Giovanni, Gwendolyn
Brooks, Etheridge Knight, and their peers absorbed the lessons of political,
poetical, and philosophical thought from the pre- and post–Cold War West,

lessons that included experiences gained in the half-century-long struggle against capitalist mass media and commodity culture, and retained in the four-century history of African slavery and its aftermath. They also absorbed the lessons of the Western poetic and theatrical traditions, avant-garde and otherwise, a definite case of Black artists knowing when not to divest from a Western cultural trend. They knew about Dada (see Baraka's "Black Dada Nihilismus"), the surrealist commitment to decolonization, modernist primitivism, Pound and Eliot, Hughes and Hurston and DuBois, phenomenology and existentialism. These same Black artists and critics were familiar with the foundational critical and artistic texts of the "negritude" movement founded by Léopold Sédar Senghor, Aimé Césaire, and Léon Damas, and were students in the associated political and ideological strategies of decolonization. They also knew the critique of negritude mounted by Frantz Fanon in *The Wretched of the Earth* (English translation, 1963) and *Black Skin, White Masks* (English translation, 1967).[26] They knew about the pretextual cultural structures of West Africa; in fact, many of them were actively involved in researching the connections between West African and African America. And they knew the Marxist tradition, including the innovations of Antonio Gramsci and Mao Zedong. Also understood was the community solidarity that had grown and matured in the intense group experience of slavery, poverty, working-class solidarity, and unparalleled economic and cultural productivity.

They knew about what we now call "performance studies," though much too early for them to call it such. The rise of folklore programs in U.S. higher education in the 1950s exposed African American intellectuals to a cultural history that extended deeply into the performative cultures of American slavery and pre-European West Africa. Zora Neale Hurston's pioneering work in the genre of ethnographic narrative was widely respected by the new generation of youthful vanguardists. Neal was a great admirer of Hurston and wrote one of the earliest critical pieces on her, introducing her to a new audience, including Cobb.[27] Jahnheinz Jahn's *Muntu: An Outline of Neo-African Culture* (1961)[28] also influenced the movement with its negritude-inspired, pan-African vision of unified ethics, aesthetics, and social structure. Nonacademic sources were just as vital; African American performance artists, whether singers, dancers, comics, actors, or jazz musicians, were a persistent influence on the movement formally and ethically. Ethnographic method was a functional part of the organizational strategies of groups like the Revolutionary Action Movement, groups intent on accurately assessing the diversity of African America and the role a revolutionary vanguard should play within that diversity.

Thus, Blackness isn't so much a concept or an entity as a field of ethical, aesthetic, philosophical, political, and economic tensions, a dynamic to be enacted. Kimberly Benston argues exactly this point in *Performing Blackness: Enactments of African-American Modernism*. He writes that the "Blackness" underwriting the Black Aesthetic is less an essential category than a site of "multiple often conflicting implications of possibility."[29] Noting the movement's reliance on varied performance idioms and a theoretically sophisticated understanding of *essence,* he argues that "any critical appraisal of the movement's effects must account for its animating tensions in terms which reduce neither their contradictory nor productive character."[30] Though Benston isn't as honest as he should be about right-wing, chauvinist, and opportunistic trends in the movement, trends that used essence as a misogynist, homophobic, anti-Semitic, and crudely racialist antiwhite bludgeon, he is absolutely correct to note that "Blackness" is not external to the larger social field in which the movement moved.

As with many other avant-garde movements of the last century and a half, the properformance bias of the BAM was frequently directed against the literary text, which was viewed as a material support for bourgeois-capitalist society. Among the critics of textuality was poet and editor Etheridge Knight, who revised the definition of "publish" to reflect the idea that the text is only one element in a larger process of production and reception, and by far the least important. He emphasizes the "public" in "publication" and advocated both a return to the oral bases of poetic creation and a closer communication between artists and the people. In an interview with Sanford Pinsker, Knight asserts that publication should be considered an act of "public utterance." Thus, when poets are "poeting the people," they are published poets.[31] It's not coincidental that Knight formulated this notion of publishing while writing the column "Lend Me Your Ear" for the house newspaper of the Indiana State Prison in Michigan City. Knight was acutely conscious of the personal responsibility he carried for what was published in that alienating and violent place. Likewise, as a poet, he composed his work in a context that was both acutely critical and a crucible of verbal inventiveness and political discipline.

Malcolm: '71, "Willie Best," and the theoretical work of critics like Knight, Neal, Charles Fuller, and James Stewart practically and theoretically engaged the power structures of textual production, circulation, and reception as they impacted the development and communication of revolutionary, performative Blackness. They all suggest that Blackness is something that one both *is* and *knows,* that such being and knowledge are inseparable from specific cultural contexts and performative gestures, and insistently transform both themselves and its "carriers." At once material, conceptual, and strategic, Blackness, rather than closing down consideration, opens onto the knottiest kinds of economic, cultural, political, and philosophical questions. Thus, rather than a simple racial designation, Blackness was an ethos, a flexible, site-specific dynamic of knowing and doing. Neal declared it as such in his seminal essay "The Black Arts Movement," commissioned by guest editor Bullins to lead off the widely read 1968 Black Theater issue of *TDR*.[32] In sum, Blackness was performance.

Roots Rhythm and Critical Metaphysics

An interesting bit of trivia: Bobby Seale, a cofounder of the Black Panther Party for Self-Defense, was at one time an actor in a San Francisco troupe run by Bullins. The fact that the Panthers and the Black Arts literally shared the stage for a brief period isn't just the kind of coincidence that warms the heart of a scholar convinced that art can serve as an effective tool for political change. Quite the contrary, it's a symptom of the contradictions of visibility politics. Hartmann's notion of hypervisibility applies well here. The rancorous split between the West Coast Panthers and the cultural nationalists who helped build the Black Arts Movement reflects a number of significant issues in the avant-garde tradition, including the relation of the intellectual to the masses, the role of art (as propaganda or aesthetic experiment), and the viability of strategic alliance with white-dominated radical groups. Both the Panthers and the BAM developed radical cultural, political, and economic strategies that effectively responded to the complications of race politics by the peculiar characteristics of the American political scene in the 1960s, a scene that was indeed hypervisible. The backlash against both movements confirms the real threat they posed to basic structures of American life. The methods used to destroy them differed, of course. The Panthers were devastated by the Nixon administration's provocateur-spreading Counter-Intelligence Program, the BAM through denigration by a generation of scholars and critics.

Both the Panthers and Black Artists found themselves on Baraka's crossroads—and cast in the same uncomfortable roles. The West Coast Panthers attempted to titillate the white-controlled mass media and wealthy liberals by way of outrageous, blatant displays of hypermasculine "Super-Blackness" (what Tom Wolfe memorably nicknamed "Mau-Mau-ing").[33] This engagement with the enforced hypervisibility of Blackness might be read as a purposeful strategy used by the Panthers to support and camouflage their unglamorous but diligent, effective work in the African American community, providing breakfast to children and monitoring local police activity to limit civil rights abuses and brutality. However, Black Artists, guided in part by the much-admired Baraka, attempted to achieve the kind of balance described in "A Poem for Willie Best" by keeping to themselves and systematically cultivating revolution through a very careful, very humble exploration of the cultural grounds upon which they walked. Rather than hypervisibility (Best's path), the Black Aesthetic was a form of "hypovisibility": Representations of Blackness produced by the movement were intended for a "closed circuit" of communication between artists and audiences. Indeed, the BAM is notable for its spectacular parades, poetry readings, and street theater, but just as notable for its attempts to control the audiences for those spectacles. Both groups focused their attention on bringing revolutionary cultural programs and material assistance (in the form of lobby pressure, meal programs, police monitors, educational programs, etc.) to locations that, they believed, could best support a mass cultural nationalist movement in African American society; for example, historically African American colleges and African American urban enclaves.

These distinct negotiations of the "society of the spectacle"—the Oakland Panthers, led by Seale and Newton, risking the doom of Best, BAM artists that of the blues traveler fleeing white eyes—were linked to very different understandings of the relationship between political radicalism and cultural identity. While the Panthers developed sophisticated alliance networks with radical and left-liberal communities of whites and basically avoided aesthetic questions in favor of programmatic ones, BAM artists, activists, and theorists generally viewed such alliances as placing in jeopardy their racial separatist strategy. The Oakland Panthers saw the benefits of art primarily as a means to an end (i.e. fund-raising or community awareness). Black Artists viewed art—as they viewed African Americans themselves—as both the means and end of the revolution. While the Panthers wanted to play the old game of propaganda versus aesthetics,[34] Black artists set about solving the contradiction: African American culture was aesthetic through and through, so any revolutionary political gesture was, inevitably, a revolutionary aesthetic event.

Risking abstraction as well as the erasure of important similarities between the two movements, we might assert that the difference between the Black Power and Black Arts movements can also be understood in terms of how they viewed their relationship to the black masses: The Panthers believed they directly represented the will and imagination of the people and utilized a model of political organization derived from Leninist vanguard theory. Black Artists, on the other hand, developed the representational and perceptual means by which the people could represent themselves. Aesthetics distinguishes the trends; and, in fact, aesthetics modeled, for the two movements, very different approaches to leadership and communication. The Black Arts Movement was a cultural-revolutionary movement underwritten by a sophisticated model of intellectual leadership premised on a careful comprehension of, and thoroughgoing respect for, the diverse cultural forms of the African American masses.

Rather than a vanguard *party*, Neal writes, it was a *movement* seeking "to link, in a highly conscious manner, art and politics in order to assist in the liberation of Black people." As with *Malcolm: '71*, the context of the statement is important to consider: *Ebony* magazine in the summer of 1969.[35] The fact that *Ebony*, a magazine catering to the African American middle classes, had devoted an entire issue to the movement stands as a high-water mark of the movement's efforts to popularize their cultural program, as the mark of a liaison of cultural revolutionaries with capitalist (better said "Black capitalist") media (African American–owned Johnson Publishing, which also published the important *Negro Digest/Black World*), and as clear evidence that, rather than aestheticizing politics, the Black Arts Movement attempted to produce a truly democratic model of cultural production.

Such revolutionary writings and reports in an ostensibly liberal publication like *Ebony* speak eloquently to the ways in which the theory and practice of cultural empowerment cultivated by a fairly small cadre of college-educated intellectuals struck a sympathetic chord with a relatively large segment of African American society, inspiring it to fight for cultural presence in unprecedented ways, including Black Studies programs, a self-invested market for distinctly African American cultural products, a celebration of formerly disparaged elements of working-class African American culture, Kwanzaa (the "Feast of the First" devised by Maulana Karenga and his cohort in 1966), and a vibrant network of arts institutions that, to some extent, still exists today. It also speaks to the innovative approaches to community organization that characterized the BAM. Neal explained in his *Ebony* essay that Black Art was nothing if it didn't strive for "intimacy with the people," a lesson he learned as an organizer for the Revolutionary Action Movement.[36] This intimacy demanded from artist and critic a self-conscious, self-critical, flexible attitude toward art, criticism, activism, and the predispositions of the masses. Though Black Artists struggled with celebrity as surely as did the Panthers or Detroit's League of Revolutionary Workers, they ultimately accomplished the kind of critical self-effacement of which the cultural revolutionaries of China could only dream.[37]

At the heart of this effort toward intimacy is a soulful articulation aptly described by Stephen Henderson as an "interior dynamism" that, he argues, shares empowering roots with the inner life of all blacks. In "The Form of Things Unknown," the introduction to *Understanding the New Black Poetry* (1984), Henderson defines what he calls a "soul field" that binds the activities of artistic production and artistic reception in a "complex galaxy of personal, social, institutional, historical, religious, and mythical meanings that affect everything we say or do as Black people sharing a common heritage."[38] Houston Baker Jr. cites Henderson's essay as a keynote in the definition of "an entirely new object of literary-critical and literary-theoretical investigation."[39] And I agree; however, Baker criticizes Henderson for "impressionistic chauvinism," a charge that must be engaged with thoughtfully and thoroughly. Baker argues that Henderson's theory fails to acknowledge the fact that reading is a cultural practice that crosses cultural boundaries: "For it is, finally, *only* the Black imagination that can experience Blackness, in poetry, or in life. As a result, the creative and critical framework suggested by Henderson resembles, at times, a closed circle" (81).

That may be true, but only "at times" and only in resemblance—and only if we ignore Scott's assertion that "blood memory" is the consequence of rigorously self-critical, decidedly public acts of ciphering and deciphering. Henderson himself is partly to blame for Baker's misunderstanding. Though steeped in performance-inflected considerations, his theory ultimately concerns the completed poetic text. The circle in which Blackness manifests poetically may indeed be an Afrocentric version of the "hermeneutic circle" in which acts of interpretation are determined by the same conditions that determine the thing being interpreted. And there is no doubt that this interpretive tautology strengthened misogyny, homophobia, anti-Semitism, and vulgar antiwhiteness. However, I would argue that the supposedly romantic essentialism of Henderson and the various other voices of cultural nationalism in the Black Arts Movement is partly mitigated when the critic considers *(a)* the larger question of grassroots organizing and cultural collaboration (again, the Revolutionary Action Movement should always be recalled as we discuss the BAM), *(b)* the more specific question of theater and performance in the movement as essentially destabilizing forces, and *(c)* the self-deconstructing lines of demarcation that manifest in aesthetic events (e.g., the hanging up in *Malcolm: '71* or the hear/here pun in "Willie Best"). Blackness is a critical practice, not a preexisting entity. Rather than relying only on a preexisting cultural identity, Black Arts performance sought to cultivate a robust, dynamic cultural identity by constructing what Leslie C. Sanders has called "the Black territory" created in the particular space-time matrix of a particular performance among a particular audi-ence.[40] Rather than simply resurrecting a preexisting culture or depending on some vulgar notion of "blood memory," Black Arts performance cre-ated, in Tejumola Olaniyan's words, "a Black dramatic voice self-con-sciously embedded in a cultural matrix."[41] Blackness, rather than being essential or nostalgic, was made "retroactively actual" through the present-oriented dynamics of performance.[42]

The status of the artist was no less dynamic. In "The Black Arts Move-ment," Neal asserts that the BAM "is radically opposed to any concept of the artist that alienates him from his community. This movement is the aes-thetic and spiritual sister of the Black Power concept. As such, it envisions an art that speaks directly to the needs and aspirations of black America."[43] Neal argues (with an eye toward DuBois's "double consciousness") that it is vital the artist reconsider his or her relationship to the art object and the lit-erary text, viewed by Neal and his colleagues as linchpins of neocolonial exploitation of African American high-, middle-, and low-brow cultural production. According to Neal, the commodity-oriented tendencies of col-onized cultural production coincided with the systematic exploitation of African Americans. Thus, a primary target of the Black Arts Movement was not simply "consciousness" but the production and circulation of *things,* particularly textual things. As surely as commodities were destroyed during the uprisings in Watts and Detroit, the entire ethos of the "white thing" was attacked by the BAM. Neal and his colleagues from the Muntu reading-per-formance group of West Philadelphia argued that objects and texts were not valuable in and of themselves, but merely as material components of a much broader cultural, political, and economic renaissance. They were art "merely incidentally," since real value was to be found in the performances, artists, and communities that surrounded the object and text.[44]

The paradox of this attack on the "white thing" is that, while Black the-orists, poets, playwrights, and performers generated an avant-garde culture of unprecedented acuity and popularity, the very success of their project has in many ways guaranteed their invisibility within literary and theater his-tory. Henry Louis Gates Jr. has repeatedly disparaged the movement, argu-ing in a 1994 issue of *Time* magazine that the Black Arts Movement was the shortest and least successful African American literary renaissance.[45] Gates not only misstates the case, he misses the point. The movement attempted to displace the very notions of value, permanence, and significance that rat-ify much of the academic establishment's sense of literariness, historicity, and success. In other words, we witness here the kinds of critical demarcations—the disengagement of critical action from mainstream critical institutions—that are typical of countercultural activism. As James Stewart, of Muntu, argued,

> In our movement toward the future, "ineptitude" and "unfitness" will be an aspect of what we do. These are the words of the established order—the middle-class value judgments. We must turn these values in on themselves. Turn them inside out and make ineptitude and unfitness desirable, even mandatory. We must even, ultimately, be estranged from the dominant culture. This estrangement must be nurtured in order to generate and energize our Black artists. This means that he cannot be "successful" in any sense that has meaning in white critical evaluations. Nor can his work ever be called "good" in any context or meaning that could make sense to that traditional critique.[46]

Stewart's essay strikes a significant note of caution—and a clear line of demarcation—to which I need to attend as I move more deeply into the Black Arts Movement's attempt to go beyond not just beyond "double consciousness," but beyond DuBois's "talented tenth" toward a truly popular revolution.

Once again, we've discovered a limit of criticism, a limit in which scholars, teachers, and editors are implicated. Looking back to *Malcolm: '71*, we should recall that Whitegirl was calling at the behest of Professor Jack Hack, "the white professor who teaches poetry and aesthetics at the new Black Revolutionary Third World City university . . . the Black Students' victory for burning down the administration building during that dreadful hassle over Black Studies." If the artists and audiences of the Black Arts Movement discovered the soul of Black liberation in the deconstruction and partial rejection of the art object and the literary text, they also discovered that such "soul" is acutely vulnerable to economic and institutional backlash. Attempting to outmaneuver the institutional and technological power of the "white thing," Black Artists formulated a theory of culture and communication that in some sense guaranteed forgetting by the elite ranks and scholarly fields of the white-dominated academic community.

Blackman, Best, and the blues traveler all contend with the problem of forgetting—in fact, politicize it. That said, the stakes of memory were very different for the BAM than they were for the Happenings and the Fluxus movement. Musician and critic Tam Fiofori captured the difference in a profile of the cosmic traveler and revolutionary Afrocentric jazz composer Sun Ra in 1967: "[M]emory, like sentiment or emotion, can be replaced, diverted, or it can simply fade away."[47] Fiofori isn't writing an elegy; he's sounding a warning. While the movement founded its critique upon performance in order to meet the complex demands of a revolutionary cultural-nationalist movement in the context of mass-mediated (or "spectacular") capitalism, its demise was due to demands placed upon it that performance practices could only inadequately address; namely, the demands of institutional permanence, mass communication, and real estate.

Total Institutions

The origins of the Black Arts Movement are instructional in this regard, for they reveal a contradictory but highly productive dynamic among organizational innovation, theoretical development, and cultural production. Moreover, they reveal a plan for institutional development that has proved extremely hardy, particularly in Chicago, where Black Arts organizations such as the Muntu Dance Company disprove the common assumption that the movement ended in the mid-1970s and demonstrate the significant presence of female leadership in Black Arts institutions.[48] Among the more interesting—if not always so long-lived—institutions were the small, distinctively local communities of poets and intellectuals that gathered in the middle years of the 1960s. These groups pursued a diverse range of projects, including research into African and African American folk, popular, and high cultures; readings of the most significant political, cultural, and aesthetic theory of their day (articulating what we would now call "cultural studies" almost a decade ahead of the Birmingham School); concrete experimentation with poetic form; self-criticism; and consciousness raising. Their sympathies, in contrast to much of the older African American middle class, were not with Martin Luther King Jr. or the Negro church establishment from and for which he spoke. *Liberator* magazine, one of the key forums for Black Arts theory, was in fact stridently anti-King. Their sympathies fell to Lumumba, Fidel Castro, Ernesto "Che" Guevara, Frantz Fanon, and (always and essentially) Malcolm X.

A list of the more significant of these reading circles would have to include the Muntu group as well as the South Side Chicago home of Gwendolyn Brooks, an engine for the city's ongoing cultural transformation. We should also note the Umbra Poets Workshop, a group of young (mostly male) writers that met weekly on New York's Lower East Side from 1962 to 1964, published a short-lived poetry journal that was regularly attentive to Afrocentric themes, and gave public readings just around the block from the famed Five Spot jazz club. Its breakup signaled a crucial shift in artistic attitudes toward interracial collaboration and the rejection of liberal politics.[49] There were also significant organizations in Los Angeles (the Watts Writers Workshop and Studio Watts), Cleveland (Karamu House), and Detroit (Concept East). That these groups were communal gatherings should not be overlooked; indeed, in the case of Muntu, relationships had existed since childhood.[50] These groups (and there were others just as important in Detroit, New Orleans, Los Angeles, and on many college and university campuses) functioned as crucial support networks, valuable sources of criticism, and, most importantly (according to Tom Dent, a founding member of Umbra and later cofounder of Blkartsouth and the Free Southern Theatre, recalled), as performative contexts that afforded a "level of communication with kindred spirits that wasn't phony or superficial."[51]

These should be understood as preparatory experiments. Though they were important in the development of social networks, critical methodologies, and activist strategy, the key organization was the Black Arts Repertory Theater/School (BART/S), founded April 30, 1965. BART/S was organized by Jones with the financial aid of the Harlem Youth Project, upon whose board African American actor-activist Roger Furman served); the practical aid of Umbra members Rolland Snellings (aka Askia M. Touré), Albert Haynes, and the intimidating proto-"gangstas" William and Charles Patterson; and the ideological aid of the *Liberator,* which that year included on its editorial staff both Harold Cruse and Neal.

At first glance, BART/S seems to lack the interdisciplinary and strategic audacity of its institutional fore- and after-runners. The fund-raising brochure for BART/S tells us that "as its name indicates, [the BART/S] will be a repertory theater in Harlem, as well as a school. As a school it will set up and continue to provide instruction, both practical and theoretical, in all new areas of the dramatic arts."[52] Appearances, as usual, are deceiving and depend on who's doing the looking. For the purposes of fund-raising, the organizers were playing their ideological cards fairly close to the chest. In fact, the "dramatic arts" that the school was exploring went far beyond the practice and theory of the putatively "phony" Anglo-Jewish mainstream theater Baraka had been vociferously criticizing for months. When we turn to texts intended for a more homogenously cultural nationalist audience, the picture is rather different. As Neal described the opening of BART/S in *Liberator,* "The idea behind . . . this event . . . is to open a dialogue between the artist and his people, rather than between the artist and the dominant white society which is responsible for his alienation in the first place."[53] This dialogue was tacitly revolutionary, a volatile, often contradictory dynamism of space, race, and representation.

What distinguished BART/S from its forerunners was its focus on the politics of space and its attempt to implement Afrocentric notions of organizational structure and community collaboration. Jones and his colleagues were attempting to spur an in-the-belly-of-the-beast decolonization movement like those that had swept through Africa, Central America, and Southeast Asia during the 1950s and 1960s, movements whose practical, conceptual, and decidedly performative force Jones first recognized during a visit to Cuba in 1960. This is not to say that the BART/S managed to evade the contradictions inherent to the idea of a revolution within. In fact, if we turn to an essay written around the same time as the founding of organization, Baraka's "The Revolutionary Theater," the contradictions can be clearly seen. The manifesto proclaims the need to

> EXPOSE! Show up the insides of these humans, look into Black skulls. White men will cower before this theater because it hates them. Because they themselves have been trained to hate . . . Even as Artaud designed *The Conquest of Mexico,* so we must design *The Conquest of White Eye,* and show the missionaries and wiggly Liberals dying under blasts of concrete. For sound effects, wild screams of joy, from all the peoples of the world.[54]

Here, Baraka attempts to imagine a kind of avant-garde hybrid, part Afrocentric nationalism, part Artaudian extremism, a critical, performance-oriented metaphysics that will place his organization's theatrical experiments beyond the horizons of Western aesthetics, ethics, and politics. His hypothetical drama *The Conquest of White Eye* riffs on the "first spectacle of the Theater of Cruelty," Artaud's *The Conquest of Mexico.*[55] Acidly punning on the familiar slur "whitey," Baraka's drama interweaves the shock of agitprop, the antioptical bias of Artaud, and the populism of street festival. It resituates Artaud in the context of colonialism and the subjective demands of decolonization described by Algerian psychiatrist Frantz Fanon.

For the authorities, such metaphysical and aesthetic nuances were far less important than the fact that angry, left-wing, agitational, vaguely "communistic" Afrocentric art was being brought to a Manhattan neighborhood dominated by impoverished African Americans. Street-corner productions of plays such as *Dutchman* were common, as were poetry readings and open-air art exhibits, not to mention impromptu performances by cutting-edge jazzmen such as Ornette Coleman, Albert Ayler, Max Roach, Sun Ra, and John Coltrane from the back of flat-bed "jazz-mobiles." The success was short-lived; BART/S lost its federal funding within a year of its founding when a federal investigation into alleged "mismanagement" of antipoverty funds was initiated, purportedly by liberal whites and African Americans out to "discredit and destroy all the militant and progressive forces in Harlem."[56] Even so, it would be an exaggeration to blame the destruction of BART/S simply on political intransigence and liberal conspiracies. The demise of the institution was catalyzed by a lack of organizational experience as well as by the in-fighting egged on by the Patterson brothers. As Baraka described it many years later, "Even while we did our heroic work of bringing the art, the newest strongest boldest hippest most avant of the swift dark shit to the streets, you could look up at that building and swear it was in flames."[57]

What BART/S ultimately represented for the movement was a commitment to organizational experiment. As Harold Cruse carefully demonstrates in his opus *The Crisis of the Negro Intellectual,*[58] unless the Black liberation movement was accompanied by "an ideological and organizational approach to . . . the administration, the organization, the functioning, and the social purpose of the entire American apparatus of cultural communication," that movement was bound to fail.[59] Cruse's comments identify a crucial survival fund for this Afrocentric avant-garde. Organizational theory had to take account of not only the ethos of Blackness, but the constant threat to organizational survival. It was lack of real estate, in particular, that pushed the movement into some of its more daring aesthetic, philosophical, and organizational directions. Wahneema Lubiano has pointed out that lacking a real "nation" in some sense forced Black radicals into the "cultural solution."[60] Lacking real estate, an ideologically unified model of community, and a sure foothold in the strategically important middle-class communities of African America, the most advanced segments of the Black Arts Movement chose ephemeral, situational, performative, local forms of avant-garde poetry, theater, and social relations.

Is it too much to speculate that interest in theater, in "Black men in transition" (to recall Neal), was related somehow to the fact that the theater is capable of transforming space and time in sites that are not owned by the theater troupe? Why were there no architects in the Black Arts Movement? Why no monumental sculptors? I don't wish to imply that real estate was *the* determinant factor for the movement; Lubiano doesn't intend this either. The Black Arts Movement can be seen, after all, as a movement within and against literary history, a movement that deemed the novel "a passive form . . . not conducive to the kind of social engagement that Black America requires at this time."[61] But there's no doubt that practical concerns over the place of art was every bit as important as the art that took place. Poetry was necessarily transformed when anchored in the contexts of performance. Neal viewed James Brown as a model performer, at once popular, conscious, and infectiously activist:

> [T]he poet must become a performer, the way James Brown is a performer—loud, gaudy, racy. He must take his work where his people are. . . . He must learn to embellish the context in which the work is executed; and where possible, link the work to all usable aspects of the music. For the context of the work is as important as the work itself. Poets must learn to sing.[62]

This isn't just a question of aesthetic form or the status of the artist vis-à-vis his or her community. Cobb describes one possible outcome of this change in aesthetics and artist status:

> Suppose we presented a play. People jam, block, the streets in order to watch or participate. That the play is written for the community, and aimed at their experiences. Suppose this happening on a number of blocks at the same time, to the point where it forces a confrontation between the community and "white power." Depending on the preparation and understanding of the people, the nature of this confrontation would range from a backing away, to a stand to hold the streets against this "white power."[63]

For Charles Fuller (Muntu member, Neal's childhood friend, and winner of the 1982 Pulitzer Prize for *A Soldier's Play*), cultural, political, and economic autonomy could only be attained by way of a complete and mutual transformation of community and artist, a transformation that would serve as a clear model for the community's need to revive traditions that preexisted the African slave trade. As he writes, "[E]ach change must of necessity produce a change in the Black writer who addresses his community."[64] Affirming Fuller's analysis, we often find that the concepts and practices of the movement were revised in order to adequately respond to the distinct political, economic, and cultural situations of geographically and politically distinct African American communities. Nevertheless, the basic urge behind its manifestations remained the same: to formulate a theory and practice of Afrocentric autonomy. This necessitated an emphatically theatrical approach to the interrelated questions of criticism and power. The critic could no longer be disengaged from the community. Criticism, Fuller asserts, is a power granted by the people to the critic, whether in direct form (as in the gathering of people in the presence of a figure of critical authority) or indirect (as in the funding of critics through state and private institutions supported by corporate philanthropy and use fees).

In the revolutionary theater described by Baraka, race politics, critical epistemology, and theatricality were coaxed into a realm where action, not merely aesthetics, was the litmus of artistic success. As he had it, "The liberal white man's objection to the theater of the revolution (if he is "hip" enough) will be on aesthetic grounds [among these, it should be noted, are issues of "success" and "longevity"]. . . . Americans will hate the Revolutionary Theater because it will be out to destroy them and whatever they believe is real."[65] If Baraka's theater showed victims and reminded its viewers "[that] they are the brothers of victims, and that they themselves are victims if they are blood brothers,"[66] it was also the place where steely resolution and a profoundly critical aesthetics took root. As Baraka concludes, "[N]ot history, not memory, not sad sentimental groping for a warmth in our despair" will create the revolutionary culture.[67]

Recalling *Malcolm: '71* and "A Poem for Willie Best," we also recall that the priority of performance in the BAM was compelled in part by economics: the real-estate market, the entertainment market, the academic market. Attitudes toward theater tend to inform all three of these markets. Artists in the movement were generally distressed by the bourgeois theater's encrypted historicism, its particular use of memory and writing, its tendency to resolve social issues in individualistic terms, and (in the post–World War II era) its marginalization by television,[68] but they were energized and empowered by the theater's capacity to shape time and space in contextually potent situations. However, put at risk by this thoroughgoing critique of Western aesthetics and space-time concepts were certainty and permanence; the theater challenges the collective capacity to define and delimit the real and the illusory, the essential and the transient, and does so, at least in the United States, mostly in unsubsidized, leased performance spaces. Along with the destructive capacity of the theater so acidly identified by Baraka came a more difficult search for the conceptual and material grounds upon which a distinctly Black body and community stand. This soulful materialism is no more or less than the politics of Blackness.

7. Blackness and Text

The "Antiobjective" Trend and the Triple Front

As I've demonstrated, the blooming of an anti-Western, antimaterialist, "antiobjective" Black Aesthetic in the 1960s can't be separated from the blooming of Black theaters across the country at the time and the effort to theoretically and practically implement a "new orality," a "Black Talk," to recall Ben Sidran.[69] Attempting to evade the materialism, rationalism, and medium-centered-art bias of white high and vanguard culture, theoretically attuned writers and critics such as Cruse, Sanchez, Neal, Giovanni, Fuller, and Stewart sought aesthetic situations that explicitly rejected the object as such and the objectivity that separated the viewer from the viewed.

It's no accident that the Black Arts Movement grounded its political theory in performative modes of culture; theater and performance can answer very specific sociopolitical needs, particularly to a community that is both economically depressed and politically advanced. This was why Cruse considers theater to be central to the question of the Black nation.[70] While Black cultural expression had been more or less forced to settle on performative forms as an expressive solution to cultural, political, economic, and historical suffocation, such necessity enabled powerful forms of resistance, among them the effervescent, efflorescent resistance of the temporary locale—of juke joint jams, theaters, church events, street-corner doo-wop, and barricades that suggest the "mobile infinity of tactics" described by Michel de Certeau.[71] As Cruse reminds his younger comrades, the struggle for African America's future was fought on the *triple front* of economy, politics, and culture. That fight, Cruse demands, had to begin in the theaters of the inner city, those in Harlem first and foremost.

Likewise, performance afforded a common conceptual ground for the triple-front struggle of antimaterialism, cultural retrieval, and urban organization. For Neal, whose untimely death in the early 1980s denied the Black Aesthetic a critical presence in academic discourse at a crucial period in the development of critical race studies, the preeminence of theater and performance in the Black Arts and Power movements was a matter of paying attention to one's history. Discussing the work of Baraka, Neal insists that theater "is inextricably linked to the Afro-American political dynamic. And such a link is perfectly consistent with Black America's contemporary demands. For theater is potentially the most social of all of the arts. It is an integral part of the socializing process."[72] Again, it is the theater that best exhibits the totality, Neal asserts, the *temporality,* of "Black men in transition."[73]

There is an important distinction to be drawn between the notions of theater/performance and its efficacy vis-à-vis the project of Black Nationalism developed by Cruse and Neal in the movement-era essays I have cited. Whereas Cruse advocates the theater for practical reasons (i.e., that it, more than any other art form, completely encompasses the cultural, political, and economic needs of Black liberation), Neal seems to be indicating that the theater *as process,* as a way of being and a way of knowing, is directly tied to Black acculturation, self-criticism, and liberation despite the existence of concrete institutions. Theater, for Neal, is literally in the skin; Blackness is a kind of phenomenological drama, an Afrocentric version of existentialist *engagé.* The theater is "a bridge between [the community] and the spirit, a bridge between you and your soul in the progression of a spiritual lineage."[74] So while Cruse focuses on essentially infrastructural concerns such as property ownership and institutional development (the practical failure of which doomed Black Art as a movement), Neal focuses on the special demands of pan-African, revolutionary subjectivity, a subjectivity that transcends the specific issues that Cruse identifies—and that has survived the short-lived institutions of the movement.

The distinction is an important one to keep in mind, particularly if we're to understand the more radical philosophical implications of Black Art; for I would argue that the Black Arts as *theory* retained a more widespread vitality after the death of the Black Arts as a revolutionary *institutional* movement. When the Nixon administration slashed government funding of experimental arts and the economic crisis of 1973 laid low hundreds of community theaters across the United States, many of the practical links forged between art and politics were sundered—but the theory survived in those educated by the Black Arts Movement. Even so, these economic trends, as well as J. Edgar Hoover's Counter-Intelligence Program, were devastating both practically and theoretically. In addition to careers and lives, many theoretical and practical openings between text, institution, and performance were foreclosed by white backlash. The Black Arts as theater transformed abstract aesthetic into movement, concept into politics, the Black Aesthetic into grassroots activism. But once the links between those revolutionary organizations and the communities that they represented were destroyed, the Black Arts Movement crossed a horizon beyond which European traditions of politics, aesthetics, historiography—and property—could not clearly see.

In the late 1960s, Maulana Karenga demanded that Black Art "remind us of our distaste for the enemy, our love for each other, and our commitment to the revolutionary struggle that will be fought with the rhythmic reality of a permanent revolution."[75] Such a rhythmic reality ill accords with the traditions and trends of European aesthetics. Reflecting this iconoclastic, jazz-inflected spirit, Stewart, in "The Development of the Black Revolutionary Artist" (the lead essay in Neal and Baraka's indispensable *Black Fire* anthology), reminds us, "The revolutionary understands change."[76] Like Baraka in *Blues People,* Stewart saw the "death of the artifact" in the Middle Passage as a conceptual and practical avenue into cultural revolution, a kind of "fortunate fall" that ensured effective resistance against racist capitalism. A revolutionary art, he concludes, must be like the legendary temples of mud "that vanish in the rainy seasons and are erected elsewhere."[77] "Likewise," he writes,

> most of the great Japanese artists of the eighteenth and nineteenth centuries did their exquisite drawings on rice paper with Black ink and spit. These were then reproduced by master engravers on fragile newssheets that were distributed to the people for next to nothing. These sheets were often used for wrapping fish. They were a people's news sheet. Very much like the sheets circulated in our bars today.[78]

"Revolution is fluidity," Stewart argues. Borrowing eclectically from Asian mystical traditions, Afro-American blues riffs, the black Baptist church, New Jazz, and Voudoun, Stewart demonstrates that the revolutionary artist is part of a proud line of "misfits estranged from the white cultural present."[79] The Black artist, therefore, could not expect to be "successful," for in the context of cultural revolution, "'ineptitude' and 'unfitness' will be an aspect of what we do."[80]

Fuller saw this spirit as energized by a "Release from Object," the title of one of a trio of articles on aesthetic theory published in *Liberator.* Thinking of the relationship between the thing and the labor to make the thing, he asks "if the sacrifice [of materials in the construction of the art object] was greater than the need, or simply a manifestation of that need—a tool, a service—something to demonstrate how much was needed and which, once fulfilling the need, was abandoned."[81] The ability to answer this question was, for Fuller, the fundamental criterion of revolutionary culture:

> If we can swallow that Black writing in this country did not begin as *object,* we can understand its present need to reflect the revolution its people are engaged in, and see a fluidity and elasticity in Black writing that can never be hoped for in the west. Black writing must twist and bend with its people, be creative because they are creative. . . . Its longevity will be limited to the nourishment it provides its people, and its writers should be considered no more than good cooks.[82]

How does this antiobjective philosophy manifest itself on stage? As an illustration, we might turn to another of Bullins's experimental pieces, *The Theme Is Blackness.* This bit of theatrical pranksterism implies that, when the theme is Blackness, the perceptual habits that underwrite our collective and individual capacity to make sense of the world—that is to say, the criteria of aesthetics and philosophy—are put at risk. The script runs complete as follows:

> *Speaker:* The theme of our drama tonight will be Blackness. Within Blackness One may discover all the self-illuminating universes in creation. And now BLACKNESS—
> *(Lights go out for twenty minutes. Lights up)*
> Will Blackness step out and take a curtain call?
> BLACKNESS[83]

It's difficult to imagine the sense of confusion and discomfort this antithetical thesis drama inspired in its predominantly white audience when it was first staged in 1967 at various sites in and around San Francisco. Even a regular goer to avant-garde theater (or a regular reader of avant-garde theatrical pranks such as those staged by the Italian futurists) would be discomfited; after all, this was the same playwright who more or less mugged his audience in the antitheater piece, *It Bees Dat Way* (1970).[84]

Read in the context of the antispectacular, antiobjective, antitextual theory articulated by Neal, Stewart, Fuller, and Baraka, *The Theme Is Blackness* can be interpreted as targeting the long history of philosophical inertia, technological expansion, and colonialism that had given Bullins and his community their riddled present. And while its totalizing urge (for nothing is more totalizing than nothingness) may push aside more concrete historical and cultural concerns (unlike Sanchez's *Malcolm/Man Don't Live Here No Mo,* which will receive attention below), its attack on the tendentiously abstracting, spectacular racism of the Enlightenment is effective indeed. Blackness, in Bullins's one-act, is a metaphysic all its own. It can't be seen— it's the theatrical equivalent of the disappearing blues traveler in "A Poem for Willie Best." However, the addition of free jazz and sound effects by the Chebo Evans Third World Three Black Trio in conjunction with the Black Arts/West company during the play's run underlines the problematic nature of *Theme*'s refusal to show and specify, to reveal anything to the eyes of its viewers—never enmeshing itself in the running intratheatrical battle of realism, naturalism, symbolism, minimalism, what-have-you-ism.

When the lights go down and Blackness comes up in *The Theme Is Blackness,* one of the central conceptual and perceptual apparatuses of white racism is hobbled: vision. The "eye of whiteness" is cast adrift, scattered on the scatological seas of a peculiarly Black history. *The Conquest of White Eye/Whitey.* Blackness swamps the viewer and her small community, the audience. Unable to claim distance from the stage, no longer able to exert its powers of judgment over the spectacle of the other, the eye of whiteness (an eye possessed not just by whites, we should note) finds itself in a context of profound ambiguity. Perhaps more significantly, Bullins's ambivalently avant-garde gesture (which recalls John Cage no less than the Greensboro sit-in) returns the viewer to his or her body. As we all know, even the most cramped theater seats can be forgotten in the face of effective theater. The discomfort of the situation in *Theme* is the result of the play's failure to alleviate the body through distracting or engaging dramatic action (not to mention having one's ankles grabbed by performers scuttling beneath the seats).

Most significant to my eyes—as inappropriate as those particular tools might be in this context—is Bullins's refusal to give his audience a sense of dramatic progression. That is to say, Bullins's play refuses to structure and thematize theatrical *time* or to make meaningful the theatrical *object*. Because the piece lacks the traditional cues of drama (visual and verbal transformations in setting, character, and thesis), it lacks the temporal shape—the pace—of traditional drama. As a result, judgment (of character or moral action, for example) can't cast its glance over the scene: It can't see at all. In the darkness, character doesn't develop, crisis and consequence don't find dialectical resolution. Drama, as it is traditionally understood, fails to take hold; time doesn't concretize, doesn't humanize. The theater, which always takes time, is pressed to its conceptual and formal limits by Bullins's one-act. The bourgeois drama, the drama of judgment, the drama of a linear, meaningful History, meets its end. The essentially linear parade of significant individuals weathering significant events—a parade we associate with both bourgeois historical narrative and bourgeois drama—is interrupted. Performativity, in the original production, was surrendered entirely to the audience; in the later, musical version, this performativity was augmented by free jazz. Having taken away its sight and its sense of temporal progression, Bullins utilizes theater to call the end of (white) History.[85] When this call was sounded before a politically astute, majority-Black audience (as it was at Black Arts/West), this act of aesthetic terrorism was given an improvisational and decidedly less anarchic shape.

But even though it strikes against the *conceptual* foundations of European culture, Bullins's play is nonetheless characterized by an *ahistorical* and ultimately *apolitical* approach to the question of Black liberation (not the first nor last time this would be the case in the movement). Certainly *The Theme Is Blackness* is a concrete critical-theatrical gesture against racism. But it fails to synthesize the freedoms of the moment with the demands of history—at least before the addition of music and sound effects for the home crowd. The deep ground, the "Black (w)hole," to cite Baker,[86] that Bullins is attempting to cultivate is given a more concrete, more historically minded spin in Baraka's *Slave Ship,* productions of which by the Chelsea Theater at the Brooklyn Academy of Music and Concept East in Detroit during the late 1960s inspired a generation of Black artists. Like Bullins's *The Theme Is Blackness, Slave Ship* simultaneously confronts, exploits, and explodes the relations of visibility, race, and theatricality. But unlike Bullins, Baraka explicitly contextualizes the "shapelessness" of Blackness in the brutality of slavery and the Middle Passage. Unlike Bullins's *The Theme Is Blackness,* which utilizes the nonobjective in a more totalizing, abstract, or "Free Jazz" manner, Baraka's play situates the nonobjective within a determinant context. Nonobjectivity is linked in *Slave Ship* both to West African culture and to a suffering that, like the Holocaust, challenges the very possibility of memory and representation.

In the Chelsea Theater's production of *Slave Ship,* the "eye of whiteness" was literally cast into the hold of racism's epitomic metaphor, the slave ship, struggling like the captured Africans in the play to find a place to stand, a place to breathe, a place from which to make sense of the sensory assault. Assaulted by smells, assaulted by the violent sonic funk of director Gilbert Moses and Archie Shepp's free jazz score,[87] the audience's ability to judge was incapacitated. The body and the community were thrown into a Blackness not unlike that exploited by Bullins in *Theme.*

But this disabling is neither portrayed as wholly negative nor as wholly a consequence of the Middle Passage. The use of the newly developed strobe light and extended periods of darkness suggest a more positive theatrical-philosophical program similar to the jazz-inflected production of *The Theme Is Blackness* at Black Arts/West, an emphasis on the ear as opposed to the eye. Ultimately, though, the strobe light simply makes concrete the conceptual strobing that Baraka explored in "A Poem for Willie Best." What Baraka allows his audience to see and hear in the flashing lights of *Slave Ship* is a shuffling Uncle Tom/liberal preacher (symbol of faith in historical progress, future justice, and white society) panicked by clamoring drums, seduced and nauseated by the rich stench of the event, trapped in the strobes and stage lights of a spectacle that threatens the very act of spectating. *Slave Ship* not only represents the act of cultural revolution, it is itself a concrete example of the Black Arts Movement's nonobjective aesthetic and its complex, often confusing relationship to history, economy, and activism.

Slave Ship is therefore not a social-protest play. It does not seek to adjust or reform existing institutions, nor is its primary address directed toward the oppressor. Likewise, it does not seek to appeal to the moral standards of the oppressor nor to those of the oppressed. Quite the opposite, in fact; the play revels in emotional excess, virtuosic jazz, intricately intertwined vocal performances, and sudden, shocking vulgarity. *Slave Ship* is a *counterspectacle* that attempts to create representational strategies to fundamentally challenge the conceptual, aesthetic, and ethical boundaries of Euro-American political drama. It does not supplicate, it deconstructs, satirizes, and destroys. The use of music, audience participation, and an offstage act of violence against an invisible "White Voice" that echoes throughout the hold of the ship reflects, in Harry Elam Jr.'s words, "the Black masses symbolically expung[ing] the visible and invisible hegemony of the dominant culture."[88] Like Bullins's *Whitegirl*, the "white thing" is never even allowed on stage.

The power of representation that Elam rightly considers one of the central critical concerns of *Slave Ship* is not only a target of proposed revolutionary action, but also a contested terrain. The antinarratival bias of Baraka's play not only revealed to its audiences that the present condition of the African American community is little different from that of slavery, but also worked to create an alternative sense or structure of historicity, community, and aesthetics. If the bourgeois tradition of protest drama, with its generally rigid narrative telos and its carefully timed deployment of ethical and progressivist assumptions, possesses any relevance in the context of *Slave Ship,* it is only in the sense of that which restrains the possibility for radical transformation. Such assumptions represent a pale, fragile bulwark against, in Gwendolyn Brooks's heady phrase, "the noise and whip of the whirlwind":

Salve salvage in the spin.
Endorse the splendor splashes;
stylize the flawed utility;
prop a malign or failing light—
but know the whirlwind is our commonwealth.
. . . .
It is a lonesome, yes. For we are the last of the loud.
Nevertheless, live.
Conduct your blooming in the noise and whip of the whirlwind.[89]

The rarely discussed plays of Sonia Sanchez utilize similarly deconstructive dramaturgical strategies to demonstrate the power available to a "whirlwind commonwealth" reclaiming a history through purposeful movement
into the future. Sanchez's *Malcolm/Man Don't Live Here No Mo* and *Sister
Son/Ji* sever the links between individualism, heroism, and the tendency all
communities have of making history into a static monument. Thereby, she
establishes a richly textured dramatic time-sense, a peculiar form of temporality that is more or less similar to what Homi Bhabha has called "future
anteriority."[90] Perhaps more importantly, they work to undermine such
"white things" as the untainted hero, the resolved crisis, phallocentrism, and
the myth of the avant-garde (things not always adequately undermined by
her male colleagues). Predicting the choreopoems of Ntozake Shange, these
plays utilize monologue and movement to highlight personality without
celebrating individuality. They are explicitly designed to cultivate memory
and inspire activism. They are, with the addition of *The Bronx Is Next*
(1968), among the most acutely self-critical, resolutely revolutionary plays
of the Black arts era, articulating a rigorously feminist attitude that one
rarely encounters among the artistic and critical works of the movement.
They accomplish what other self-critical revolutionary dramas (such as
Richard Wesley's *Black Terror* [1970], the four plays by Edgar White col-
lected in *Underground* [1970], Oliver Pitcher's *The One,* and Bullins's *We
Righteous Bombers*) fail to accomplish: they deconstruct and question without in any way diffusing the commitment to action. And like *The Theme Is
Blackness* and *Slave Ship,* her plays challenge the relationship between the
"seen" and the "scene."

Malcolm/Man is a notable children's play in a movement that valued
highly such plays and organized many theaters exclusively for children, a
tradition that continues today in such places as Chicago's Chocolate Chip
Theater. And like all effective children's plays, it manages to be profound
without sacrificing simplicity. The piece is essentially a dance-drama that

takes place in a never-ending "Now" that reflects an urge much like that of *Theme* and *Slave Ship:* to render time more malleable. A chorus of "3 sistuhs," a "brotha (bout 14 or 15)," and a "sistuh (bout 12, 13, or 14)" retell the life of Malcolm X. The tale is told by the sistuh and brotha, who take on a variety of roles, the girl various female characters ("wite/amurica," "malcolm's future wife"), the boy variously aged versions of X. The telling of the life is counterpoised to the chorus, who take the play into and out of its narratively structured movements by singing, "we be's hero / worshippers . . . we be's death / worshippers . . . we be's leader/ worshippers . . . BUT: we should be blk / people worshippers . . . AND: some of us are leaderless toooooday . . . our homes are empty cuz . . . MALCOLM / MAN DON'T LIVE HERE NO MO."[91]

As in her other plays, Sanchez complements a major theme (X as exemplum) with one or more minor themes (here the loss of individuality caused by hero worship and the lack of political and familial leaders). This complementary dyad of major and minor theme is itself triangulated within a "feminine focus," to paraphrase Enoch Brater.[92] X's life is counterpoised in the text by the strong presence of the sistuh and in performance by the female chorus members. And, as in her other plays, Sanchez does not conclude but rather articulates a question. If *The Bronx Is Next* locates its central question in the lies and violence directed toward women marginalized by the revolution (single mothers, prostitutes, elderly women), the centering question of *Malcolm/Man* is the origin of X: "Malcolm, Malcolm, where did u come from."[93] This question of origins is presented by Sanchez as inseparable from a community of growing young women: the rotating, fluid X is composed of five dancers, four of them female, moving around a single male performer.

Thus, this search for the origins of X's revolt—an emblematic origin of the Black Arts Movement—is not presented in hagiographic terms, is not viewed as the rise of a heroic masculine individual, nor is it portrayed as a crisis resolved by the traditional forms of dramatic dénouement: tragic death or comic marriage (though it does, like *Son/Ji,* view the revolution in decidedly heterosexist terms). Quite the contrary, the primary purpose behind Sanchez's use of dance and music in *Malcolm/Man* is to place the heroic example of X within reach of the Black child and his or her memory, to transform the historic figure of X into a kind of "revolutionary spirit," and to quite literally frame that life within the transient, beautiful motions of dancing children. The transformation of X into an accessible figure was accomplished by utilizing a child actor to portray the man and by surrounding him with female performers to remind the viewers of the crucial importance of women to the liberation of Black men. The transformation into performative spirit of the heroic individual constructed by X and Alex Haley in the *Autobiography* is enabled by having the five performers periodically return to the slowly rotating X-formation with which the performance began, momentarily obliterating the individual and foregrounding the icon-as-dance. The hero's name is transformed into the space of dance.

By transforming the potentially intimidating example of a revolutionary hero into a role that could be performed by any child and that had to be performed in careful cooperation with other actors, Sanchez avoids the potentially antidemocratic tendencies of hero worship. By utilizing dance and iconography, she foregrounds the importance of community cooperation and collective beauty. (Moreover, the child-viewer will probably never view the end of her alphabet lessons in the same way again.) Intended for those in transition—children—Sanchez's play deconstructs the traditions of hero worship that can distance heroes from the people. The history of which X was such a significant part is transformed by Sanchez into a fluid, embodied icon that cannot survive outside the context in which it is sung and danced. "X" in *Malcolm/Man* is not as much a hero to be worshipped as an ethos to be embraced in the spirit of the drum or an initial to replace the last name and pull one from the genealogy of white Euro-Americans (e.g., "Marvin X"). This spirit is rather more gentle than that which informs Bullins's *Theme* or Baraka's *Slave Ship,* but it is no less impatient with the conceptual limitations and narrative habits of Western metaphysics.

We move from youth to age, yet *Sister Son/Ji* suggests a message just as surely tied to the question of memory, the separation of individuals from their community bases, the vanguard attitude, and the future-minded sense of anteriority that shaped the movement. It shows us a more positive, empowering vision of the dialectic of embodiment and disembodiment experienced by the poet in "Willie Best" and by Blackman in *Malcolm: '71,* one that, like Baraka and Bullins's texts, places the burden of resolution on the reader/viewer. Son/Ji quite literally: "Anybody can grab the day and make it stop. can u my friends? or may be it's better if i ask: will you?"[94] The question, here, is explicitly about time, the control and command of time through a dynamic movement of claims, reclaims, forgettings, and expropriations. However, even with that, a strong note of caution is suggested by *Sister Son/Ji*'s dynamic of dramatic structure and audience knowledge; the play's circular structure is offset by the linear development of the onstage character's identity, revealed to us in a series of temporally, musically, and gesturally distinct moments. Lastly, the play launches a pointed critique of the avant-garde myth by focusing on the elderly, the female, and the family—all viewed by Sanchez as intrinsically committed to revolutionary collectivity and consistently forgotten by the avant-garde and its boosters.

The play opens and closes with an elderly African American woman alone, "dressed in shapeless blk / burlap dress, blk / leotards & stockings; gray natural wig,"[95] stage empty except for a narrow spot, a dressing table, and mirror. In between, she changes accessories and makeup. We have a sense, initially of great poverty—and a fairly brutal antielderly message. The poverty signified by the burlap dress is complemented by the poverty signified by the gray natural wig and deep lines of the actor's face. However, this message is undercut by the first scene shift. This shift takes us from the present of the theatrical performance—a moment of bluesy audience/performer communication as Son/Ji declaims herself to the crowd—to a remembered past whose set and other characters are experienced directly by the college-age Son/Ji, indirectly by the audience through her dialogue with "Nesbitt," a man who, like Son/Ji, is militant, and who gets her pregnant. Two interesting implications of this moment might be noted. The dramatic trick Sanchez uses here—giving us only the onstage character's side of a dialogue—allows her to play with names. Unlike Nesbitt, we never discover Son/Ji's "Negro" name, despite the fact that most of the dialogue concerns her description of an action she carried out against a white professor who "don't even know my name unless I raise my hand when u spit out three/black/names."[96] Despite being named, the males are no less problematic: Is Nesbitt the same as "brother Williams," the Black Power heavy whose organizational duties are taking him away from Son/Ji, or the unnamed "he" whom Son/Ji excoriates before a revolutionary council for having a relationship with a white "devil/woman"? Does Son/Ji stay with the same man throughout her revolutionary development, made to "go through changes" with his fickle, unfocused character? Or does she move from man to man, abandoning each with the same decisiveness with which she dealt with earlier stages of her political consciousness?

The theatrical cues of the shift between the old and young woman are worth noting—Son/Ji removes her elderly makeup and wig, puts on a "straightened / black / wig," a belt, necklace, and ankle bracelet over her burlap dress, picks up a notebook, and transforms, suddenly, from a "slow-oldish" performer, to a young woman running across the stage in elation over her first act of militant, racially conscious resistance. Son/Ji has struck her first iconic pose here, and will strike several more (Black Power activist, revolutionary fighter, woman in labor, mother, survivor, inmate, elder). We should note that the taking on and off of costume accessories and props demonstrate her authority over the signifiers of age and politics. It also communicates a message comparable to the conclusion of Audre Lord's poem "Naturally":

> But I've bought my can of
> Natural Hair Spray
> Made and marketed in Watts
> Still thinking more
> Proud beautiful black women
> Could better make and use
> Black bread.[97]

These props and baubles get tangled in the same kind of questions and uncertainties surrounding the men's names. We are unsure whether we are witnessing a series of disconnected passions or the slow, persistent growth of a revolutionary elder. Maybe we think a moment about the gray "natural wig" worn by Son/Ji in the first scene: as a signifier of youth, radicalism, and personal politics, the natural didn't make any sense in a senior hue. The complications concerning stage properties and absent characters are reflecting some odd shadows back to the concluding lines of the first scene: "today i shall be what i was / shd have been and never can be again. Today i shall bring back yesterday as it never can be today. as it shd be tomorrow."[98]

These potentially positive, strengthening messages are, however, constrained by the second scene's narrative arc, which carries us from Son/Ji's account of her action in class to a night of love with her man. The scene, which we might assume would focus on Son/Ji's ideological development, concludes with a rather haunting emphasis on love: "*(Softly.)* nesbitt do u think after a first love each succeeding love is a repetition?"[99] In two brief scenes, Sanchez has sculpted a theatrically complex, emotionally vivid dramatic line. She welds together the old woman's isolation with the young woman's intense moment of fellow feeling. She has drawn the audience's attention to the reification of Blackness, but has also opened the reified signifiers (the natural, the straight hair, the ankle bracelet) to a memory performance not unlike that experienced by the audience/participants of *Eighteen Happenings in Six Parts*. She has shown memory to be a restoration of embodied vitality but also an inevitably partial, biased perspective (specifically, a feminist perspective whose partiality enables her to identify the successes and failures of Black men as she tells her own life story and the story of a revolution not so much in the future, as in an "age and now and never again").[100] In sum, she takes the traditional African American literary trope of naming, yokes it to a self-conscious use of stage devices, and interweaves it in an authoritatively told performance of a life already lived but not yet justified. The concluding lines of the poem—"Anybody can grab the day and make it stop. can u my friends? or may be it's better if i ask: will you?"[101]—take us through a similar set of changes as in "Willie Best" and *Malcolm: '71:* the question of our revolutionary commitment is inseparable from the conventions of theatrical encounter.

Soul and the Commodity of Blackness: The Strange Case of [Ed.] Bullins

Thus far, I've explored three dimensions of performativity in the Black Arts Movement: as a tactic to effectively maneuver across Cruse's triple front, as a practical mechanism for revisioning precolonial West-African aesthetics and philosophy, and as a perceptual mechanism that manifests a critique of Euro-American Enlightenment traditions (and its antagonist, the avant-garde). I've shown how these performative modes systematically undermine the racist colonialism of Euro-American commodity culture, especially through its subversion of text. The results of this subversion are the kinds of self-dramatizing texts that lined the walls of Blackman's study in *Malcolm: '71* and that line the study of that play's readers. However, though it's tempting to celebrate only the success of performance against the forces of textuality, we need to take careful note of how various modes of textuality undermined and deflated claims about the efficacy of performance. In the following pages, I'll turn back to the role of *editing* in the Black Arts Movement, particularly as practiced by Bullins. The first Black Theater issue of *The Drama Review* and *Black Theatre* magazine (the house journal of the New Lafayette Theatre) served the role of public enunciations and spread a very particular textual construction of revolutionary subjectivity intended for very specific communities of readers.

Editing served as a weapon for Bullins, a former Minister of Culture for the Black Panther Party who was well versed in the possibilities of rhetorical action, a weapon to be turned both against the oppressor outside and against ignorance inside the community. Though his work as an editor in the Black Arts Movement has rarely been discussed,[102] it stands as one of the more self-critical moments in the movement's history and in the larger history of the text-performance dynamic that has been so important in the avant-garde tradition. This becomes clear when we turn to an emblematic crisis of the BAM, a crisis that exposed power structures and conceptual limits *within* the Black arts community: the discovery in 1969 that the play *We Righteous Bombers,* supposedly written by a young Black revolutionary martyr, was a plagiarism of a widely available English translation of Albert Camus's *Les Justes* and an act of authorial disguise.[103] Examining both the plagiarism as a performative act of textual manipulation as well as Bullins's editorial negotiation in *Black Theatre* of the scandal the play caused, we can acquire a more nuanced understanding of the role of both textual and performance power in the Black Arts Movement.

As we recall, Harold Cruse continually pressed his younger colleagues to conceive and pursue their struggle on the triple front of culture, economics, and politics. We also recall how Neal agreed with Cruse that the struggle was best waged through the strategic construction and affiliation of Afrocentric institutions. But we also recall that Neal revised Cruse's pragmatist approach to institution building by linking it to a more Afrocentric vision. Like Cruse, Neal saw theater and performance as the best organizational and aesthetic practices to link the three fronts of the struggle and the specific qualities of revolutionary transformation in the African American community. However, at the same time, they both understood that the *text* served a range of indispensable functions for the movement. Pragmatically speaking, it was also a medium for communicating among the widely dispersed revolutionary communities of the BAM; textual exchanges were a crucial medium for articulating national consciousness. But both Cruse and Neal saw the text as a double-edged sword, prone to cut the wielder as much as his opponent.

One particularly important component of the movement's institutional development was the command and control of textual production, exchange, and reception. For example, the selling of poetry supplied revenue to Black cultural organizations and kept the hunger for foundation funding dulled. In addition to being an important source of revenue, selling texts with the right message by the right authors to the right communities could significantly aid the development of the kind of total institutions and Black subjectivity I have described already. Just as importantly, the production, distribution, and reception of texts created a sense of virtual community, bringing many individuals together in an intimate and significant way through the mediation of text. The ambiguities of the trade in textualized Blackness is captured by Nikki Giovanni in her marvelously theatrical poem "Our Detroit Conference (for Don L. Lee)":

> We met in
> The Digest
> Though I had
> Never Known You

Tall and Black
But mostly in
The Viet Cong
Image

You didn't smile

Until we had traded
Green stamps
For Brownie Points

The text is rife with vertiginous contradictions produced by its desire to make visible its politics and its community while maintaining a selective but dearly valued invisibility—and it's text that produces these decidedly theatrical contradictions. The poem's use of insider references (the conference, the "Digest") complements Giovanni's effort to mark out a place for individualism in a movement always trending toward orthodoxy. It plays in paradox. The poem is a public document dedicated to an individual; it describes a community convocation in terms of distinctively private experience; and it represents the meeting of two highly celebrated, well-known writers in terms that deny the ability of the reader to read them clearly. And all of this is wrapped in the language of exchange, the objectifying gaze of the poet enabling the trading of . . . well, what exactly gets traded here?

Whatever community is created between the poet and the iconic, macho-man poet is bound up with meetings in pages (the Digest), with indexical signifiers (the Viet Cong image) that lack referent (what does a subguerilla insurgent look like?), and with the exchange of "green stamps" and "brownie points," the lattermost understood less as commodities than as signifiers (coupons) of an unspecified exchange of intensely personal experiences. The objectifying, simplifying pressures of the short poetic text are used by Giovanni to indicate a poetic referent (that which is possessed by the poet and her primary addressee, Don Lee [aka Haki Madhubuti]) while at the same time maintaining that referent in a state of curiously inalienable privacy. The overtly visual quality of the poets' meeting (the visuality of the journal page, the visual titillation of meeting one's peers at conferences, the militant-poet's chic signification of anger and revolution, the smile, the Pop-like invocation of the Green Stamp) turns, at the end of the poem, into a value represented by empty, but highly charged icons of bourgeois exchange: coupons and favors, quantity and quality.

Giovanni's poem exemplifies a much larger problem for the movement. The production and circulation of guiding texts such as critical studies, poetry collections, historical studies, and model dramas were vital to the health of institutions that sought, paradoxically, a kind of mythologically pure, separate community where all shared in a common and inalienable soulfulness. Much like *Malcolm: '71*'s Blackman, the BAM required textual models to sustain its essentialist force. There could be no "soul" without the printing press. Like the stamps and points of Giovanni's poems, texts served the BAM, to recall Knight, as forms of public enunciation that brought together a message and a movement in a paradoxically exclusivist fashion. Along these lines, we might think of the superb collection *For Malcolm,* published by Broadside Press in 1969.[104] The public enunciation in this collection of feelings peculiar to the Black community runs with the grain of Giovanni's transformation of a social, historical movement into something that belongs exclusively to her and Lee. In addition, the fact that a number of contributors to the volume are white complicates this exclusivity in a fashion also similar to Giovanni's poem. The conference is "ours," just as the poem, a textual form available to all who buy her book, belongs to a single reader: Lee. But it can never be simply theirs. As shown in *For Malcolm,* the public event of X's death results in the formation of a separatist poetic movement founded on a culturally specific emotional response—but a response that is available, as text, to all who can read.

However, given the impossibility of ever fully controlling the movement of texts, and given the benefits of selling "Black" texts to as wide an audience as possible to ensure more robust revenue streams, the notion of a truly nationalist textual economy would seem both conceptually and practically untenable. The burden carried by the Black nationalist writer in this kind of situation is difficult to imagine and important to examine since basic concerns of the avant-garde, the counterculture, and the critical demarcations between activist and scholars come to light. Bullins is emblematic in this regard. As Minister of Culture for the Black Panthers and Black House from 1966 to 1967, he was in a pressured position practically and personally. In practical terms, he was compelled to spend much time fund-raising instead of working on plays; in essence, performing the iconic, "Viet Cong / Image" role of the Black militant to raise money. Moreover, the theater of provocation Bullins utilized for fund-raising events was too one-sided, too one-dimensional for him; he wanted to explore less pedantic forms, forms that could support a more ironic, self-critical, and less elitist drama. The opportunity for this kind of exploration came when he was invited to join the New Lafayette Theatre, where he cemented his fame not only as a playwright and public intellectual, but as an editor, organizing and producing four groundbreaking texts of the modern American theater: *The Drama*

Review's 1968 issue on Black Theater, two major collections of Black Arts Movement drama *(New Plays from the Black Theatre* and *The New Lafayette Theatre Presents)*, and the potent and precise house journal of the New Lafayette, *Black Theatre.*

Bullins's work as a playwright, activist, and editor during the 1960s occurred in contexts in which the ethical questions and communicative possibilities of performance were entangled with the production and circulation of texts. Keeping an ear to the contradictions unearthed by Bullins through his editorial practices, we discover that he predicted by some three decades recent developments in performance studies that have challenged a number of common assumptions concerning the critical efficacy of performance. During the last few years, discussions of authority, textuality, and performance—notably that initiated by former *Theatre Journal* editor William Worthen in the pages of *TDR*[105]—suggest that research on the relationship of politics and theater is best sited in contexts in which power, textuality, and performance are the objects of sustained theoretical and practical critique and development. However, by and large, consideration of such sites have tended toward rigidity, regarding performance as an inherently liberating practice and text as a prison house. Worthen calls for a more critically sophisticated understanding of performance as a cultural practice; specifically, for research into the ways that performance can serve as a disciplinary power as opposed to a purely decentering or deconstructive practice. Bullins's work as an editor of the Black Arts Movement epitomizes such a site.

The notion of editing as a form of performance might inspire skepticism, especially considering the occasionally loose ways that the term *performance* gets used across disciplines. But being conscious of the construction of public subjectivities (the Best/bluesman paradox), the shifting geographies of textual enactment as they are made visible in a play such as *Malcolm: '71,* and the dynamics of audience reception as they function in the editorial process gives to scholars a number of effective critical levers for interdisciplinary performance scholarship. George Bornstein writes, in *Representing Modernist Texts: Editing as Interpretation,* "Textual scholarship must necessarily always remind us that any embodied form of a text is a contingent product of concrete historical and economic institutions rather than a transparent conduit of an author's unmediated words."[106] Bornstein implies that editorial work is an embodied, public negotiation of possibility and prohibition that enables both effective deconstructive strategies and the construction of forms of political and cultural power. This would come as no surprise to Bullins, whose work as an editor coincided with his greatest celebrity as a

Black activist, artist, and public intellectual. He had no choice except to perform since he was always exposed to the close scrutiny of his comrades and enemies. Bullins played both sides of this game; as an African American, he lived within the imposed theatricality of racist society; as a Black editor and playwright, he worked behind the scenes, out of view. Bullins-the-Editor is both producer and product of texts.

Though his response is unique, Bullins was not alone in his recognition of the power relations surrounding these activities. Black artists and critics of the 1960s and 1970s never viewed questions of textual production, circulation, and reception as anything but politically and economically situated. Carolyn Gerald has argued that the little magazines of the BAM such as *Black Dialogue, Journal of Black Poetry, Liberator, Negro Digest,* and *Soulbook* represented a concrete "literary enactment of the crisis of the Sixties: the Break with the West."[107] Abby and Ronald Johnson note that "[t]hose who identified with the [BAM] wanted their little magazines to go to the heart, or the essential reality, of blackness. Thus, they insisted the journals be black at all levels of involvement, from owner to reader."[108] Following the lead of Gwendolyn Brooks, who left Random House for Dudley Randall's nationalist Broadside Press in 1967–68, Black Arts writers published in presses such as the Free Black Press, Journal of Black Poetry Press, Black Dialogue Press, Jihad Press, and Third World Press, many of which were affiliated with Black theater cooperatives.

It's a reasonable speculation that Bullins was less than confident that such presses could ultimately succeed in overcoming the contradictions of a textually supported antitextual movement. His experience with the New Lafayette was, for example, impacted by the chronic financial difficulties typical of politically and ethnically exclusive theaters and presses—and the kinds of compromises such difficulties compelled (in the case of the Lafayette, support from the Ford Foundation in order to supply free tickets to Harlem residents). Moreover, it is reasonable to assert that Bullins was less than confident that the Black community was unified enough to support such theaters and presses since his work as playwright and editor was profoundly and repeatedly impacted by the ideological divisiveness within that community. And finally, it is clear from examination of his writings that Bullins had little patience with the chauvinist essentialism of many of his colleagues, even though he could not fully abandon a notion of Blackness that was basically essentialist. (Certainly, Bullins himself has veered into chauvinism if not outright misogyny at times.)

When Bullins left San Francisco in 1968, he could not have known that the tensions that had torn Black House to pieces would reappear. But this time, Bullins had a new form of power with which to negotiate those tensions, one not available to him on the West Coast, where his work as political organizer and playwright consumed most of his energies. Not expected to raise funds as playwright-in-residence for the Lafayette, Bullins was able to develop new skills as an editor.[109] Ironically, by the end of the next year, the contradictory dynamic of text, performative blackness, and institution would reassert itself, this time with Bullins pulling off an astounding feat of strategic, self-deconstructing, coyly public editorial performance. In May 1969, New Lafayette founder and director Robert Macbeth organized a panel discussion of Kingsley G. Bass's *We Righteous Bombers,* supposedly in order to forestall a threat to firebomb the New Lafayette Theatre because of the "reactionary" nature of the play (a threat all the more threatening given the fact that the Lafayette had been burned down in 1967, possibly due to ideological conflict). During the panel, it was revealed that Bullins had actually written the play; "Bass" was a hoax. In addition, Neal discovered that the play was a plagiarism of a popular English translation of Camus's *Les Justes.*

By exploring such examples of Bullins's editorial and dramatic work together, we can better understand the impact of the text/performance dynamic on the movement and its triple front. Bullins's editorial work has never been considered a form of critical activity as significant as his work as a playwright, but his efforts as editor and playwright were mutually informative. To illustrate the ways in which art, economics, and politics informed Bullins's varied labors, I'll briefly examine his editorial negotiations of *The Drama Review*'s varied audience expectations. But my main focus will fall on his most significant undertaking as an "editorial performer": the plagiarized *We Righteous Bombers* and the fourth issue of *Black Theatre.* The lesson taught by these works is that ultimate power rests in the hands of those who can artfully manipulate text, performance persona, and institution; in this case, [Ed.] Bullins.

Late in 1966–67, Bullins corresponded with *TDR* editor Richard Schechner concerning a special issue on recent developments in Black theater. Schechner thought the idea a timely one, especially given the playwright's recent celebrity and the increasing visibility of the Black Power movement, so when Bullins arrived in Manhattan, he got to work. The issue would prove to be unique; *TDR*'s editorial board granted Bullins complete control of the issue, even giving up the right of final editorial veto. As Schechner put it, "'Telling it like it is' is a particularly difficult task—if 'it' isn't happening to you. In this issue we sought a precise measurement of a certain aspect of black awareness. To achieve that, we removed the white hands from the blue pencils."[110] The issue is notable for three things, aside from the fact that it was the first on African American theater published by a white-run academic journal. First, the theoretical and critical content is in itself significant, including essays by Bullins, Neal, Concept East cofounder Woodie King Jr., Adam David Miller, Free Southern Theater's John O'Neal, Henrietta Harris, and Jones. His assemblage of texts shows that Bullins recognized the importance of theory and criticism to the articulation of a revolutionary cultural project. Likewise, the assemblage reflects an ecumenical tolerance of aesthetic and ideological diversity unusual for the fractious BAM, a tolerance that was certainly the fruit of Bullins's unpleasant experience of Black House's demise. In short, editorial decisions are structured by a polemical position and the strategic construction of revolutionary subjectivity.

Second, the dramatic material was organized by Bullins under two headings, "Black Revolutionary Theater" and "Theater of Black Experience," two varieties of Black drama and performance that differ fundamentally in terms of the communities and institutions for which they were written (roughly stated, the former was intended for the unorganized and undecided, the latter for the true believers). Bullins clearly is not willing to reject one or the other form. This distinction reflects an understanding of how dramatic genres can differentially respond to the tactical needs of revolutionary confrontation and community consolidation. If essence is strategic, to recall Fuss again, then it must be able to respond to the slippery, shifting strategic decisions necessitated by Cruse's triple front. Such an editorial decision also stands in tacit support of the ironic, nondogmatic, critical, and experimental forms of theater Newton, Karenga, Cleaver, and Touré viewed as counterrevolutionary.

Lastly, Bullins's choice of essays and plays was significant beyond its attempt to intervene in discussions concerning revolutionary drama; the critics, playwrights, and theaters he included were necessarily limited in number and generally unknown within both the American and African American theater communities. Unfortunately, this gives the impression that the movement was both limited in scale and sui generis.[111] The mentors of the movement are essentially erased. Moreover, established theaters such as the Negro Ensemble Company and Karamu received only oblique mention, if mention at all. Such editorial bias against older generations was not unusual for a young radical of the 1960s, of course. Like many of Bullins's plays (e.g. *Clara's Ole Man*, *The Electronic Nigger*, *The Corner*), the special issue implied that they were irrelevant, even harmful, to revolutionary Black youth. However, the vision of the BAM as a product of the "generation gap" underserves both the ideological complexity and the cross-generational communication that made it so powerful and innovative.

The older generations were not the only ones to feel Bullins's editorial barbs; the issue seems to be designed specifically to clash with the editorial tendencies of *TDR*. Schechner notes the differences:

> As I read over the material for this issue it became clear to me that the aesthetics most commonly debated in *TDR*—happenings, environmental theater, new kinds of criticism, regional theater, actor training—are most lively in the context of a certain segment of white American society. Most of these movements are irrelevant to black theater. And some of them are viewed as "decadent," others as "oppressive."[112]

Schechner incorrectly states that "happenings, environmental theater, new kinds of criticism, regional theater, actor training" are not part of Black theater; he needed to look uptown to Barbara Ann Teer's National Black Theater, or in the pages of *Liberator, Black Theatre,* or Bullins's experimental theatrical works to recognize the oversight. However, the error was not entirely his fault.

Schechner's assertion is determined both by the closed communications circuit of the BAM as well as Bullins's strategically minded editorial performance. Though the special issue became something of a holy text for the BAM, like all performances it gives a selective perspective on both its subject matter and its performers. *TDR* was, at the time, read predominantly by liberal and liberal-activist whites, a great many of whom were affiliated with academic institutions. Thus, it was important that Bullins take advantage of the opportunity while avoiding the doglike domestication satirized in *Malcolm: '71*. Much like Baraka's public performances while at BART/S, the multiaccentual representation of the Black singer in "A Poem for Willie Best," or the early poetry of Nikki Giovanni, Bullins's editorial work on *TDR* is structured by the need to perform before a politically and ethnically diverse readership, to actively negotiate and exploit double consciousness in order to get the right message across to the right people. Like *Malcolm: '71*'s Blackman, Bullins had to maintain his vigilance against the seductive threat of co-optation. This very public editorial performance addressed distinct publics by way of rhetorically coded textual manipulation. For the reader who keeps an ear toward the racial and political rhetoric of the Black Arts, the special issue's presentation of theorists, plays, and documents reveals itself to be a highly self-conscious performance of textual Blackness.

Bullins was definitely skeptical of the kinds of theater and performance theory regularly featured in *TDR,* precisely what he criticizes in his essay "The So-Called Western Avant-Garde"; however, he was also sympathetic to the antitextual theories of the BAM, theories that, while clearly rooted in the diverse performance traditions of the African diaspora, were not unlike the kinds of theater favored by Schechner and his white colleagues. Given this ambivalent address, we can begin to see how Bullins's work as an editor can be viewed as a concrete, often ironic negotiation of a contradictory rhetorical and political terrain. But Bullins didn't only perform before politically and racially mixed audiences; these same tactics of presentation and disguise were also utilized before the more politically, geographically, and ethnically homogenous community of the BAM.

The 1970 issue of *Black Theatre* embodies the paradoxes and possibilities of the movement's commitment to performance, with Bullins as editor playing a complicated and public game of signifying backstage.[113] The cover of the magazine (designed by Ed Sherman) hints at the complex dynamic of economic, political, and cultural nationalism that had determined the course of a revolutionary cultural movement already five years old and stumbling toward political and economic exhaustion. On that cover, we find a stereotypical anarchist bomb, its fuse spitting sparks, a triangular decal affixed to it, each point a different symbol: Egyptian ankh, Islamic star-and-crescent, and the mathematical signifier for square root. But it is unclear what the relation is between the bomb and the signifiers on its surface. Is the bomb explosive because it emblematizes the combined force of Black spirituality, Black Nationalist militancy, and Black science? Are the emblem and the unity itself threatened by the potential violence of the bomb? Or is it the magazine itself that is threatening to explode?

The text of the cover is no less polyvalent. Written in chalk are the words "Get OFF THE SiDewAlk!" The warning is repeated by Baraka inside the magazine: "If we're—supposed to be so hip and intelligent—at least carry as much information as somebody on the sidewalk, saying, 'Get off the sidewalk.'"[114] As we'll see, this concern with the spaces outside text and theater structures the magazine as a whole.

Inside the front cover, the reader finds a quote from Karenga, "To play revolution is to get put down," but this is a rather unsettling statement to find in a journal devoted to the production, dissemination, and criticism of revolutionary *plays.* Ambivalency and signifying are the keynotes here. Even as it pokes fun at the tradition of Black revolutionary drama, the placement of the quote in this particular issue of the journal puts Karenga at the service of a kind of Black drama that, at least on a theoretical level, he could hardly tolerate.

"The cover of the magazine (designed by Ed Sherman) hints at the complex dynamic of economic, political, and cultural nationalism . . ." (Reprinted with permission of Ed. Bullins.)

This is more than just rhetorical playfulness. Among the reports of regional black theater activity in the issue is Naima Rashidd's, which warns the reader about the institutional impact of the very kinds of textual tricksterism that structures the issue:

> After reading *Black Theatre* #2, I immediately recognized the urgency of writing this note regarding the article on the Detroit Repertory, by Bruce Millian. . . . I wish to inform you that this man is a fraud. First of all, ". . . this very articulate brother," as you incorrectly described him, is an Anglo-Saxon Caucasian. Secondly, the Detroit Repertory Theater is only a sect of the "American" theater, and has survived with the same traits, purposes and indifferences of its ancestors as far as the needs of Black culture are concerned.[115]

Compromised by an act of textual forgery, a falsification of "Blackness," Bullins can only highlight the hazards: "Oop! . . . sorry, Brothers and Sisters. But it has been rumored that the devil does quote revelations to his advantage. [Ed.]" (3). Not only the devil, it would seem. The centerpiece of the issue is a discussion devoted to an act of textual tricksterism perpetrated by Bullins himself that is not unlike Millian's. As Marvin X revealed, "Brother Ed wrote the play . . . in an attempt to suggest the type of play that a brother killed in the Detroit Revolution would have written. And he wrote it in an attempt to suggest some of the rhetoric that is used, you know, among so-called revolutionaries."[116]

As I have already discussed, the Black Theater issue of *TDR* helped secure a revolutionary Black identity against ethnically and ideologically nonBlack readers through a self-conscious presentation of the Black Arts Movement and Bullins himself. In the fourth issue of *Black Theatre* magazine, Bullins arranges texts in a similarly self-conscious way in order to place the entire movement at a moment of decision not unlike the one we experience as readers in Baraka's "A Poem for Willie Best" or at the end of *Sister Son/Ji*. However, the dynamic of text and performance that played such a potent role in those texts is not used here to safeguard Blackness from a nonBlack audience; rather, the dynamic is exploited to deconstruct a particular theoretical/ideological interpretation of Blackness, specifically the "social realist" vision that favored idealized images, heroic plots, and the like. In addition, the issue partly deflates the belief that performance is an effective way to secure Blackness from nonBlack eyes. The audiences of *TDR* and the *Black Theatre* issue differ, but the exploitation of the text/performance dynamic to flush out ingrained, insufficiently criticized assumptions about Blackness remains the same.

Exploiting the ironies of textual production and circulation, [Ed.] Bullins effectively subverts some of the hotly debated principles of the movement, not least of these the insistence that a revolutionary drama be an ideologically prescriptive, mimetic drama.[117] Touré criticizes *Bombers* for exactly these reasons; though sympathetic to its soulful qualities, he saw it as neither socially committed nor sufficiently "realistic": "There is confusion among the people because the author's intentions are not clear. . . . The playwright fails to distinguish between the fool and a true revolutionary . . . thus further contributing to the counter-revolutionary aspects of the play by alienating and/or confusing the Black audience."[118] Likewise, Touré criticizes the play for its lack of positive images and role models—a classic concern for the social realist, though in the case of Touré, the term "soulful realist" is much more appropriate, given his profound understanding of the function of signifyin' in African American culture. Unlike Bullins, whose work might best be considered "soulfully materialist" since it grounded Blackness in deeper, more central, but also highly fluid, transformative contexts of production and consideration, Touré feels that the unambivalent, didactic indication of a clear-and-present reality, linked to the emotional intensity of soulful exchange, is the best way to chart the paths toward the Black Revolution.

Bullins tacitly asserts his disagreement with Touré and the soulful realists by including in the issue Baraka's poem "For Maulana Ron Karenga & Pharaoh Saunders":

Describe beauty brother-lover, create worlds of dazzling sweet color
Speech, image in the sand, the water pulls up, cloud sketch a colony of
    other kinds of life, rain waving thru the middle air as a heart
describes,
the momentary taste of picture
the God Thot
arrived
sweet seeing
and then, behind that,
we did another thing[119]

According to the poem, "sweet seeing" is not sufficient for political clarity; rather than the eye, a soulful evocation of essential knowledge determines the quality of "Black" perception. Seeing discloses Blackness while at the same time threatening to disguise it. Black art interrogates the lines between disclosure and disguise, in fact activates the subversion of the two in order to restore creative authority to the Black artist and the Black community. Black "essence," as it plays out in the pages of *Black Theatre,* is a shared transformative power rooted in history and memory, always open to sudden shifts in the form and contexts of community and communication.

Baraka's trust in the rhythmic and spiritual metastructures of the community's orature as an empowering opening onto Blackness ("Speech, image in the sand . . . . behind that, / we did another thing") is seconded by Karenga's "On Black Art," a collection of aphorisms that follows Baraka's poem in the issue and precedes Neal's introduction to the transcript of the *Bombers* debate. Karenga, too, argues that "the object [is] not as important as the soul force behind the creation of the object."[120] However, we shouldn't assume that Bullins is putting his editorial weight wholly behind the essentialists and against the realists. As is all too clear from the examples of literary falsification identified by Rashidd, Neal, and X, the transformative power of "soul force" is just as prone to the counterfeit textual object and the textual disguises of writers and editors as is the supposedly objective perceptions of Touré and his ideological compeers.

In short, the first pages of *Black Theatre* number 4 establish a self-deconstructing matrix of textual and performative Blackness that (1) implicitly criticizes those who hold an insufficiently self-conscious attitude toward textuality, (2) deconstructs both the essentialist and realist positions, and, as we'll shortly see, (3) establishes a homology between the movement (represented in the issue by the discussion panel transcript) and *We Righteous Bombers*. The struggle of the panel's participants mirrors the struggle of the characters in *We Righteous Bombers*. In the play, the shifting lines between truth and lie define the shifting boundary between revolution and self-delusion, between essence as a source of self-recognition and essence as an illusion created by racist media. As a result, the characters are never certain whether they are creating a revolution or, to recall Karenga, playing at revolution. They are never sure where the play ends and the revolution begins. That the central character of *Bombers* is a poet forced to become a television performer (specifically, the executioner for the state) is no accident. To recall Karenga once again, the assassins may in fact be playing at revolution and, therefore, fated to be "put down."

The spectator and scholar is no less prone to confusion than the characters of the play they watch and study, for "Kingsley B. Bass" is a charade, a complex pun on the name of a character from the old *Amos 'n' Andy* radio and television show, a version of whom appears in the play itself as an acid reminder of what Bullins saw as a tendency toward self-deception and self-exploitation within the African American community.[121] Bullins's choice of a pseudonym reflects a number of pressing concerns: it supplied a revolutionary pedigree to his play (this recognized by X, who understood that

Bullins's own "Blackness" was undermined by his affiliation with Macbeth's Ford Foundation–supported theater), it addressed the limitations on his work as a playwright caused by his status as a representative Black revolutionary writer, it reflected his concern with the lack of historical and literary understanding of his peers, and it fulfilled his desire to criticize a movement to which he was deeply committed. The disguise was also necessitated by plagiarism; the BAM's critical establishment (clued in by Neal) quickly recognized *Bombers* as a word-for-word rip-off of Stuart Gilbert's 1958 translation of Albert Camus's *Les Justes*. Neal, who spent much of the 1960s warning his colleagues away from precisely this kind of reliance on European models of dramatic construction, thought the implications dire. "This is serious shit," he writes in the preface to the transcript of the *Bombers* panel discussion. "What we have on our hands is the first literary hoax of the Black Arts Movement. Bad scene. We have all lost something."[122]

But again, Bullins makes his presence felt through editorial intrusion and the textual manipulation and framing of his colleague's public pronouncements: Neal's diatribe is punctuated by a footnote: "Our innocence [Ed.]" (15). Ed, indeed. Neal's public call for honesty, new artistic and analytical forms, and criticism of "Brother Bass" (had Neal not been informed? Was he playing along with the joke?) is undercut by Bullins, who manages by editorial subterfuge to have both the last word and the last, bitter laugh. Below the footnote, Bullins places a box containing the announcement of Kingsley B. Bass Jr.'s, receipt of "The Harriet Webster Updike Theater Award" for literary excellence. But the award is also a sham. Neal's criticism of a textually fabricated comrade is juxtaposed to a bit of textual fabrication that tries to lure the reader into yet another trap. The bait: an ingrained assumption (unconsciously upheld by those panel members who insisted on textual analysis as opposed to analysis of the role of the play as a tactical maneuver on Cruse's triple front) that the true value of the dramatic text is the text itself, and not the community in and for which the text is performed, discussed, and challenged.

In the case of *Bombers,* Bullins manipulates text with the same kind of strategic, audience-minded irony that we witnessed in his *TDR* editorship. Interestingly, the play opens with a possibly unintentional gaff: the introduction of the "stone revolutionary soul sister" Bonnie Brown, who tells us that she is "gonna be with yawhl this evening as we go through some Black Revolutionary changes."[123] However, the promise of Bonnie's presence as a central, onstage shaper of the narrative (a unique presence in Bullins's work) doesn't pay off. Her character is the most confused in the play—her final declaration, "Oh, the sun is out brothers, it is spring . . . and how suddenly happy I am" (25), rings absurdly hollow because the audience is unsure at that point whether her martyred comrade Murray Jackson has been executed or has become, via an act of behind-the-scenes subterfuge, the new state executioner. Her desire to join Jackson in an act of spectacular sacrifice on television is based on a fundamental misunderstanding of the struggle she and her comrades are waging, as well as an inability to recognize that what she sees and what she feels are in part the illusions generated by lies, secrecy, and the spectacle of mass-mediated revolution. Little wonder that Touré considered her a "vacillating, schizophrenic character."[124] But Touré's criticism—as accurate as it is—misses the point. Bonnie's tentative existence as an empowered narrator (a reader of her own text) runs afoul not of the ideological confusion of the playwright but of the complex set of narrative frames Bullins erects around both Camus's well-made existentialist drama as well as the play itself as it occurred in the New Lafayette Theatre.

Bullins's literary-historical and practical knowledge of the absurdist theater (as revealed in his essay "The So-Called Western Avant-Garde Theater")[125] puts him in excellent stead for the complex act of appropriation and *détournement*[126] of existential "truths" that constitutes *Bombers*. Camus's play, after all, is a creature of the dramaturgical contradiction first identified by Martin Esslin: "If Camus argued that in our disillusioned age the world has ceased to make sense, he did so in the elegantly rationalistic and discursive style of an eighteenth-century moralist, in well-constructed and polished plays."[127] But unlike the theater of the absurd, which "renounced arguing *about* the absurdity of the human condition [and] merely *presents* it in being—that is, in terms of concrete stage images" (6), *Bombers* is still concerned with the possibility of community empowerment, social transformation, and the moral uses of violence—this despite its deeply cynical vision of revolutionary activity. Bullins does to the tradition of Black revolutionary drama what the absurdists did to the plays of Sartre and Camus. By transposing the dramatic structure and philosophical tenets of those texts into a context of riddling and fluid theatricality, specifically the hazardous terrain of the "so-called avant-garde," Bullins is able not only to criticize the nihilism of Black revolutionaries but also the certainties of revolutionary Blackness and its proponents and opponents.

It is important that we recognize *Bombers* not simply as plagiarism, but as a public act of textual manipulation on par with Bullins's other editorial performances. While it is certainly true that he appropriates passages wholesale from Gilbert's translation, he also makes crucial changes in the structure and thematic emphases of the play, controverting Neal's assertion that the play apes European dramatic conventions. These changes foreground two themes of only secondary importance to *Les Justes*: the paradoxes of "just" action and judgment (emblematized by the prison poet forced to perform in the spectacle of terrorism) and the spectacle of revolution (the theater). As concerns the first, Bullins expands the fourth act of Camus's text—the crucial prison scene in which the poet-turned-bomber Kaliayev undergoes a series of temptations by the Guard, the Chief of Police, and the Assassinated Grand Duke's widow—into a framing device for the entire play. So while Camus's play begins with the reunion of the revolutionaries in their hideout (a hideout that, because it exists in a pre-electronic era, is implicitly free of surveillance devices), Bullins's begins in the dark with the sounds of urban apocalypse, the voice of a military announcer summarizing the realities of fascist America, and the slowly rising lights that reveal Murray Jackson sitting in his cell, surrounded by "numerous less distinguishable shapes" that "move and make sounds—choking, gagging, hisses, laughter, whimpers, coughs."[128] And while the passionate ideological debate of Camus's Stepan, Anenkov, and Voinov pierces confusion and defines the precepts of moral action, Bullins's Jackson, Brown, Cleveland, Banes, and Burk's recital of the "Black Revolutionary Codes of War" are theatrically linked to the line-call of the concentration camp guard.

As with the theme of imprisonment, theatricality also plays a minor role in the source material. While it is true that the Grand Duke is killed on his way to the theater, the words and actions of Camus's revolutionaries are never consciously ironized as theatrical. In fact, quite the contrary. The reference to theatricality in *Les Justes* supplies the negative ground for the characters' foregrounded discovery of moral truth and authentic fellowship supposedly beyond the gaze of the audience. In Camus's play, it is the conservative establishment that is theatrical—and therefore, immoral. Nontheatrical truth and moral certainty are to be found in the "authentic" words and emotions of the revolutionaries. That such language and emotion is *staged* is not acknowledged by Camus; the theater tacitly functions as a transparent, nonideological medium. In Bullins's play, however, theatricality is the *only* context, the continuum that binds and bounds their conflict and infuses irony into all they say and do. Bullins's revolutionaries are emphatically *theatrical,* his revolution clearly *staged.*

In this world of constant surveillance, the revolutionary movement has become quite literally theatrical and its fighters unwitting actors in a prison production. Sissie feels the actor's burden most acutely:

But it was the eyes . . . the electric eyes . . . I could feel them on me as I stood on look-out. All the time I could feel them . . . look at me . . . through me . . . as if I didn't have no clothes on. They could see through my disguise . . . could see my skin, brothers and sisters.[129]

While she delivers her apology to the assassins, a guard sits nearby with a copy of *Playboy* magazine "with a bunny on the cover."[130] Sissie's paranoia, her sense that her skin is no protection from the powerful, is not the result of schizophrenia, is not the pathological consequence of extremism. In text (magazine) and theater (light), she is compelled into forms of visibility that she cannot control—or even fully comprehend.

Moreover, less radical elements in Harlem are also being watched—and put on view. The theater the Grand Prefect is attending is none other than the New Lafayette. Sissie's paranoia spreads like a virus. Later in the play, Bullins asks that the projection screens that border the stage space "show images of the areas surrounding the theater, and the local black community: the barber shops, attending meetings, of well-known local figures photographed unsuspectedly, etc."[131] Like *Malcolm: '71, Bombers* systematically expands the theatrical frame. The transparency of the theater in Camus's play is denied in Bullins's by textual manipulation and institutional power, both of which simultaneously produce and undermine the revolutionary blackness of the bombers. Existence precedes essence (as existentialists such as Camus claimed), but the printing press precedes all.

The textual manipulation of Camus's emblematic existentialist drama pitches both the play and the special issue of *Black Theatre* into the precincts of the black existentialist tradition. In this sense, his editorial work doubles Fanon's representation of acts of revolutionary crisis in *Black Skin, White Masks,* as well as his sympathetic critique of French existentialism. Commenting on Fanon's work as writer and activist, Lewis R. Gordon notes that Fanon's existential standpoint rests on the interrelated concerns of the lived body, the problem of self and other, and the anguish over freedom and unfreedom—typical existentialist concerns. However, Fanon ultimately departs from Sartre, Beauvoir, and Camus by demonstrating that the objects and gestures in the colonial situation possess dimensions that are highly unstable conceptually and politically and always prone to the situational demands of military and ideological conflict. For example, Gordon notes that the Algerian woman's veil, in a period of revolutionary struggle, "goes through a dialectic [among] colonized signification, traditional Muslim signification, and its purely functional role as an opportune mode of concealment."[132] The instability of the veil should recall the special issue of

Black Scholar and the gray wig of Son/Ji. In Bullins's editorial work, the text is run through a dialectic among its roles as pillar of racist culture, liberatory weapon, and functional purveyor of radical theory and cultural memory.

Ironically, Jackson's failure to understand the economic and political conditions of his words, actions, and identity is mirrored by the response to *Bombers* within the Black Arts community. The irony of the symposium sparked by Bullins's play is that it closes with a call for clarity by Baraka similar to Bonnie's self-deluded celebration of revolutionary spring and the essential bonds of Black Nationalism. As in his poem for Karenga and Sanders, here Baraka calls for soulful community and the supposed immediacy of speech that can escape the ironies of performance. His words are infused with the call-and-response traditions of African American orature conjoined with the kind of reticence characteristic of oral communication among peers:

> And that's what I'd like to see. That . . . evolution to the point where, it's like, you know, as simple as a commercial. You know what I mean? But beautiful. Like, "Get off the sidewalk." You know what I mean? But done with a great deal of—artistry and feeling. You know what I mean?
>
> I don't think—I think the mysticism of art is—is like jive, you know? The mystical part of it is that finally we don't know anything, you know.[133]

Do we know that we don't know? Baraka, as a contributing editor to *Black Theatre,* surely knows that his performance will be transcribed by his editor. But he may not know that the empowering theatricality of his call and response will be reduced to syntactical gaps and stage directions, his potent repertoire of physical gestures and his situational responses to the audience elided. Bullins-the-editor turns Baraka into a woefully incomplete script with vague indications of audience ("[LAUGHTER]," "[APPLAUSE]"), a faltering technology ("[DISCONTINUITY IN TAPE]"), and an elliptical ending that begs the question of exactly what a "community of feeling" could possibly be given the economic, political, and cultural contradictions identified, but never fully synthesized, by the Black vanguard.

That said, Baraka's performance isn't fully contained by the text. Baraka's comments carry a heavy and contradictory burden—again, a freight of signification that reveals the intertwined, contradictory dialectic of culture, politics, and economics, a dialectic grounded in revolutionary performativity. *Sidewalk,* like the term *street,* is rooted in African American urban vernacular of the 1960s. The street, specifically the sidewalk, is one of the places where the African America comes to terms with his or her place within the community, within the overlapping public spheres of America and African America. The place of the sidewalk in African American performance has been more than a little significant in helping to promote such coming to terms; for example, radical oratory, doo-wop, break dancing, and rap emerged from the streets of predominantly African American neighborhoods. It was also a key site for Black Arts performance, for drama, jazz, and the display of visual art.

In African American vernacular, the question, "What do you do on the street?" signifies, "What do you do for a living? What do you do to earn money?" The street, or sidewalk, is one of the potent sites where capitalism intersects the political, economic, and cultural interests of African America—and it is also the site where ideas are exchanged, bartered, and communicated in site-specific, embodied fashion. In a racist, capitalist United States of America, the sidewalk stands as the tangled, fluid site where both individual subjectivity and material objects are produced, circulated, and consumed in public fashion. The term *sidewalk* is, to put it mildly, freighted with contradictory signification.[134]

Thus, when Baraka says that he'd like to see the phrase "Get off the sidewalk" evolve "to the point where, it's like, you know, as simple as a commercial," he is making a densely packed allusion to capitalism, commercialism, the economic realities of the street, and their capacity to be appropriated and transformed through acts of public symbolic and materialist action, acts that, like his own poetry, is "bullshit unless they are teeth or trees or lemons piled on a step."[135] It is a self-conscious, self-reflexive comment on the capitulations and compromises of Black Nationalist capitalism; but it is simultaneously a celebration of the specific qualities of urban, African American culture that stand in uneasy relationship to commodity culture, Black Nationalist or otherwise.

However, placed in the same issue whose cover tells its reader to get off the sidewalk, Baraka's comment proves at least partly blind to the political, economic, and cultural dynamics of his own place in the text-performance dialectic of *Black Theater* number 4. Even the momentary collectivity of the panel and its audience is put to the stake when that soulful collectivity is transformed into a text full of the kinds of gaps and uncertainties that make the drama such a potent, if uncertain, form of performative text. Bullins flirts with the contradictory powers of textuality and performance, demonstrating that both can easily become the techniques of a self-deceptive, egotistical, commodifying power. Like Jackson and Bonnie's dialogue in the play, which is projected onto the film screens that define the stage space of the prison, the panel members assembled for the symposium (Bullins not present but continually invoked) are themselves rendered prone to the ironies of performance, theatricality, and the textual commodity. In a sense, Bullins takes on the role of Whitegirl in *Malcolm: '71:* absent, invisible, seductive, disembodied, powerful. Even so, Baraka correctly identifies the most significant effect of *Bombers:*

> Now, I say the play is successful on the level that there are, like, 200 and some Black people in here talking about the play. In other words, it opened us up, which is about all you can expect in the sense of art . . . You don't need me to tell you the play was correct or incorrect, that the play was bothering you . . . I don't have to validate it in a positive or a negative way for you. You know. You know. You're here. (19)

Baraka expresses profound faith in audience presence, unaware that he has been cornered by the ironies of the *Bombers* event, pressed to defend a communal spirit that is deconstructed by the very play he defends, that is denied by his rivals on the panel and in the audience who continually and intentionally misunderstand one another, and that is compromised by the textual commodity in which it is reproduced. At the same time, he bears witness to the living fact of the movement, a vital, transformative vanguard that continues its work to this day.

8. Was the Black Arts Movement an Avant-Garde?

The Avant-Garde as Racist Model of Cultural Production

The "righteous bombers" of the Black Arts Movement—the writers, performers, artists, and critics who conceptualized and implemented the Black aesthetic—appear from all accounts to be an emblematic vanguard. Notwithstanding their persistently critical attitudes toward the white-dominated avant-garde tradition, a tradition rooted in racist aspects of Euro-American capitalism, the movement nevertheless seems to fall well within the theoretical boundaries established by critics such as Poggioli, Bürger, Hewitt, and Mann. Furthermore, the movement seems to replicate the founding metaphor of the tradition; like the military vanguard, the BAM moved very much like a war machine into unmapped territory, territory that was both conceptual and material. Baraka's call in "Black Art" for poems that were like fists, daggers, and strafing airplanes exemplifies the activist understanding of violence that is typical of the avant-garde as a whole, as is evidenced by such widely read plays as Jimmy Garrett's *We Own the Night* (1967) and Sanchez's *The Bronx Is Next*. Most importantly, and much to its credit, the BAM established deeply rooted relations with the African American community in both urban and academic settings; in this respect, they were indeed a vanguard along a range of theoretical lines (at times Leninist, Gramscian, and Maoist), leading their community into a better future. From all appearances, understood in the historically conscious, critically self-conscious fashion I've tried to maintain throughout these case studies, the BAM appears to be a typical, even emblematic avant-garde.

But we can't trust appearances. Historians and critics of the avant-garde need to remember Willie Best and the bluesman slipping into the thicket. Scholars, critics, and teachers are never outside the struggle waged under the banner of the Black Aesthetic; they are always haunted by *Malcolm: '71*'s Professor Jack Hack. Benston makes precisely this point when he writes that

"any critical appraisal of the movement's effects must account for its animating tensions in terms which reduce neither their contradictory nor productive character."[136] In part, the animating tensions among the critic, the
avant-garde, and the BAM—tensions that structure consideration of the
textual evidence—are due to the fact that the movement was a radical aesthetic trend that was both "inside" and "outside" Euro-American aesthetic,
philosophical, and critical traditions.

This is true of other identity-based countercultural movements. But, like
those movements, the BAM negotiated and mediated cultural boundaries in
a specific fashion. On the one hand, this inside/outside status enabled the
complicated form of signifying that we see in the works of Baraka, Neal,
Stewart, Giovanni, and Sanchez. The renegade wears a mask, and even the
mask is a renegade disguise—a perfect description of the way that Black
artists used the myth of the avant-garde as a mask that openly revealed its
refusal of the mainstream but also kept the secrets in the hands of the Black
community. On the other hand, the idea of being both inside and outside
Euro-American history (in short, suffering compulsory poverty while producing great profits for others) compelled careful attention to more practical, day-to-day affairs. The poet in "Willie Best," Blackman, and Son/Ji all
put revolutionary action and revolutionary identity into play with the material conditions of revolutionary art: the text, the theater, the audience, the
institution. As with every counterculture, the avant-garde myth established
in postrevolutionary France and developed by the great wave of vanguard
activism in the first two decades of the twentieth century is made to conform to the affective, material, and structural characteristics of the now.

Even so, the Black Arts Movement was never wholly *of* the avant-garde,
even if it maintained fairly close (if carefully informal) contacts with other
avant-garde trends and communities within the counterculture. The Muntu
group, for example, read extensively in the kind of Western philosophical,
aesthetic, and political traditions that gave rise to the avant-garde, and were
in regular contact with nonBlack intellectuals with similar interests, but it
read those traditions in systematic comparison to West African philosophy,
the nonobjective, the cultural politics of African America, and Black radicalism. In part, this reading and counterreading was an effort to redefine the
role of the vanguard intellectual. By the time the Black Arts Movement
came into being, a generation of African American leaders (the generation
of Jesse Jackson, Neal, Baraka, Louis Farrakhan) had absorbed the lessons of
four waves of political, cultural, and economic leadership (Abolition and
Reconstruction, with Frederick Douglass and the coalition of African
American congressmen from the South taking the lead; the Popular Front

generation of the 1930s and 1940s; the post–World War I era of DuBois, Alain Locke, the Pullman Porters, and Garvey; the civil rights movement of King, Fannie Lou Hamer, and X). However, and as contradictory as it might sound, this reading and counterreading were also an effort to step outside the myth of vanguard leadership altogether.

The issue I'm attempting to describe here isn't entirely about how Black artists viewed their relationship to the history of radical culture, whether avant-garde or not. The issue here is how scholars, critics, and teachers conceptualize the BAM's role in the culture wars of bourgeois-liberal society. This note of caution must be even more insistently sounded when we use that key term *avant-garde*. As a tradition peculiar to the West, the avant-garde possesses an uneasy and at times embarrassing proximity to racism. The cultural turn of the avant-garde engineered in the 1840s by the Parisian "bohemians" pivoted on the discursive erasure of the Roma. The birth of modern experimental theater, as another example, was formulated in terms that do not fit well the demands of antiracist struggle. We might recall the metaphoric toploading of "darkness" by the symbolists, particularly in Maurice Maeterlinck's *The Intruder* (1890), which explicitly links the conceptual and existential horizons of European bourgeois culture (death, the extra-familial, the timeless) with darkness.[137] Maeterlinck's exploration of darkness, which recalls the swirling grays and blacks in Joseph Turner's cataclysm paintings, generates its pathos by placing in our view a fathomless darkness. Conrad's great novella *The Heart of Darkness* (1899) only confirms the deep structural connections of race, culture, critical philosophy, and deeply experienced emotional states during the fin de siècle. And yet, this romantic, essentially sublime vision of "darkness" would seem to have met with sympathy among Black artists and audiences. Darkness is similarly freighted by Bullins in *The Theme Is Blackness,* by Baraka in *Slave Ship,* and by Sanchez in the manless/childless/madness sequence of *Sister Son/Ji.*

There are deep structural connections between the Euro-American and modernist fascination with "nothingness" and its fascination with dark-skinned peoples. Fredric Jameson, for one, has convincingly argued that modernism developed in response to the failure of European culture to "contain" the cultural, historical, and epistemological challenges of the colonial system.[138] Both the explicit allusions in Picasso's *Les Damoiselles d'Avignon* (1907) to African sculpture on display in the collections of André Derain and the Musée d'Ethnographie du Trocadéro and the self-styled negritude of the Dada movement, especially in its Swiss and German incarnations, mark a profound—and profoundly problematic—interrelation of the avant-garde and Africa.[139] There's no doubt that a Dada drummer such as Richard Huelsenbeck had a genuine interest in and sympathy with West African drum aesthetics, that he understood the distinctions between West African and European aesthetic systems, and that he despised colonialism of all kinds. But just as surely he was playing in the ambivalent currents of modernist racist aestheticism, an aestheticism explicitly criticized by Stewart and Fuller.

These more esoteric concerns shouldn't be forgotten as we recall the far less subtle actions against non–Western Europeans in the societies the symbolists and Dadaists were trying to revolutionize. Just as surely, I don't want to overlook the explicitly antiracist avant-gardes that battled capitalism before World War II; surrealism, for example, which developed explicit, persistent, and theoretically sophisticated strategies to address racism, colonialism, and commodity culture. (In fact, the group's first engagement with practical politics was in response to France's war on anticolonialist insurgents in Morocco.) Even so, race and racism remain troubling concerns for any scholar and critic seriously examining the theory and practice of the avant-garde.

This is especially true when we turn to Italy, where the enormously influential Italian futurists linked the revolutionary mythos of the avant-garde to a thoroughly racist vision of self, community, and nation. The racism of the futurists hardly needs to be argued. But as is true of all forms of racism, futurist racism was complicated, determined by local structures, and filled with odd tensions. See, for one example, "The Foundation and Manifesto of Futurism,"[140] in which Marinetti makes explicit references to his childhood nurse as he describes a moment of Dionysiac ecstasy following the overturning of his automobile in an explicitly "black" creek of filth flowing from a factory:

> O maternal ditch, almost full of muddy water! Fair factory drain! I gulped down your nourishing sludge; and I remembered the blessed black breast of my Sudanese nurse. . . . When I came up—torn, filthy, stinking—from under the capsized car, I felt the white-hot iron of joy deliciously pass through my heart![141]

The manifesto represents futurism as both nourished by the Blackness of modern industry and repelled by it, self-consciously wallowing in the shock value of incestuous, misogynist, miscegenist innuendo, and punctuated by the masochistic self-penetration of a white man by an ego-driven mechanized whiteness and doused in a deliciously viscous excretion of mechanized blackness. White car and black muck come together in a moment of lyricized, sexualized violence, haunted by memories of a Sudanese woman. This is a truly *avant-garde* racism, one that manages to step outside of the competing narratives of ethnicity (racism and constructivism) in one agonizing moment of automotive impact.

The explicitly racist imagery of the "Foundation and Manifesto" isn't a mere ploy to shock. The Italian futurists' disdain for "sentimentalism," for the optical bias of postimpressionist painting, and for symbolist poetics neatly complemented the modernist propaganda they produced for the invasion of Ethiopia, an issue Marinetti hoped to ride to political victory in the elections of 1919. Just as the racist imagery of the manifesto is linked to the political ebb and flow of colonial politics, it is also linked to the history of colonial resistance. There are deeper currents to the futurists' hawkish attitudes than mere political opportunism or macho bluster. Italy's humiliation by Ethiopia in 1896 at the Battle of Adwa, a victory celebrated across the African diaspora and gasped at by other colonialist nations in a fashion reminiscent of American slaveholders after the Haitian revolution, is surely close to the anxious heart of the futurists' tough-guy rejection of *art pour l'art*. Marinetti—a macho, militaristic white supremacist—wasn't just espousing modernization and machines in the abstract. His call for a cataclysmic modernization of the Italian army and its supporting industries was echoed by his extreme hatred for the antiracist, prolabor, democratic-humanist currents in Italy. This typically fascist attitude was spiced with a desire for payback for the humiliations suffered at the hands of Africans. Futurism's heavy-handed treatment of impressionism and symbolism gains an added dimension when viewed with an eye toward Ethiopia: *l'art pour l'art* failed to supply adequate ideological support for the plundering of Africa. Had Italy won victory on the plains of Adwa, the Italian avant-garde might never have made it out of the nineteenth century.

The terms of the twentieth-century avant-garde tradition were substantially set by the futurists. Movements as ideologically diverse as constructivism, vorticism, Dada, the Lettriste and Situationist internationals, Gutai, and concrete poetry developed the discoveries of the Italians and critiqued them, unwittingly committing themselves to a long-term conversation whose vocabulary and history they didn't fully comprehend. The primacy of futurism is also typical of avant-garde scholarship and criticism; Marinetti and his cronies appear in virtually every scholarly history of the avant-garde as a founding moment. And not by accident—their impact, progressive and reactionary, devastated a number of crucial ideological strongholds for bourgeois hegemony, and produced an aesthetic theory that effectively disrupted a significant number of national, ideological, and disciplinary boundaries. After the futurists, every avant-garde, every movement that attempted to produce a meaningful relationship between aesthetic form and political need, had to confront the question of racism, colonialism, and antiparliamentarianism—and, more often than not, they didn't even realize they were doing so.

So what about the Black Arts Movement? Was the BAM an avant-garde?

This question, rather than foreclosing further discussion, actually opens a number of critically interesting twists and turns, lines of consideration that extend back beyond Ethiopia and Marinetti's circle to the four-century history of African slavery and, beyond that, to the myths of blood right and the prejudice against foreign merchants so typical in the age of European feudalism. As I hope to demonstrate, by framing the avant-garde in a much longer history of racist slavery, the Black Aesthetic and the Black Arts Movement can come to be seen as holding a position in vanguard history not unlike that held by Black radicalism as it is described in Cedric Robinson's *Black Marxism,* a critical history of the Black radical tradition to which I'll devote a fair amount of space in this case study's conclusion.

Robinson's book is invaluable to the effort of any scholar-critic to reflect critically his place and identity as a scholar-critic. Robinson interrogates the work of scholars and historians in an effort to better understand their periodically pivotal relevance to radical political action in the West. Specifically, Robinson focuses on the scholarly misrecognition of the Black radical tradition. He defines the ultimate goal of his study as the description of "the failed efforts to render the historical being of Black people into a construct of historical materialism, to signify our existence as merely an opposition to capitalist organization."[142] As he defines it, the problem is that the Black tradition is both inside and outside the critical categories and methods of Euro-American radical thought, especially Marxism. Much as Bullins or Sanchez open a space within the avant-garde so that the specificity of Blackness can interface with the demands of Cruse's triple front and demarcate itself from similar developments beyond the Black cultural revolution, Robinson attempts to open a space within Marxism, intellectual history, liberatory struggle, and critical theory for the specific accomplishments and cultural conditions of African-diasporic resistance. And just as with Bullins and Sanchez, contradictions are present both in the acts of resistance and in their reception and conception by those who write and teach the history of that resistance. Robinson agrees with Marx, Mao, and Lenin that non-European radical movements in the industrial and postindustrial eras have proven to be "negations" of capitalism; however, capitalism "was hardly the source of their being."[143] I will discuss this fairly complicated idea in more detail shortly, as well as how it describes the role of scholars in the misrecognition of Black radicalism's negation of racist capitalism.

The structural similarities between the Black radical tradition writ large and the more specific case of the BAM (which should not be considered merely a subset of Black radicalism, given that it fundamentally altered the very terms of radical activity in the African diaspora) suggest that Robinson's historical and critical rethinking of the radical tradition can be usefully applied to the avant-garde tradition, which is what I'll attempt to do as I draw this case study to its end. The historical and social conditions that gave rise to the avant-garde are especially important if we wish to demarcate the Black Arts Movement from an avant-garde tradition that, while serving as an effective model for the Black Revolution, was hardly the source of its being. According to Robinson, the development of radical thought in the West and the history of radical activism have been portrayed in disingenuous ways by mainstream intellectuals. More specifically, the tradition of Western radicalism has consistently effaced the constitutive role of nationalism and racism in the development of Western radical thought and strategy.

Robinson asserts what is by now a fairly commonsensical idea: Marxism is a construct "emergent from the historical experiences of European people's mediated, in turn, through their civilization, their social orders, and their culture" (2). Meticulously tracking the role of race in the formation of early capitalist trade, of the industrial working class, of the modern nation-state, and of the revolutionary party, Robinson is able to demonstrate that, as the "determinant form" of anticapitalist critique, Marxism has "incorporated theoretical and ideological weaknesses which [stem] from the same social forces which provided the bases of capitalist formation" (9).

One particular weakness is its inability to comprehend the Black radical tradition's contradictory inside/outside status. The great historian C. L. R. James was among the first to identify this blind spot. In *The Black Jacobins* (revised edition, 1963), a work assiduously studied by young African American radicals in the 1960s, James explored the relationship of the Haitian revolution to the tradition of French radicalism born in the revolutionary years of 1791–1804. According to Robinson, James's book should be read as not just about eighteenth-century slaves in San Domingo, but also about Ethiopian peasants and workers transforming themselves into liberation forces capable of repelling the Italian army at Adwa. James's book is enormously important to any discussion of the avant-garde and the BAM. Robinson writes that, for young African Americans in the 1960s, "[f]irst the book and then the author would help . . . to confirm their ideological struggle with bourgeois culture" (396). Let's take careful note of this fact. James's ingenious hybridization of meticulous historiography, acute polemics, and self-reflexive criticism served young, increasingly countercultural African Americans as a model for critical activity at the service of cultural activism.

Though to my knowledge he never mentions futurism in this or any of his other works, James does spend significant time discussing that kissing cousin to the avant-garde: the revolutionary party. James makes clear that the development of vanguard political theory by the Left was conditioned by the theory and practice of non-European revolutionaries. Indeed, the broader history of European radicalism was conditioned by the slave rebellions aboard the *Amistad* and *Diane;* by the Maroon settlements; by Haiti; by slave insurrections; by black rebels in South Africa; by the great migration that occurred in the United States, rapidly swelling the populations of northern urban areas; and by the series of wars waged by European nations in Africa during the 1800s and 1900s. Robinson assesses James's counterhistory as a precise critique of the great theories of revolutionary vanguard practice generated by Marx, Engels, Lenin, and Trotsky. Reflecting on his own past as part of an elite in training, James notes that "the leaders of a revolution are usually those who have been able to profit by the cultural advantages of the system they are attacking."[144] Having enjoyed those advantages himself and felt their temptations, James advises caution and a careful monitoring of the vanguard by the people. He advised the masses to, in Robinson's words, "preserve to themselves the direction of the revolutionary movement, never deferring to professional revolutionists, parties, or the intelligentsia" (388–89). Neal's call for "intimacy with the people" is, in this light, a call for an opening for critical commentary between groups of African American separated by clear, if porous, caste lines.

Though, again, the avant-garde is to my knowledge never mentioned by James, we find many connections between the avant-garde and the radical tradition of political thought implicitly criticized while never wholly rejected by James. We can't even imagine a Black Arts Movement without the tradition of freedom from governmental interference, freedom of expression, and freedom of historical determination theorized by the great bourgeois and liberal-activist thinkers of the eighteenth century. But then, what do we do with the fact that, from the perspective of Black radicalism, European radicalism was profoundly suspect? The institutions of liberty, property, and individualism developed in the bourgeois revolutions of the late 1700s were basically funded by the profits of slave trade and slavery. Maurice Jaures writes, "Sad irony of history: the fortunes created at Bordeaux, at Nantes, by the slave-trade, gave to the bourgeoisie that pride which needed liberty and contributed to human emancipation."[145] In England, the free trade and antislavery movements, so crucial to the development of modern theories of human right and radical prerogative, were in part a response to the decline in profitability of the slave trade and of its coincident economic policies, especially as they related to the Jamaican sugarcane industry. The success of these movements belies the fact that "they could never have succeeded a hundred years before when every important capitalist interest was on the side of the colonial system."[146]

There's another level of complication here that relates more specifically to the question of the Black Arts Movement's status as an avant-garde. As is often noted, the avant-garde as an activist tendency is historically grounded in the military imagination of Napoleonic France and the specific innovations in infantry warfare developed to support French liberal imperialism; the theory of vanguard leadership that cultivates that tendency is grounded in the life and death of François-Noël Babeuf (aka "Gracchus") and, thus, in the peculiar characteristics of radical activity in France during the rule of the Directory, a period that witnessed the abolition of most of the radical and egalitarian policies decreed in 1793. Fleeing underground, radicals formed secret societies and clubs, while tradesmen formed unions. At this moment of sharp division between the intellectuals, the working class, peasants, and the new government, there arose the "Conspiracy of Equals," an abortive revolution that would in time come to hold a special place in the hearts of Leftists around the world. During the trial of Babeuf and his coconspirators, a plan was revealed in which a small revolutionary group would, through carefully targeted acts of audacious, courageous violence, establish a revolutionary government and, with it, the national assembly mandated by the constitution of 1793. Robinson notes that, their bravery notwithstanding, "at no point had the conspiracy become a popular or mass movement" (65). It found support mainly in the larger urban areas, especially Paris, where it gathered around itself a fringe of militants and fellow travelers, including left-wing artists—the same fertile cultural mulch that would settle in Parisian cafés and later launch attacks against bourgeois propriety and the annual Salon exhibitions.

Gracchus would warm the hearts of more than a few radicals during the long exile into futility that would characterize left-wing politics for the next half-century. Frankly, Robinson understates the constructive theoretical and ideological impact of Babeuf; he is not the ideologically fortified illusion of an isolated socialist movement that Robinson would have him be—at least not entirely. That said, Robinson draws our attention to the indisputable fact that when mass social movements and socialist theory collided in the three great waves of European radicalism, the 1840s, 1870s, and early

1900s, "each had assumed forms and prerogatives only slightly tolerable to those of the other."[147] The myth of Gracchus, ensconced in the exciting new theory of the revolutionary party, would paper over the fault lines. Lenin, Marinetti, Antonio Gramsci, Hans Richter, Abbie Hoffman, Rosa Luxemburg, Mao, Lukács, and, most recently, Ernesto Laclau and Chantal Mouffe all spent significant time and energy attempting on the level of theory to solve a dilemma as old as the vanguard itself. It is the mythically healed split between the intellectuals and the masses that is Gracchus's most long-lived legacy.

The mythic status with which Gracchus has been endowed would help to promote significant kinds of blindness in the critics, scholars, and teachers who worked on the history, theory, and practice of radicalism in Europe and abroad. No better example of such blindness can be found than in the analysis by European military and legal authorities of the "Baptist War" that scourged Jamaica in 1831, only a few years after Henri de Saint-Simon bestowed the mantle of vanguard leadership on the progressive visionaries (i.e., artists) so rarely acknowledged by the military and bureaucratic functionaries of the Napoleonic state and so little cared for by the peasantry in a nation that was developing industry at a rate far slower than any other in Europe. After the rebellion was quashed, 626 men and women were tried; 312 of them were executed. The spirit of Gracchus haunted the efforts of the authorities to make sense of the rebellion and the radicals to celebrate it, blinding them to the specificity of the uprising. The Jamaican Assembly's Commission of Inquiry concluded that a "clever," "relatively privileged elite" of slaves led the rebellion.[148] As a consequence, Samuel "Daddy Ruler" Sharpe, George Taylor, George Guthrie, and the "Black Regiment" were granted pride of place in both radical and reactionary accounts of the events.

Robinson disproves this elevation of an elite. He shows, without downplaying Sharpe's charisma, audacity, and strategic acumen, that any claim that he and his men were the leaders of the rebellion must be tempered by the fact that Sharpe's reliance on Baptist missionary networks alienated many slaves who were neither "culturally or ideologically identified" with the Baptists.[149] Even the heroic role of the Black Regiment, 150 men armed with five dozen guns, a force that had successfully resisted the forces of Napoleon only a few years before, has to be viewed in light of the fact that most of the estates involved in the uprising were neither part of the rebels' military organization nor organized by Sharpe for passive resistance.[150]

The lack of fit between the myth of the avant-garde and the more specific history of black radicalism has, until relatively recently, been overlooked or misrecognized by most scholars and historians. Robinson writes, "Before the African and New World Black liberation movements of the post–second world war era, few western scholars of the African experience had any conception of an ideologically or epistemologically coherent historical tradition of Black radicalism" (95). Of course, Neal, Baraka, Sanchez, Giovanni, and their fellow Black Artists were crucial players in this ideological and epistemological renewal. The importance of aesthetic concerns to this renewal can be attributed to the fact that this same group of scholars, artists, critics, and enthusiasts recognized that *culture,* not just economics and politics, would mediate the revolution in the United States. In fact, the Black Aesthetic can best be described as the first great wave of the cultural studies revolution that had such a profound impact on the American system of higher education in the latter half of the twentieth century. A decade before the pivotal Birmingham Centre for Contemporary Cultural Studies, the Muntu group had effectively synthesized vanguard leadership theory, avant-garde aesthetic experiment, and popular culture studies. Muntu was not alone by any means. For example, we should take a moment to consider the fact that Kingston's Yard Theatre, run by Marina Maxwell and featured in the 1971 issue of *Black Theatre,* sat just around the corner from the great dub-reggae producer Lee "Scratch" Perry's Black Arts Studio. The implications of this connection are intriguing. Through Perry, a local variant of the Black Aesthetic, heavily influenced by the rhythm and blues music broadcast from New Orleans, transformed Jamaican popular music and spread—via ska, rock steady, and the groundbreaking reggae revolution of Bob Marley—to neighborhoods throughout the African diaspora. It was exactly this phenomena—British kids grooving to the kinky, millennialist beat of Kingston Yard culture—that would inspire Stuart Hall, Dick Hebdige, and their colleagues to develop what is now a contested but fairly mainstream academic method.

Does our perception of the function and trajectory of cultural studies change when we restore the Black Aesthetic to its rightful place in the development of such studies? The answer would seem to be, emphatically, yes. As Mae G. Henderson argues, the restoration of the BAM's "formal and vernacular traditions," "indigenous principles and methodologies," and "geographical and historical specificities" can be achieved only through the application of cultural studies methodologies. However, such an application, in turn, opens up critical perspectives on cultural studies itself, particularly the gaps in its historical memory.[151]

James asserts that misapprehension of Black radicalism is due to "a different set of conventions in Western historiography" that frame events according to belief in qualitatively distinct stages of human development, a belief that tends "to trivialize or diminish the significance of precedents of too longstanding account," and individualize what were genuinely popular, decentered democratic uprisings.[152] One has to wonder how the BAM managed to be so systematically excluded from academic memory. Could there even be critical race or cultural studies without the radical acts of Black artists and audiences? That said, critics and scholars, especially conservative ones, have played on occasion a purposeful role in obscuring the history and continuity of Black radicalism. In *Black Jacobins,* James writes, "Haiti burned the ears of the slave-owners in the new world at the beginning of the 19th century. They whispered its name, futilely conspiring to deny its legend and its very existence to their properties. But it was their ideologues, their intellectuals, and their academics which succeed in the larger suppression of the fact."[153] Already mystified by the lack of detailed accounts of uprisings in colonial Africa, Black radicalism was highly vulnerable to tendentious treatment by scholars, historians, and critics. DuBois notes this in *Black Reconstruction in America, 1860–1880* (1969). There he writes that "the real frontal attack on Reconstruction, as interpreted by the leaders of national thought in 1870 and for some time thereafter, came from the universities and particularly from Columbia and Johns Hopkins," where John W. Burgess and William A. Dunning served as professors of political science and history, respectively.[154] This scholarly and intellectual reaction complemented the development of neocolonial practices in the twentieth century, which based themselves explicitly on the formation of native elites, what Robinson describes as "an appropriate contingent of clerks and a limited number of professionals, not nationalistic intellectuals."[155]

In this respect, Neal's assertion that the Black Arts Movement "is radically opposed to any concept of the artist that alienates him from his community" stands as not simply a critique of the garreted artist, but also as a critique of the avant-garde itself, a tradition that, as Hewitt has argued, incorporates into itself a binary division between politics and aesthetics, the intellectual and the people.[156] When Neal then asserts that the movement "is the aesthetic and spiritual sister of the Black Power concept," he is tacitly placing Black Art in precisely the tradition of Black radicalism first identified by James and later expanded by Robinson, a tradition that doesn't so much exorcise the ghost of Gracchus as simply move onto a wholly different cosmology, where ghosts like Gracchus have no spiritual or material substance.

It's here that I wish to conclude, at the moment when the Black Arts Movement is fully demarcated from the histories that have contained it: the avant-garde, the revolutionary party, critical-race and cultural studies. Neal writes, "The Black Arts Movement proposes a radical reordering of the Western cultural aesthetic"; it "proposes a separate symbolism, mythology, critique, and iconology."[157] Stewart further strengthens the links between cosmology, aesthetics, and politics in "The Development of the Black Revolutionary Artist." His critique of the covertly linear, qualitative logic of the art world, begins by addressing the question of cosmological models. He writes, "It is imperative that we construct models with different basic assumptions" than "white paradigms or models," which "do not correspond to the realities of black existence." "Our models," he writes, "must be consistent with a black style" reminiscent of West African worship systems, which do not differentiate between the art object and the process of making art.[158] It's hard to imagine a more radical suggestion: Black Art exists only in the instantiatory moment. Any scholarly or critical consideration of Black Art must account for its own instantiation.[159]

Though the most immediate source for Stewart's comments is Jahn's book *Muntu,* studied intensively by the Muntu group, he is also referencing the fact that, as a consequence of the transport of African labor to the Americas, "African ontological and cosmological systems; African presumptions of the organization and significance of social structure; African codes embodying historical consciousness and social experience; and African ideological and behavioral constructions for the resolution of the inevitable conflict between the actual and the normative" fundamentally structured the Black radical tradition.[160] Cosmology played no small role in the development of the larger Black radical tradition. Obeah priests were significant players in many slave rebellions as well as in the founding of the economically, politically, and culturally autonomous Maroon populations of the Americas. Obeah men and women administered oaths of secrecy and also distributed the sacred objects that protected the revolutionaries. Interesting to note is the fact that Congolese and Angolan societies banned Obeah magicians due to the fact that they were perceived as contrary to the interest of kings and royal bureaucracies.[161]

The effort by the Black Arts Movement to invent a theory of revolution, a theory that could successfully guide action on Cruse's triple front while also manifesting the mythical, Afrocentric unity of social structure, aesthetics, ethics, and cosmology theorized by Jahn and Stewart, ensures that scholars, critics, and teachers will inevitably be led to misrecognize the movement. As I've noted previously, the issue here isn't the political sympathies or cultural identities of the critic-scholar in question; a self-proclaimedly "Black" critic may just as surely misrecognize the BAM as his nonBlack colleague will. While our political sympathies, actions, and institutional affiliations must always be considered, the fact is that the BAM has successfully separated itself from the mainstream of academic discourse in order to fulfill its function as an ongoing mode of cultural transformation, reclamation, and demarcation. Though it is certainly less revolutionary now than it was from 1965 to 1975, it is much more institutionally robust. Chicago, in fact, can plausibly claim that the Black Aesthetic enjoys a more significant presence in 2001 than it did in 1970. The bluesman's magic paper sack, Blackman's enveloping textuality, Son/Ji's baubles and paint sticks, Bullins's editorial signifying, and Neal's James Brownian revolutionaries are the milestones marking a line of cultural development that has fundamentally altered the terrain of race in the United States and abroad while remaining beyond the view of capitalism's voracious gaze.

At least, that is the way it has been until now, when we are witnessing the rapid growth of interest in the 1960s and the Black Aesthetic among students and teachers. When Blackman hangs up the phone, who's left hanging on the other end? Is it Jack Hack? Or is it the addressee of "A Poem for Willie Best":

> Can you hear? Here
> I am again. Your boy, dynamite. Can
> You hear? My soul is moved. The soul
> You gave me. I say, my soul, and it
>   Is moved. That soul
>   You gave me.
>
>   . . . .
>   I mean
>   Can you?[162]

Notes

Introduction

1. See Sayyid Qutb, *Milestones* (Cedar Rapids, Iowa: Mother Mosque Foundation, 2003); and Paul Berman, *Terror and Liberalism* (New York: Norton, 2003).

2. Donna Haraway, "A Manifesto for Cyborgs," in *The Norton Anthology of Theory and Criticism,* ed. Vincent B. Leitch (New York: Norton, 2001).

3. Most recently in Arnold Aronson's *American Avant-Garde Theatre: A History* (New York: Routledge, 2000).

4. Marcelin Pleynet, "The Readability of Sade," in *The Tel Quel Reader,* ed. Patrick French and Roland-François Lack (New York: Routledge, 1998), 119.

5. Roland Barthes, "The Death of the Author," in Leitch, *Norton Anthology.*

6. Roger Shattuck, introduction to Maurice Nadeau, *The History of Surrealism,* trans. Richard Howard (Cambridge: Harvard University Press, 1989), 14.

7. Which is not to imply that internal debate about art and art institutions isn't significant and productive work, only that it tends to foreclose larger questions of political action. Hal Foster's *The Return of the Real: The Avant-Garde at the End of the Century* (Cambridge: MIT Press, 1996) is a perfect example of the kind of insight generated by careful attention to the gallery and museum system's ambivalent relationship to the avant-garde. On the other hand, his attack on identity politics, interdisciplinarity, and invocation of nonart issues in "The Artist as Ethnographer" reminds us that intrainstitutional critique forecloses consideration of issues that have never had a secure place in those institutions.

8. Renato Poggioli, *Theory of the Avant-Garde,* trans. Gerald Fitzgerald (Cambridge: Belknap Press of Harvard University Press, 1981); Paul Mann, *The Theory Death of the Avant-Garde* (Bloomington: Indiana University Press, 1991); Kristine Stiles, "Synopsis of the Destruction in Art Symposium (DIAS) and Its Theoretical Significance," *Act* 1 (spring 1987): 22–31; Stiles, "Sticks and Stones: The Destruction in Art Symposium," *Arts,* January 1989, 54–60; Stiles, "Never Enough Is Something Else: Feminist Performance Art, Avant-Gardes, and Probity," in *The Contours of the Theatrical Avant-Garde: Performance and Textuality,* ed. James Harding (Ann Arbor: University of Michigan Press, 2000). I should also mention Jack Burnham, whose essay "Problems of Criticism," in *Idea Art: A Critical Anthology,* ed. Gregory Battcock (New York: E. P. Dutton, 1973) (originally published in *Art Forum* 9.5 [1971]) was among the first to thoroughly address the avant-garde as a "linguistic structure." Hans Magnus Enzensberger attempted the first historical and critical analysis of the term *avant-garde* in his 1962 essay "The Aporias of the Avant-Garde"

(reprinted in Enzensberger, *The Consciousness Industry: On Literature, Politics, and the Media,* ed. Michael Roloff [New York: Seabury Press, 1974]). Enzensberger asserts that the spatial/military metaphor returns us inevitably to the avant-garde's "original temporal significance" (23). Finally, I should acknowledge the contributors to a special issue of *Theatre Survey* 43, no. 1 (2002), "Self-Reflexive Approaches to International Radical Theater, Drama, and Performance of the 1960s."

9. Gregory Battcock, "Reevaluating Abstract Expressionism," *Arts,* December 1969–January 1970, 48.

10. Robert Motherwell, qtd. in Dore Ashton, *The New York School: A Cultural Reckoning* (New York: Viking, 1973), 162.

11. Shattuck isn't fair to Sartre, though he is more fair to the perspective Sartre's work was viewed from by Shattuck's fellow academics during the 1960s. In fact, Sartre is a significant influence on poststructuralism. See Mark Poster, *Existential Marxism in Postwar France: From Sartre to Althusser* (Princeton: Princeton University Press, 1975).

12. Theodore Roszak, *The Making of a Counter Culture: Reflections on the Technocratic Society and Its Youthful Opposition* (Berkeley and Los Angeles: University of California Press, 1968), xii.

13. Malcolm X, "The Ballot or the Bullet," in *The Sixties Papers: Documents of a Rebellious Decade,* ed. Judith Clavir Albert and Steward Edward Albert (New York: Praeger, 1984),

14. "SNCC Speaks for Itself," 119.

15. Frederic Jameson, "Periodizing the 60s," in *The Ideologies of Theory: Essays, 1971–1986,* vol. 2, *The Syntax of History* (Minneapolis: University of Minnesota, 1988), 208.

16. Peggy Phelan, *Unmarked: The Politics of Performance* (New York: Routledge, 1993).

17. Jean-Jacques Lebel, "On the Necessity of Violation," *TDR* 13, no. 1 (1968): 96.

18. It is Paul Mann who has suggested this connection (*Theory Death,* 16). I'll discuss Mann's book at length below.

19. Stiles, "Never Enough," 265–66.

20. RoseLee Goldberg, *Performance Art: From Futurism to the Present,* rev. ed. (New York: Harry N. Abrams, 1988), 1.

21. Ibid., 7.

22. Ibid., 9.

23. Andrew Hewitt has carefully explored the conceptual structure of the avant-garde's radicality, especially as it manifested itself in ultra-right-wing vanguard movements such as Italian futurism and German National Socialism. Restrictions of space keep me from considering and critiquing his provocative *Fascist Modernism: Aesthetics, Politics, and the Avant-Garde* (Palo Alto: Stanford University Press, 1993).

24. Jerry Rubin, from *Just Do It!* in Albert and Albert, *Sixties Papers,* 107.

25. Qtd. in Rick Perlstein, "Who Owns the Sixties? The Opening of a Scholarly Generation Gap," *Lingua Franca,* May–June 1996, 36.

26. Ellen Maddow, "The Otrabanda Company," *TDR* 20, no. 2 (1976): 44.

27. Otrabanda Company, "Discussion," 1974, Audio Reel 2, Collection of Susan Horowitz.

28. Lloyd Steele, review of *Stump Removal* by Tone Brulin and the Otrabanda Company, *Los Angeles Free Press,* February 9, 1973, 7.

29. David Riley, "Bringing Theatre to the People," *Daily Rag,* October 5, 1973. Document in Otrabanda Archive, Antioch University, Yellow Springs, OH.

30. Clifford Geertz, "Blurred Genres: The Refiguration of Social Thought," *American Scholar* 49 (spring 1980): 23.

31. Jon McKenzie, *Perform or Else: From Discipline to Performance* (New York: Routledge, 2001), 18.

32. Foster, *Return of the Real,* 3.

33. Ibid., 5.

34. Paul Ricoeur, *Freud and Philosophy: An Essay on Interpretation,* trans. Denis Savage (New Haven: Yale University Press, 1986).

35. Foster, *Return of the Real,* 5.

36. Ibid.

37. Erwin Piscator, *The Political Theatre,* trans. Hugh Rorrison (New York: Avon, 1963), 46.

38. Stiles, "Sticks and Stones," 56.

39. Heidegger writes, "In our dealings with the world [*welt*] of our concern, the un-ready-to-hand can be encountered not only in the sense of that which is unusable or simply missing, but as something un-ready-to-hand which is *not* missing at all and *not* unusable, but which 'stands in the way' of our concern. That to which our concern refuses to turn, that for which it has 'no time,' is something *un*-ready-to-hand in the manner of what does not belong here, of what has not as yet been attended to. Anything which is un-ready-to-hand in this way is disturbing to us, and enables us to see the *obstinacy* of that which we must concern ourselves in the first instance before we do anything else." *Being and Time,* trans. John Mac-Quarrie and Edward Robinson (San Francisco: HarperSanFrancisco, 1962), 74.

40. Graham Holderness, introduction, *The Politics of Theatre and Drama,* ed. Holderness (London: Macmillan, 1992), 13.

41. See the film *Black Theatre: The Making of a Movement,* dir. Woodie King Jr., California Newsreel, 1978.

42. Herbert Blau, *The Audience* (Baltimore: Johns Hopkins University Press, 1990), 237.

43. André Breton, "Legitimate Defence," in *What Is Surrealism? Selected Writings,* ed. and trans. Franklin Rosemont (New York: Monad Press, 1978), 40.

44. Teresa de Lauretis, *Technologies of Gender: Essays on Theory, Film, and Fiction* (Bloomington: Indiana University Press, 1987), 130.

45. Ibid., 131.

46. Ibid., 136.

47. Stiles, "Never Enough."

48. Theodore Shank, *American Alternative Theater* (New York: Grove Press, 1982), 2.

49. Sue-Ellen Case, "A Case Concerning Hughes," *TDR* 33, no. 1 (1989), qtd. in Lynda Hart, "Identity and Seduction: Lesbians in the Mainstream," in *Acting Out: Feminist Performances,* ed. Lynda Hart and Peggy Phelan (Ann Arbor: University of Michigan Press, 1993), 120.

50. Ibid.

51. Ibid.

52. Hart, "Identity and Seduction," 134.

53. Stanley Fish, *Is There a Text in This Class? The Authority of Interpretive Communities* (Cambridge: Harvard University Press, 1980).

54. Situationist International, "Preliminary Problems in Constructing a Situation," in *Situationist International Anthology,* ed. and trans. Ken Knabb (Berkeley: Bureau of Public Secrets, 1981), 43.

55. Homi K. Bhabha, "The Commitment to Theory," in Leitch, *Norton Anthology,* 2395.

56. Martin Duberman, *Stonewall* (New York: Plume, 1993), 126.

57. Ibid.

58. Judith Butler, *Gender Trouble: Feminism and the Subversion of Identity* (New York: Routledge, 1990), 134.

59. Ibid., 135.

60. The notion that the avant-garde is a method of probity comes from Stiles. She writes, "The radical act represented in the cultural construct of the avant-garde *is the concentrated attentiveness to the conditions of being and making wherein personal subjectivity and social reality themselves converge toward acts of probity*" ("Never Enough," 276). Though I disagree with Stiles that such attentiveness needs to be "original" or needs to "contribute something substantial to the social order within which it is involved (279), I do very much agree that the avant-garde is both a form of critical thought and an ethical problematic and not merely a desire to shock, to recall Robert Hughes's paraphrase of Ezra Pound and one of the more threadbare tropes in avant-garde scholarship, "the shock of the new."

61. Manfredo Tafuri, *Architecture and Utopia: Design and Capitalist Development* (Cambridge: MIT Press, 1992), ix. Originally published as *Progetto e Utopia* in 1973.

62. Daniel Herwitz, *Making Theory/Constructing Art: On the Authority of the Avant-Garde* (Chicago: University of Chicago Press, 1993), 6.

63. Ibid., 2.

64. Ibid., 9.

65. Fred Orton and Griselda Pollock, "Avant-Gardes and Partisans Reviewed," in *Pollock and After: The Critical Debate,* ed. Francis Frascina (New York: Harper and Row, 1985), 167.

66. Stiles, "Never Enough," 267.

67. Stiles, "Sticks and Stones," 56.

68. Susan Suleiman, *Subversive Intent: Gender, Politics, and the Avant-Garde* (Cambridge: Harvard University Press, 1990).

69. Walter Kalaidjian, *American Culture between the Wars: Revisionary Modernism and Postmodern Critique* (New York: Columbia University Press, 1993), 1.

70. Ibid., 2.

71. Hilton Kramer, *The Age of the Avant-Garde: An Art Chronicle of 1956–1972* (New York: Farrar, Straus and Giroux, 1973).

72. See Alan M. Wald, *The New York Intellectuals: The Rise and Decline of the Anti-Stalinist Left from the 1930s to the 1980s* (Chapel Hill: University of North Carolina Press, 1987).

73. Daniel Bell, *The End of Ideology: On the Exhaustion of Political Ideas in the Fifties* (Glencoe, Ill.: Free Press, 1960).

74. Wald, *The New York Intellectuals*, 218.

75. Ibid., 226.

76. Robert Hughes, *The Shock of the New* (New York: Knopf, 1991).

77. Diana Crane, *The Transformation of the Avant-Garde: The New York Art World, 1940–1985* (Chicago: University of Chicago Press, 1987), 9.

78. Stewart Buettner, *American Art Theory, 1945–1970* (Ann Arbor: University Microfilms International Research Press, 1981), 125, qtd. in Crane, *Transformation of Avant-Garde*, 9.

79. Crane, *Transformation of Avant-Garde*, 137.

80. The notion that social struggle and time changed during the 1960s is argued by David Harvey in *The Condition of Postmodernity: An Enquiry into the Origins of Social Change* (Oxford: Blackwell, 1989); Fredric Jameson, *Postmodernism; or, The Cultural Logic of Late Capitalism* (Durham, N.C.: Duke University Press, 1991); and Ernesto Laclau and Chantal Mouffe, *Hegemony and Socialist Strategy: Towards a Radical Democratic Politics* (London: Verso, 1991).

81. Herwitz, *Making Theory/Constructing Art*, 3–4.

82. Yolanda Broyles-González, *El Teatro Campesino: Theater in the Chicano Movement* (Austin: University of Texas Press, 1994), xii.

83. Michel Foucault, *Power/Knowledge: Selected Interviews and Other Writings, 1972–1977*, ed. and trans. Colin Gordon (New York: Pantheon, 1980), 127.

84. For a spirited critique of Aronson's theoretical and historiographical limitations, see Daniel Mutson's review in *American Theatre*, April 2001, 47. Mutson, as I do, considers *American Avant-Garde Theatre* to be a fine piece of historiography that shows both a sustained effort to avoid critical jargon and commonplaces and to honestly confront the difficulties that attend the effort to define something as broad as the "avant-garde." However, Mutson also notes that Aronson relies on a limited notion of cultural antagonism (opposed to some nebulous "mainstream") and a highly suspect idea of the "average viewer." Mutson also draws attention to Aronson's rather glib dismissal of artists who receive governmental or corporate funding and his tendency to foreclose consideration of the non-U.S. roots of American cultural antagonism. These are significant flaws, the consequence, ultimately, of failing to consider the cultural function of avant-garde scholarship.

85. Peter Bürger, *Theory of the Avant-Garde*, trans. Michael Shaw (Minneapolis: University of Minnesota, 1984).

86. Mann, *Theory Death*, 3.

87. Ibid., 7.

88. Ibid., 7.

89. Ibid., 12.

90. Louis Montrose, "Professing the Renaissance: The Poetics and Politics of Culture," in *Literary Theory: An Anthology*, ed. Julie Rivkin and Michael Ryan (Oxford: Blackwell, 1998), 777.

91. Ibid., 782.

92. Meiling Cheng's forthcoming *Mutating Performance Art* characterizes critical scholarship as a "prosthesis" of performance. Cheng presented her work at a Fresh Print Series panel for the Association for Theater in Higher Education conference (Chicago, 2001).

93. Kalaidjian, *American Culture*, 2.

Case 1

1. Qtd. in C. W. E. Bigsby, *A Critical Introduction to Twentieth-Century American Drama,* vol. 3, *Beyond Broadway* (New York: Cambridge University Press, 1985), 81.

2. Sally Banes, *Greenwich Village, 1963: Avant-Garde Performance and the Effervescent Body* (Durham, N.C.: Duke University Press, 1993), 41.

3. Antonin Artaud, "The Theater and the Plague," in *The Theatre and Its Double,* trans. Mary Caroline Richards (New York: Grove Press, 1958), 15.

4. Susan Sontag, introduction to Antonin Artaud, *Selected Writings,* ed. Susan Sontag (New York: Farrar, Straus, and Giroux, 1976), lviii.

5. Antonin Artaud, "No More Masterpieces," in *Theatre and Its Double,* 75.

6. David Graver, "Antonin Artaud and the Authority of Text, Spectacle, and Performance," in Harding, *Contours,* 48.

7. John D. Lyon, "Artaud: Intoxication and Its Double," *Yale French Studies* 50 (1974): 120–29.

8. Roszak, *Making of Counter Culture,* 156.

9. Roszak makes this claim (*Making of Counter Culture,* 170). For documentation on addict populations in the nineteenth century, see David T. Courtwright, *Dark Paradise: Opiate Addiction in America before 1940* (Cambridge: Harvard University Press, 1982), 6–64.

10. For discussion of Rutgers, see Joan M. Marter, *Off Limits: Rutgers University and the Avant-Garde, 1957–1963* (Rutgers, N.J.: Rutgers University Press, 1999).

11. Serge Guilbaut, *How New York Stole the Idea of Modern Art: Abstract Expressionism, Freedom, and the Cold War,* trans. Arthur Goldhammer (Chicago: University of Chicago Press, 1983), 3. For extensive discussion of advertising and organizational innovation during the 1960s, see Thomas Frank, *The Conquest of Cool: Business Culture, Counterculture, and the Rise of Hip Consumerism* (Chicago: University of Chicago Press, 1997).

12. Two important statements on this phenomenon were presented at a seminar I cochaired with James Harding at the 2000 American Society for Theatre Research convention. Alan Filewod's "Postcolonial Surrogation and American Theatrical Radicalism in Canada" argues that countercultural groups working with Newfoundland unions and development organizations were both enabled and hampered by the textual models that circulated in Canada via journals such as *TDR, Theatre Quarterly,* and *Gambit.* Graham White pursues a similar line in "Digging for Apples: Reappraising the Influence of Situationist Theory on Theatre Practice in the English Counterculture," Seminar on Research and Pedagogy for a Turbulent Decade: Self-Reflexive Practice and Radical Performance of the 1960s, American Society for Theatre Research, New York, November 12, 2000.

13. Guy Scarpetta, "The American Body: Notes on the New Experimental Theatre," in *The Tel Quel Reader,* ed. Patrick French and Roland-François Lack (New York: Routledge, 1998), 215.

14. James Harding, "Dissent behind the Barricades: Radical Art, Revolutionary Stages, and Avant-Garde Divisions," in *Contours.*

15. Norman Mailer's *The White Negro: Superficial Reflections on the Hipster* (San Francisco: City Lights, 1957) makes the claim that jazz and jazz clubs were promoting a new kind of rebellious subjectivity, a rebellion that, to Mailer, seemed pecu-

liarly devoid of moral, political, and historical concern. This, as we'll see, is a typical way to represent deviant music and drug subcultures, as I'll demonstrate below.

16. Guilbaut describes the role of the United States Information Service in promoting abstract expressionism abroad. He also supplies a brief, but useful summary of the sources upon which he builds his history (*How New York Stole*, 237–38 n. 174).

17. Jack Gelber, "Julian Beck, Businessman," *TDR* 30, no. 2 (1986): 6–29.

18. Qtd. in Pierre Biner, *The Living Theatre* (New York: Horizon Press, 1972), 50.

19. Qtd. in ibid., 43.

20. Judith Malina, *The Enormous Despair* (New York: Random House, 1972), 145.

21. Artaud, *Theater and Its Double*, 102, 103.

22. Artaud, *Selected Writings*, 72.

23. The clearest indication of the close relations between Artaud and jazz can be found in the work of LeRoi Jones/Amiri Baraka. His essay "The Revolutionary Theatre" (*Liberator* 5.7 [1965]: 21) explicitly references both Artaud and avant-garde jazz as linchpins for the black revolution.

24. For a rigorous, fascinating analysis of this impact, see Kimberly Benston's comments on John Coltrane in *Performing Blackness: Enactments of African-American Modernity* (New York: Routledge, 2000).

25. Julian Beck, *The Life of the Theatre: The Relation of the Artist to the Struggle of the People* (San Francisco: City Lights, 1972), 129.

26. Julian Beck, "Storming the Barricades," introduction to Kenneth Brown, *The Brig* (New York: Hill and Wang, 1965), 30.

27. John Tytell, *The Living Theatre: Art, Exile, and Outrage* (New York: Grove Press, 1995), 160.

28. James Schevill, *Breakout! In Search of New Theatrical Environments* (Chicago: Swallow Press, 1973), 352.

29. Victor Turner, *From Ritual to Theatre: The Human Seriousness of Play* (New York: PAJ Publications, 1982), 24.

30. Bonnie Marranca, introduction to Gertrude Stein, *Last Operas and Plays*, ed. Carl Van Vechten (Baltimore: Johns Hopkins University Press, 1977), xi.

31. Gertrude Stein, "Plays," in *Last Operas and Plays*, xxix.

32. Daniel Belgrad, *The Culture of Spontaneity: Improvisation and the Arts in Postwar America* (Chicago: University of Chicago Press, 1998), 15.

33. David H. Rosenthal, *Hard Bop: Jazz and Black Music, 1955–1965* (New York: Oxford University Press, 1992), 79–80.

34. Qtd. in ibid.

35. Peggy Phelan, "Reciting the Citation of Others," in Hart and Phelan, *Acting Out*, 15.

36. Banes, *Greenwich Village, 1963*.

37. Qtd. in Michael Smith, *Theatre Trip* (New York: Bobbs-Merrill, 1969), 12.

38. Paul E. Willis, "The Cultural Meaning of Drug Use," *Resistance through Rituals: Youth Subcultures in Post-war Britain*, ed. Stuart Hall and Tony Jefferson (London: Routledge, 1993), 106.

39. Qtd. in Biner, *The Living Theatre*, 116.

40. Dick Higgins, "Boredom and Danger," in *foew&ombwhnw: A Grammar of the Mind and a Phenomenology of Love and a Science of the Arts as Seen by a Stalker of the Wild Mushroom* (New York: Something Else Press, 1969), 115.

41. Jerry Tallmer, review of *The Connection, Village Voice,* July 22, 1959, 9.

42. Kenneth Tynan, review of *The Connection, New Yorker,* October 10, 1959, 126–29.

43. Louis Calta, review of *The Connection, New York Times,* July 16, 1959, 30:2.

44. Judith Crist, review of *The Connection, New York Herald Tribune,* July 15, 1959.

45. Robert Brustein, "Junkies and Jazz," review of *The Connection, New Republic,* September 28, 1959, 29.

46. Tynan, review of *The Connection,* 129.

47. Lorenzo Thomas, "'Communicating by Horns': Jazz and Redemption in the Poetry of the Beats and the Black Arts Movement," *African American Review* 26, no. 2 (1992): 291.

48. Lewis MacAdams, *Birth of the Cool: Beat, Bebop, and the American Avant-Garde* (New York: Free Press, 2001).

49. Qtd. in Rosenthal, *Hard Bop,* 78–79.

50. Qtd. in Scott DeVeaux, *The Birth of Bebop: A Social and Musical History* (Berkeley and Los Angeles: University of California Press, 1997), 25.

51. Ibid., 26.

52. Qtd. in ibid., 89.

53. Qtd. in ibid., 173.

54. Qtd. in Rosenthal, *Hard Bop,* 72.

55. Ben Sidran, *Black Talk* (New York: Holt, Rinehart and Winston, 1971), 88.

56. Qtd. in MacAdams, *Birth of the Cool,* 206.

57. Qtd. in Belgrad, *The Culture of Spontaneity,* 188.

58. Michael James, qtd. in Rosenthal, *Hard Bop,* 121.

59. Rosenthal, *Hard Bop,* 121.

60. Qtd. in ibid., 80.

61. Qtd. in ibid., 81.

62. Belgrad, *The Culture of Spontaneity,* 183.

63. Rosenthal, *Hard Bop,* 123.

64. Banes, *Greenwich Village, 1963,* 41.

65. Jonathan Crary, "Spectacle, Attention, Counter-Memory," *October* 50 (fall 1989): 100.

66. Barbara Hodgson, *Opium: A Portrait of the Heavenly Demon* (San Francisco: Chronicle Books, 1999), 108.

67. Courtwright, *Dark Paradise,* 126.

68. Umberto Eco, "Semiotics of Theatrical Performance," *TDR* 21 (spring 1977): 107–17.

69. Marvin Carlson, *Performance: A Critical Introduction* (New York: Routledge, 1996), 54.

70. Christopher Innes, "Text/Pre-text/Pretext: The Language of Avant-Garde Experiment," in Harding, *Contours,* 58–75.

71. Marshall Berman, *All That Is Solid Melts into Air: The Experience of Modernity* (New York: Penguin, 1982).

72. Alfred Jarry, "L'Opium," discussed in Hodgson, *Opium*, 91–93.

73. Qtd. in Hodgson, *Opium*, 93.

74. Qtd. in Rosenthal, *Hard Bop*, 83.

75. Qtd. in ibid., 84.

76. Sidran, *Black Talk*, 113.

77. Qtd. in ibid.

78. For extended discussion of modern drama's disciplining of the spectator, see W. B. Worthen, *Modern Drama and the Rhetoric of Theater* (Berkeley and Los Angeles: University of California, 1992). Worthen writes that the modern drama can be characterized by its attempts to construct a particular audience and valorize a certain approved interpretive activity. Likewise, Georgy Lukács characterized the "new drama' as determined by the needs of "value judgment": "In the new drama not merely passions are in conflict, but ideologies . . . as well. Because men collide who come from differing situations, value judgments must necessarily function, as importantly, at least, as purely individual characteristics" ("The Sociology of Modern Drama," trans. Lee Baxandall, *The Theory of the Modern Stage,* ed. Eric Bentley [New York: Penguin, 1986], 426).

79. Qtd. in Bigsby, *Critical Introduction*, 63.

80. Graver, "Authority of Text," 54.

81. *The Dividend, The Shanghai Gesture,* and *The Chink and the Child* are discussed in Hodgson, *Opium,* 63, 112.

82. Laurence Senelick, "Text and Violence: Performance Practices of the Modernist Avant-Garde," in Harding, *Contours,* 17.

83. Ibid., 21 ff.

84. The manifestation of "deviancy" was not always coincident with the dissemination of the drug. Opium addiction, acquired and maintained through the erstwhile assistance of medical professionals, had long been present in the upper classes. As Courtwright points out, Mary Tyrone, the martyred, well-mannered mother in Eugene O'Neill's *Long Day's Journey into Night* (1956), exemplifies this class of addict: middle-aged, middle or upper class, white, female, and the most common addiction demographic in the United States prior to 1895 (*Dark Paradise,* 1).

85. Interview with Thomas C. Sell (Commander, U.S. Public Health Service, ret.), June 6, 1996. Congressman Stephen G. Porter, sponsor of the 1928 legislation that created the "farms" at Lexington and Fort Worth, Texas, called addicts "a serious menace." He defended the farms in terms that made analogy with the confinement of the mentally ill: "it is just like the situation a long time ago, when there was no provision made for lunatics, idiots, and feebleminded people. Fortunately, the humanity of that time brought about what is known as the insane asylum. These people are confined for their own welfare and for the protection of society" (qtd. in Courtwright, *Dark Paradise,* 141–42). However, the first head of the Lexington hospital, Lawrence Kolb, took great offense at the carceral nature of the place and housed addicts as far as possible away from the criminal population, a courageous gesture given that some high-level officials were suggesting that the only solution to addiction was a bullet (Courtwright, 135).

86. Jack Gelber, *The Connection* (New York: Grove Press, 1960), 21.

87. Antonin Artaud, "The Theater and Culture," in *The Theater and Its Double*, 7.

88. Sontag, introduction to Artaud, *Selected Writings*, xvii.

89. Malina, *The Enormous Despair*, 48.

90. Artaud, *Theater and Its Double*, 80.

91. Artaud, "To Have Done with the Judgment of God," in *Selected Writings*, 565.

92. Artaud, "The Theater and the Plague," 24.

93. Michael Smith, *Theatre Trip* (New York: Bobbs-Merrill, 1969), 122.

94. "Infinite plasticity" is a phrase of Stanley Crouch's, qtd. in DeVeaux, *The Birth of Bebop*, 82.

95. Qtd. in Edward Lucie-Smith, *Symbolist Art* (London: Thames and Hudson, 1972), 50.

96. Qtd. in ibid., 76.

97. Qtd. in Frantisek Deak, *Symbolist Theatre: The Formation of an Avant-Garde* (Baltimore: Johns Hopkins University Press, 1993), 167.

98. Qtd. in Courtwright, *Dark Paradise*, 127.

99. Author unknown, "The Addict Psychology," qtd. in Curtiss, unpublished manuscript.

100. Lyon, "Artaud," 120–21.

101. Lee Edelman, "Homographesis," in Rivkin and Ryan, *Literary Theory*, 732.

102. Jacques Derrida, "The Rhetoric of Drugs: An Interview," *differences* 5, no. 1 (1993): 1–25, 14.

Case 2

1. For discussion of the subjective in performance scholarship, see Colin Turnbull, "Liminality: A Synthesis of Subjective and Objective Experience," in *By Means of Performance: Intercultural Studies of Theatre and Ritual*, ed. Richard Schechner and Willa Appel (New York: Cambridge University Press, 1990).

2. Bürger writes, "For it is in the historical avant-garde movements [futurism, Dada, surrealism] that the totality of artistic means becomes available as means" (*Theory of the Avant-Garde*, 18).

3. The genealogy reflects another bias, being modeled on Alfred Barr's genealogy of abstract expressionism, a map placed on the cover of a 1936 Museum of Modern Art catalog and hanging, since then, in the museum's library. The desire for a historical and institutional permanence is one more subcurrent in Maciunas's vexing diagram. Barr's genealogy is reprinted in Marc Aronson, *Art Attack: A Short Cultural History of the Avant-Garde* (New York: Clarion, 1998), 105.

4. A similar notion of singularity is developed by Jean-François Lyotard in *The Libidinal Economy*, trans. Iain Hamilton Grant (Bloomington: Indiana University Press, 1993). Geoffrey Bennington has written about how Lyotard develops Pierre Klossowski's discussion of popular religion in the late Roman Empire: "Here there is a paroxystic multiplication of gods and goddesses for every act and object of daily life, not subordinating such acts and objects to a single principle or meaning or cause . . . but naming them as intense singularities, 'sufficient to themselves in their

self assertion.'" See *Lyotard: Writing the Event* (New York: Columbia University Press, 1988), 27.

5. The notion of "dangerous boredom" is formulated by Dick Higgins in "Boredom and Danger."

6. Michael Kirby, ed., *Happenings: An Illustrated Anthology* (Topanga, Calif.: Boulevard Books, 1965).

7. Allan Kaprow, "Happenings Are Dead," in *Essays on the Blurring of Art and Life*, ed. Jeff Kelley (Berkeley and Los Angeles: University of California Press, 1993), 61. Kaprow studied the works of John Dewey and knew them well. Not surprisingly, he characterized his work as antiart, but in a distinctly American, distinctly pragmatic tradition of antiart that recalls Dewey explicitly: "[A]nti-art isn't something the dadas invented. There's a whole thread of 'life is better than art' dating at least to the time of Wordsworth, right through Emerson and Whitman, to John Dewey and beyond, emphasizing art as experience, trying to blend art back into life—this tradition [Dada] influenced me very much. But anti-art is an old Western theme." See Susan Hapgood, *Neo-Dada: Redefining Art, 1958–62* (New York: American Federation of Arts in association with Universe Publishing, 1994), 115.

8. Samuel Delaney, *The Motion of Light in Water: Sex and Science Fiction Writing in the East Village, 1957–1965* (New York: Arbor House, W. Morrow, 1988), 186.

9. Michael Kirby, "The New Theatre," *Tulane Drama Review* 10, no. 2 (1965): 32.

10. Paul Lafargue, quoted in Walter Benjamin, *The Arcades Project,* trans. Howard Eiland and Kevin McLaughlin (Cambridge: Belknap Press of Harvard University Press, 1999), 497.

11. Roland Barthes, *S/Z,* trans. Richard Miller (New York: Farrar, Straus and Giroux, 1974), 3–4.

12. In this respect, Delaney's autobiography does anything but demonstrate the "self-preconceptions that narrative convention imposes on remembering with false, epistemological positivity," a claim made by Diane Chisholm in her remarkable essay "The City of Collective Memory" (*GLQ* 7.2 [2001]: 197). Chisholm underestimates the emblematic role played by Kaprow's event throughout Delaney's text.

13. Kirby, "The New Theatre," 26.

14. Frank, *The Conquest of Cool.* For a discussion of the role of the avant-garde and spontaneity in American capitalism in the 1940s and 1950s, see Belgrad, *The Culture of Spontaneity.*

15. Susan Sontag, *Against Interpretation and Other Essays* (New York: Farrar, Straus and Giroux, 1966), 14.

16. Jill Johnston, "Dada and Fluxus," in Hapgood, *Neo-Dada,* 93.

17. Allan Kaprow, "The Education of the Un-Artist, Part I," in Kelley, *Essays on Blurring,* 98–99.

18. Oldenburg and Williams, *Store Days,* 110.

19. W. B. Worthen, "Disciplines of the Text/Sites of Performance," *TDR* 39, no. 1 (1995): 13–28. Worthen writes, "I am interested in the ways that notions of authority are covertly inscribed in recent discussions of performance, often at just those moments when the supposedly liberating 'textuality' of performance is most

urgently *opposed* to that Trojan horse of the absent author, the text. Reconsidering how, or whether, texts are actually opposed to performances, is one way to rethink the disciplinary instruments that map the contours of drama/theater/performance studies today" (14).

20. Jean-Joseph Goux, *Symbolic Economies: After Marx and Freud,* trans. Jennifer Curtiss Gage (Ithaca, N.Y.: Cornell University Press, 1990), 44.

21. Naomi Schor, "Fetishism and Its Ironies," in *Fetishism as Cultural Discourse,* ed. Emily Apter and William Pietz (Ithaca, N.Y.: Cornell University Press, 1993), 95.

22. Susan Stewart, *On Longing: Narratives of the Miniature, the Gigantic, the Souvenir, the Collection* (Baltimore: Johns Hopkins University Press, 1984), xii.

23. Roland Barthes, "From Work to Text," in *Art in Theory, 1900–1990: An Anthology of Changing Ideas,* ed. Charles Harrison and Paul Wood (Oxford: Blackwell, 1993). Barthes writes that the text "cannot be contained in a hierarchy, even in a simple division of genres. What constitutes the Text is . . . its subversive force in respect of the old classifications" (942).

24. Laura Mulvey, "Visual Pleasure and Narrative Cinema," *Screen* 16 (autumn 1975): 7.

25. Michael Kirby and Richard Schechner, "An Interview with John Cage," *Tulane Drama Review* 10, no. 2 (1965): 53.

26. Stiles, "Sticks and Stones," 54.

27. Situationist International, "The Avant-Garde of Presence," in Knabb, *Situationist International Anthology,* 110–11.

28. Karl Marx and Friedrich Engels, *The Manifesto of the Communist Party,* trans. Samuel Moore (Chicago: Charles H. Kerr, 1947), 1.

29. Henri Lefebvre, *Critique of Everyday Life,* vol. 1, trans. John Moore (New York: Verso, 1991).

30. Jameson, "Periodizing the 60s," 208.

31. The Happenings peaked during the transitional period between abstract expressionism and pop. They can therefore be understood as a form of "hand-painted pop," as the title of a 1992 Los Angeles Museum of Contemporary Art exhibit suggested. See R. Ferguson, ed., *Hand-Painted Pop: American Art in Transition, 1955–62* (Los Angeles: Museum of Contemporary Art, 1992).

32. Qtd. in Benjamin, *The Arcades Project,* 502.

33. Benjamin, *The Arcades Project,* 10.

34. Katie O'Dell, "Fluxus Feminus," *TDR* 41, no. 1 (spring 1997): 43–60.

35. The playwright Doric Wilson has also argued this point. Special Panel: "Excavating the Underground: Towards an Archaeology of Off-Off-Broadway," Association for Theater in Higher Education Conference, New York, August 8, 1996.

36. Andreas Huyssen, *After the Great Divide: Modernism, Mass Culture, Postmodernism* (Bloomington: Indiana University Press, 1968), 168.

37. Qtd. in Hapgood, *Neo-Dada,* 126.

38. See Al Hansen, "Muscle Art and Whiplash: Walter Gutman," in *The Gutman Letters* (New York: Something Else Press, 1969), 36 (originally published in the *East Village Other*).

39. Michael Benedikt, introduction to *The Gutman Letters,* vii.

40. Ibid., ix.

41. Ibid.

42. Gutman, *The Gutman Letters,* 15.

43. Ibid., 23.

44. Ibid., 32.

45. Higgins, *foew&ombwhnw,* 133; emphasis added.

46. Allan Kaprow, "O.K.," in *Manifestoes* (New York: Something Else Press, 1966), 188 ff.

47. Stiles, "Sticks and Stones."

48. Huyssen, *After the Great Divide,* 170.

49. Kristine Stiles, "On Tuna and Other Fishy Thoughts on Fluxus Performance," in *FluxAttitudes,* ed. Cornelia Lauf and Susan Hapgood (New York: New Museum of Contemporary Art, 1992).

50. For extended discussion of *Zyklus,* see Stiles, "Between Water and Stone: Fluxus Performance, a Metaphysics of Acts," in *In the Spirit of Fluxus,* ed. Janet Jenkins (Minneapolis: Walker Art Center, 1993).

51. Gregory Ulmer has characterized the moiré effect as a major influence on poststructuralism generally and the work of Derrida in particular. Ulmer characterizes the project of grammatology as "based on the conceptualization of the nonobjective senses," a conceptualization that depends on "[t]he experimental production of optical illusion directly in abstract forms (rather than indirectly, as in the mimetic tradition, in forms subordinated to representational demands)." See *Applied Grammatology: Post(e)-Pedagogy from Jacques Derrida to Joseph Beuys* (Baltimore: Johns Hopkins University Press, 1985), 39. The Group for Research in the Visual Arts (GRAV), which developed op art, was founded in France in 1960 as a means for experimenting with the confluence of philosophical conception and optical perception.

52. For discussion of the signature's deconstruction of the text/context divide, see Jacques Derrida, "Signature Event Context," in *A Derrida Reader: Between the Blinds,* ed. Peggy Kamuf (New York: Columbia University Press, 1991).

53. A term I borrow from Hall and Jefferson's *Resistance through Rituals.*

54. Janet Jenkins, frontispiece, *In the Spirit of Fluxus,* 37.

55. Kaprow, "The Legacy of Jackson Pollock," *Art News,* October 1958, 56–57.

56. Kaprow, "The Artist as Man of the World," in Kelley, *Essays on Blurring,* 51.

57. Al Hansen, *A Primer of Happenings and Time/Space Art* (New York: Something Else Press, 1965), 72.

58. See Jean Baudrillard, *The System of Objects* (New York: Verso, 1996); and Georg Perec, *Things: A Story of the Sixties* (London: Collins Harvill, 1990).

59. Qtd. in Hansen, *Primer,* 84.

60. Bürger, *Theory of the Avant-Garde,* 54.

61. Ibid., 114 n. 21.

62. Qtd. in Perlstein, "Who Owns the Sixties?" 37.

63. Frank, *The Conquest of Cool,* 13.

64. Connections between the Fluxus group and identity politics have been established by Stiles, "Between Water and Stone," and O'Dell, "Fluxus Feminus."

65. Jameson, "Periodizing the 60s," 208.

66. Kirby and Schechner, "Interview with John Cage," 53.

67. Johnston, "Dada and Fluxus," 93.

68. Delaney, *Motion,* 189.

69. Oldenburg and Williams, *Store Days,* 44.

70. Kirby, "The New Theater," 32.

71. Qtd. in Hapgood, *Neo-Dada,* 129.

72. Claes Oldenburg, interview, in Hapgood, *Neo-Dada,* 126.

73. Walter Benjamin, "The Work of Art in the Age of Mechanical Reproduction," in *Illuminations,* ed. Hannah Arendt, trans. Harry Zohn (New York: Schocken, 1969).

74. Susan Hapgood, "Neo-Dada," in *Neo-Dada,* 25.

75. Kaprow, "Man of the World," 47.

76. Ibid., 48.

77. Ibid., 49.

78. For a useful history and critique of the categories of "work," "play," and "leisure," and their role in the practice of art, philosophy, and production, see Victor Turner's "Liminal to Liminoid in Play, Flow, Ritual" in *From Ritual to Theatre.* Unfortunately, there is not space to examine the "mythologization of work" within the Happenings community (nor in Warhol's "Factory"), which seems to reflect both a sense that a society of abundance had been achieved in the United States, but also a kind of ironic class consciousness among these prototypical intellectual laborers. See, among other useful documents, Walter De Maria, "Meaningless Work," in *An Anthology,* ed. La Monte Young (New York: Something Else Press, 1963). For a discussion of the economic and pedagogical conditions of art education in the 1940s and 1950s, particularly as it functioned in the "flash lab" of Ohio State's Hoyt Sherman, see David Deitcher, "Unsentimental Education: The Professionalization of the American Artist," in Ferguson, *Hand-Painted Pop.*

79. Qtd. in Hapgood, *Neo-Dada,* 43–44.

80. Kaprow, "Education of Un-Artist," 98–99.

81. Thomas Crow, "Modernism and Mass Culture in the Visual Arts," in *Modernism and Modernity,* ed. Benjamin H. D. Buchloch et al. (Nova Scotia: Nova Scotia College of Art and Design, 1983), 215.

82. Arjun Appadurai, introduction to *The Social Life of Things: Commodities in Cultural Perspective,* ed. Arjun Appadurai (New York: Cambridge University Press, 1986), 26–27.

83. Ibid., 27.

84. Charles Mackay, *Extraordinary Popular Delusions and the Madness of Crowd* (London: Wordsworth Reference, 1995), 95.

85. Appadurai, introduction to *Social Life of Things,* 28. For a similar perspective on the relationship between subversion, market expansion, and moral shock, see Greil Marcus, *Lipstick Traces: A Secret History of the Twentieth Century* (Cambridge: Harvard University Press,1989).

86. Laclau and Mouffe, *Hegemony and Socialist Strategy,* 7.

87. Ibid., 9.

88. Ibid., 47.

89. Marx and Engels, *Manifesto of Communist Party,* 5.

90. See Guilbaut, *How New York Stole*.

91. "So did he then envision to merchandise wishes to pioneer an emporium of material banalities, fantastic from the pressure of actualities—not available—and of dreams exceeding the reality of existing objects. Yes! He did." Carolee Schneeman, "About Claes Oldenburg's Store," in *More Than Meat Joy: Complete Performance Works and Selected Writings,* ed. Bruce McPherson (New Paltz, N.Y.: Documentext, 1979), 17. Once again, a metaphorics of inflation and conceptually inaccessible causality dominates description of the Happenings context.

92. Ina Blom, "Hiding in the Wood," in *The Fluxus Performance Workbook,* ed. Ken Friedman (http: www.panix.com/~fluxus).

93. For a useful review of the publications and activities of various "pro-Situ" groups during and after the era of the Happenings and SI, see Simon Ford, ed., *The Realization and Suppression of the Situationist International: An Annotated Bibliography, 1972–1992* (San Francisco: AK Press, 1995).

94. Stiles, "Sticks and Stones," 54.

95. Ibid., 56.

96. Ibid., 60. Stiles further specifies that such a split is the result of the problems raised by the entry of "destruction" into aesthetic practice. Reflecting on the importance of the Destruction in Art Symposium held in London during 1966, Stiles argues that the rupturing of aesthetic distance in destruction art is simply unrepresentable by theory, which inevitably preserves distance, even if it works its own form of linguistic or conceptual destruction (ibid., 59).

97. Situationist International, "The Avant-Garde of Presence," 110–11.

98. Ibid., 110.

99. Louis Althusser, "From Capital to Marx's Philosophy," in Louis Althusser and Etienne Balibar, *Reading Capital,* trans. Ben Brewster (New York: Pantheon, 1970), 60.

100. Readers of Walter Benjamin's "The Work of Art in the Age of Mechanical Reproduction" and critical responses to Benjamin's essay by Saul Friedlander (*Reflections of Nazism: An Essay on Kitsch and Death,* trans. Thomas Weyr [New York: Avon, 1984]) and Alice Yaeger Kaplan (*Reproductions of Banality: Fascism, Literature, and French Intellectual Life* [Minneapolis: University of Minnesota, 1987]) will flinch at the idea of viewing the "aestheticization of politics" as a progressive political tactic. The explicitly and implicitly antifascist ends of early American performance art remind us that the problem is not the distinction of aesthetics and politics per se, but that distinction put at the service of self-blindness and violence. As Vivian M. Patraka has written in regards to the representation of fascist ideology in theater, any aestheticization of politics must be attended to with great rigor; however, any representation of the dynamic of aesthetics and politics "must ask for what purpose and to what effect" the dynamic is utilized. See "Fascist Ideology and Theatricalization," in *Critical Theory and Performance,* ed. Janelle G. Reinelt and Joseph R. Roach (Ann Arbor: University of Michigan Press, 1992), 347. Hewitt, in *Fascist Modernism,* suggests a variety of readings of the aesthetics/politics divide.

101. Louis Althusser, "Ideology and Ideological State Apparatuses: On Ideology," in *Critical Theory since 1965,* ed. Hazard Adams and Leroy Searle (Tallahassee: Florida State University Press, 1986).

102. Ibid., 241.

103. Ibid., 245.

104. Ibid., 243.

105. Guy Debord, *The Society of the Spectacle*, trans. Donald Nicholson-Smith (New York: Zone, 1995).

106. Althusser and Balibar, *Reading Capital*, 40.

107. Ibid., 41.

108. Tafuri, *Architecture and Utopia*.

109. Althusser and Balibar, *Reading Capital*, 95 ff.

110. Burnham, "Problems of Criticism," 50.

111. Ibid., 57.

112. Ibid., 69.

113. Antonio Negri, *The Politics of Subversion: A Manifesto for the Twenty-first Century* (Cambridge, Mass.: Polity Press, 1989), 52.

114. Ibid., 53.

115. Ibid., 77.

116. Ibid.

117. Ibid., 89.

118. Ibid., 90–91.

Case 3

1. Ed Bullins, *Malcolm: '71, or Publishing Blackness*, in *Black Scholar*, June 1975, 84.

2. Ibid.

3. Ibid.

4. Michael Fried, "Art and Objecthood," in Harrison and Wood, *Art in Theory*.

5. Andrew Sofer, "Felt Absences: The Stage Properties of Othello's Handkerchief," *Comparative Drama* 31 (fall 1997): 370. For other pieces in this vein, see *The Stage Life of Props* (Ann Arbor: University of Michigan Press, 2003).

6. Anna Scott, "It's All in the Timing: The Latest Moves, James Brown's Grooves, and the Seventies Race-Consciousness Movement in Salvador, Bahia-Brazil," in *Soul: Black Power, Politics, and Pleasure*, ed. Monique Guillory and Richard C. Green (New York: New York University Press, 1998). I discovered Scott's essay and Gillory and Green's groundbreaking book in September 2001 and so was unable to reference it in my earlier publications on the movement.

7. Ibid., 20.

8. Ibid., 22.

9. Larry Neal, "The Black Arts Movement," in *Visions of a Liberated Future: Black Arts Movement Writings*, ed. Michael Schwartz (New York: Thunder's Mouth Press, 1989), 62–63; W. E. B. DuBois, *The Souls of Black Folk: Essays and Sketches* (Chicago: A.G. McClurg, 1903).

10. Saidiya V. Hartman, *Scenes of Subjection: Terror, Slavery, and Self-Making in Nineteenth-Century America* (New York: Oxford University Press, 1997).

11. LeRoi Jones, *Dutchman* in *The LeRoi Jones/Amiri Baraka Reader*, ed. William J. Harris (New York: Thunder's Mouth Press, 1991), 97.

12. Amiri Baraka, "A Poem for Willie Best," in *Jones/Baraka Reader*, 58.

13. Ibid., 56.

14. Baraka, "The Revolutionary Theatre," 4–6.

15. Baraka, "Poem for Willie Best," 54.

16. Ibid., 55; emphasis added.

17. Ibid.

18. Ibid., emphasis added.

19. V. N. Vološinov, from *Marxism and the Philosophy of Language,* in Rivkin and Ryan, *Literary Theory,* 280–81.

20. Baraka, "Poem for Willie Best," 57.

21. We should note that Debord's theory of counterspectacular activism was formulated partly in response to the violent uprisings in African American communities that occurred throughout the middle and late sixties. See "The Decline and Fall of the Spectacle-Commodity Economy," in Knabb, *Situationist International Anthology.* Debord argues that the uprisings were explicit responses to and attacks on commodity culture.

22. See Howard L. Sacks, "Cork and Community: Postwar Blackface Minstrelsy in the Rural Midwest," *Theater Survey* 41, no. 2 (2000): 23–50. The *Amos 'n' Andy* show ran on television in some local markets as late as the middle 1960s.

23. Charlie Cobb, "Ain't That a Groove," in *Black Fire: An Anthology of Afro-American Writing,* ed. LeRoi Jones and Larry Neal (New York: Morrow, 1968), 522.

24. Ibid., 520.

25. Ibid., 524.

26. Frantz Fanon, *The Wretched of the Earth,* trans. Constance Farrington (New York: Grove Press, 1963); *Black Skin, White Masks,* trans. Charles Lam Markmann (New York: Grove Press, 1967).

27. Larry Neal, "Eatonville's Zora Neale Hurston: A Profile," in Neal, *Visions.*

28. Jahnheinz Jahn, *Muntu: An Outline of Neo-African Culture* (London: Faber and Faber, 1961).

29. Benston, *Performing Blackness,* 51.

30. Ibid., 4.

31. Etheridge Knight and Sanford Pinsker, "A Conversation," *Black American Literature Forum* 18, no. 1 (1984): 12.

32. Neal, "The Black Arts Movement," 64.

33. Tom Wolfe, *Radical Chic and Mau-Mauing the Flak Catchers* (New York: Farrar, Straus and Giroux, 1970).

34. See Samuel Hay, *African American Theater: An Historical and Critical Analysis* (New York: Cambridge University Press, 1994).

35. Larry Neal, "Any Day Now: Black Art and Black Liberation," *Ebony* August 1969, 54.

36. Ibid., 55.

37. For an account of the League of Revolutionary Workers, see Dan Georgakis, Marvin Surkin, and Manning Marable, *Detroit, I Do Mind Dying: A Study in Urban Revolution* (New York: South End Press, 1975).

38. Stephen Henderson, *Understanding the New Black Poetry: Black Speech and Black Music as Poetic References* (New York: Morrow, 1973), 41.

39. Houston Baker, *Blues, Ideology, and Afro-American Literature: A Vernacular Theory* (Chicago: University of Chicago Press, 1984), 74.

40. Leslie C. Sanders, *The Development of Black Theater in America: From Shadows to Selves* (Baton Rouge: Louisiana State University Press, 1988), 102.

41. Tejumola Olaniyan, *Scars of Conquest/Masks of Resistance: The Invention of Cultural Identities in African, African-American, and Caribbean Drama* (New York: Oxford University Press, 1995), 4.

42. "Retroactively actual" is a phrase that should remind one of Richard Schechner's notion that, in some forms of collaborative, end-oriented theater work, "the project coming into existence through the process of rehearsal . . . determines the past: what will be kept from earlier rehearsals or from the 'source materials.' . . . [R]ehearsals make it necessary to think of the future in such a way as to create a past." Richard Schechner, *Between Theater and Anthropology* (Philadelphia: University of Pennsylvania, 1985), 39.

43. Neal, "The Black Arts Movement," 62.

44. Larry Neal, "And Shine Swam On" in *Black Fire,* ed. LeRoi Jones and Larry Neal (New York: William Morrow & Co., 1968), 649.

45. Henry Louis Gates, "Black Creativity: On the Cutting Edge," *Time,* October 10, 1994, 75.

46. James T. Stewart, "The Development of the Black Revolutionary Artist," in Jones and Neal, *Black Fire,* 6.

47. Tam Fiofori, "The Illusion of Sun Ra," *Liberator* 7.12 (1967): 13.

48. When I asked Joan Gray and Nora Brooks Blakely, two leading figures in the contemporary Chicago black art scene, what they thought was the primary responsibility of scholars of the black arts movement, they agreed on the importance of describing the continuity of the movement both with the past and the present. "A Conversation with Black Arts Movement Women," Association for Theatre in Higher Education, Chicago, August 5, 2001.

49. For a detailed, sensitive description of the rise and fall of Umbra, particularly the scandal caused by Ray Durem's anti-Kennedy poem "A Decoration for the President," see Michael Oren, "The Umbra Poets' Workshop, 1962–1965: Some Socio-Literary Puzzles," in *Belief vs. Theory in Black American Literary Criticism,* ed. Joe Weixlmann and Chester J. Fontenot (Greenwood, Fla.: Penkevill, 1986).

50. For discussion of the Muntu group, see James Spady, *Larry Neal: Liberated Black Philly Poet with a Blues Streak of Mellow Wisdom* (Philadelphia: PC International Press, 1989), 11–12.

51. Qtd in Oren, "The Umbra Poets' Workshop," 193.

52. LeRoi Jones, "The Black Arts Repertory Theater School," *Liberator* 5.4 (1965): 21.

53. Larry Neal, "The Cultural Front," *Liberator* 5.6 (1965): 27.

54. LeRoi Jones, "The Revolutionary Theater," *Liberator* 5.7 (1965): 5.

55. Antonin Artaud, "The Conquest of Mexico," in *Theater and Its Double,* 128. An excellent and thorough discussion of Baraka's appropriation of Artaudian dramaturgical-philosophical concepts can be found in Sanders, *Development of Black Theatre,* 126–31. See also Mance Williams, *Black Theater in the 1960s and 1970s* (Westport, Conn.: Greenwood Press, 1985), 20–24.

56. Daniel H. Watts, "Cong. Powell-HARYOU-ACT," *Liberator* 5.11 (1965): 3.

57. Amiri Baraka, *The Autobiography of LeRoi Jones* (Chicago: Lawrence Hill, 1997), 458.

58. Harold Cruse, *The Crisis of the Negro Intellectual* (New York: Morrow, 1967).

59. Ibid., 14.

60. Wahneema Lubiano, "Black Nationalism and Black Common Sense: Policing Ourselves and Others," *The House That Race Built: Black Americans, US Terrain*, ed. Wahneema Lubiano (New York: Pantheon, 1997). I'd note that Lubiano's criticism does not take adequate account of the "nonobjective" aesthetics of the movement, which causes her to make two strong a distinction between the materiality of space and the conceptuality of space, the local enclave and the global movement. Other considerations of the land issue include the letter from Rolland Snellings (Askia Touré) to Larry Neal, June 2, 1967 (Larry Neal Papers, New York Public Library) in which Snellings argues for renewed attention to the South and a carefully planned deployment of Black Arts leaders to all parts of the country. As he puts it, "Our 'nationalism' only extends to Harlem, Philly, or Detroit for the most part. We are really *regionalists* using the rhetoric of nationalists" (8). Touré's argument in favor of the deployment of leaders ironically reveals his lack of knowledge about regional developments that were actually quite robust. For further discussion of the "Southern Shift" of the movement after 1970, see the discussion of the "Southern College Poets" in Henderson, *Understanding New Black Poetry*, 185 ff.; Addison Gayle Jr., "The Black Aesthetic Ten Years Later," *Black World*, September 1974, 20–29; and Larry Neal, review of *The Sound of Soul*, by Phyllis Garland.

61. Larry Neal, "The Black Writer's Role," *Liberator* 6.6 (1966): 8.

62. Neal, "And Shine Swam On," 655.

63. Cobb, "Ain't That a Groove," 520.

64. Charles Fuller, "Black Writing Is Socio-Creative Art," *Liberator* 7.4 (1967): 10.

65. Ibid.

66. Ibid., 6.

67. Ibid.

68. Georgy Lukács criticized the bourgeois theater of his time in exactly such terms. "The new drama . . . is bourgeois and historicist; we add now that it is a drama of individualism. And in fact these three formulas express a single point of demarcation; they merely view the parting of ways from distinct vantage-points." As a result, the drama "increasingly becomes an affair of the spirit [and] increasingly misses the vital centre of personality." See "Sociology of Modern Drama," 430.

69. Ben Sidran, *Black Talk* (New York: Da Capo Press, 1981).

70. Cruse, *Crisis of Negro Intellectual*, 68.

71. Michel de Certeau, *The Practice of Everyday Life*, trans. Steven Rendall (Berkeley and Los Angeles: University of California Press, 1984).

72. Neal, "The Black Arts Movement," 68.

73. Ibid., 69.

74. Neal, "And Shine Swam On," 649.

75. Maulana Ron Karenga, "Black Cultural Nationalism," in *The Black Aesthetic*, ed. Addison Gayle (Garden City, N.Y.: Doubleday, 1971), 38.

76. Stewart, "Black Revolutionary Artist," 5.

77. Ibid., 3–4.

78. Ibid., 4.

79. Ibid., 6.

80. Ibid.

81. Charles H. Fuller, "Black Writing: Release from Object," *Liberator* 7.9 (1967): 20.

82. Ibid.

83. Ed Bullins, *The Theme Is Blackness,* in *The Theme Is Blackness: "The Corner" and Other Plays* (New York: Morrow, 1973). For further discussion of Bullins's life and work, see Samuel Hay, *Ed Bullins: A Literary Biography* (Detroit: Wayne State University Press, 1997).

84. Bullins, *It Bees Dat Way,* in *The Theme Is Blackness.* The influence of Jack Gelber's *The Connection* on Bullins is acutely visible in this piece, which features a trio of stereotypically threatening blacks who harass the bourgeois spectators systematically and with increasing intensity.

85. For other discussions of historicism and its limitations, see Hayden White, *Metahistory: The Historical Imagination in Nineteenth-Century Europe* (Baltimore: Johns Hopkins University Press, 1973) and *The Content of the Form: Narrative Discourse and Historical Representation* (Baltimore: Johns Hopkins University Press, 1987). See also Dominick LaCapra, *Rethinking Intellectual History: Texts, Contexts, Language* (Ithaca, N.Y.: Cornell University Press, 1983). For an overview of White's and LaCapra's work and critical responses to it, see Lloyd S. Kramer, "Literature, Criticism, and Historical Imagination: The Literary Challenge of Hayden White and Dominick LaCapra," in *The New Cultural History,* ed. Lynn Hunt (Berkeley and Los Angeles: University of California Press, 1989).

86. Baker, *Blues, Ideology,* 5.

87. For discussion of the role of music in several productions of *Slave Ship,* see Harry Elam Jr., "Social Urgency, Audience Participation, and the Performance of *Slave Ship* by Amiri Baraka," in *Crucibles of Crisis: Performing Social Change,* ed. Janelle Reinelt (Ann Arbor: University of Michigan Press, 1996). See also Kimberly Benston, "Vision and Form in *Slave Ship,*" in *Imamu Amiri Baraka (LeRoi Jones): A Collection of Essays,* ed. Kimberly Benston (Englewood Cliffs, N.J.: Prentice-Hall, 1978). Benston characterizes *Slave Ship*'s music (composed by Ornette Coleman) as reflecting "the entire historical and mythical process of Afro-American being" (174).

88. Elam, "Social Urgency," 22.

89. Gwendolyn Brooks, "The Sermon on the Warplane," *Blacks* (Chicago: Third World Press, 1989).

90. Homi K. Bhabha, *The Location of Culture* (New York: Routledge, 1994), 238.

91. Sonia Sanchez, *Malcolm/Man Don't Live Here No Mo,* in *Black Theatre* 6 (1972): 24.

92. Enoch Brater, ed., *Feminine Focus: The New Women Playwrights* (New York: Oxford University Press, 1989).

93. Sanchez, *Malcolm/Man,* 24.

94. Sonia Sanchez, *Sister Son/Ji,* in *New Plays from the Black Theatre,* comp. Ed Bullins (New York: Bantam, 1969), 107.

95. Ibid., 98.

96. Ibid., 100.

97. Audre Lord, "Naturally," *The Black Woman,* ed. Toni Cade (New York: Mentor, 1970), 18.

98. Ibid., 99.

99. Ibid., 101.

100. Ibid., 98.

101. Ibid., 107.

102. The exception being Samuel Hay, whose comments concerning Bullins's work with Erika Munk on *TDR* are brief, but insightful (*Ed Bullins,* 31 ff.). Hay's book carefully explores Bullins's work as a playwright and organizer and, in this respect, affords editorial scholarship of the Black Arts Movement a foundation upon which to build. Absence of discussion of *Black Theatre* magazine mars Abby A. Johnson and Ronald M. Johnson's otherwise indispensable *Propaganda and Aesthetics: The Literary Politics of Afro-American Magazines in the Twentieth Century* (Amherst: University of Massachusetts Press, 1979). Lastly, for in-depth discussion of Broadside Press, see Julius E. Thompson, *Dudley Randall, Broadside Press, and the Black Arts Movement in Detroit, 1960–1995* (Jefferson, N.C.: McFarland, 1999).

103. Albert Camus, *The Just Assassins, Caligula, and Three Other Plays,* trans. Stuart Gilbert (New York: Vintage, 1958).

104. Dudley Randall and Margaret S. Burroughs, eds., *For Malcolm: Poems on the Life and the Death of Malcolm X* (Detroit: Broadside Press, 1969).

105. Worthen, "Disciplines of the Text." Worthen writes, "I am interested in the ways that notions of authority are covertly inscribed in recent discussions of performance, often at just those moments when the supposedly liberating 'textuality' of performance is most urgently *opposed* to that Trojan horse of the absent author, the text. Reconsidering how, or whether, texts are actually opposed to performances, is one way to rethink the disciplinary instruments that map the contours of drama/theater/performance studies today" (14).

106. George Bornstein, *Representing Modernist Texts: Editing as Interpretation* (Ann Arbor: University of Michigan Press, 1991), 8.

107. Qtd. in Johnson and Johnson, *Propaganda and Aesthetics,* 165.

108. Ibid.

109. This was not the first time Bullins worked as an editor. While at Los Angeles City College in 1961, the year he began writing, he founded a campus literary magazine called *Citadel.*

110. Richard Schechner, "White on Black," *TDR* 12, no. 4 (1968): 25.

111. See Hay, *Ed Bullins,* 28 ff.

112. Schechner, "White on Black," 26.

113. The tropological history of "signifyin'" in African American letters is established and criticized by Henry Louis Gates, Jr., in *The Signifying Monkey: A Theory of African-American Literary Criticism* (New York: Oxford University Press, 1988).

114. "Lafayette Theatre Reaction to Bombers, May 11, 1969," *Black Theatre* 4 (1969):25.

115. Naima Rashidd, "Black Theater in Detroit," *Black Theatre* 4 (1969):3.

116. "Lafayette Theater Reaction," 16.

117. This is a long-standing debate in African American theater. For extensive

discussion of the issue, see Hay, *African American Theater*. It is notable that Bullins has recently declared, "Today is the time of August Wilson" in "Black Theatre 1998: A Thirty-Year Look at Black Arts Theatre," in *A Sourcebook of African-American Performance: Plays, People, Movements*, ed. Annemarie Bean (New York: Routledge, 1999), 11. This would seem to imply a return to a less experimental form of theater; Wilson's work is firmly in the line of Euro-American theatrical realism that extends back to Ibsen. However, the page-long quote that ends Bullins's essay makes no mention of Wilson's plays (though doubtless Bullins greatly admires them; many of Bullins's own works are realistic); rather he quotes Wilson at length to grant authority to the continued *institutional* vitality of black nationalism in the American theater scene.

118. "Lafayette Theater Reaction," 17.

119. Amiri Baraka, "For Maulana Karenga & Pharaoh Saunders," *Black Theatre* 4 (1969):7.

120. Maulana Karenga, "On Black Art," *Black Theatre* 4 (1969):10.

121. Hay discusses the *Amos 'n' Andy* reference in *Ed Bullins*, 258 n. 55.

122. Neal, "Toward a Relevant Black Theater," *Black Theatre* 4 (1969):15.

123. Ed Bullins, *We Righteous Bombers*, in *New Plays*, 25.

124. "Lafayette Theater Reaction," 17.

125. Ed Bullins, "The So-Called Western Avant-Garde Drama," *Liberator* 7.12 (1967): 16–17.

126. *Détournement* is a mode of inversive appropriation whose best-known practitioner was the Situationist International. Typically, the SI would take popular comic strips such as Steve Canyon, erase the content of the word balloons, then fill the empty space with their own revolutionary writings. The SI defines *détournement* as "first of all a negation of the value of the previous organization of expression" ("Détournement as Negation and Prelude," *Situationist International Anthology*, 55).

127. Martin Esslin, *The Theater of the Absurd* (Garden City, N.Y.: Doubleday, 1961), 6.

128. Bullins, *We Righteous Bombers*, 22.

129. Ibid., 46.

130. Ibid., 29.

131. Ibid., 52.

132. Lewis R. Gordon, *Fanon and the Crisis of European Man: An Essay on Philosophy and the Human Sciences* (London: Routledge, 1995), 45, 64.

133. "Lafayette Theatre Reaction," 25.

134. Thanks to David Krasner for suggesting the deeper, layered meanings of the term *sidewalk*.

135. Amiri Baraka, "Black Art," in *Jones/Baraka Reader*, 219.

136. Benston, *Performing Blackness*, 4.

137. Maurice Maeterlinck, *The Intruder, Doubles, Demons, and Dreamers: An International Collection of Symbolist Drama*, ed. Daniel Gerould (New York: Performing Arts Journal, 1985).

138. Fredric Jameson, "Modernism and Imperialism," in *Nationalism, Colonialism, and Literature*, ed. Seamus Deane (Minneapolis: University of Minnesota, 1990).

139. Qtd. in Goldberg, *Performance Art*, 38.

140. Filippo Tommaso Marinetti, in Harrison and Wood, *Art in Theory*, 145–48.

141. Ibid., 146–47.

142. Cedric J. Robinson, *Black Marxism: The Making of the Black Radical Tradition* (London: Zed, 1983), 1.

143. Ibid., 4.

144. Qtd. in ibid., 386.

145. Qtd. in ibid., 158.

146. Robinson, *Black Marxism*, 212.

147. Ibid., 63.

148. Qtd. in ibid., 216.

149. Ibid.

150. Ibid., 218–19.

151. Mae G. Henderson, "'Where, by the Way, Is This Train Going?': A Case for Black (Cultural Studies)," *Callaloo* 19, no. 1 (1996): 60–67.

152. Qtd. in Robinson, *Black Marxism*, 251.

153. Qtd. in ibid., 202.

154. W. E. B. DuBois, *Black Reconstruction in America, 1860–1880* (Cleveland: World Publishing, 1969), 718.

155. Robinson, *Black Marxism*, 256.

156. Hewitt, *Fascist Modernism*.

157. Neal, "The Black Arts Movement," 62.

158. Stewart, "Black Revolutionary Artist," 3–4.

159. For an intriguing discussion of this dynamic, see Fred Moten, review of *Soul: Black Power, Politics, and Pleasure*, ed. Monique Guillory and Richard C. Green, *TDR* 43, no. 4 (1999), 169–75.

160. Robinson, *Black Marxism*, 174.

161. Ibid., 189.

162. Baraka, "Poem for Willie Best," 57.

Index

315